NEW VIEWS

ON

AMERICAN ECONOMIC
DEVELOPMENT

NEW VIEWS

ON

AMERICAN ECONOMIC

DEVELOPMENT

A Selective Anthology of Recent Work

Edited, compiled, and with introductions

by Ralph L. Andreano

SCHENKMAN PUBLISHING COMPANY, INC.

CAMBRIDGE, MASSACHUSETTS

Copyright © 1965

Schenkman Publishing Company, Inc.
Cambridge, Massachusetts 02138

Printed in the United States of America
Library of Congress Catalog Card Number: 65–20307

To Harold F. Williamson, Sr.

A Bridge Between the "Old" and
the "New" Economic History

ACKNOWLEDGMENTS

The articles reprinted here first appeared in the sources listed below. The editor wishes gratefully to acknowledge the permission of the authors and editors of the journals to reprint them here.

1. Abramovitz, M.; Hearings Before the Joint Economic Committee, 86th Congress, First Session, Part 2; April 10, 1959; pp. 411-466. (Reprinted with permission of the author.)

2. Chandler, A. D., Jr.; *Business History Review, XXXIII*; Spring 1959; pp. 1-31. (Reprinted with permission of the author.)

3. Fishlow, A.; *American Economic Review,* LIX; May 1964; pp. 352-364. (Reprinted with permission of the author.)

4. Fogel, R. W.; "Discussion," *American Economic Review,* LIX; May 1964; pp. 377-381. (Reprinted with permission of the author.)

5. Fogel, R. W.; "Railroads," was originally presented to the Annual Meeting of the Mississippi Valley Historical Association in 1963. (Reprinted with permission of the author.)

6. Gallman, R. E.; *Economic Development and Culture Change,* IX; April 1961; pp. 397-412. (Reprinted with permission of the author.)

7. Goldsmith, R.; Hearings Before the Joint Economic Committee, 86th Congress, First Session, Part 2 — Historical and Comparative Rates of Production, Productivity and Prices; April 7, 1959; pp. 229-279. (Reprinted with permission of the author.)

8. Hughes, J. R. T.; *Explorations in Entrepreneurial History,* Second Series, I; Spring 1964; pp. 213-231. (Reprinted with permission of the author.)

9. Lebergott, S.; Hearings Before the Joint Economic Committee, 86th Congress, First Session, Part 3 — Historical and Comparative Rates of Labor Force, Employment and Unemployment; April 27, 1959; pp. 577-586. (Reprinted with permission of the author.)

10. Lester, R. A.; *Journal of Political Economy,* XLVI; June 1963; pp. 324-375. (Reprinted with permission of the author.)

11. North, D.; *American Economic Review,* LIII; March 1963; pp. 128-130. (Reprinted with permission of the author.)

12. Taylor, G. R.; *Journal of Economic History,* XXIV; December 1964; pp. 427-444. (Reprinted with permission of the author.)

13. Williamson, H. F., and Andreano, R.; in *Oil's First Century;* Har-

vard University Graduate School of Business Administration; Cambridge, Mass.; 1960; pp. 71-84. (Reprinted with permission of the author.)
14.   Wright, C.; *Journal of Political Economy,* XXXXVI; October 1938; pp. 688–701. (Reprinted with permission of the author.)
15.   Fishlow, Postscript, was prepared for the present volume. The editor is deeply grateful to the author for granting permission to print this material.
16.   Fogel, Am. Interregional Trade, was prepared for the present volume. The editor is deeply grateful to the author for granting permission to print this material.

I also wish to acknowledge the generous support and criticism of Evan I. Farber, Head of the Lilly Library at Earlham College. Miss Joyce Jackson performed in her usual efficient and cheerful manner the difficult task of typing the editorial introduction and certain of the articles. My deepest debt is to Prof. Harold F. Williamson, Sr. of Northwestern University for sharing with me his wisdom, wit, and generosity.

R. L. A.

TABLE OF CONTENTS

PART IV

Industrialization: The Civil War to 1914

PART V

The Long View of American Economic Development

EDITOR'S INTRODUCTION TO THE VOLUME

This book was to be originally a set of essays by the editor combining and interpreting for the general historian the new research developments that have occurred in the decade in American economic history. So much of the important research is so recent, and continues to come forth in books, articles, and Ph. D. theses, that my original conception of a book of essays synthesizing the new research for students and teachers of American history had to be restructured. What I have done instead, is to bring together a collection of articles, some mine but mostly from others, bearing on the long-term economic development and welfare of the American economy, for this is one of the topics most in need of fresh thought.

Books of readings in recent years have either attempted to explore one facet in depth, present opposing views on the same subject, or to cover all phases and aspects of American economic history from Colonial times to the present. I have chosen a quite different approach in this volume. In point of time all the readings collected here cover American economic development from the 18th to the 20th Century. But in terms of the issues discussed by the authors whole blocks of relevant information bearing on our long-term development are not treated at all. Rather, what I have attempted to do in this book, is to provide for teachers and students of American history a flavor of the kind of work being done by economic historians today as it bears on the long-period performance of the American economy. It should be emphasized that the book is not a text in American economic history; at its best it is a preview of the new research which has been opened up by scholars whose methodology is traditional and by those who have pioneered in what has come to be known as the "New Economic History." At its worst, this collection may be the rumblings of an iconoclast editor.

I have tried to provide something more than a collection of important articles. Indeed, some of the authors represented in the volume have done work more important than what is reprinted here. For myself, I have tried in the editorial introductions to go beyond mere explanations and background material necessary for an understanding of the articles in each part of the book; rather, I pose questions, present other relevant information, and explore issues not examined, at least explicitly, by any of the other authors. What I hope this has produced is a useful and introductory book for teachers of American economic history at the undergraduate level who have been trained in traditional historical discipline. I have tried to include in my introductions and in the articles subject matter about which teacher and student can argue, explore in student research papers, or refute in lectures. In short, it is a book which is meant to be used by teacher and student and not just read.

The book is broken into five major units. Part One is devoted to the methodology of economic history emphasizing the approach of the New Economic History, its continuity with traditional historical method, and a tentative appraisal of the proper scope and method for the writing of economic history. Part Two explores the long term expansion of the American economy from the beginning of the 18th Century until, roughly, the period of the Revolutionary War. Part Three deals with matters of personal and national economic welfare before the Civil War, the geographical flow of commodities and their importance to our growth pattern, the influence of the railroad on economic growth, the impact of the Revolutionary War, and various explanations of antebellum economic development. Part Four concentrates on issues related to large scale industrialization in the last quarter of the 19th Century. An assessment of the economic impact of the Civil War, an analytical framework for appraising the historical role of the entrepreneur in American economic development, and a detailed examination of changes in selected and major industries. This part also contains one non-historical paper designed to nudge historians into reading the work of a famous theoretical economist — Alfred Marshall — not for economic theory but for his historical observations on the growth and industrialization of the American economy. The final unit, on Long-Term Economic Performance — presents three papers in which the long view of the American economic record is the focal point of analysis. The three articles read together come as close to being a "theory of American Economic Development" as anything yet written can be said to have done. But this work is not theory in the conventional sense but rather theory (laws?) as empirical observation and generalization.

PART ONE

Methodology: The New Economic
History and The Old

[1]

EDITOR'S INTRODUCTION
The New Economic History/What is new?/An appraisal

[2]

DOUGLAS NORTH
Quantitative Research in American Economic History

[3]

RALPH ANDREANO
Four Recent Studies in American Economic History

[4]

CHESTER W. WRIGHT
The Nature and Objectives of Economic History

EDITOR'S INTRODUCTION

The New Economic History was born in conflict. One is hard pressed to point to a specific time and place from which the rebirth of economic history is to be dated. The most obvious battlegrounds were the annual meetings of the Economic History Association where the perennial conflicts between the traditional historian and the new breed of economist-historian appeared in the papers given and in the general floor discussion. In the discussion following one of the more brilliant papers of the Cliometricians, as they were to be called later, virtually the entire body of the Association's membership rose as one to defend the traditional, literary tradition in economic history. This occurred at a meeting in 1960; a similarly slashing attack on the old economic history today would hardly create a ripple of disturbance, so commonplace has the work of the Cliometricians become in the assimilated kit of tools of the modern economic historian. The revolution has come and gone, and what one sees in the scholarly literature now is that the new economic history is not new, that its revolutionary impact was long foretold by the work of the great masters of the past, and that the traditional literary methods of historical scholarship were never as loose and non-rigorous as the revolutionists had claimed. What is indicated of course, is that partisans on both sides of the debate had much support for their respective views. But a revolution has taken place nonetheless, and economic history will never again be the same as it was even in the days of the great solitary scholars such as Clapham, Unwin, Toynbee, Usher, and the like.

The condition of the field, as proclaimed above, is an idealized state. The new economic historians continue to question the approach and the findings of the conventional wisdom of traditional historical scholarship; and the reverse is equally true. In one of the selections that follows, published originally in 1963, a major economic historian, Douglas North, challenges the traditionalists to join battle with the new methods and approaches of the modern economic historian and to rewrite American economic history and development. The focus of the other selection, by Andreano, suggests that the revolution may be taking place with some sort of historical "blinders" on the researchers. The two selections are not to be interpreted as an outline of the methodology of the new economic history but rather as an agenda for research and criticism of both the old and the new history and a guideline to the creative turmoil now at work in the study of American economic history.

Partisan debates aside, the student of American history ought to know in more general terms what it is that has caused the writing of American economic history to be once again a field of lively imagination attracting some of the most talented scholars in both economics and history. The selections by North and Andreano provide some of this flavor but in neither case are the fundamental linkages and cleavages with the historical scholarship of the past fully developed.

[II]

What Is New?

Despite disclaimers by the Cliometricians, many scholars viewing the work of the New Economic History declared that only the "numbers" were new. Some support of the view that quantification was now the hallmark of economic history scholarship could be found in statements of the practitioners. Other methodological foundations were also indicated, but Davis, Hughes and Reiter, in one of the first statements of the new work, did leave the impression that quantification of relevant economic magnitudes was the fundamental difference between traditional literary economic history and the new approach.[1] One could also draw a similar conclusion from Douglas North's statement in the selection following that accepted "truths" of United States Economic history "are inconsistent with elementary economic analysis . . . and would not survive . . . testing with statistical data." If it is the numbers that are new then the linkages with the past, and with traditional economic history, are indeed many: Alfred Marshall, J. H. Clapham, Guy S. Callendar, Arthur H. Cole and many others pioneered in the use of quantitative information. In the case of America one could also mention the 19th Century contemporary statisticians, Tenche Coxe, Adam Seybert, Ezra Seaman, George Tucker and Samuel Blodgett. But of course, the New Economic History is more than quantification.

Robert Fogel, one of the most brilliant and pioneering of the Cliometricians, has correctly noted that the distinctiveness of the New Economic History is not simply measurement but a redirection of quantification in ways that reconstruct economic data which might have existed but are

---

[1] See Lance E. Davis, Jonathan R. T. Hughes, and Stanley Reiter; "Aspects of Quantitative Research in Economic History," *Journal of Economic History,* XX; December 1960; pp. 539-547.

not now available, and in making measurements that were never before made.[2]

Underpinning a redirection of quantitative measurement is the emphasis on economic theory and on models of rational economic behavior which is made explicit in the work of the New Economic History. Thus Fogel suggests in the following passages the nature of the distinctiveness in this regard between the traditional and the new.

> Theory enters, first, in the determination of what it is that needs to be measured. . . . Theory enters even more obviously in the attempt to measure indirectly those things which cannot be measured directly. . . . The reliance of the new economic historians on theory is fostered by their desire to determine the extent of the contribution of particular changes in economic institutions, in factor supplies, in technology, etc., to the observed growth of an economy. (pp. 380-81)
>
> . . . It seems clear that what is most novel and most important in the New Economic History is not the increased emphasis on measurement but the reliance on theory to measure that which was previously deemed unmeasurable. (p. 381) [3]

What is of course meant by economic theory has tended to vary depending on the wishes and the value system of the investigator. That is why one can point to previous flirtations with economic theory in the construction of economic history — Schumpeter, for example — to debunk the newer emphasis now placed on models of hypothesis and deduction. But it is not the same; even though earlier work, as Fogel has noted, of the past masters of economic history almost by default employed logical and deductive methods of economic reasoning in the quest for statistical "truth."[4]

[III]

How Good Is It?

The final test of the New Economic History, *qua* economic history, is whether or not it yields returns in understanding and generalization unquestionably superior to alternative methods of research and conceptualiza-

---

[2] See Fogel's "Discussion" in *American Economic Review,* LIV; May 1964; pp. 377-89, esp. 378-79.

[3] from his "Discussion" in *Ibid.* Fogel has also argued that the visible result of the work being done in the New Economic History is the final reunification of economic history with the mainstream of economic theory. This is a statement open to dispute. See Fogel's "The Reunification of Economic History with Economic Theory," paper delivered at the Chicago, Dec. 1964 meeting of the American Economic Association, *American Econ. Review,* LV (May 1965), pp. 92-98.

[4] An article relevant to the above is Alfred Conrad and John Meyer, "Economic Theory, Statistical Inference and Economic History," *Journal of Economic History,* XVII, December 1957; pp. 524-544.

tion. There are several levels of appraisal which are relevant. First, has the new economic history yielded results in a narrow sense (time, space, or for an economic magnitude or institution) not previously available? The answer to this question is affirmative. Some of the work cited in the articles collected herein as well as a dozen or so doctoral theses in the final stages of completion suggest that the new economic history has indeed upset much of the conventional historical wisdom relating to narrowly defined issues in American economic development.[5] Larger synthesis, or generalizations, relating to theories of economic growth or, more especially, to the process, pattern and pace of American economic development have been notably lacking. Perhaps Douglas North's, *Economic Growth of the United States, 1790-1860* (New York: 1961), Robert Fogel's, *Railroads and American Economic Growth* (Baltimore: 1964), and a textbook or two have attempted to fit all the pieces of the new economic history into the old grooves honed by the traditional scholarship. But on any grander scale of generalization, no scholar has yet woven the interrelated developments of United States national history as did, for instance, two of the older economic historians, Charles A. Beard and Louis Hacker. In the final analysis, the present large expenditure of research resources to put American economic history on a "solid statistical foundation" will be in vain if it does not lead to broader generalizations concerning our past and our place in the loom of history.

[IV]

It is against the background of the previous introductory material that a few additional words now may be written concerning the third selection in this unit on the methodology of economic history. It has already been noted that economic history can never be the same again as a result of the work of the new economic historians. To the editor there is some lament in that statement tempered with a bit more than equal dose of affirmative relief. The following selection by Chester Wright, written almost forty years ago, demonstrates the bottleneck that the writing of American eco-

---

[5] It would be an exhausting task to compile a bibliography of work done and under way by the new economic historians; it would be equally tedious to appraise individual contributions. At the risk of oversimplification let me suggest that the following areas of research interest relevant to United States economic history have been investigated by one or more members of the profession in the past decade: national income and product accounts in the 19th Century, transportation — canals, railroads, commodity movements in international and inter-regional trade, sources of industrial borrowing, productivity growth in agriculture and selected manufacturing industries, the historical role of investment in human capital, negro slavery and plantation agriculture, the Role of Tariffs. The list grows longer each year.

nomic history found itself in until the Cliometricians broke the cork. But Wright's article also contains much wisdom which is a joyous legacy of the old economic history. For, as he indicates in this article and at even greater length in his still valuable textbook (*Economic History of the United States,* second edition, New York: 1949), the study of economic history ought not to be so rigorous as to exclude any relationship with "life."

This is the main reason for reprinting this article in this volume: the modern student of economic history, imbued with the rigor and scientific methodology of economic theory and statistics will surely be impatient with what on the surface appears to be outdated normative judgments about what is after all only a fragment of human experience. Cautious judgment, however, is urged, for what will rigor have gained us if we do not better understand what and how and who we are as a national people? In the final analysis, inclusion of the article by Chester Wright is the editor's method of pleading for the continuance of the outlook of the old economic history but not for its methodology.

People, living and dead, are the stuff of economic history. Despite the show of age, the article by Wright has much to recommend to the student of this subject. For, though one can labor *in vacuo* in positivistic economic history and garner just rewards, the relevance of scholarship to the human condition of the past and present is the ultimate test of our contribution as intellectuals in the on-going network of ideas called civilization. Perhaps the conspectus of objectives laid out by Wright claim too much for economic history, but even so they are ideals which any intellectual discipline ought to strive to fulfill. One is reminded of an equally broad definition of the scope of economic history offered by Guy S. Callendar nearly a half a century ago. Callendar set three objectives for the economic historian: to explain and describe the economic life at all stages of development of a nation, to investigate the interrelationship of economic affairs to politics, and to show the influence of economic life upon the social evolution of a nation.[6]

[V]

Discussions about methodology can easily slip into redundancy and the currently artificial distinction between a new and an old economic history is no exception. Little is to be gained by further promoting differences of research interest and methodology; the new economic history has pushed the frontiers of possible knowledge outward at some significant rate but

---

[6] Guy S. Callendar; Selections From the Economic History of the United States, 1765-1860; Ginn and Company, New York; 1909; p. iv-vi.

the stereotyped old historical scholarship still continues to offer data and interpretations of relevance to our national history. That is what really counts, for all scholars are united in the same effort to produce "truth" in the purest and most exact form possible.

Quantitative Research in American Economic History

Douglas North *

Publication of the revised and expanded *Historical Statistics* [1] in 1960 was a notable achievement in bringing together the available quantitative information on the historical aspects of the U.S. economy. A comparison of the new volume with the first *Historical Statistics*,[2] published in 1949, amply testifies to the impressive accomplishment of the Bureau of the Census, the Committee on Historical Statistics of the Social Science Research Council, and the various consultants in this specialized field who were responsible for the new volume.

The introduction to the 1960 volume stresses that the original *Historical Statistics* was intended as a "working document" to pave the way for the "more comprehensive and definitive volume." In good part the data for the earlier volume were the result of research efforts over time by a variety of government agencies and by the National Bureau of Economic Research. The contribution of professional economic historians — with some notable exceptions such as the Committee on Price History — was not impressive.

The new *Historical Statistics* reflects a fundamental change in this respect. While the consultants responsible for individual sections were predominantly of governmental or National Bureau origin, there was more than a scattering of professional economic historians. A number of the most important series added to the new volume stem from the 1957 Conference on Income and Wealth held jointly with the Economic History Association.[3] Some of the papers at this conference were devoted primarily to a criticism of existing statistics. Others, such as the commodity output figures from 1839-99, the regional income estimates from 1840-1950, and

---

*Douglas North is Professor of Economics at the University of Washington, Seattle.

[1] U.S. Bureau of the Census, *Historical Statistics of the United States, Colonial Times to 1957*. Washington 1960.

[2] U.S. Bureau of the Census, *Historical Statistics of the United States, 1789-1945*. Washington 1949.

[3] *Trends in the American Economy in the Nineteenth Century*, Nat. Bur. Econ. Research Stud. in Income and Wealth, Vol. 24. Princeton 1960.

the balance-of-payments figures from 1790-1900, were net additions to our knowledge.

This conference heralded a growing interest in quantitative research in U.S. economic history. It has been followed by annual conferences at Purdue University which have been working sessions devoted to research in progress. The growing attendance at these sessions has reflected the increasing volume of quantitative research.*

A revolution is taking place in economic history in the United States. It is being initiated by a new generation of economic historians who are both skeptical of traditional interpretations of U.S. economic history and convinced that a new economic history must be firmly grounded in sound statistical data. Even a cursory examination of accepted "truths" of U.S. economic history suggests that many of them are inconsistent with elementary economic analysis and have never been subjected to — and would not survive — testing with statistical data. A number of major reappraisals have already been undertaken. The unprofitability of slavery in the ante-bellum South,[4] the indispensable role of the railroads in nineteenth-century American development,[5] and the importance of the Civil War in accelerating U.S. industrialization,[6] are three illustrations of this critical scrutiny, and they are just the beginning of the reassessment of our economic past.

If we are learning what U.S. economic history is not, it is a more difficult task to reach positive conclusions. A reconstruction requires far more comprehensive knowledge of our past than we currently possess. This knowledge, whenever possible, must be made available in the form of the quantities that have constituted the external manifestation of economic change in the United States. If the new *Historical Statistics* gives evidence of our relative richness with respect to quantitative data, it is still true that we are far from well endowed with the quantitative information necessary to outline the contours and patterns of American economic change from the past. We have only scratched the surface. Even a cursory examination of the wealth of material available in the form of early price data, offi-

[4] A. H. Conrad and John R. Meyer, "The Economics of Slavery in the Ante-Bellum South," *Jour. Pol. Econ.,* April 1958, 66, 95-130.

[5] Robert W. Fogel, "A Quantitative Approach to the Study of Railroads in American Economic Growth, a Report of Some Preliminary Findings," *Jour. Econ. Hist.,* June 1962, 22 (2), 163-97.

[6] Robert E. Gallman, "Commodity Output 1839-1899," *Trends in the American Economy in the Nineteenth Century,* pp. 13-72; Thomas Cochran, "Did the Civil War Retard Industrialization," *Mississippi Valley Historical Review,* 1961, *48,* 197-210; Douglas C. North, *The Economic Growth of the United States, 1790-1860,* Englewood Cliffs 1961.

*Ed. Note: Papers presented at the 1963 Conference on Income and Wealth in the Nineteenth Century were published as Vol. 29 in the Income and Wealth Series of the National Bureau of Economic Research.

cial documents of many kinds, local historical materials, and state statistics, indicates that possibilities for a much firmer reconstruction of the quantitative estimates of our past are available to us. While any single time series may be subject to a wide range of error, the gradual accretion of independent series lends greater confidence in our ability to arrive at careful judgments about the characteristics of our economic development in previous years.

A more difficult problem faces us in the development of the theoretical hypotheses necessary for shaping the direction of quantitative research. A decade or more of concentrated research on economic growth has yielded meager results for the quantitative economic historian. The tools of the economist provide initial hypotheses to explore a wide range of questions posed by the economic historian, but for those concerned with the great question of the economic rise and fall of nations the fare is still thin. Perhaps the major result so far has been to disabuse the economic historian of any simple ready-made explanation of U.S. economic growth, and to encourage more intensive investigation of the varying sources of changing productivity in the economy. In this area the tentative exploratory hypotheses of economists offer useful starting points for further work. Recent research on technical change,[7] investment in human capital,[8] and economies of scale,[9] all offer the economic historian starting-points from which to develop further hypotheses and undertake quantitative research. On a somewhat breathtaking scale, the study of E. F. Dennison [10] is an imaginative effort to provide a more comprehensive analysis of the contribution of different sources of increasing efficiency to the growth of the U.S. economy.

Economic history has been, and will continue to be, a field in which historians and economists combine their efforts to contribute to our knowledge of the economic past. Moreover, this new emphasis in no way vitiates the contributions of the nonquantitative historian. It does promise to provide both the historian and economist with important new support. For the political and social historian, the basic revisions of our economic history should suggest some fundamental reinterpretations in political and social history.

The economist can expect that the quantitative research and analysis of

---

[7] A suggestive study for the economic historian is W. E. G. Salter, *Productivity and Technical Change,* Cambridge 1960.

[8] "Investment in Human Beings." *Jour. Pol. Econ.* Suppl., Oct. 1962, 70 (5), Pt. 2.

[9] George Stigler, "Economic Problems in Measuring Changes in Productivity," *Output, Input, and Productivity Measurement,* Stud. in Income and Wealth, Vol. 25, Princeton 1961, pp. 47-78.

[10] *The Sources of Economic Growth in the United States and the Alternatives Before Us,* Suppl. Paper No. 13, Committee for Economic Development, New York 1962.

the economic historian will provide him both with improved data to test hypotheses and with a cumulating number of analytical insights into the process of past economic change which are the essential prerequisite to evolving sound theoretical propositions about long-run economic development.

Four Recent Studies in American Economic History: Some Conceptual Implications

RALPH ANDREANO

For quite a long time, the study of economic history in American colleges and universities and, indeed, the study of American economic history generally, has occupied a secondary position in the related disciplines of economics and history. In the past ten to fifteen years, however, economic history has assumed a vitality which few of the early pioneers in the field suspected would ever come to pass. Economists, statisticians, and historians have vigorously attacked long-held interpretations of American economic history, and a flock of researchers has turned up — in attics, basements, and old plantation mansions — enough raw material to keep everyone occupied for many decades to come. Never before has the subject seen such intensive scrutiny of economic institutions, entrepreneurs, individual business firms, industries, regions, economic policies, and the determinants and barriers to the process of economic development. And not since the middle of the nineteenth century have we had such large-scale efforts to construct historical quantitative series on wages, prices, output, national income and product, income distribution, labor force mobility, and productivity levels. The sheer volume of this work taxes the capacity of the individual scholar to absorb even a small proportion of it.

The recent survey article by Douglas North, reprinted in this section, provides the best statement of the current vitality of the field. "A revolution is taking place in economic history . . . ," North writes, "It is being initiated by a new generation of economic historians who are both skeptical of traditional interpretations of United States economic history and convinced that a new economic history must be firmly grounded in sound statistical data. Even a cursory examination of accepted 'truths' of United States economic history," North continues, "suggests that many of them are inconsistent with elementary economic analysis and have never been subjected to — and would not survive — testing with statistical data." [1]

Robert Fogel, one of the most gifted scholars working in the field, has

---

[1] Douglas North; "Quantitative Research in American Economic History" *American Economic Review,* LIII; March 1963; pp. 128–129. [Reprinted in Part I.]

amplified North's statement, suggesting that the tenets of the new economic history are not an abrupt change from the past — though there are marked dissimilarities in method and content — but part of an extended development from the best traditional scholarship in economic history. As Fogel has written:

> "The new economic history is the contemporary continuation of [the] theoretical-quantitative tradition, fortified by the methods developed and the experiences gained in recent empirical studies of economic growth, by the increasingly powerful tools of mathematical economics and econometrics, by the increasingly varied models of economic theory, and by the improved understanding of the possibilities that exist for the adaptation of models to the analysis of problems and situations other than those that prompted their invention."[2]

The new economic history has had a startling impact on traditional scholarship. Work by Conrad and Meyer, North, Fogel, and others has cut through a virtual tonload of traditional generalizations concerning the course and dimension of American economic history.[3] Nonetheless, it is my judgment that this newer quantitative, theoretical work has been accepted far too uncritically; as economic history it has just as many deficiencies as the work of non-theoretical, non-quantitative institutional economic historians. It is, however, facilitating the approach of that time when synthesis of United States economic history based on solid empirical logic and data will be possible.

Nevertheless, I think the growing tendency in the profession is for the newer economic historian to reject outright the approach and the findings of the pure institutional, unstructured economic historian. I, for one, deplore this tendency, and it is to this proposition that the following pages are directed. I have selected four studies, all of recent vintage, two each from the new quantitative and from the non-quantitative institutional literature of nineteenth century American economic history, and I propose to scrutinize both the findings and the conceptual implications that all four

---

[2] Discussants' remarks of papers by Ransom, Temin, and Fishlow in American Economic Association, *Papers and Proceedings;* May 1964; p. 389. [Part of this article is reprinted in Part III.]

[3] Conrad and Meyer; "Economics of Slavery in the Ante-Bellum South", *Journal of Political Economics,* LXV; April 1958; pp. 95-130. Another investigation using somewhat different primary data and an alternative set of assumptions arrived at essentially the same conclusions as Conrad and Meyer. See National Bureau of Economic Research, *Aspects of Labor Economics;* Princeton, 1962, Robert Evans, Jr., "The Economics of American Negro Slavery," 184-243; North, *The Economic Growth of the United States, 1790-1860;* New York, 1961, Robert Fogel, "A Quantitative Approach to the Study of Railroads in American Economic Growth: A Report of Some Preliminary Findings; *Journal of Economic History,* XXII; June 1926; pp. 163-197.

have upon the direction toward which the study of American economic history is tending.

The First Merger Wave

One of the most intensively researched periods of American economic history is the last quarter of the nineteenth century. There is no particular need to recount the scope and depth of such scholarly investigation. I have arbitrarily selected one particular aspect of this period, what has been termed by Ralph Nelson in his recent study "The First Merger Wave." [4] Institutional economic historians know the First Merger Wave under a variety of names: The Trust Period, the Combination Movement, the Consolidation Era, and others. The non-quantitative economic historians have been imprecise in the dating of the merger wave: estimates range from the late 1870's and the formation of the Standard Oil Trust to the middle 1880's and 1890's. Traditional explanations of the causes that gave rise to the movement, whatever name is used to describe it, range widely. There were the farsighted, though avaricious, entrepreneurs who had a vision of the "industrial progress" of America; there was the overextension of railroad capacity, the knitting of local and regional markets into a national framework by transportation and other communications improvements; there are the facts of sheer efficiency and profitability associated with size of firm and size of plant. The availability of a well-developed capital market is also thrown in for good measure as an explanation. [5]

Nelson's study of the First Merger Wave is an excellent sample of a quantitative approach. He gives a specific dating to the First Merger Wave, namely, 1894-1905, with the peak of activity in 1899-1901. Having described the quantitative dimensions of the rate and absolute level of merger activity centering in a ten-year period, Nelson attempts to test, statistically, four of the traditional causal explanations of the movement: (1) the retardation of industrial growth, (2) the immediately preceding expansion of the national railroad system, (3) the growth of a highly organized capital market, and (4) the increase of motivation toward market control. There is no need to recount his techniques in devising statistical tests for each of these propositions; his work is in the very best National Bureau tradition, involving careful scrutiny of the reliability of the data and putting the data against logico-deductive tests.

---

[4] Ralph Nelson, *Merger Movements in American Industry;* Princeton University Press, Princeton, New Jersey, for the NBER, 1959.

[5] A textbook widely used by historians who teach economic history in which all the points noted above are treated without discrimination or precision is Gilbert Fite and James E. Reese; *An Economic History of the United States;* Boston 1959; pp. 360-366.

Nelson's conclusions, however, are of considerable interest for our purposes here. First, he rejects the industry retardation hypothesis: "The years preceding the merger wave," he writes, "saw a reversal of the pattern of retardation, especially in the very industries where merger activity was highest" (p. 104). Moreover, a comparison of merger activity and industry growth rates enabled him not only to reject the retardation explanation but to affirm with some confidence that the overwhelming proportion of merger activity occurred in industries with accelerating growth rates. Second, Nelson discounts the importance of transportation growth as a "major cause of the merger movement" (p. 105). He finds that geographically concentrated industries did have high merger rates, but other tests failed to confirm the hypothesis. Third, the development of the capital markets is assigned a major role as a causative factor. Nelson found a high correlation between merger activity and stock prices, and further examination indicated that capital market factors proved statistically more significant than the level of industrial activity in influencing mergers. "This suggests," Nelson tells us, "that cost-price relationships in business firms were a less important influence than many students believed" (p. 105). Finally, Nelson concluded that the desire for market control played at least a permissive role in the merger movement. The large proportion of merger activity resulting in market control suggested to him that the desire for the protection thus afforded to profits was a factor of substantial importance in inducing firms to merge. With the growth of capital markets this desire found an effective means of implementation. Coupled with the expectation of gains to be reaped from a rising stock market, the added promise of protected profits represented a compelling argument for independent firms to join into consolidations.[6] Nelson is unable to develop any statistical tests for the existence of economies of scale, a fifth possible causal explanation of the First Merger Wave.

I find several points worth mentioning in regard to Nelson's findings:

(1) Do his findings square with interpretations of this period advanced by non-quantitative economic historians? I think the answer to this question is obvious: the institutional explanation most often recurring is the market control-capital market hypothesis. That is to say that the existence of large capital markets made the possibilities of promotional profits both possible and attractive. But the institutional literature has stressed: (1) the

---

[6] It may be recalled that a common explanation of the "increased desire for market control" in certain industries in the 1890's was the downward pressure on prices caused by what was thought to be declining demand for the product, aggravated by too much productive capacity. It was probably this phenomenon that influenced the development of the retardation explanation. See J. Bain in H. F. Williamson, ed.; *Growth of the American Economy*; Prentice-Hall, Inc.; New York 1947; Chapter 22.

social aspirations of industrial entrepreneurs; (2) the role of technology in breaking down the sectoral or geographical market boundaries; and (3) the influence of shifts in overseas demand for American commodities finished and raw, upon domestic resource patterns of use. All of these factors, and others, are qualitative in impact and differential in effect. But all have bearing on an hypothesis that a peak in merger activity had as its primary cause a desire and drive for market control. It is not inappropriate, I think, to raise a fundamental objection, that of causality. Did high rates of merger activity cause the development of the capital markets or vice versa? Isn't it equally likely that the growth and development of the capital markets were facilitated by the increased supply of securities fostered by the increased desire to finance firm expansions and acquisitions by non-internal financial sources? In other words, why shouldn't the hypothesis, i.e., *that the existence of well-developed capital markets was a major contributory cause to the first merger wave,* be turned around, to read: the first merger wave made possible the development of large-scale capital markets? In fact, if one examines the securities markets independent of any causal relationship to the merger wave, it is possible to read the data this way. A recent, non-quantitative study of the compelling forces in the development of an industrial securities market offers just such an interpretation.[7]

(2) Nelson's finding with respect to the market control hypothesis is also debatable. He tells us that the preponderant proportion of merger activity occurred not in industries with falling demand, but rather in growth industries. To be sure, growing industries are plagued frequently by violent short-term capacity/effective demand adjustments, by differential rates of growth for the various subsidiary industries or subsectors providing the major inputs, and by radical instability in market shares. Thus, the apparent desire to mitigate the tensions and pressures exerted by these market forces make firms turn to mergers of existing as well as potential facilities. This proposition opens the Pandora's Box called "market success" and economic rationality. Was it a rational entrepreneurial motive to believe that mergers in fast growing industries was the most desirable method of mitigating the "ravages" of new competition? That is, was such a market strategy one which had much of a chance in succeeding? On the surface the answers seem affirmative; but there are still questions of causality which need to be asked.

The really critical factor to be discussed here is what Bain and others have called the "Condition of Entry." Joe Bain's own analysis of the First

---

[7] T. R. Navin and Marion Sears, "The Rise of a Market for Industrial Securities, 1887-1902," *Business History Review;* June 1955.

Merger Wave conforms to Nelson's except in the important detail of weighting the importance of external economies and plant scale generated by the buildup of a national transportation network. But Nelson has not examined entry conditions in the industries he has studied.[8]

To confuse matters further, let me suggest still another hypothesis: even if the drive for market control is genuine and the immediate impact of mergers on market dominance is successful, industry structure may still prove to be unstable because entry conditions preclude any outright market control short of predatory and collusive action. My own investigations in the petroleum industry over the same period as the Merger Wave, for example, show that barriers to entry even in the face of Standard Oil (before dissolution) — in refining and crude oil production — were not overwhelmingly great. It was for this reason, in fact, that Standard Oil, even though it employed predatory and possibly collusive tactics, could not impede or blockade the entry of vertically integrated firms.[9]

Now, what is the point of talking about the First Merger Wave? First, let me say that Nelson's imaginative and obviously backbreaking quantitative investigation established only two points conclusively — that there was a cluster of mergers between 1894-1905 and that the overwhelming proportion of such mergers occurred between firms in growing industries. These are findings which I think have never been fully stressed by non-quantitative economic historians. But Nelson does not explain why this is so nor does he examine alternative motives which could be offered to frame reverse hypotheses. Let me suggest several additional factors and questions bearing on the problem and which economic historians of this phenomena ought to consider: To what extent, for example, did political institutions and the prevailing political climate toward business condition the particular timing and magnitude of the First Merger Wave? What effect did tariff levels have upon merger activity? (Several institutional historians have pointed out in a general way the close relationship between the increase in tariff levels — particularly dating with the Dingley Tariff in 1897 — and the rate of mergers consummated.) And finally, what common relationships, if any, are there between the First Merger Wave in America and the almost identical occurrence — in magnitude and timing — in England? That is, what were the international influences on the rate and level of domestic mergers?

If we are to understand the First Merger Wave, it must first be sufficiently described. Ideally, one must frame an analytical *a priori* argument

---

[8] See, J. S. Bain; *Industrial Organization;* Wiley Press; New York 1959; pp. 191-194.

[9] R. L. Andreano and Harold F. Williamson; "The Competitive Structure of the American Petroleum Industry, 1880-1911: A Reappraisal," in *Oil's First Century;* Boston 1960; pp. 70-84. [Article reprinted in Part IV.]

of economic and relevant non-economic motives and results of merger activity. And finally, empirical evidence — quantitative and non-quantitative — must be weighted within the context of the phenomenon being examined. It is not my intention to say that the Nelson study should have been a non-quantitative piece of work. On the contrary, just the description of data and the compilation of non-controversial data series make it a valuable contribution to American economic history. But in its own impressive way the study is just as narrow in focus and outlook as the work of the so-called institutional economic historians. This does not make the work of either group a more or less valuable contribution to our understanding of American economic history.

The Controversy over Income and Output, 1799-1839

One of the most interesting quantitative controversies that has developed in recent years is over the interpretation and veracity of national output and income data measuring the performance of the American economy from 1799 to 1840. The major national income series available for the period before 1860 is the work of R. F. Martin, whose study was published by the National Industrial Conference Board in 1939.[10] The Martin data showed two very surprising results: (1) the total national output and income did not increase more rapidly than population between 1800 and 1840 and (2) that the growth of income and output was particularly slow in the decade 1810-1820 and failed to exceed population growth during the 1820's, i.e., real per capita output and income fell. These results seemed to shatter some long held illusions about the uninterrupted, almost linear, pattern of economic growth in the United States.

Some years ago Simon Kuznets seriously questioned the acceptability of the Martin data and the conclusions drawn from it.[11] Kuznets argued that the Martin data should be discarded not only because the estimating procedures and sources of the data are questionable but also because of the inherent logical improbability of falling real *per capita* income between 1800 and 1840. He cites six pieces of evidence to support his case:

1. A rise in the share of nonagricultural occupations in the total of the gainfully employed from 27.2 to 31.4 per cent.

2. A rise in the ratio of workers to total population from 0.29 to 0.32, or by about 10 per cent.

3. A greater rise in the output of cotton, wheat, lumber, grain, and in

---

[10] R. F. Martin; *National Income in the United States, 1779-1938;* National Industrial Conference Board; New York 1939; 6, Table I.

[11] S. Kuznets, "National Income Estimates for the Period prior to 1870," *Income and Wealth of the United States: Trends and Structure,* Cambridge 1952; pp. 221-241.

the number of horses, cattle, and sheep on farms than in the increase in population; a lesser rise only in tobacco output.

4. An apparent rise in labor productivity in wheat, corn, and cotton production.

5. An increase in the real wages paid to farm workers in Vermont.

6. Somewhat greater declines in wholesale prices of manufactures than of farm products, indicating a relatively greater rise in per worker productivity in manufacturing.

The Kuznets argument boils down to this: Assuming the same relative labor productivities of 1799 in agriculture (.50) and manufacturing (2.34), two structural changes — an interindustry shift from agriculture to the manufacturing sector and an increase in the labor force participation ratio — would show an increase in aggregate product per worker in constant prices of 19 per cent between 1799 and 1839.

William Parker and Franklee Whartenby, in a searching critique of Martin's statistical methodology, while persuaded that Martin's data leave much to be desired, are not fully convinced that history, or Kuznets, has upset the correctness of his (Martin's) conclusion. "The evidence appears to be too weak," they argue, "to support Kuznets' inference that per capita real income followed a rising trend from 1800 to 1840. The validity of his [Kuznets'] contention depends upon the assumption of a constant or rising level of productivity in agriculture. . . . A small fall in agricultural productivity would have sufficed to wipe out any such gains [i.e., a 19% increase in real product per capita]." [12]

The latest to be heard from is Douglas North in an article published a few years ago.[13] North's own contribution is a cyclical analysis of the period, drawn largely from his suggestive earlier work on the role of the foreign trade sector in setting the pace for growth in United States national income.[14] His qualitative conclusion is that "although Martin's methods will not stand scrutiny, his conclusion that per capita real income was higher in 1799 than it was to be again for a half century appears to be correct." [15]

---

[12] William Parker and Franklee Whartenby; "The Growth of Output before 1840," in Conference on Research in Income and Wealth, *Trends in the American Economy in the Nineteenth Century*. Studies in Income and Wealth, Vol. XXIV; Princeton University Press; Princeton, New Jersey 1960; pp. 211.

[13] Douglas North; "Early National Income Estimates of the United States," in *Economic Development and Cultural Change*, IX; April 1961; pp. 387-396.

[14] Douglas North, *The Economic Growth of the United States, 1790-1860;* Prentice-Hall, Inc.; New York 1959; esp. pp. 24-35.

[15] Douglas North; "Early National Income Estimates," pp. 387. The late Sumner Slichter, extending productivity estimates for 1869 backward, came to the independent conclusion that the Martin data vastly understated the gains in per capita real product realized before 1850. See, Sumner Slichter, *Economic Growth in the United States: Its History, Problems and Prospects;* Louisiana State University Press; Baton Rouge, Louisiana 1961; pp. 48-51.

I have added certain suggestions of my own in the appendix to my paper in Part III.

Now, where does this leave us? Did output grow faster than population? And how steady was the increase in output between 1800 and 1840? The answer to both questions is that we don't know for sure and possibly never will if the present approach to the problem is maintained. The forty-year period under review includes a war, two protracted depressions, the westward migrations, the first appreciable immigration movement since colonial times, and the build-up of a stock of social overhead capital not to be equalled in magnitude until the latter years of the century. The period also includes substantial increase in governments' (federal, state, local) contribution to national income, output, and employment. Paul Trescott's recent study, for example, has shown that federal government expenditures alone over the same period were increasing at an average annual rate of 4 per cent. (The original Martin data measure only "private" production income and output.)

Most modern students of the period have singled out the years 1800-1840 as especially significant in conditioning the subsequent pattern and pace of American economic development. The desire to know whether or not real per capita output and income fell during this period also has contemporary relevance. Recent studies by Deane and Cole of British Economic Growth for example, have shown that "most, if not all, of the advance in average real incomes which had been achieved between the end of the seventeenth and the beginning of the nineteenth century had been achieved by 1770, before the Industrial Revolution had well begun. In the last three decades of the eighteenth century, that is, in the period which saw the unmistakable beginnings of rapid industrialization, the rate of increase in average real incomes was apparently negligible, if indeed there was not a positive decline." [16]

Perhaps the direction in which this controversy leads is the use of economic history for predictive purposes; that real income and output per capita must fall substantially before the industrialization process can acquire momentum. Whether or not such was the case in America, however, has not yet been proved or disproved. (Also, the passage quoted above notwithstanding, the issue for the English economy is far from settled.[17]) From the vantage point of contemporary interest in underdeveloped econo-

---

[16] Phyllis Deane, "The Industrial Revolution and Economic Growth," *Economic Development and Cultural Change;* January 1957; page 107.

[17] J. R. T. Hughes has seriously challenged the later work of Deane on which the above quotation is in part based. See Hughes' version of Deane and Cole, *British Economic Growth, 1688-1959: Trends and Structure;* Cambridge University Press; New York 1962 in "Measuring British Economic Growth," *Journal of Economic History,* XLIV; March 1964; pp. 60-82.

mies, to discover the course of American real income and output before 1840 seems eminently useful. But suppose acceptable quantitative results of the problem are achieved, will the fact that per capita output and income fell, or increased linearly, or remained constant, increase our basic understanding of the causal underlying forces of American economic development? Quantitative measurement of these economic magnitudes is essential, but in my judgment it is still only the starting point of further quantitative and non-quantitative investigations.

If economic history has any meaningful insights for contemporary problems of economic development, it is imperative that we hypothesize and test the causal relationships affecting output and income movements over time. And in order to do this the scope of investigation will have to be much broader and deeper as regards the structure of the economy and the socio-political-institutions that are responsible for change than is evident in the present debate. To mention only one factor which must be integrated into the income and output discussion — namely, the impact of the Westward Movement on agricultural productivity — does not exhaust the possibilities. In short, the work of the non-quantitative economic historians must ultimately be linked to the behavior of time series data (and vice versa) if the study of American economic history is to yield any useful insights into the processes of economic development. The current debate stimulated by the inadequacies of the Martin data is a necessary first step to a possible synthesis; but standing alone the research results so far indicate a narrowness in focus equal to the conventional historical wisdom about this period. A later essay in the present book examines this controversy in more detail.

The New York Canals

Our third example of recent research deals with a topic which falls squarely in the time period of the income and output controversy already discussed. Nathan Miller's *The Enterprise of a Free People: Aspects of Economic Development in New York State during the Canal Period,* co-winner of the Beveridge Prize of the American Historical Association for 1959, is a study tied to the theme of economic development though it has no *a priori* conceptions and no well-articulated analytical framework.[18] Miller examines in great detail the records and decisions of the Commissioners of the Canal Fund — state officials who administered the revenues and expenditures of the canals — and attempts to trace the way the Canal Fund (which he modestly calls a Development Bank) siphoned revenues from the canals into the private sector of the economy. The Canal Fund, he points out, used revenues as a sort of regional counter-cyclical weapon,

---

[18] The volume was published by Cornell University Press in 1962.

by easing pressures of local and New York City banks during periods of financial stringency. He concluded, after a very thorough examination of the documents, that initial investment in Canal securities came primarily from small savers and that only when the enterprise appeared successful were larger holders of capital funds, foreign and domestic, induced to commit their funds to canal projects. Miller also suggests that the canals could have been built without foreign capital imports, a proposition which, in theory at least, can hardly be denied.

It is a fascinating, well-written book. But its deficiencies, in my judgment, are critical. First, the study presents no information on the real magnitudes involved: one does not know the relative contributions of Canal Fund capital formation to, say, the totals for the state or region. One gets no impression of the relative size of the movement of funds between regions of the state. There is no attempt to appraise the investment criteria used (or lack of them) by the commissioners or to differentiate between the direction of Canal Fund investments into growing, lagging, or neutral sectors of the economy. There is no analysis of the structure of the state's (or region's) economy and no analysis of how it squares with the national picture. Simple measures of performance of the state's economy are ignored and there is no attempt to incorporate the findings of Harvey Segal and others on social returns of Canal Fund investments. Moreover, one gets from Miller's study no feeling whatsoever of the interrelationship of the sectors of the economy in the state or economic region which the Canals served.

It is impossible to find any meaningful links between Miller's study and a national framework of an underdeveloped economy. There is no attempt to compare his qualitative results with the work of others, for example, with that of Carter Goodrich and his students on investments in canals; there is no attempt to trace the backward linkage effects of revenues generated by the transportation input; finally, the study is treated in almost complete ignorance of over-all economic history of the United States between 1792 and 1838. The Miller study covers essentially the same period as does the Martin-Parker-Kuznets episode noted earlier, but it does not add any insights to this controversy except to highlight the "qualitative" importance of government's role in the western half of one state of the Federal Union.

I do not mean to be so negative about the Miller study, but I find it particularly distressing to see limited research resources being badly allocated. Actually, the study is good institutional history. But my point is that it could have been nearly ideal economic history had the author had a conception of magnitude and proportion and had he adapted the useful findings of the newer economic historians who have written on canals. If one is going to use economic history as a vehicle for analyzing the process of economic development, it is incumbent upon the investigator to give to central issues the weights appropriate for the time period under investigation. Had Miller concentrated more on the uniqueness (or lack of it) of the historical phenomenon he examined and less on the "apparent" similarities of the phenomenon to contemporary problems of development, the study would have been better economic history and would very likely have yielded more rewarding insights on the inner structure of the process of economic development in America.

Clifton Yearly's Study

Miller's book dealt with an entire state, or at least, the western half of a state. My second example of institutional economic history examines a single industry of a single country, in one state. I am referring to a study by Clifton Yearly, *Enterprise and Anthracite: Economics and Democracy in Schuylkill County,* 1820-1875 (Baltimore, 1961). Yearly, through a study of a *single* Pennsylvania County, argues that social beliefs conditioned, indeed determined, the pattern of exploitation of one of the world's three great anthracite coal fields (the other two being in adjacent Pennsylvania counties). Yearly writes that "frontier democracy," that is, "the promise of unfettered creativity, dynamism, hope, class mobility, individual opportunity . . . [and] equalitarian culture," conditioned the population of Schuylkill to demand a small-scale, highly competitive, individual pattern of mining development. This, Yearly argues, mitigated against technological progress in mining in the county and resulted in a distorted allocation of the county's resources committed to mining development. The only conceivable development path, Yearly argues, was one in which industry structure was much more highly concentrated. Specifically, he maintains that the "large corporation" was necessary, for only in this way could the capital requirements necessary to finance technological improvements be accumulated and the debilitating influence of price and output instability be overcome.[19]

The Yearly argument is, I think, not very well formulated; simple economic analysis, logic, and empirical observation contradict his findings. Let me mention just a few points.

1. When Schuylkill's mines did come under the control of a single major corporation — the Reading Railroad — it proved no salvation for either the Reading (which twice went into bankruptcy) or for the population of the county dependent on the economic performance of the county's mines.

---

[19] A superb, critical, and penetrating review of Yearly's book by Stephen Salsbury in *Business History Review,* XXXVI; Spring 1962; pp. 116-118, is far more complete than the brief comments I can make in this paper.

2. The entry conditions — low initial capital requirements, property laws, ease of access to deposits, low level of technology required — probably had more influence on conditioning the structure of the county's mining industry than did the social-democratic beliefs of the population.

3. The two adjacent counties, Luzerne and Northumberland, developed industry structures much more highly concentrated than did Schuylkill. Were the inhabitants of these counties more or less democratically inclined than Schuylkill's? Since all of the three counties developed simultaneously, it would seem crucial to explain these county-wide social differences if there were any.

4. In my judgment, the author, because of a lack of knowledge of competitive theory and the theory of industrial organization, failed to ask the really critical questions of his data: (1) What was the character of market forces that shaped industry structure? (2) What impact did the income and price elasticity of demand for coal have on industry structure and performance? (3) What cost disadvantages, if any, did firms of varying size face? and (4) What were the alternative social costs of county mine development associated with the existing pattern of industry development as opposed to the actual pattern of development?

The Uses and Objectives of Economic History

The gist of what I have been saying in my criticism of both quantitative and institutional economic historians is that ideal economic history, from my vantage point at any rate, is that which employs the best of both approaches. One need not be *ipso facto* opposed to the use of theory or quantitative materials; similarly, those who measure, should not be suspicious or have their minds closed to untidy, unconnected, institutional and qualitative facts. This is hardly a startling conclusion; people on both sides of the scholarly fence quickly affirm it. Yet, having once paid lip service to the assertion, too many scholars go their own merry way. This is to be regretted.

The larger issue which is implicit in my criticisms relates to the proper scope of economic history and to the use it has. "Economics," Jacob Viner once defined as "what economists do." Thus one answer to my question is: "economic history is what economic historians do, however they may do it." But one needs a bit more to go on than this. Economic history *is* descriptive, and proscriptive. As description it reconstructs the content and course of some economic magnitude or institution over time. Causal, dependent, and independent relationships and the like, hopefully may be drawn from such information; and these relationships may even dictate the form or content of the data. Descriptive economic history is the raw material for broader conceptualizations. Economic history as proscription not only tests contemporary economic theory with empirical proofs from the past but in its best moments offers basic conditions and premises for more predictive theory.

The integration of analysis and description as the proper scope for the economic historian can be accomplished, however, only if we line our research with what the great economic historian Clapham called "marked, quantitative interests." It is hard to improve upon another of Chapham's dicta: "Every economic historian should . . . have acquired what might be called a statistical sense, the habit of asking in relation to any institution, policy, group or movement the questions: how large? how long? how often? how representative?"[20]

The study of economic history in the United States is at a very critical point. We seem to be so fascinated by economic development that most quantitative and non-quantitative work is tied, however tenuous the connection, to this theme. From my point of view this emphasis is justified. The attempts to understand the process as well as the results of capital formation, to assess the importance of income distribution and resource mobility, and to appraise the contribution of non-economic forces to the changing structure and performance of the American economy are all attempts worthy of support. However, judging by the sample of current work in economic history on which this paper is based, a sample admittedly small and select, I think that progress in understanding the driving forces and results of American economic development will be stymied so long as institutional and quantitative economic historians plod along in general ignorance of each other's respective contributions.

---

[20] John H. Clapham, "Economic History" in *Encyclopedia of the Social Science,* reprinted in Fritz Stern, ed.; *Varieties of History;* New York 1962; pp. 308-313.

The Nature and Objectives of Economic History

CHESTER W. WRIGHT *

The nature and objectives of economic history can best be made clear if we first describe its position among the other branches of the study of economics. The study of economics can be subdivided into (1) the science of economics, which is concerned with the formulation of economic laws or principles; (2) the techniques of (a) accounting, which deals exclusively with economic phenomena; and (b) statistics, which, though most extensively used and developed in dealing with economic data, is by no means confined to this use and may, perhaps, be more properly classified as a branch of logic; (3) the study of economic history in the broad sense, which covers all the facts of economic life and development of the past whether recent or remote. This field of facts however, is commonly subdivided into (a) the more specialized studies of so-called applied economics and (b) economic history in the more customary sense of the term. Though no sharp differentiating line can be drawn, the practical difference between these two branches of history is that applied economics commonly studies a contemporary problem in a limited field of economic activity and is often specifically directed toward laying down some line of action for dealing with the problem. The economic historian, on the other hand, is expected to cover the whole range of economic life and development of a nation or group of nations and over a considerable period of time, though his monographic studies may be limited to a small sector of the field. Its all-inclusive scope and its primary concern with the evolutionary development of the whole economic order chiefly distinguish economic history from applied economics.

To understand the objectives of economic history it is essential to make clear the underlying problem with which it is concerned. This is the more necessary since the study and writing of economic history have been largely undertaken by two groups, one approaching the subject with the training and point of view of the political historian and the other with the training and point of view of the economist. The historian's chief interest in the subject is ordinarily based upon the light which it can throw upon

---

* Chester Wright was Professor of Economics at the University of Chicago from 1907 to 1944. He now resides in Chicago.

political or social history — in short, the influence of economic conditions and forces upon history. The economist, on the other hand, looks upon economic history as primarily a study of how a given people have proceeded in their endeavors to supply their economic wants, as an analysis of the means they have employed and the institutions and economic order they have evolved in their effort to raise their standard of living. For just as the main objective of the study of economics is to aid man in his struggle to supply his economic wants, so economic history, by describing and analyzing man's past efforts to raise his standard of living, seeking to explain wherein and why he has succeeded and where and why he has failed, is directed toward indicating how he may do still better in the future. This may be called the functional approach to the study.

Obviously, since history must be founded upon facts, the first task of the economic historian must be the establishing of the facts. But the determination of the facts is only the first step; those facts and the trends of development which they portray must, so far as possible, be explained and interpreted if the study is to make its most valuable potential contribution to human progress. The student of economic history is often appalled, if not repelled, by the mass of factual detail with which he is confronted. Yet these facts are full of human significance if the student will but inquire as to their broader meaning and seek to formulate the ideas that lie hidden within them. As the historian Ranke once said, particulars carry generalities within them. Just as Isaac Newton, seeking to explain the fall of a particular apple, evolved the general, so the student of economic history in dealing with its mass of detail must constantly ask the question: What light does this or that little fact throw upon the problem of how this people proceeded in their efforts to maintain or to raise their standard of living? Only thus can the essential unity and coherence of the many topics covered be brought out and the mass of factual detail be made interesting, humanly significant, and valuable.

In order to appreciate the relation of these facts to this central problem the student must fully understand and constantly keep in mind the main factors involved. The standard of living of any people depends, first, upon what they produce or can secure through exchange of their products with other groups, and, second, upon how that product is distributed among them. What they produce is determined, first, by the quantity and what, for lack of a better term, may be called the quality of the four factors of production: natural resources, labor, capital, and business management; and, second, by the efficiency with which these factors are combined for purposes of production. The latter, in turn, is determined by the economic order with its institutional framework, including the related background of social organization in general, within which the given entrepreneurship must function. How the product is divided is also determined by this same economic and social environment.

No general economic history has ever been written, so far as I am aware, where the material was clearly organized along lines suggested by these basic factors in the underlying problem. To do so would be difficult and probably would not serve the various objectives of the study in the best manner. The histories that have been written typically are organized on the basis of the various fields of economic activity such as agriculture, manufacturing, commerce, finance, etc., or center about the more general changes in the organization of industrial society or simply seek to portray the economic background of political and social history. This often results either in the omission of important material bearing on the fundamental factors in the underlying problem or else in the failure of the reader to trace the connection between those factors and the material presented. Yet it is certainly possible to avoid these defects in an economic history where the material is organized on any of these different bases, and taking care to do so would greatly add to the reader's understanding and appreciation of the human significance of that material.

In this connection, however, the warning should be given that the promotion of the means for satisfying man's economic wants which must be the central problem and the primary objective of the study of economic history is not to be confused with advancing welfare. Whether the satisfaction of any specific economic want contributes to the advancement of human welfare is a problem beyond the province of the economist as such, just as is the question what determines man's wants in the first place. The chief social justification for the study of economic history, as of economics in general, must rest on the assumption that whether man wants much or little of economic goods, whether he is a sybarite or an ascetic, and whether the satisfaction of a particular want promotes his welfare or not, it is always desirable, other things remaining equal, that these wants be satisfied at the minimum cost. It must also be equally obvious that the economic historian, just as the economic theorist, can never say what ought to be done except where the ultimate ends have been determined on the basis of valuations established or accepted by some system of religion, ethics, or philosophy of life. But with the ultimate social objectives agreed upon, the economic historian, aided by theory, can say that past experience indicates that on line of procedure will presumably further the attainment of the desired objective in the most economical manner while another line of procedure will not.

At this point it may be pertinent to indicate what this conception of the nature of economic history implies as regards the training and equipment of the economic historian other than the possession of the attributes

of scholarship in general. Since no important nation or group lives in economic isolation, the economic historian must know the main developments,
economic, political and social, of the rest of the world in so far as they had
an appreciable reaction on the country or group with which he is primarily
concerned. Obviously he must possess a knowledge of generally accepted
theory, while an acquaintance with the content of current controversy will
of course also prove useful. Familiarity with the essentials in the techniques
of accounting and statistics is necessary, while on occasions where refine-
ments are called for the aid of specialists in these fields may be required.
To be fully competent in contemporary as well as more remote history it
would be desirable to possess the knowledge of all the applied fields of
economics that is commanded by the specialists in those varied fields. In
short, the ideal economic historian would possess most of the knowledge
to be found in a large and well-rounded department of economics. Unfortunately this is not all, for he must have some knowledge of the whole
of the social and natural orders in which the economic order was set in so
far as the former exercised significant reactions upon the latter. Among
the social studies political history thus becomes especially important,
though the sociological, legal, religious, and other cultural factors cannot
be ignored. In the field of the natural sciences an equally broad background
will be found useful. The whole history of the sciences, both natural and
biological, and of the application of their contributions to knowledge as
they reacted upon the process of co-operation between man and his environment in man's efforts to provide for his economic wants thus becomes significant for the economic historian. Finally, if he seeks to delve
into the economy of certain periods and peoples, he will require the assistance of various other disciplines such as anthropology, epigraphy, pale-
ography, etc. That an individual possessing even a near approach to this
ideal equipment of the economic historian will seldom, if ever, be found is
obvious. But, if those who feel that the economic historian's products fall
short of much that could be desired will only recollect the magnitude of the
task confronting him, they may be disposed to be more lenient in their
judgments.

I now turn to what I conceive to be the main objectives of the study
of economic history or the chief purposes which it can serve. My previous
statement as to the nature of economic history has indicated my idea as to
its primary objective — that is, the raising of the standard of living through
the knowledge gained from a study of the past and applied to social guidance in the future. The economic problems confronting any country or
people today are largely a product of developments extending back over
a long period of time, and they cannot be dealt with effectively except as
we understand the historical and causal background out of which they have

arisen. Moreover, though we may accept the statement that history never repeats itself in the literal sense that all the factors entering into a given historical event are never exactly duplicated, yet it is equally true in the less literal sense that history is always repeating itself. This, for reasons subsequently indicated in more detail, is much more frequently the case in the field of economic history than in the field of political history where the more incalculable factor of individual, as contrasted with mass, action plays a larger role in determining the course of events. Thus in the field of economic history a study of the past is peculiarly fruitful in throwing light upon the present.

Undoubtedly the experts in those fields of applied economics where specialization has occurred will be better prepared to provide guidance, each in his own peculiar field, than the economic historian. The contribution of economic history to the specialist will consist in providing analogous situations from past experience, making clear the general background, indicating the complex interrelationship between the various specialized lines of economic activity, and suggesting the trends in the evolving economic order as a whole. The marked advantage gained through the study of economic history, in addition to the sense of evolution and relativity, is that breadth and scope of general background which necessitates a view of all the factors, economic and noneconomic, which enter into such specialized problems, while it alone surveys the economic process as a whole.

If we turn from this major objective of economic history to consider other objectives there appear several of sufficient importance to justify separate consideration.

One may be called the nationalistic objective — the study of economic history for the light which it can throw upon such economic factors as tend to augment the power of a country in the struggle for survival or aggrandizement among the nations. If we look back over the ages we see few nations that have risen to a position of dominance which have been able to maintain that position for any great length of time; one after another has fallen from its high estate. Hence, if we have any interest in the survival and success of the nation as a political unit and whatever it stands for, we must concern ourselves with a study of the conditions which tend to make for such survival. In this struggle the economic factor, always important, has had its importance vastly increased in modern times, chiefly through the rapid advance in the mechanization of warfare. Add to this the remarkable intensification of the spirit of nationalism which has recently swept the world and we can appreciate more clearly the importance which may be attached to this second objective. It must be noted, however, that while it is true, generally speaking, that conditions promoting an advance in a nation's standard of living will also augment its political power, there are numerous cases where the two objectives do not, or are believed not, to coincide; certainly not in the short run. Witness contemporary Germany or Italy, though every nation will afford frequent illustrations of the point.

A third objective served by economic history is to provide such knowledge of the economic conditions and background as may be essential for the understanding of any phase or period in the civilization of any people — in short, to provide a basis for the economic interpretation of history, using that phrase in the broad rather than the narrow Marxian sense. Just how important the economic factor may be in the interpretation of the political or any other phase of the social process doubtless always will afford opportunity for dispute, so long as there is no accurate basis for measuring the influence of any one of the infinitely complicated mass of factors entering into the problem. I believe most economic historians would also readily admit the possibility of various other so-called interpretations of history, such as the geographic or the spiritual; and I am confident that a biochemical or an astronomical interpretation could be worked out if one deemed it worth while to stress the importance of some such factor. But, regardless of the dispute as to the exact degree of importance of the economic factor in history, there will probably be few today who will deny it a position of any importance; the whole trend in historical writing during the last half-century is sufficient evidence on the point. While the economic historian may be called upon to provide such economic material for the background of general history as others require, it does not seem to me to be his function as such to undertake the interpretation of this history, that being a task for which the political historian, or better still the historian covering all aspects of a given civilization, should be better qualified.

A fourth objective is to further the development of economic theory and to fructify that theory. Of course it is perfectly possible to develop a system of theory based on assumptions which have no relation to facts or economic history if it is thought worth while to do so; but I assume there are few theorists who do not hope to make their theory of greater use than as pure mental gymnastics. If so, they cannot ignore economic history. This does not mean that the theorist must make the whole range of economic history his laboratory, and yet that vast store of material is full of data of which he can well make use. Economic history fructifies economic theory just as theory fructifies history; they cannot make their most valuable contributions to knowledge without each other. Together they provide the basic elements for the study of economics.

The ways in which history and theory fructify each other are various.

Theory should provide much of the explanation for the course of developments in economic history; and without an understanding of why things developed as they did the facts lose much of their value. Theory also suggests what facts to look for as particularly significant. The economic historian, I fear, has not made the use of theory that he should; and this can be attributed only in part to the two main difficulties with which he finds himself confronted in the effort to do so. The first arises from the frequent lack of general agreement among the theorists as to what is correct theory. The second is due to the fact that the premises upon which much theory is built differ so from the actual conditions in a given historical case that the use of theory in explaining the situation is greatly limited.

Economic history aids theory by providing the only laboratory in which a practical test of its validity is possible. Occasionally the theorist may be in a position to initiate an experiment on a small scale in private business or on a much larger scale under governmental auspices, as in Soviet Russia or in our own recent alphabetical progeny. Unsatisfactory as this may be from the point of view of the ideal, the historical data thus resulting have to be employed as best they can. If the facts, assuming they are accurate and adequate, cannot be explained by theory, then either the theory is wrong, of if correctly deduced from the premises, it is useless for practical purposes, or at best simply suggestive. History then implies that the theory be revised or that it be developed upon premises that correspond to the factual situation. The picture of the institutional framework of any given period and of the evolution of that institutional background through the centuries is particularly important in making clear the relativity of any theory with its fixed premises for the practical purposes of explanation or guidance in action. The extent to which the trends of development in theory have been shaped by history is only too obvious, from the controversies of the mercantilist period through the physiocrats and the English classical school down to the economic history of the post-World War period with its impetus to the resurvey of monetary, banking, and cycle theory and the belated awakening to the need for a theory of imperfect competition.

A fifth objective is to provide the student of economic history with at least some guidance in meeting the problem of getting a living. He faces that problem in a business world which has been largely shaped by economic history, and through his life his efforts to get a living will be reacted upon by historical developments. The typical content of historical study will throw little or no light upon the problems connected with the internal organization of a business enterprise or upon the technique of an occupation. But the general trends in economic development may have powerful reactions upon a business, an occupation, or an investment; and it behooves the individual who would be successful to try to understand what those reactions are likely to be. For this purpose more remote history also provides many a lesson of value. The farmer or manufacturer who knew something of the economic reactions following the Civil War would have been better prepared to meet those that followed the World War. Though this objective is stated in terms of private gain, it is obvious that, in so far as it results in decreasing waste and increasing economic efficiency, it furthers social objectives as well.

A sixth objective would be a better understanding of ourselves. We are in part the product of the economic age in which we live, of the economic conditions in the country and section where we reside, of the economic class in which we are brought up, and of the pursuit whereby we strive to earn a living. Our aspirations, our ideals, and our notions on problems of economic and social policy are inevitably in some measure shaped by these influences or by our reactions against them. One of the outstanding lessons which the study of economic history must bring home to us is the extent and power of such influences and the undesirable consequences of social action that is so frequently the outcome of the biased ideals and judgments which ensue therefrom, though these may be as sincere and honest as our convictions on most other issues. If we can learn to study and understand the influences of this character to which we have been subject, and then have the reason and the will to endeavor, as best we can, to counteract any bias resulting therefrom, we can accomplish much in furthering economic and social progress.

Possibly there should be included as a seventh objective a purely cultural one — the acquisition of such knowledge of economic history as may be considered essential in a well-rounded education, quite independent of its use for social objectives. The important part played in human history by the economic factor would appear to justify considering some knowledge of economic history, particularly that of one's own country, as a desirable part of one's cultural equipment. In addition, the subject can be pursued in more detail for the mere satisfaction of intellectual curiosity.

As a final objective there may be listed the formulation of laws of economic development or a philosophy of economic history. I list this last because I do not believe that in our present stage of knowledge it is possible to formulate laws of economic development that have universal validity. The nearest approach to such a law that I can suggest is the age-long tendency toward greater functional specialization or division of labor. The efforts to formulate a certain sequence in the stages of economic development have been shown to be still less valid generalizations. Yet such generalizations, imperfect as they may be, are still useful. Their utility suggests the possibility of developing what may be called, in the sense in which Cournot used the term, a philosophy of economic history.

Cournot, approaching history from the standpoint of one interested in the theory of probabilities, declared that the factor chance, which he defined as the product of the several mutually independent series of causes and effects which accidentally meet to produce a result, was so prominent in history that the formulation of scientific laws of historical development was impossible. Yet he held that it was possible, by using statistical or other technique to abstract the abnormal or accidental, get at the average or the usual, and so to pick out the dominant forces and the more persistent tendencies in history. Thus, by distinguishing the general or essential forces and tendencies from the particular, individual, or accidental it would be possible to draw philosophical inductions and to form hypotheses which would enable us better to explain the past and to predict future trends with a greater degree of accuracy. In this manner, he held, we may formulate a philosophy of history, frankly recognizing that its generalizations lack the universality of a scientific law.

As I view it, there are various reasons which render this method particularly applicable to economic history, especially as contrasted with political history. My reasons for so thinking can be briefly summarized as follows. The fundamental factors in history are man and the physical universe; but for our purposes we may make a further rough subdivision into (1) the individual man, each unique; (2) the masses, reflecting the more essential and common traits of man; (3) the whole institutional fabric evolved by society; and (4) the physical universe. Each of these is reacted upon by the rest.

The influence exerted by the unique personality of individuals upon the course of political history is vastly greater than in the case of economic history. You find no counterpart of an Alexander, a Caesar, or a Napoleon in economic history; a Fugger, a Rothschild, or a Morgan does not appreciably alter its general course, even for a brief time. It would be difficult to write a political history without some account of the character of the men who played the leading roles. Economic history can be written with few of such characterizations and vastly less mention of even the names of individuals; while a goodly fraction of those that may be named will be noted because of action in the political arena which affected economic conditions. This is not asserting the big-man interpretation of political history, or denying that the individual is largely a product of his times and exerts an influence chiefly as he acts in harmony with social trends. It is only saying that his influence is greater in the field of political than in that of economic history and that because each individual is unique, the product of chance, his action and its results are less certain and predictable. Its corollary is that in economic history mass action is relatively more important than in political history.

The influence of this second factor; mass action, is obviously great in the political field as well. But here it is determined by a vastly wider range of human instincts and emotions than in the economic field. In the latter, the field of purely business relations, there is one simple dominating motive, that of the economic man. The sway of this motive is not absolute; it will vary as between groups or peoples and as between periods among a given people. Nor is rational calculation always present even in strictly business relations. But the motive is sufficiently dominant so that the lines of mass action in economic affairs in the past can be analyzed and for the future can be predicted with a fair degree of accuracy, certainly greater than is possible in the political field.

In the case of the third factor, the institutional background, we also have a better basis for analysis and prediction in the economic than in the political field. The general framework of economic institutions has a greater degree of fixity and continuity than that of the political order. You cannot have a revolution overnight in the economic order. It is too complex, too interdependent, and too vast, and its continuous functioning too essential to human existence to permit such sudden sweeping change. The so-called Industrial Revolution was spread over at least sixty years. The experience of Russia well suggests the difference between the difficulties incident to carrying through a political revolution and an economic revolution — the latter is still in process.

In the case of the fourth factor, the physical universe, we have such basis for certainty of prediction as the present state of the natural and biological sciences provides. There the only element of uncertainty assuming the accuracy of our present knowledge, arises from such advance in knowledge as the future may achieve. But whether this more certain factor can be said to be of greater influence in the economic than in the political field, as I strongly suspect is the case, I would hesitate to assert.

If this analysis be correct it indicates that economic history provides much greater prospects for developing a philosophy which will prove valuable in interpreting the past and in forecasting the general trend of developments in its field with more accuracy and for a somewhat longer period of time than is possible in political history. This, it seems to me, is what Karl Marx did; not accurately or on the basis of reasons that were always sound, yet with unusual success considering the difficulties of the problem. And I would not minimize those difficulties. The greatest factors of uncertainty upsetting prediction are likely, however, to arise outside the field of economics: first, in the political field, notably war; second, and in the long run more fundamental and far-reaching, from the progress of science and invention. Despite the difficulties, the development of a philosophy of history in the sense previously indicated may well be included among the objectives of the economic historian. So far as it can be developed, it will serve to throw a great light upon the interpretation of the past. Whether the still greater service of attempting to forecast future trends which it may provide is a task which the economic historian should assume may be left as an open question. Trends in particular lines may be better foreseen by the specialists in the various branches of applied economics; but outlining the more general trends can be attempted only by those whose breadth of view of the economic order is as great in scope as that which the economic historian should possess. The task, by whomsoever assumed, has become the more vital and pressing in these days when the world so belatedly is first engaging in comprehensive social planning on the grand scale.

In conclusion: If I were to choose a philosophy of history I should look upon the history of civilization as the record of man's struggle for more complete self-development and self-expression along the lines contributing to the enduring satisfactions of life. This should suggest the fundamental forces and factors which shaped the records of civilization and provide the master-key for their interpretation. In this struggle for self-expression we of the Western world at least have chosen a mode of living that involved an ever increasing dependence upon economic means for its support. The simple life of the ascetic, the Buddhist ideal of minimizing wants dependent upon material things and finding the highest and most enduring satisfactions in a life of contemplation have made little appeal to us. We have chosen, whether rightly or wrongly, what we consider a richer, a fuller life. But whether that life be spent in play or in pursuit of the more sensual and momentary pleasures or be devoted to the cultural arts and higher self-development, it requires increasing economic means, both to make possible the greater leisure for such activities and to provide for their support. In pursuit of this ideal we of the United States have been fortunate enough to attain the highest standard of living any important country has ever known. The analysis of how that result was attained constitutes the fundamental problem of the student of our economic history. But we must also face the stark fact that the whole of this attainment in national income, when equally divided, is only sufficient to provide us all with a standard of living little higher than what has been called the minimum of decency. How this can be increased constitutes the practical problem toward the solution of which the economic historian's analysis of the past is primarily directed. Pursued with the objectives I have indicated, the study of economic history, in co-operation with the other branches of economics and with advancing knowledge in general, may hope to promote that higher standard of living so essential in furthering the more complete realization of man's aspirations. This faith must be the *apologia pro vita sua* of the economic historian.

PART TWO

Economic Growth in the Colonial Economy

CONTENTS

I.

EDITOR'S INTRODUCTION

It has become an issue of some priority in recent years to examine the origins of economic development, and in particular, the beginnings of industrialization. Walt Rostow's celebrated yet heavily criticized essays on the stages of economic growth typified a vast yearning on the part of practitioners in underdeveloped areas for a framework of analysis to fit the early and rich experience of economic history (of the West, primarily) to the urgent needs of the present. Before and after Rostow a huge literature was developing aimed at understanding the mechanisms and processes of economic development. But it has now become obvious to many scholars that the early excitement and promise of the study of the dynamic elements in economic development in already industrialized societies for today's "Third World" failed to materialize. Economic history and economic development, though they have much to offer each other, must now stand or fall as separate spheres of human and institutional study. The policy results of the almagamation of the two can be at best only nominally rewarding.

These prefatory statements are made in a unit on American colonial economic development because this period — the most unexplored in American economic history — has much to commend itself to the policy-minded scholar of today's underdeveloped world. Yet the fruits of such a search are not to be identified with the search itself. The semi-autonomous growth of the American colonies premised on a large export sector, incredibly sharp entrepreneurial attitudes and favorable economic, social, and political institutions would appear to most underdeveloped countries of today (non-Communist ones, in any case) as a bill of particulars by which a society can break the circle of poverty. Unfortunately this is not the entire case: the study of economic development of the American colonies is intertwined with the study of economic development in the abstract, but policy implications must rest on results for a particular case at a particular time.

The noted historian Clarence Ver Steeg has recently chastised his fellow historians for having neglected the colonial 18th century (1693 to 1763) and suggests that the reasons for this are to be found in the absence of a unifying theme.[1] Yet all serious writers of colonial history have noted that the 18th century was one of unparalleled economic growth — a period in which the horizontal and vertical extensions of the colonial economy made progress far ahead of any reasonable expectations. Here is a theme worth extended development; and yet scholarly accounts of the colonial 18th Century economy have in the main fallen into an historian's no-man's land.

II.

The two selections that follow, by Taylor (see pp.   ) and Lester, (pp.   ), are not offered as an answer to the grander scheme of analysis pleaded for by Ver Steeg. As a matter of fact, one piece is merely exploratory (Taylor), and the other (Lester) is a quarter-century old and only deals with a topic of importance in a restricted time period and place. Certain contours of American colonial growth are outlined below but it should be pointed out here that no period of our national development remains as untouched by testable generalizations as does this one. It is for this reason that the piece by Taylor, originally given as a Presidential address to the Economic History Association, deserves the attention of American historians. Scholars simply do not know all the details of the long path of economic expansion from the founding of the American colonies to the Revolution. Taylor suggests a number of potentially testable interpretations relying exclusively on qualitative information, or at best on fragmentary quantitative data. If the development of the American colonies is to be studied from the vantage point of the economics of underdevelopment — and most importantly if it is to have relevance to the stream of American history — one simply must know the dynamic elements at work in the process of economic development and growth.

The article by Lester dealing with a much neglected yet important historiographic topic also deserves to be noted by the current generation of American historians. The role of paper money and financial institutions in our national life is still subject to untenable clichés and shibboleths. This is equally true of the prevailing historical wisdom concerning the colonial use of and experimentation with novel financial institutions and monetary policies. For a bearing on the pace of American colonial economic growth the issues discussed by Lester were of uppermost priority.

[1] "The North American Colonies in the Eighteenth Century, 1688-1763" in *31st Yearbook, National Council for the Social Studies,* Chapter III, pp. 24-37. In a most rewarding book, *The Formative Years, 1607-1763;* New York 1964, Ver Steeg has done a wonderful summary of the Structure and Performance of the Provincial Economy. See especially Chapters 7 and 8.

III.

In the following sections, and in order to provide some reference framework for the articles by Taylor and Lester, I intend to sketch out some of the outward evidence concerning the path of colonial economic expansion. The topics to be commented on are population, international and interregional trade, certain indexes of physical output, growth, prices, and the supply of money.

Population

In the colonial statistics collected in the compendium, *Historical Statistics of the United States From Colonial Times to the Present,* for the first time there is now available to historians a population series for the colonies based on extrapolations from reasonably reliable reference dates. An independent compilation by the editor from one of the major sources of population data conforms quite closely with the series given in *Historical Statistics.* Both series are shown in Chart I. In any case, one is primarily interested in trend of growth rather than annual or decadal differences, and although for the nearest comparable years the two series diverge somewhat for the years before 1680, they are moving on roughly equal trend paths. An independent check of the population for New York province against the data in *Historical Statistics* (shown in Table I) will confirm this.

The components of population growth were the natural rate of increase of the population and net immigration. The former was both absolutely *and* relatively the more important component during the colonial period, but there were important peaks of net immigration in the last two decades of the 17th and the third and fourth decades of the 18th Centuries. Immigration was nonetheless an important component of population growth and, as Ver Steeg has noted, "without it the growth of the American provinces in the eighteenth century could well have been retarded." [2] However, aside from being able to identify the major ethnic sources, it is also necessary to estimate the volume of immigration. Between 1710 and 1770 perhaps as many as 200,000 non-English white persons had already migrated to the Provinces. It is usually noted that by 1776 one-third of the provincial population had non-English native origin, which would suggest a quite high numerical importance of immigration to population growth. Ver Steeg and others have questioned this figure, arguing that it could only be accepted if one included the slave population. Of the white population

---

[2] Ver Steeg, *The Formative Years;* Hill and Wang; New York 1964; p. 169.

Chart I.

POPULATION TRENDS IN COLONIAL
AMERICA, 1630-1740; TWO VIEWS

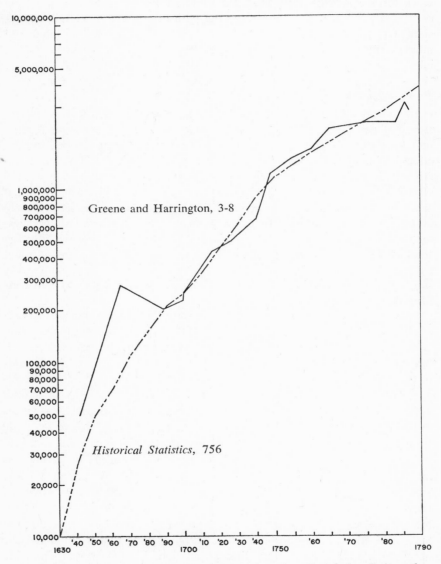

Sources: E. B. Greene and V. Harrington, *American Population Before the Fed. Census of 1790* (N.Y., Col. U. Press), pp. 3-8; *Historical Statistics of the U.S.: From Colonial Times* to the Present (GPO, Washington, 1960) Series Z1 - 19, p. 756.

TABLE I.

POPULATION OF NEW YORK PROVINCE, 1703-1771

Year	Total (inc. Slaves)		Slaves	
1703	20,049	[19,107] (c)	1,625 (a)	[2,256] (c)
1712	(14,851) (a)		2,237 (a)	
1723	40,564	[36,919]	6,171	[5,740]
1731	50,289	[48,594]	7,231	[6,956]
1737	60,437		8,941	
1746	61,589		9,107 (b)	
1749	73,448	[76,696]	10,692	[11,014]
1756	96,765		13,542	
1771	168,007	[162,920]	19,883	[19,112]

Notes:
  (a) Only includes New York, Kings, Richmond, Orange, Westchester, and Ulster and Dutchess (Data for 1714) Counties. Slave figures for Ulster and Dutchess at 1700 and 1714.
  (b) Does not include City and County of Albany.
  (c) Bracketed figures are population at nearest even decadal year as given in *Historical Statistics of United States*, p. 751.
SOURCE: E. B. O'Callaghan, (comp.) *The Documentary History of the State of New York*, Vol. I (Albany, 1849), pp. 691-697.

alone, perhaps 10 to 15% were of non-English origins on the eve of the Revolution.

International Trade

The total values of imports and exports by the American colonies to and from England are plotted in Chart II. These are in official values, pound sterling, and do not therefore include so-called invisible items. Nonetheless, again being only interested in sketching out trend relationships, it will suffice to use official value figures. A greater disadvantage, however, is that trade with England accounted for perhaps 80% of the combined value of total colonial international trade by the 1750's and 1760's. There are no published trade figures for the other regions, mainly the British and French colonies of the West Indies and Southern Europe, but the volume was large and the importance was great in balancing international payments of the American colonies. It is not necessary here to examine the traditional notions concerning the colonial trade balance with England, either in the aggregate or for individual colonies. Many statements have been made about both matters but until a unified balance of payments account is available most of what is concluded is at the level of informed conjecture. But three points deserve mention in regard to the figures in Chart II: (1) the unmistakable upward trend, (2) the break

Chart II.

TOTAL VALUE OF EXPORTS TO ENGLAND FROM AMERICAN COLONIES, 1700-1770 (in pounds sterling)

TOTAL VALUE OF IMPORTS FROM ENGLAND TO AMERICAN COLONIES 1700-1770 (in pounds sterling)

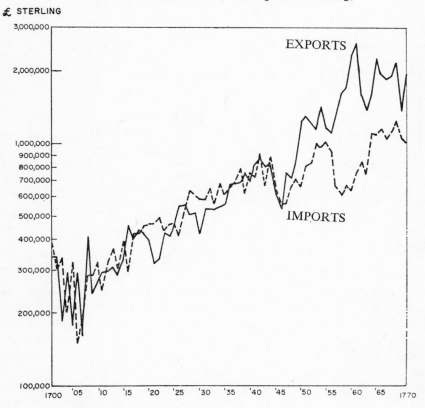

Source: *Historical Statistics of the U.S.,* 757.

in the aggregate trade balance with the mother country which began in 1745, and (3) the relative stability in the range of annual fluctuations in the trade balance between 1710 and 1745. All three points, of course, have much to do with any appraisal of the secular growth of the colonies. The increasing divergence of imports and exports after 1745 suggest a firmer footing for interpretations one might place on the change in British Colonial policy, more or less coinciding with the break in the trade data.

Relating these trade figures to per capita measures (which may be taken here as a rough approximation of secular changes in personal economic welfare) reveals a somewhat more sober picture than is evident from Chart II alone. There is about a 50% decline in the combined value of imports and exports from and to England between 1700 to 1720, virtually no change in per capita levels for the next two decades, about a 10% increase in the 1740's, and a 20% increase in the 1750's. Imports per capita, which may be a better approximation to changes in the level of living, behaved slightly differently: imports from England to all the colonies and adjusted by a wholesale price index, rose by 10% in the 1720's, 22% in the 1730's, 1% in the 1740's, and 30% in the 1750's. If the import balance is indeed a rough approximation to changes in personal consumption of market produced goods, and if this in turn is in some sense relevant to personal welfare, it can be said that the level of living in the colonies in per capita terms was about one and one-half times greater in 1760 than in 1715 or 1720. What is more, this advance appears to have been spread relatively evenly throughout all the colonies, although from about 1745 on, the northern group (New England, New York and Pennsylvania) accumulated imports per capita at an appreciably faster rate than did the southern group of colonies (Virginia, Maryland, and the Carolinas).

Inter-colonial trade

The volume of inter-colonial trade is known to have been extensive, especially from the 1740's on. Table Z56-75 on page 759-760 of *Historical Statistics* does, however, collect tonnage figures of outward and incoming ships by destination for the major ports of the thirteen colonies. Without reproducing such figures here, it should be noted that continued outward and incoming tonnage from the ports of Boston, New York, Philadelphia, Hampton, and Charleston grew about five-fold between the 1730's and 1770's.

Physical Output

The known production of important raw and semi-finished commodities in the American colonies is, by and large, limited to only a few items. The best available data are to be found in *Historical Statistics*. It is suggested that for certain raw material and food products, these crudely illustrative measures indicate an output growth in excess of total population growth. Pig iron exported to England, which by 1768 probably accounted for about

3/4ths of colonial pig iron output, rose from a per annum average (1731-35) of 2,300 tons to slightly over 3,200 tons by the middle years of the 1760's. Converting Bining's well-known figures on colonial and world iron production of all types (with 1775 as the base year) shows a rise in the colonial index of from 5 in 1700 to 30 in 1750, while our share of world iron production increased from 1.5% at the beginning of the 18th Century to 14% on the eve of the Revolution.[3] One should not be misled into believing that the existence of an important iron industry constituted a base upon which modern industrialization could be founded. This was not the case. Rather the industry should be considered as one providing both a large volume of domestic employment and a steady and consistent earner of foreign exchange; it is the latter which ties the output of the domestic iron industry to colonial economic welfare, for it was the earnings from exports that enabled the provinces to finance the growing and relative volume of imports. The same comments also hold for all the mix of products that were produced domestically, and exported by the colonials; tobacco, rice, indigo, furs, silk, timber and timber products (ships and naval stores), and the heavy grains of the middle colonies all served as sources of domestic employment and income generation, as well as being earners of foreign exchange by which imports were ultimately financed. Though one can discern differential rates of growth in the output of these respective commodities throughout the 18th Century, the trend was unmistakably one at rates equal to and in most cases in excess of population growth rates.

Prices

Fortunately, there is extant a great deal of information about colonial prices — the major series being collected in *Historical Statistics*. The series presented in Chart III are Ethel Hoover's on wholesale prices. The trend of prices (as indicated in the chart) was a rising one throughout the pre-Revolutionary period. However it should be noticed that the amplitude of price fluctuations was remarkably narrow, considering the underdeveloped nature of the colonial economy. The relationship of the price level to economic development is one that has been widely debated by development economists. The balance of opinion seems to favor the conclusion that a rising price level is most consistent with high rates of growth in national income and output, although one can easily suggest historical cases (for example, the United States in the 1869-1894 period) where this was not the case.[4] Nonetheless, it is of great interest to the general historian to

---

[3] Arthur C. Bining; *British Regulation of the Colonial Iron Industry;* Thesis at University of Pennsylvania, Philadelphia 1933; p. 134; raw data also cited in *Historical Statistics,* p. 746.

[4] A book which historians could well profit from on this point is Geoffrey Maynard; *Economic Development and the Price Level;* Macmillan, London 1962.

Chart III.

INDEX OF WHOLESALE PRICES FOR
COLONIES AND UNITED STATES, 1720-1780
(1850-59 equal 100)

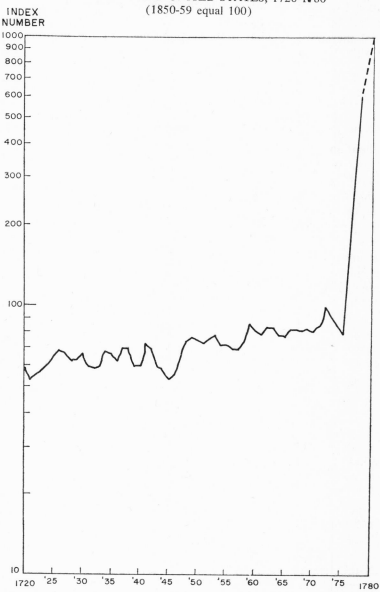

Source; *Historical Statistics*, 772.

consider the movement of prices in colonial times, for so much of the qualitative literature on the political relationship of social classes turns on a discussion of the relative impact of changing economic conditions. This is a point directly relevant to the issue of paper money in colonial times and the debtor-creditor controversy concerning the use of such financial measures. Judging from the movement of the wholesale price index, the fears of runaway inflation during the 18th Century on the part of those provincials opposed to non-traditional monetary expedients seem not to have materialized. But there is more discussion on this matter both in the section on the role of money and in Richard Lester's article.

Long-term growth rates

Without any statistical series on national income, and its level, structure, and composition, or on capital formation and the relative efficiency and growth of productive factors, one can only speculate about the long-term performance of the colonial economy in terms of growth rates of income or product per capita. Taylor, in the article reprinted here (p. 57), speculates about these matters, and it may therefore be instructive to suggest some numerical relationships which may give some "feel" to our understanding of probable rates of growth in the 18th Century. The trend rate of population growth between 1650 and 1770 was 3.30%, compounded annually. To keep total output growing at the same rate as population therefore implies an annual rate of growth of 3.30%. If an increase of 1% in national output requires that 3½% must be invested (an assumption made for illustrative purposes only), then in the previous example the colonial economy would have to have invested annually 15.05% of its national product. To allow for a 1% increase in income or output per head would require annually investing 18½% of national product. It seems improbable that the colonial economy could have achieved these levels of capital investment or of the implied expansion in total output. This suggests, therefore, that the average per capita per annum increase in national output must have been below 1%, and more than likely in the range of zero to .5% per annum. These rates are, however, statistically significant: a compound annual rate of 1% in per capita national product would result in a doubling in 64 years and a ½% annual rate would double per capita income in about a century.

These numbers are merely illustrative; it is well known that the outward evidence of the expansion of total output is impressive. The colonies made enormous economic advances in ways more relevant to our national history than can be related to probable long-term growth rates. One needs also to consider, in ways not yet done, the effect of the mercantilist legislation on the long-term growth rate of the colonies. Harper has made some calculations relevant to this point, but the frame of reference he adapts is generally inappropriate. One needs to know whether or not the structure of resource allocation in the colonies would have been fundamentally different in the absence of mercantilist restrictions. One then needs to know whether or not mercantilist laws significantly retarded or accelerated the forced flow of colonial resources into market patterns that were critical to its long-term growth rate.[5]

IV.

Supply of Money

It is alleged, and with some justification, that there was always a "shortage of money" in the American colonies, especially during the 18th Century. As James Ferguson has recently written, however: "The accepted view of the financial and monetary history of the American colonies needs revision. It owes too much to the influence of 19th century scholars who were themselves partisans in currency disputes".[6] The land banks and public bills of credit, institutions most severely criticized by 19th century writers, were recognized by Richard Lester in the 1930's and much earlier by Guy Callendar as not being villians in a predetermined policy of subversion against "sound money" but as practices logically arising in an economic situation where capital was scarce. The colonials' use of paper money, Callendar wrote, " . . . does not arise from any exceptional ignorance of monetary science on the part of the inhabitants, nor to a dishonest desire to defraud creditors, but is the natural result of their economic situation." [7]

The economic situation was determined by the trade patterns of the respective colonies. For areas such as Conn. and New Jersey, where the predominant direction of trade was internal and the accumulation of imports was from either Boston, New York or Phila., the degree of scarcity of specie tended to be greater than was the case of those areas of international trade (such as the three cities above). On the other hand, even the main centers of international trade in relative terms also felt the so-called shortage of money, although on an absolute evaluation the stock of money

---

[5] Harper's article is reprinted in Harry Schreiber; *United States Economic History: Selected Readings;* New York 1964; p. 42-78 and in Richard B. Morris, (ed.); *The Era of The American Revolution* (Harper Torch Book, 1965), pp. 3–39.

[6] E. James Ferguson; "Currency Finance: An Interpretation of Colonial Monetary Practices," in *William and Mary Quarterly,* 3rd series, Vol. X, No. 2; April 1953; p. 153.

[7] Guy S. Callendar, ed.; *Economic History of the United States;* Ginn and Company, New York 1909; pp. 8-9.

was greater there. This occurred because the volume of imports and re-exports passing through these cities both from international trade and from the intra-colonial and inter-colonial trade made the demand for money transactions purposes much higher than was the case in the relatively trade-locked colonies as New Jersey and Connecticut.

The level of economic transactions would have been undoubtedly facilitated had there been a responsive money stock in the colonies. But any shortage should be looked upon as one indigenous to the patterns of trade. It is clear that the pattern and level of economic activity valued other forms of investment higher than it did a larger "money supply." In the extreme case, had the colonies desired to have a flexible money supply, they could only have acquired it by giving up some imports. But other requirements and other investments had higher priorities in colonial economic development and consequently financial institutions as well as the supply of money had to get along as best they could.

It is really in this context that the use of paper money, either as emissions from land banks or as bills of credit from the colonial governments, must be considered. In a sense, colonial emissions of paper currency were an overt attempt to provide a money supply in a relatively painless and costless manner. It was most definitely to provide a money stock without having to give up any existing trade patterns, and hopefully it would also open up new ones. Extended debate, especially in Massachusetts Bay Province, over whether or not the sinews of trade were lubricated by paper money emissions, shows that the colonials were probably well aware of possible barriers to their economic development because of inadequate financial institutions and an inflexible money supply. Callendar wrote what most of the informed colonialists felt when he commented as follows:

> "Specie is no doubt the most perfect instrument to serve as a medium of exchange, but it is a very expensive one, and a new country may for some time be too poor to afford it. The same necessity, which induces the inhabitants to use inferior tools of husbandry, induces them to adopt a like policy with regard to their currency. It was not economic delusion simply that caused Franklin and Dickinson to regard colonial paper money with favor and its prohibition by the mother country as an act of tyranny. Poor as the paper money was, in Pennsylvania, at least, it seemed to them more economical than specie. It is always a question how far the losses do to an inferior currency outweigh its economies, and in a new country men are always prone to consider that question and test it by experience." [8]

Similarly, as the antagonism between the colonies and the mother country became more intense, many writers in England articulated what the

---

[8] Callendar, ed.; Ibid., p. 9.

colonists had been arguing for nearly a century. Lord Pownall in his book, *The Administration of the Colonies* (1764) well illustrates this point.

"The British-American colonies have not, within themselves, the means of making money or coin. They cannot acquire it from Great Britain, the balance of trade being against them. The returns of those branches of commerce, in which they are permitted to trade to any other part of Europe, are but barely sufficient to pay this balance. By the present Act of Navigation, they are prohibited from trading with the colonies of any other nations, so that there remains nothing but a small branch of African trade, and a scrambling profits of an undescribed traffic, to supply them with silver. However, the fact is, and matters have been so managed, that the general currency of the colonies used to be in Spanish and Portuguese coin. This supplied the internal circulation of their home business, and always finally came to England in payments for what the colonists exported from France. If the Act of Navigation should be carried into such rigorous execution as to cut off this supply of the silver currency to the colonies, the thoughts of administration should be turned to the devising of some means of supplying the colonies with money of some sort of other . . . . " [9]

Finally a statement by Jonathon Dickinson sums up the point of view which is being expressed here. After assessing both the necessity for a flexible money supply and its relation to the level of economic activity, Dickinson presents several well known arguments in defense of the colonies' use of paper money. He ends this discussion by appealing to British authorities to allow the colonials to develop such a money system.

"If it could be possible," Dickinson writes, "to establish a currency throughout the colonies, on some foundations of this kind, perhaps greater benefits might be derived from it, than would be generally believed without the trial." [10]

How is it then, that legend persists that the colonies were reckless as regards the use of paper currency? In part the accepted textbook accounts of colonial finance are based on the work of a group of scholars in the last quarter of the 19th Century whose own views toward paper money, of whatever form of issue, can only be called conservative. With the exceptions already noted for Richard Lester and Guy Callendar, nearly all the standard treatments of colonial finance, including the standard work by Curtis Nettels, argue that paper currency was not used successfully in the colonies, primarily on the basis of evidence drawn from the outstanding cases of its misuse in Massachusetts, Rhode Island, and South Carolina. But it is easy to establish, as Lester has done in the article reprinted here, that Pennsylvania, New Jersey, New York, and, to a certain extent, Del-

---

[9] Pownall. The Administration of the Colonies, as quoted in Callendar, ed.; loc-cir., p. 65.

[10] Dickinson, Political Writings, Vol. I, as cited in Callendar, ed.; loc-cit., p. 68.

aware, all used the emissions of bills of credit and the land bank institution with a considerable degree of success. One might even argue that the experience in the New England colonies, undoubtedly contributing to a somewhat inflated price structure, also provided a money stock which proved of some considerable assistance in the area's inter-Colonial trade patterns. The same might also be said for the experience with bills of credit in South Carolina, although in this case the final record of paper currency is totally unfavorable.

There is no desire to recount the separate experience with the use of paper currency in the individual colonies, for that has been done by other scholars. What is being suggested, however, is that the traditional notions by which the institutions of finance in the colonies are appraised by modern scholarship are considerably in error. There was an inadequate money stock as well as inadequate financial institutions, but this is true only because the direction of trade and the economic structure of the colonies made such institutions less desirable forms of capital investment than say, import balances or land holdings. On the other hand the issuing of paper currency *per se* does not indicate that the colonists were ignorant of what they were doing, but rather suggests that they sought a method of providing for an instrument of inter-and intra-Colonial trade in relatively short supply. Similarly, if one examines the effect of paper money issues on the level of economic activity in those colonies which had relatively good experience (as Richard Lester has done), one is able to associate increases in the stock of money very closely with increases in the level of economic activity. It does not suffice for critics to argue that ultimately most of the paper money issues did suffer severe depreciation relative to the British pound sterling, or even to other colonial currencies. What is important is that the issuance of paper currency during periods when the level of economic activity was expanding rapidly (as was the case especially in Pennsylvania from 1720 to 1745) greatly facilitated the process of internal and external exchange. On this basis one needs to view the colonial's use of paper currency as a low cost way of liquidizing available assets in order to facilitate trading from the back country to the seaports and from seaports to international markets.

In per capita terms, paper money outstanding did not appear to be excessive (shown in Table II) in the years before the Currency Act of 1750 was in effect. For New England, where a fairly reliable estimate of the paper money supply can be constructed, the growth in the paper money outstanding against population growth does show a slightly higher trend rate for the former. (See Chart IV, on p. 56.)[11]

---

[11] The basic data included in Brock and not in *Historical Statistics* are Boston Merchant's notes. See Leslie Van Horn Brock, *The Currency of the American Col-*

TABLE II

PAPER MONEY OUTSTANDING IN THE AMERICAN COLONIES
1710-1739

(all figures in colonial pounds)

Year	Paper Money Outstanding	Per Capita
1710	123,000	.4
1715*	395,000	1.02
1725*	581,000	1.06
1730	892,000	.42
1735*	586,000	.76
1739	1,296,000	1.43

*Data for these years was divided by an estimate of the population figures for the mid-decade point. It was assumed that one-half the increase between decades took place equally in the first and second five-year intervals.

Source: Compiled from data in *Historical Statistics*, p. 774.

Indeed, if one takes a look at the admittedly inadequate figures on paper money outstanding, as reported in *Historical Statistics,* the general conclusion reached for New England can be extended to the entire 13 colonies. The paper money stock grew about three times as fast in the aggregate as did the paper money stock in per capita terms. What is relevant here is not that the volume of paper money emissions was negligible, but rather that the necessity for a money stock was so urgent and was so tied to the patterns of trade that one would be foolhardy to suggest that these emissions had only bad effects on the level of economic activity in the colonies. Indeed, in per capita terms the paper money outstanding would seem to be very small. But one must remember that these data are by no means complete, though for at least those colonies that resorted quite frequently to issues of bills of credit or that had Land Banks, the paper money stock figures are reasonably accurate.

One final note should be made concerning the Land Banks institutions which materially contributed to the paper money supply. The Land Banks were widely used in the 18th Century and, as Lester notes below, with considerable success in certain colonies. Although a number of articles have appeared since Lester's (most notably one by Theodore Thayer), no one has yet written an economically sound analysis of the Land Banks. What is needed is an assessment of the economic functions of the Land Bank as a financial intermediary (aggregating savings for productive investments) as well as bank of issue. One certainly needs to know the rela-

onies, (Unpublished doctoral dissertation, University of Michigan, 1941), esp. Table II, Part B.

tionship of the bank to agricultural development in regard to loan and credit policies. And finally, an assessment of the respective bank's contribution to the stabilization of the inter-colonial trade and payments balance would be most helpful in understanding the undoubtedly important role played by these institutions in the economic life and growth of the American Colonies.

Chart IV.

NEW ENGLAND PAPER MONEY

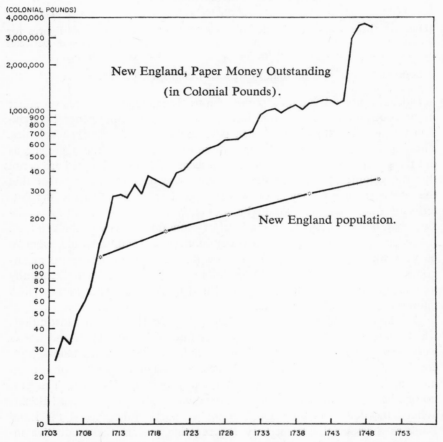

Sources: Van Brock, *Colonial Currency,* Table II, Part B; *Historical Statistics,* p. 756, 114.

American Economic Growth Before 1840:
An Exploratory Essay

GEORGE ROGERS TAYLOR *

In developing the subject of this paper, "American Economic Growth before 1840," I shall, relying for the most part on familiar materials, propose the hypothesis that economic growth per capita in the Thirteen Colonies of Britain in America advanced at a relatively rapid rate from about 1710 to 1775. I shall also suggest that the level of living remained relatively low in these colonies as late as about 1710 and that for the new nation over the years 1775 to 1840 output per capita improved slowly if at all.

Quantitative studies in economic history, and particularly those having to do with growth over appreciable periods of time, necessarily involve, to an extent often forgotten or ignored, basic assumptions and value judgments. Even under the most favorable circumstances data, never complete, have to be *manipulated* on the basis of *reasonable* assumptions. And price indices require *adjustment* because the importance of the items included changes over time. Moreover rates of productivity or growth should, if one is to be precise, be designated as rates of *measured* growth, for much of the contribution made to better living standards, for example by improved technical knowledge and business organization, defines quantification. So, as students well know but sometimes forget, growth rates computed over appreciable time spans imply a spurious exactness.

Nevertheless, if the limitations are kept in mind, attempts to determine numerical rates of growth may prove interesting and useful even where considerable reliance must be placed on non-quantitative material. Despite faulty and imperfect information students have combined careful analysis and bold assumptions to determine numerical values for the rate of economic growth in the United States since 1839. This accomplishment stimulates curiosity as to the rate of growth before that date in a period when data were even less complete. Many detailed studies need to be made before important questions can be answered with assurance. This essay consti-

---

* George Rogers Taylor was Professor of Economics at Amherst College and past president of the Economic History Association. He is now Research Prof. of Econ. History at the Eleutherian Library.

57

tutes merely a probing of this area — an effort primarily directed to making a tentative estimate of the rate of per capita growth from about 1710 to 1775 using the quantitative and qualitative materials readily at hand. It is hoped that the speculative conclusions sketched will provoke further investigation.

Raymond W. Goldsmith in his testimony in Washington before the Joint Economic Committee in 1959 focused his attention on the period 1839-1959. He concluded that the national product per head adjusted for price changes had averaged in the one hundred twenty years since 1839 close to one and five-eighths per cent per year. Incidentally, he raised the question as to the rate of American economic growth before 1839 — a period for which quantitative data did not permit reliable measurement. He concluded, on the basis of two alternative lines of reasoning, that the long run rate of one and five-eighths per cent could not be extended backward into the pre-1839 period. His two lines of reasoning are briefly summarized.[1]

First, assuming that the average real income per person in 1760 could not have been less than half the level of 1860, it follows that the average rate of growth per person from 1760 to 1839 was only about six-tenths of one per cent per annum. If this estimate approximates the true picture, it then follows that the trend line of growth from 1760 to 1839 was much flatter (rose less sharply) than it did thereafter. In fact, under this assumption it equalled only about one-third the subsequent annual growth rate.

Following an alternative line of reasoning, Goldsmith concluded that a continuous rate of per capita growth as high as one and five-eighths per cent per year was inconceivable for the pre-1839 period. Assuming the post-1839 growth rate projected backward from that year implies cutting in half the per capita income every forty-three years. So, if the average income per person in 1839 was about $400 based on present prices (as he suggests), the income per capita would have been $145 in 1776, $80 in 1739, and $30 in 1676. Studies of American living levels indicate that these average incomes are absurdly small for the late Colonial period and for seventeenth century America as well.

On such reasoning Goldsmith concluded:

> There seems little doubt, then, that the average rate of growth of real income per head was much lower than 1⅝ percent before 1839. If we consider periods of at least 50 years' length, it is questionable that we would find an average rate of growth as high as 1 percent in any one of them. There thus must have occurred a fairly sharp break in the trend of

---

[1] Hearings before The Joint Economic Committee, Part 2 — *Historical and Comparative Rates of Production, Productivity, and Prices* (Washington: Government Printing Office, 1959), pp. 277-8. [Reprinted in entirety in Part V.]

real national product per head some time before 1839. . . . I would hazard a guess . . . that the break occurred not very long before 1839 and that it reflects both the transition of the United States from a predominately agricultural to a more and more industrial country and the advent of the railroads.[2]

Goldsmith's suggestions (he clearly regarded them as no more than that) open up interesting lines of inquiry. Though his general deductions as to pre-1839 growth are acceptable, I question his supposition that 1839 may have been preceded by an extended period of gradual growth at a rate of 0.6 per cent per year and also his conclusion that in no period of fifty years duration before 1839 was the annual growth rate as high as one per cent. My own hypothesis is that until about 1710 growth was slow, irregular, and not properly measured in percentage terms; that from about 1710 to 1775 the rate of growth was relatively rapid for a preindustrial economy (perhaps one per cent per capita or even a little higher), and that from 1775 until 1840, or possibly a decade earlier, *average* per capita production showed very little if any increase.

I.

More than a century intervened between the first permanent settlement in Virginia in 1607 and the chartering of the Colony of Georgia in 1732. In any meaningful sense economic growth in the British continental colonies must have been relatively slow and uneven during most of the seventeenth century. Not only did the machinery of government have to be established and gradually adapted to meet local conditions but the early years were devoted to pushing back the Indians, learning to exploit immediate sources of income from fishing and trading in furs and deer skins, experimenting in raising agricultural crops, and the slow development of trade and communications both at home and with the rest of the empire. By the Peace of Utrecht (1713) or a little later, the early costs of economic experiment had, in most colonies, become largely a matter of the past. The colonies stood at the beginning of an era of remarkable development. Growth before this time was, of course, important in laying the basis for future development but it does not appear to have been generally very great in any absolute sense. Measurement in percentage growth rates for the seventeenth century is on the whole rather meaningless because increases must be computed from zero or at least from a very small base.

If productivity is measured by exports, the English West Indian possessions greatly surpassed the British North American colonies. But if size of population, the extent of settled territory, the number of independent

---

[2] *Ibid.*, p. 278.

farmers, or the development of an indigenous commerce and industry are compared, then, at least by the eighteenth century, a decided advantage lay with the mainland colonies of Great Britain. Perhaps the best overall evidence for the rapid increase in the gross product of the British North American colonies lies in the rapid population increase. It is estimated that the population in 1700 consisted of about 224,000 white persons and 28,000 negroes. By 1774 the whites numbered about 2,100,000 and the negroes 500,000.[3] The large size of this white population of European origin on the eve of the Revolution deserves emphasis. It equalled more than one-fourth that of the mother country and was perhaps sixty times that of the British Caribbean. In fact the white population of the Thirteen Colonies attained a rapid and sustained growth in the first three-fourths of the eighteenth century unique in colonial history.

If measured by gross product or per capita productivity of the free population a strong case can be made out for the conclusion that rapid economic growth characterized the plantation areas of the Southern Colonies for the sixty years beginning about 1710 or a little later. If the slaves be included in the reckoning the rate of per capita output would be reduced for the number of slaves increased more rapidly than the whites during these decades.

Tobacco became the staple produce of tidewater Virginia and Maryland soon after these colonies were founded early in the seventeenth century. Though the white population grew rapidly and a few great planters prospered, judging from contemporary reports, the average level of living for the white population improved slowly if at all until toward the end of the seventeenth century. But the second and third quarters of the eighteenth century brought rapid growth and the great age of colonial tobacco culture. European markets for tobacco expanded greatly and the increasing importation of African slaves after about 1680 apparently lowered the cost of tobacco production. By 1700 the slaves in Virginia totaled about 16,000. Their numbers had risen to 30,000 in 1730 (about 26 per cent of the total population); over 100,000 in 1750, and nearly 300,000 by 1790. The Maryland experience was similar. By 1770 the population of that colony reached 203,000 of which 64,000 were slaves.[4]

This prosperous tobacco economy depended on slave labor. Most independent yeoman farmers either drifted out to the frontier or became the

---

[3] Evarts B. Greene and Virginia D. Harrington, *American Population before the Federal Census of 1790* (New York: Columbia University Press, 1932), p. 7 and U.S. Bureau of the Census, *Historical Statistics of the United States, Colonial Times to 1957* (Washington, D.C., 1960), p. 756.

[4] U.S. Bureau of the Census, *Historical Statistics of the United States*, p. 756; Greene and Harrington, *American Population*, p. 142.

owners of at least a few slaves. The large plantations, some with hundreds of slaves, now increased in number and proved the most profitable producing units. Thomas J. Wertenbaker describes the situation as follows:

> . . . the Eighteenth century was the golden age of the Virginia slave holders. It was then that they built the handsome homes once so numerous in the older counties, many of which still remain as interesting monuments of former days; it was then that they surrounded themselves with graceful furniture and costly silverware, in large part imported from Great Britain; it was then that they collected paintings and filled their libraries with the works of standard writers; it was then that they purchased coaches and berlins; it was then that men and women alike wore rich and expensive clothing.[5]

In the more southern plantation area, that centering in tidewater South Carolina, settlement came late in the seventeenth century and plantation rice culture expanded rapidly in the opening decades of the eighteenth century. To this plantation slave economy, indigo was added as a profitable crop in the late 1740's. The economic growth in this region after about 1715 appears to have been even more rapid than in the tobacco colonies. The average annual Carolina rice crop increased fourteen times from 1716-20 to 1771-75.[6] Indigo production expanded tremendously after 1753. From 1747 to 1754 annual exports from Charleston averaged only about sixty-five thousand pounds but by 1772-75 the average had grown by more than twelve times.[7] In commenting on the prosperity of this area just preceding the Revolution, Lewis C. Gray cites an estimate which places the return on rice production at nearly thirty per cent on the capital invested and even higher for indigo.[8]

David Ramsay, a respected authority on South Carolina history, states that:

> Few countries have at any time exhibited so striking an instance of public and private prosperity, as appeared in South Carolina between the years 1725 and 1775.[9]

According to him, frugal and industrious planters doubled their capital every three or four years, "laborers on good lands cleared their first cost and charges in a few years," and immigrant settlers "commonly left their children in easy circumstances."[10] These statements appear extreme and

---

[5] *The Planters of Colonial Virginia* (Princeton: Princeton University Press, 1922), pp. 158-9.

[6] *Historical Statistics* (1960), p. 768.

[7] Lewis C. Gray, *History of Agriculture in the Southern United States* (Washington, D.C.: Carnegie Institution, 1933), II, 1024.

[8] *Ibid.*, I, 193.

[9] *The History of South Carolina from its First Settlement in 1670 to the Year 1808* (Charleston, S.C., 1809), I, 123.

much further study is needed. But it seems probable that South Carolina during these years enjoyed a more rapid economic growth per capita than any other American colony — and perhaps than that of any other colony or country in the world. This statement seems justified if production growth is measured per white person. If all persons, both slave and free, are counted it may still be true for the South Carolina plantation area and possibly for the whole southern plantation region.

II

The farming area of the Thirteen Colonies extended from the banks of the Kennebec River in southern Maine (then a part of Massachusetts) along the seacoast to Maryland in a strip of varying depth and then inland beyond the coastal plantations down the western piedmont and the mountain valleys to the Savannah River in Georgia. This vast region varied greatly as to time of settlement and development of population density. Individual ownership of small family-sized farms was the rule. And though many farms, especially those on the more remote frontier, were self-sufficient, this must not be overstressed. The colonial farmer, seldom far-removed from water transportation, always sought to produce some marketable items. These he often supplemented by part-time activities such as hunting, trapping, and fishing; exploiting the forests for masts, ashes, and naval stores; and in some of the northern colonies by digging iron from bogs and ponds.

Available clues point to rapid growth in this farming area following the initial difficulties of settlement and adjustment to new conditions. Population increased tremendously. Excluding persons living in the plantation region and in cities of 2,500 or more, the inhabitants of the colonial farming region numbered by 1775 approximately 1,700,000 making up about 80 per cent of the total white population of the thirteen colonies. Both immigration and rapid natural increase brought this white population (there were very few negroes) to a total actually greatly exceeding the number of settlers of European origin living in all other colonies at that time.

Along with this population expansion came a growing tide of products from land and sea. Although returns from hunting and trapping declined as the settled area spread, forest products increased greatly and iron production, after growing slowly until about 1750, expanded so rapidly thereafter that by 1775 one-seventh of the world's annual iron production came from the American colonies. Except for such items as iron, forest products and ships, Great Britain took very little of the surplus production of the Mid-

---

10 *Ibid.*, I, 114-8.

dle and New England Colonies. But other markets expanded during the eighteenth century — Southern Europe, the West Indies, and the northern cities. Increasingly after about 1700 merchant traders operated a growing fleet of small trading vessels on the navigable rivers and on the bays and little harbors along the extended American coast exchanging a variety of items from the outside world for local products.

Clearly the gross product of this farming region expanded greatly after the early decades of settlement. But determination of the per capita growth rate presents unusual difficulties. Perhaps two confident statements may be made. First, the farming population made up such a large proportion of the total that its per capita productivity assumes special importance. Second, the great extent of the farming area, the variety of products, and the differing conditions of production make estimates of productivity very difficult. A tremendous amount of study will be required before reliable conclusions can be drawn.

Some negative factors may be noted. Farming methods, whether cultivation of crops or the breeding of animals, improved very little during the colonial period and appear to have lagged behind those adopted in England during the eighteenth century. On the other hand, colonial farm procedures often suited American conditions better than contemporary British critics realized. Soil exhaustion became a problem as the century advanced in areas where good nearby lands could not be cleared. In eastern New England, where this situation early became most troublesome, wheat-growing soon gave way to corn or rye and the raising of cattle and swine.

On the whole I find the indications favorable to substantial economic per capita growth in the sixty years preceding the Revolution. The growth of population and the expansion of settlement point in this direction. The records left by contemporaries, though imperfect and at times contradictory, indicate an average level of living on farms in the Thirteen Colonies which was rising during the eighteenth century and probably was higher than in England in the decades preceding the Revolution. An indirect approach supports this conclusion. Richard B. Morris estimates that real wages of labor exceeded by thirty to one hundred per cent the wages paid in England at the time.[11] But urban workmen, even skilled craftsmen, were reportedly leaving the city to become farmers. Perhaps the freedom and independence of farm life helped to draw away these city workers, but they were also attracted by the high returns from farming.

It may also be argued that the people themselves, the farmers and their families, possessed characteristics favorable to economic growth. The

---

[11] *Government and Labor in Early America* (New York: Columbia University Press, 1946), p. 45.

colonial farmers appear to have been relatively healthy and, at least in most of the New England and Middle Colonies, better educated than the general run of farm laborers in England. On small, individually owned farms, said Crevecoeur, the owners developed a "restless energy" and a strong incentive to industry. Their vigor and achievement orientation undoubtedly contributed to their productivity. In a recent study Theodore W. Schultz concludes that not land or the quantity of material capital but ". . . differences in the capabilities of the farm people are most important in explaining the differences in the amount and rate of increase of agricultural production." [12]

Had the wealth and economic potential of the thirteen Atlantic colonies depended solely on farming, their growth history might have paralleled that of many another slowly developing agricultural settlement. However, along with increasing agricultural output and acting as an essential stimulant to it, urban centers arose in the New England and the Middle Colonies. Under the leadership of local merchants an indigenous commercial economy developed unique in colonial history and conducive to sustained growth.

The great commercial cities of Western Europe played a major role in the colonial empires of the sixteenth and seventeenth centuries. But in none of the continental European empires did colonial cities or the merchants living in them play a significant part in promoting and organizing colonial trade. This also held generally for the British colonies. Privileged English companies monopolized the trade to India and to Hudson Bay and English and Scotch merchants held so firmly to the tobacco trade with Virginia and Maryland that colonials were largely excluded. Nor, despite the magnitude of the sugar trade, did independent centers of commercial activity spring up in the British West Indies. Bridgetown in Barbadoes, although the largest center of ocean trade in the British Caribbean, had only a few thousand inhabitants and its commerce was largely directed by merchants living in England or New England.

The single exception developed in New England and the Middle Colonies where flourished not only major commercial cities like Boston, New York, and Philadelphia, but a host of smaller ones like Newport, Rhode Island; Albany; and Salem. By 1760 Boston, long the largest city in the Thirteen Colonies, had about 16,000 inhabitants, New York 18,000 and Philadelphia 24,000. By 1775 these three cities were major world trading centers and seventeen other American cities exceeded three thousand in population. These figures become most impressive when it is realized, as

---

[12] *Transforming Traditional Agriculture* (New Haven: Yale University Press, 1964), p. 16. See also Chapter VIII.

Carl Bridenbaugh points out, that Philadelphia in 1775 with 40,000 inhabitants exceeded in size every English city save only London.[13]

The rise of these commercial cities forms an important and complex story. Here it may merely be pointed out that the nature of the farming area made possible the rise of an indigenous colonial commerce just as commerce simultaneously encouraged and forwarded the growth of the farming and extractive economy. The surplus products of the colonial farms did not consist of recognized staples with an assured English market but were diverse in their nature, collected over an extensive area, and shipped to many widely-scattered home and foreign markets. Here was a commerce not well-suited to monopolization as was that from India or Hudson Bay nor easily dominated by great British merchants as was the direct trade from the tobacco and sugar colonies. The British merchants had little difficulty in retaining the lion's share of the commerce in enumerated commodities with the plantation areas. But in the export of various farm products and fish to Southern Europe and the West Indies, in the growing intracolonial trade, and in the marketing of imported goods up and down the Atlantic coast, the Boston, New York, and Philadelphia merchants had the advantage of being on the spot and so able accurately to judge market needs and product quality, of dealing in small shipments and miscellaneous cargoes, and of relying less on factors, agents, and super-cargoes than did the merchants of the mother country.

From their mentors, the British merchants, the American traders acquired a wealth of accumulated knowledge of management, of accounting, of communications, and of techniques essential to trading. The merchants of Boston, New York, Philadelphia, and other commercial centers provided leadership and promotion indispensable to the economy. Much more than wholesale dealers, exporters, importers, and shipowners, they performed most of the services which later became special branches of marketing, insurance, and finance. At almost every colonial seaport but especially in New England, they promoted shipbuilding and, thanks in part to cheap and abundant raw materials, sailing vessels became a leading colonial export. Directly or indirectly they promoted manufacturing activities supplementary to commerce and shipbuilding and employed many workmen in ropewalks, candle-making and cooperage establishments, sail-lofts, flour mills, bakeries, and distilleries. As long as the American merchants continued to enjoy wide trading privileges within the British Empire and the protection of the British navy, they prospered greatly and American port cities increased in population and productivity. The available statistics on the commerce of the Thirteen Colonies, though incomplete

---

[13] *Cities in Revolt* (New York: Alfred A. Knopf, 1955), pp. 216-7.

and fragmentary, give many indications of relatively rapid growth after about 1710. No summary or sampling will be attempted here though it may be pointed out that, as a market for British exports, the Thirteen Colonies surpassed the British West Indies for the first time in 1726-30 and that their share of the total British exports rose from 4.4 per cent in 1701-5 to 12.9 per cent in 1766-70.[14] And this came about at a time when British exports were expanding greatly.

So, what estimate can be made of the rate of per capita growth in the Thirteen Colonies as a whole? I hazard the opinion that the average level of living about doubled in the sixty-five years before the Revolution. This implies an average rate of increase of slightly more than one per cent per annum. This largely speculative conclusion finds some indirect support from the consideration of the post-Revolutionary years which now follows.

III

During the Revolutionary War, productivity fell off and remained relatively low during the Confederation period. Then it appears to have risen rapidly during the 1790's so that by the first five or six years of the new century the average level of living was about where it had been in the early 1770's. Conditions continued good to 1807 but thereafter embargoes, non-intercourse acts, and the War of 1812 definitely depressed living standards. A brief expansion following 1814 ended with a sharp reaction in 1819-20. A period of slow growth followed in the twenties giving way to rapid improvement in the thirties. By 1836-40 the level of living had, I believe, risen to, or somewhat above, the average reached in 1770-74 and 1799-1804. Some of the chief developments from 1775 to 1839 supporting this conclusion may be briefly reviewed.

Little need be said of the final twenty-five years of the eighteenth century. The American Revolution, like most wars, brought unexpected results. Caused in part at least by colonial resentment of British attempts to tax Americans and restrict their commerce, the struggle established independence (an object not generally sought when the war began) and resulted in considerable physical destruction, reduced foreign trade, and generally increased taxes. Freedom from foreign rule may be above price. But Americans following 1783 discovered, as have many newly independent nations in more recent times, that political freedom, far from stimulating economic growth, may, at least for a time, actually retard it.

The gross product of the colonial economy apparently declined during the war years and made at best only a partial recovery by 1789. As popu-

---

[14] D. A. Farnie, "The Commercial Empire of the Atlantic, 1607-1783," *The Economic History Review,* Second Series, XV, No. 2 (1962), 214.

lation increased by about seventeen per cent during this difficult period the average per capita income was doubtless lower in 1789 than it had been in 1774. In the decade before the break with England, the growing productivity of the rice and indigo plantations had continued without serious interruption. In the tobacco area soil exhaustion and an increasing shortage of suitable new lands had begun to slow growth in the late colonial years. The Revolutionary War seriously hurt production in both plantation areas. The British armies in the South, following victories in 1779 and the capture of Charleston in February, 1780, wrought widespread destruction from Georgia to the river valleys of eastern Virginia, and plantation production halted over wide areas when the British carried away 30,000 slaves from Virginia and nearly as many from South Carolina. During the period of the Confederation plantation conditions improved slowly. Tobacco production in Virginia did not regain its prewar level until 1786. Wheat replaced tobacco as the chief product of eastern Virginia as tobacco-growing spread into the far piedmont and the valley. Virginia tobacco exports in 1783-90 averaged only slightly higher than in 1760-75. Annual rice exports, 1783-85, totaled less than half the average for 1770-74 and indigo production fell off drastically with the withdrawal of the British bounty.[15]

The war and its direct aftermath brought less positive damage in the Middle and Northern States. Some immediate benefits accrued. The French and British military forces provided an unusual market for the products of American farms. A new trade, formerly forbidden to Americans, developed with European Atlantic ports and with the non-British West Indian Islands. Wartime needs promoted the manufacturing of such products as iron, gunpowder, linens, cottons, and paper. And at least for a time, New England ports and Philadelphia increased their commercial activity. Nevertheless influences detrimental to productivity appear to have predominated. The aggregate population of the five leading commercial cities fell by more than fifty per cent during the first year of the conflict.[16] The war disrupted coastwide trade, and foreign commerce became increasingly difficult as the British blockade of the coast became more effective.

With the return of peace in 1783 the newly independent country lost important colonial advantages. The British navy no longer protected American commerce and Britain imposed trading restrictions including virtual

---

[15] L. C. Gray, *History of Agriculture in the Southern United States*, II, 589-99, 1022-4; Curtis P. Nettels, *The Emergence of a National Economy, 1775-1815* (New York: Holt, Rinehart and Winston, 1962), pp. 49-51; W. A. Low, "The Farmer in Post-Revolutionary Virginia," *Agricultural History*, XXV (July 1951), 122-27.

[16] Bridenbaugh, *Cities in Revolt*, p. 216.

exclusion from commerce with the British West Indies. Shipbuilding slumped as American-built ships were denied British registry and whaling and fur trading declined also in part due to British measures. Although Great Britain remained America's best customer, the market value of American goods imported by that country 1784-89 averaged less than for the years 1771-75. Currency troubles, internal disorders including Shay's Rebellion, and interstate rivalries placed obstacles in the path of growth. A retardation of the rate of urban growth reflected the slowed economic development. From 1775 to 1790 the aggregate population of the three largest cities, Philadelphia, New York and Boston rose by less than three per cent while the total population of the new nation increased by about forty per cent. American cities of 5,000 or more population at the outbreak of the Revolution numbered twelve. No increase in this total had taken place by 1790.[17]

For more than a decade the Napoleonic Wars greatly stimulated the American economy. Rapidly rising prices and expanding trade characterized the early 1790's, and despite a brief setback in 1797-98 conditions had improved so much by 1799-1800, that the general level of living probably approximated that of the early 1770's. For the years 1799-1839, data on which to base estimates of economic growth, while still fragmentary, became more abundant and a number of attempts at measurement have been made. In 1939 Robert Martin published a statistical study purporting to show average per capita income to be less in 1839 than in 1799. An index of per capita income based on his calculations shows the following:

1799 — 100; 1809 — 96; 1819 — 79; 1829 — 77; and 1839 — 92.[18]

Martin's results and his methods in securing them were re-examined in 1952 by Simon Kuznets who concluded that, contrary to Martin, productivity per capita showed a rising trend over this period.[19] Recently more elaborate and detailed studies have been made of the statistical

---

[17] *Historical Statistics of the United States,* pp. 7 and 14; Bridenbaugh, *Cities in Revolt,* pp. 216-7; Bureau of the Census, *A Century of Population Growth,* p. 11. Bridenbaugh's estimates for 1775 seem high but even so urban population growth clearly lagged in this period. For a description of economic conditions during the war and postwar years, see Nettels, *The Emergence of a National Economy,* Chps. II-IV.

[18] Robert F. Martin, *National Income in the United States, 1799-1938,* National Industrial Conference Board Studies No. 241, 1939, pp. 8-12; William N. Parker and Franklee Whartenby, "The Growth of Output Before 1840," in *Trends in the American Economy in the Nineteenth Century, Studies in Income and Wealth,* XXIV (Princeton: Princeton University Press, 1960), 191.

[19] "Long Term Changes in the National Income of the United States of America since 1870," in *Income and Wealth of the United States,* International Association for Research in Income and Wealth, Income and Wealth Series, II (Cambridge, England: Bowes and Bowes, 1952), 221-39.

materials available for this period. Parker and Whartenby on re-studying the whole problem found the available statistics inadequate to support either Martin's or Kuznets' conclusions.[20] Their calculations appear to throw real doubt on the assumption of a rising secular trend over this period, a conclusion challenged in a later study by Douglas C. North.[21] My own estimate is that the average level of living in 1799-1806 was not again reached until the early 1830's at the earliest and, although some improvement came in that decade, the average for 1836-40 was at best not much higher than that for the prosperous years around the beginning of the century. Only the chief considerations leading to this conclusion can be summarized here.

As late as 1840 about two-thirds of the persons gainfully employed were in agricultural production. Therefore farm productivity trends take on special significance. An extensive statistical study made of this sector by Marvin W. Towne and Wayne D. Rasmussen found the average output per worker in agriculture very nearly the same in 1840 as in 1800.[22] The authors make it clear that results for these years rest partly on the fragmentary statistical data available and very largely on assumptions regarded as reasonable. Their persuasive, nonquantitative arguments in support of their conclusions are followed in part in the paragraphs which follow.

In Maryland and Virginia the yield of tobacco and wheat fell off as the fertility of the soil became exhausted. Farther south, the invention of the cotton gin in 1793, the great European demand for raw cotton, and the suitability of considerable portions of the piedmont for cotton culture offset for a time the failure of other products, especially rice, to expand with population growth. But by the 1820's and probably earlier most cotton growing in the South Atlantic States yielded reduced per capita returns on increasingly impoverished soils. On the other hand, the migration of cotton growing to large plantations on the rich lands of the Deep South brought an increased output per worker. At the same time throughout the South, small independent farmers and so-called poor whites increased in numbers and settled on marginal lands. Many, too poor to own slaves, engaged largely in subsistence farming seldom producing more than enough to provide a meager living for their large families. I find little here to persuade me that average per capita productivity was rising in the southern states.

Nor does agricultural production in the North clearly demonstrate an upward trend per capita during this period. Most of the fertile river valleys

[20] "The Growth of Output Before 1840," pp. 191-212.

[21] "Early National Income Estimates of the U.S." *Economic Development and Cultural Change,* IX (Apr. 1961), 387-96.

[22] "Farm Gross Product and Gross Investment in the Nineteenth Century" in *Trends in the American Economy in the Nineteenth Century,* XXIV, *Studies in Income and Wealth* (Princeton University Press, 1960), pp. 258-60.

leading down to the Atlantic had been cleared and cultivated even before the close of the Colonial Period. But population continued its rapid increase and in the decades following the Revolution the areas with poorer soils in the Middle Atlantic States and upland New England became dotted with farms. Not only were these lands often stony and difficult to clear but their initial fertility soon disappeared and transportation to market presented burdensome costs. By 1830 most of the upland areas of the New England and some of the Middle Atlantic States had reached and passed their population peaks. The hard work of clearing the land, building roads and bridges, constructing houses and barns — all this had brought disappointing returns to the hopeful settlers. Individuals, families, and on occasion whole settlements now abandoned their homes in these areas and sought better lands in western New York and the Ohio River Valley.

Three new developments in farming partially offset these unfavorable conditions. First the growth of eastern cities brought some prosperity to nearby farmers by expanding the local market for perishable products. Second, at least after 1820, some increased yield may have resulted from the use of improved farm tools and machinery, especially the iron plow with interchangeable parts. But, although many improvements were being developed during this period, their use did not become sufficiently widespread appreciably to affect production until after 1840.

The growing migration westward to the rich soils and cheap lands of the Ohio Valley probably did little immediately to increase per capita productivity. The clearing of the land and the construction of dwellings, barns, roads and bridges, was neither a quick nor easy process and the sparseness of settlement denied the advantages of specialization and the economies of scale. Moreover, the bulky farm products of the West had to be marketed a thousand miles or more down the river systems to New Orleans. And even though steamboats and canals reduced somewhat the transportation difficulties, effective relief did not come until after 1840 when the expanding demand of eastern cities and Western Europe created the necessary market and railroads began to contribute toward solving the transportation problem. All three of these mitigating factors developed too late appreciably to affect per capita farm production before 1840.[23]

Probings in a number of other areas indicate that product increased less rapidly than population. This is evident for example in shipbuilding and the merchant marine engaged in foreign trade. Re-exports from the United States reached their peak in the first decade of the eighteenth century and

---

[23] If the quality of the northern farmers contributed to productivity in the Colonial Period, why, it may be asked, was it not important later? The answer seems clear enough. The most ambitious and able gave up the struggle against overwhelming odds and moved to the cities or to the frontier.

declined thereafter. And the average value of domestic exports from 1798-1802 to 1838-42 failed to increase as rapidly as population.[24]

On the other hand it is obvious that in some sectors of the economy productivity expanded at a rapid rate between 1800 and 1840. Internal commerce experienced such an increase both coastwise and on the rivers, lakes, and canals. [25] Turnpikes, canals, steamboats, and at least the beginnings of the railroads must have contributed toward increasing per capita output. Manufacturing also grew rapidly. Manufactures in homes under the putting-out system became extensive in New England and New York State during the first three or four decades of the nineteenth century and helped at least to some extent to offset declining agricultural productivity by providing part time employment for women and children and winter employment for the men. But the chief productivity gains in manufacturing came from the introduction of improved machines and the factory system. Though important for the future, factory manufacturing constituted before 1840 a small fraction of total output. Also the rapid growth of cities especially after 1820 contributed to the substantial enlargement of both regional and local markets, making possible economies of scale whose growing importance must not be overlooked even though they cannot be exactly measured.

As in Colonial times and at least down to 1840, the great majority of Americans were farmers. The proportion of the gainfully employed in agriculture, after rising during the decade 1810-1820, appears to have declined thereafter. This shift of employment from agriculture to other sectors after 1820 contributed toward increased per capita productivity as it has in more recent times. But the gains cannot be accurately measured and they came fairly gradually. They will surely be greatly exaggerated if attention is focused on the increased output of workers in textile factories. In absolute terms the growth in factory employment was much less than in construction, in trade, and even in domestic service.

Sometime shortly before 1840 and probably during the decade of the thirties the per capita productivity of the American economy began a strong upward trend. This improvement had by 1840 raised the average income to or even moderately above the level enjoyed in 1770-74 and the first years of the nineteenth century. This income level was a relatively high one. It was by about 1840 clearly above that for France and not far below the English average. The estimate of $400 per capita (in dollars of current purchasing power) accepted by Goldsmith is actually well above the level now enjoyed in most Asian, African, and South American countries. As

---

[24] Computed from *Historical Statistics of the United States*, pp. 7 and 538.

[25] Douglas C. North, *The Economic Growth of the United States* (Englewood Cliffs, N.J.: Prentice-Hall, Inc., 1961), pp. 250-54.

Gallman points out, "It is quite clear that the United States was not a poor country in 1839, even by modern standards."[26]

Recognition of the high level of productivity attained by 1840 accords well with the hypothesis already developed that rapid economic growth took place in the period 1710-1775. Thus if per capita income was relatively low in 1710, as I believe plausible, and if per capita income in 1840 was about the same or at least not substantially higher than in the early 1770's, as was concluded above, then it follows that relatively rapid growth must have characterized the years from 1710 to 1775.

Like other attempts to estimate economic growth over long periods of time the conclusions drawn in this paper depend partly on statistical measurement but largely on value judgments. They differ from calculations of growth rates for recent years chiefly in that they are more tentative and that they depend of necessity less on actual measurement and more upon qualitative judgment. The conclusions have been presented as plausible hypotheses. Their purpose is less to provide answers than to suggest tasks awaiting the best efforts of students — both those trained in statistical procedures and those more at home with an institutional approach.

[26] Robert E. Gallman, "Estimates of American National Product Made before the Civil War," *Economic Development and Cultural Change,* IX (Apr. 1961), 399-401; Goldsmith, *Hearings before the Joint Economic Committee,* p. 278; and Simon Kuznets, "Quantitative Aspects of the Economic Growth of Nations," *Economic Development and Cultural Change,* V (Oct. 1956), 24–5. [Gallman and Goldsmith articles reprinted in Parts III and V, respectively.]

Currency Issues to Overcome Depressions in Pennsylvania, 1723 and 1729

RICHARD LESTER*

The connection between the quantity of money and business conditions has received considerable attention recently. The Economic Intelligence Service of the League of Nations has pointed out that in the years since 1929 the turning-point from depression to economic revival in practically every country was "characterized by an increase in the supply of money."[1] In his 1937 report the director of the International Labour Office remarks that "the revitalizing effects of monetary expansion have been the same everywhere" and adds:

> The demonstration that in one country after another the upturn in business and employment coincided not with the reduction of wage-rates, the cutting of costs or the deterioration of working conditions but with the abandonment of deflation and the adoption of monetary expansion has made a deep impression upon the world. [2]

Professor James W. Angell believes that

> it is perhaps not even too rash to suggest that much of the decline in world economic activity between 1928 and 1933, possibly more than half, could have been avoided by stabilizing the quantity of circulating money at around the 1928–1929 peaks, or (still better) by causing it to increase gradually from those peaks, say with population.[3]

This paper deals with two attempts to overcome depressions in Colonial Pennsylvania by expanding the money supply. The first of these experiments was in 1723 and the second in 1729. The character and severity of the depression that preceded each of these currency issues are discussed in detail, along with the alleged objections of Colonial authorities to gold and silver money. The nature of the recovery that followed the currency issues in both periods is treated in detail, especially by means of quotations

---

* Richard A. Lester is Professor of Economics and Chairman of the Department of Economics at Princeton University.

[1] *Money and Banking*, 1935-1936, Vol. I: *Monetary Review* (1936), p. 56.

[2] *Report of the Director* (Geneva: International Labour Office, 1937), pp. 41 and 45.

[3] "The General Objectives of Monetary Policy" in *The Lessons of Monetary Experience*, ed. A. D. Gayer (New York, 1937), pp. 56-57.

from contemporary publications and letters; and business conditions in Pennsylvania are contrasted with conditions in other colonies and in England. An attempt is also made to determine the effect of the currency issues in 1723 and 1729 upon internal prices, foreign-exchange rates, foreign trade, and, by means of deductions from the foreign-trade figures, upon the domestic market. Finally, there is a more general section indicating the colony's subsequent currency experience and later views on the success of Pennsylvania's experiments with currency issues to stimulate business expansion. In Pennsylvania a little currency inflation did not lead to extreme currency inflation, and the price level during the fifty-two years prior to the American Revolution that Pennsylvania was on a paper standard was more stable than the American price level has been during any succeeding fifty-year period.

Though this paper is necessarily confined to the experience of Pennsylvania with currency issues, it should be stated that the other middle colonies also issued paper money to combat depressions. New Jersey did so in 1723 and 1733, Delaware in 1723 and 1729, Maryland in 1733, and New York in 1737. Even the New York currency issues in 1715 and 1717 were designed "to restore the public Credit, and add new Vigour to a then languishing Trade." [4] The author plans to publish soon in book form an account of the experience of these other middle colonies with currency issues as an antidote for depressions.[*] According to contemporary accounts and the available statistical data, all the middle colonies had surprisingly successful experience with monetary expansion as a method for stimulating the return of prosperity, and in all of them, except Maryland for the first few years, the exchange value of the currency seems not to have fallen more than about 30 per cent in terms of gold and silver for any year during the period of fifty or sixty years that these colonies were on a paper standard prior to the Revolutionary War.

It might be well to add that the currency experience of Pennsylvania discussed in this paper (as well as the experience of the other middle colonies) throws grave doubt on such statements as the following, which have been culled from recently published textbooks:

> Historical evidence demonstrates that in no case has a paper currency ever been managed properly or ever existed as a satisfactory standard *for any great length of time.*[5]

Historically the world's experience with fiat money has been, almost

---

[4] *Journal of the Legislative Council of the Colony of New York, April 9, 1691 to September 27, 1743* (Albany, 1861), p. 434, dated October 9, 1718.

[*] [Ed. Note: Published as *"Monetary Experiments, Early American and recent Scandinavian"; Princeton University Press; Princeton, New Jersey 1939.]

[5] W. E. Spahr in *Economic Principles and Problems,* ed. Spahr (3d ed.; New York, 1936), I, 566.

without exception, disastrous. The principal exceptions now cited in support of the managed money proposal are the irredeemable paper monetary systems which have prevailed in Great Britain and Sweden since 1931.[6]

A rise in prices caused by currency inflation cannot end in a state of economic equilibrium. It can culminate only in business liquidation and currency deflation or in repudiation, or in devaluation. It always causes heavy social losses.[7]

Once inflation has been engaged in, deflation is inevitable sooner or later.[8]

Mild doses of inflation have no material effect upon a depressed business situation, whereas generous applications cause prices to rise with a bound. . . . Even if it [inflation] is brought under control before it brings complete economic disaster as it did in Germany and Russia, there follows a period of most painful readjustment.[9]

BACKGROUND OF THE CURRENCY QUESTION

Scarcity of coin. — Scarcity of money was one of the common complaints in the North American colonies. Gold and silver were not mined or minted in the English colonies, and one English government after another prohibited the export of gold and silver to the colonies. When the colonists did acquire gold or silver coin, they soon sent it to England in exchange for English products, which they needed much more than they did expensive money. Gold and silver coins were a luxury in the colonies, where the population was sparce, where there were no banking facilities, and where the natural rate of interest was high.

Also the conditions at that time permitted the colonies to be almost drained of their coin without much immediate change in their balance of trade. In the first place, most of the colonies exported a few staple agricultural products or pelts (tobacco from Maryland and Virginia, beaver skins from French Canada, and wheat, flour, and pelts from Pennsylvania and New York). Changes in the world-prices of their exports would not cause the colonists to change to another line of production for many years. Transportation and communication took so much time that the colonists did not know what prices abroad were until months later. In the meantime prices might have changed. Consequently, merchants often shipped goods to a country without knowing about the current market conditions there.[10]

---

[6] F. R. Fairchild, E. S. Furniss, and N. S. Buck, *Elementary Economics* (3d ed.; New York, 1936), 698.

[7] Spahr, *op. cit.*, p. 595.

[8] A. L. Meyers, *Elements of Modern Economics* (New York, 1937), p. 293.

[9] G. W. Dowrie, *Money and Banking* (New York, 1936), p. 476.

[10] As Governor Crosby of New York wrote to the British Board of Trade in December, 1734: "Whenever a market in Spain, Portugal or other parts of Europe has encouraged the sending thither [of] Grain, the adventurers have often suffered

Under such circumstances it might require years for a full adjustment in the balance of trade to take place with an outflow of gold and silver coin from the colonies. Therefore, it is not surprising to find that the colonists, even before any paper money was issued, were at times so short of coin that they had to pay their relatively small tax bills in jewels, gold rings and earrings, gold plate, or in agricultural produce.[11]

The Colonial authorities complained that gold and silver, "being also Subject to the Rise and Fall of Markets," did "not conveniently answer the Ends of a Currency in our Home Trade."[12] Even before the issue of paper money in Pennsylvania, the exchange rate on London sometimes rose to a premium of 7 or 8 per cent above parity.[13] It is not surprising, therefore, to find the Governor of Pennsylvania advocating "an imaginary Specie [paper money] which fully answers the End of a permanent Currency and Measure of Trade amongst Ourselves." To him it was "evident that a fluent Currency of Paper, will render the Market Here more frequent and contribute exceedingly to his [the merchant's] Dispatch" in collecting his outstanding debts.[14]

Finally, the general trend of prices in Europe and America in terms of gold and silver was downward during the first three or four decades of the eighteenth century. This downward trend in prices seemed to prove that there was a general scarcity of money relative to goods. With the decline of prices, people tended to hoard coins. In Pennsylvania the complaint about the "scarcity of money" became especially loud during the early 1720's, when the colony was suffering from a severe business depression and prices were falling rapidly. The governor of Pennsylvania realized that there was "not a sufficient quantity of gold or Silver in these Countries to Quicken & Promote a mutual Exchange" and to stop the tendency for coins to be hoarded. He therefore lent his support to the proposal for an issue of currency. In his opinion, "the natural effect" of the issue of "a Sufficient Quantity" of paper money, which "is not of its Nature exportable and not Lyable to be Hoarded up," would be to discourage hoarding and to

---

by the undertaking, for at this remote distance the intelligence of a demand reaches us so late, that the marketts are supplyed before our vessells come there" (*Documentary History of the State of New York,* ed. E. B. O'Callaghan [Albany, 1850], I, 491).

[11] See a letter from Governor Burnet of New Jersey to the British Board of Trade, May 12, 1724, in *Archives of the State of New Jersey* (1st ser.; Newark, N. J., 1882), V, 87.

[12] Sir William Keith to the British Board of Trade, December 12, 1723, in *British Board of Trade Papers, Proprieties,* Vol. XI, R 47. (There is a transcribed copy of these unpublished papers at the Historical Society of Pennsylvania, Philadelphia, Pa.)

[13] See Table 3.

[14] Sir William Keith to the Board of Trade, December 12, 1723, *op. cit.*

speed up spending, so that the planter in Pennsylvania would "find a ready Sale for the whole produce of his Farm."[15]

Business depression. — In September, 1720, there was a serious crisis or panic in England, following the collapse of the speculative orgy known in history as the South Sea Bubble.[16] England then began to suffer from a slump in trade; a business depression set in, and prices fell. A price index for cereals in England fell 30 per cent from 1719 to 1721, and an index for the cost of living declined 14 per cent during those two years.[17]

Whether the business depression in Pennsylvania really began before September, 1720, is difficult to determine from the available data. Imports into Pennsylvania from Great Britain decreased 10 per cent from 1719 to 1720 and 12 per cent from 1720 to 1721. However, exports from Pennsylvania to Britain, normally amounting to about one-third or one-fourth the sum of imports from Britain, increased each year from £4,499 in 1716 to £8,037 in 1721.[18]

Pennsylvania's imports from Great Britain included a great variety of commodities to which the settlers had been accustomed in the Old World. Practically all clothing and manufactured goods in Pennsylvania as well as some foodstuffs like spices, tea, fine salt, and loaf sugar, were imported from Great Britain. According to a Philadelphia merchant, the ships brought from England

> all kinds of British manufactories in great abundance and India goods, etc. In the last of the winter or early in the spring [we] choose to import our linens and other things fit for summer, the latter end of which we should have our woolen goods of all kinds ready for the fall sale to use in winter. The spring is the best time for iron mongery, cutleryware, furniture for furnishing houses, and all other brass and iron work. Our imports of those articles are very large, the people being much employed in agriculture, husbandry, clearing and improving lands, but slow progress is made in the manufactories here. Good grindstones assorted, and sometimes a quantity [of] Newcastle coal, would sell readily.[19]

Because of the importance of British imports into Pennsylvania, they seem to be a fairly good index, with some lag perhaps, of the rate of consumption

---

[15] *Ibid.*

[16] William R. Scott, *The Constitution and Finance of English, Scottish and Irish Joint-Stock Companies to 1720* (Cambridge, 1910), Vol. I.

[17] E. W. Gilboy, "Cost of Living and Real Wages in Eighteenth Century England," *Review of Economic Statistics,* August, 1936.

[18] See Table I, p. 88. Most of Pennsylvania's exports were to the West Indies and the Madeira Islands.

[19] Thomas Clifford to Abel Chapman, July 25, 1767, quoted in A. Bezanson, R. D. Gray, and M. Hussey, *Prices in Colonial Pennsylvania* (Philadelphia, 1935), p. 263.

and the condition of the market for commodities in Pennsylvania at that time.[20]

A monthly index of wholesale prices of twenty commodities in Philadelphia (1720-75) shows that the price level dropped 9 per cent from January to September, 1720, in Philadelphia.[21] Boston figures for the price of wheat, deflated by an index for the price of silver, indicate that wheat had been falling in price since 1718. Wheat in terms of silver fell in value 30 per cent between 1718 and 1721 and fell 34 per cent between 1718 and 1724.[22]

In the latter part of 1720, Philadelphia merchants in their letters to English correspondents mention the depression in England without reporting similar conditions in Pennsylvania. On September 24, 1720, a Philadelphia merchant wrote to London: "Wee are inform'd mony is Scarce with you . . ."[23] and in another letter to London on December 24, 1720: "If any prospect of trade mending with you please to give us notice."[24]

In December, 1726, the Pennsylvania assembly reported to the authorities in England that, because of

> the general Damp that was given to Trade in the Year 1720, and the great Fall [in the price] of our Produce, about the same Time, we were, in the Years 1721 and 1722, so effectually drained of our Coin, which, for want of other Returns, was generally ship'd off to Britain, that the Inhabitants of every Degree were reduced to the greatest Straits; Debts could not be discharged, nor Payments be made; the Rents of Houses fell, many whereof were deserted; and the Value of Lands and Improvements sunk considerably; Families who had lived well could scarce find Means to purchase necessary Provisions for their Support; and therefore both Artificers and Traders were obliged to quit the Country, in Search of Employment and Sustenance elsewhere; But, above all, our Shipping, by which the most advantageous Returns for Britain had been made, was so greatly declined, that our Yards appeared almost empty, and all Trade discouraged. Such was the distressed Condition to which this Country was at that Time unhappily reduced.[25]

In November, 1721, Pennsylvania merchants wrote letters to London correspondents stating: "Of late years the Ballance of Trade hath so much ran against us with Brittain that when any thing is recover'd [from out-

---

[20] For a further discussion of this point see pp. 98-99.

[21] Bezanson, Gray, and Hussey, *op. cit.*, p. 429.

[22] Ruth Crandall, "Wholesale Commodity Prices in Boston during the Eighteenth Century," *Review of Economic Statistics*, XVI, No. 6 (June, 1934), 121.

[23] Thomas Griffitts to George Griffitts, September 24, 1720, in *Letters of Isaac Norris, 1719 to 1756*. (MS at Historical Society of Pennsylvania.)

[24] Thomas Griffitts to John Eastwick and John Gale, December 24, 1720, *ibid.*

[25] *Pennsylvania Archives* (8th ser.; Philadelphia, 1931), III, 1828.

standing debts in Pennsylvania] tis very Difficult to procure Bills or such remittances as will give Satisfaction there [in England]" [26] and "I intended to have sent some Wheat but the Country Debtors have been backward & mony is so Extreamly Scarce that we begin to be or rather have been for some time pinch'd for Want of some proper medium for Currency without which Commerce is a perplexing Employment." [27] At the same time (November, 1721), another Philadelphia merchant wrote:

> We have scarce any Cash here but Gold, and that exceeding scarce at present. Gold passes with us at £5:10 per oz. If it be true therefore that with you it is fallen to £3:17—the exchange is near 43 per Cent besides freight & Insurance, which will bring it to near 50 per Cent tho we generally account the Par but 33 1/3 because it really is so in silver Money.[28]

From James Logan's letters it seems that the exchange rate on London, with the par at 133 1/3, was at least as high as 143 on November 14 and 19, 1721, and at least as high as 137½ on November 1, 1722; November 13, 1722; July 4, 1723; and September 23, 1723.[29]

Of this period, Francis Rawle, a prosperous Philadelphia merchant, wrote in 1726:

> For such was the Scarcity of Gold and Silver, that the Farmer not able to purchase it with his Crop, forc'd the Shops to take it [country produce], and they again impos'd the same on the Merchant till it became pretty current in Trade; but at so low a Price, the Farmer could not live by it. The Silver had been bought up for Merchandize, so that none pass'd in common payments, and Gold so far exhausted, that little but Cut Pieces, and some scraps passed, and That melting up for Remittances [to England], before Paper-Money came out; . . . .[30]

In 1721, Rawle published anonymously in Philadelphia a pamphlet entitled *Some Remedies Proposed for Restoring the Sunk Credit of the Province of Pennsylvania with Some Remarks on Its Trade*. This is said to be the first publication in America on political economy and its application to local conditions,[31] and it is interesting to note that the publisher, Andrew Bradford, was summoned before the Pennsylvania council on February 1, 1722, and told by the governor that in the future he was not

---

[26] Isaac Norris to Charles Loyd, November 12, 1721, in *Letters of Isaac Norris, 1716 to 1730*, p. 277. (MS at Historical Society of Pennsylvania.)

[27] Thomas Griffitts (Norris' son-in-law) to Benjamin Bartlett, November 24, 1721, *Letters of Isaac Norris, 1719 to 1756*.

[28] James Logan to John Andrews, November 19, 1721, in *Letter Book of James Logan, 1717 to 1731*, p. 227. (MS at Historical Society of Pennsylvania.)

[29] *Ibid.*, pp. 223, 227, 284, 294, and 326, and *Letters of Isaac Norris, 1716 to 1730*, p. 337.

[30] *A Just Rebuke to a Dialogue betwixt Simon and Timothy, Shewing What's Therein To Be Bound* (Philadelphia, 1726), p. 15.

[31] See "Francis Rawle" in *Dictionary of American Biography*, XV (1935), 400 and *Pennsylvania Magazine of History and Biography*, III, No. I (1879), 118-20.

to "publish any thing relating to or concerning the Affairs" of the Pennsylvania government "without the permission of the Governor or Secretary of this province." [32] In this pamphlet Rawle, "expatiating on the low State of this Province" and "proposing a reasonable Way for her Recovery," wrote:

> It is melancholly to tell the miserable Condition of this Province, occasioned by a Neglect in this last Particular [sufficient money]. How deplorable are the Lives of the Common People! Their trades and Callings discouraged and valued at nought; What real Estates they have had are mortgaged, eat out and consumed; and the whole Province look'd upon by all Foreigners, as a Country beggarly and scandalous, not worth Trading with. But the melancholy Decay of Credit in this Province requires not much Time to demonstrate, for every Dealer is too sensibly convinced of it; nor need we dive any farther than into our own Pockets, to convince us, that a running Stock of Money now wanting is the Cause of this Decay: The common Necessaries for Families brought to the Market are not bought, because Change (as Silver and Copper is commonly called) is not to be had; all our Domestick Trade is become nothing but Discount, *A miserable Make-shift* good for Nought, but to *enrich* Knaves and *beggar* Fools.[33]
>
>   . . . . it is to be hoped, as every Inhabitant of this Province cannot but be sensible of the said Decay and Credit, that they will be as ready to encourage every Thing, that may tend to restore the same to its former happy State, when our Produce was preferred before any others of the same kind in the *West-Indies,* and our payments at Home ready and punctual: So good was their Credit, and so generous the Inhabitants in their Dealings one with another, that *Dunning,* the Bane and Destruction of all Trade, was not heard of in *Pennsylvania*: But where is there, at this Time, a Country more behind in their Payments, and more careless of the Goods they export; and consequently of worse Credit at Home and Abroad? [34]

In this same pamphlet Rawle pointed out that it is not necessary for money to have a high commodity value. "The Dutch," he wrote, "by Virtue of a Stamp, impress'd on a base Metal, have raised a Running Stock of Money, which is frequently imported into other Countries; but the intrinsick Value of this Money is near One Fifth short of the Value it commonly passeth for." [35] He advocated the issue of "Stamp'd Paper" whose value would be "secured" by "some visible Fund" of loans on "real Security," the loans of paper money to be made "at an Office appointed by Public Authority for that Purpose," and the interest on the loans becoming "the Publick's Advantage." This would provide, in Rawle's opinion, "really a Money not inferior to the best Silver and Gold

[32] *Colonial Records* (Philadelphia, 1852), III, 145.
[33] *Some Remedies, etc.,* signed "By a Lover of this Country," pp. 6-7.
[34] *Ibid.,* pp. 19-20.
[35] *Ibid.,* p. 10.

for Domestick Trade" and would help "to restore our Credit, and encrease our Trade both at Home and Abroad." [36]

The business depression in Pennsylvania became worse in 1722 and 1723. In August, 1722, James Logan, a Philadelphia merchant and chief representative of the Penn interests in the province, wrote:

> Our trade is sunk and very little of any thing to be done. [37]
>
> I have received about 1/3 of the pay by Discount, but not one farthing in Money and the rest will be long out for the Trade of this place is exceedingly sunk. . . .[38]

In November, Logan wrote:

> I must acquaint thee that this Country Since it was a Province has never been under such low Circumstances for want of Trade and Money as at present So that Lands will sell for Scarce any thing but a very long Trust, and in Jersey they are yet more dull than here.[39]

While business conditions were going from bad to worse in Pennsylvania, apparently business in England had emerged from the depression by the fall of 1722. In November, 1722, Logan wrote in a letter to a London merchant:

> I was much concerned to hear by Eli Crocket of the many Removes & changes amongst you and the late calamitous times you have known by the sinking of Trade. Tis now our case in this Province to as great a degree I believe as it was yours tho not so many drop by it, much longer Credits being given here. But I am pleas'd to hear your affairs are mended which I fear is more than will very soon be paid of us. . . .[40]

Political situation and trade. — Many "doleful Complaints" were made to the Pennsylvania assembly late in 1722 and early in 1723 about "the scarcity of money" and "the evident Decay of this Province in general, for want of a Medium to buy and sell with." [41] The inhabitants were reported as "being nonplus'd in a regular Dispatch of Affairs for Want of Pay when due" and statements were made that "many families were likely to be ruined" because the values of lands and products were "brought so low by the Scarcity of Money." [42] Officials and residents of Philadelphia, Chester County, Bucks County, and other places throughout the province sent numerous petitions to the Colonial legislature "complaining of the

---

[36] *Ibid.,* pp. 14, 19, 20.

[37] Logan to John Askew, August 13, 1722, *Letter Book of James Logan, 1717 to 1731,* p. 254.

[38] Logan to John Andrews, August 14, 1722, *ibid.,* p. 255.

[39] Logan to Amos Strettle, November 12, 1722, *ibid.,* pp. 297-98.

[40] Logan to John Hop, November 12, 1722, *ibid.,* p. 297.

[41] *Pennsylvania Archives* (8th ser.), II, 1460, 1461.

[42] *Ibid.,* 1483 and 1762.

great Decay of Trade and Credit, and requesting a Paper Currency." [43]

In the meantime, the general discontent against the existing government which accompanies hard times and the demand for some "relief" from the depression led to a considerable change in the composition of the Colonial assembly. In 1721 and 1722 a wealthy coterie, representing the Proprietary party, lost their seats in the assembly to members of the Democratic or anti-Proprietary party, of which Francis Rawle, although a prosperous merchant, was one of the leaders. The Proprietary party was made up mostly of wealthy residents of Philadelphia who were members of the creditor class and had strong aristocratic interests, whereas the Democratic party represented the rural areas and people of small means and had, at this time, what the well to do claimed was a "levelling spirit."

Two leaders of the Proprietary party were Isaac Norris and James Logan, the chief representatives of the Penn interests in the province. Norris was a wealthy merchant and landowner who had helped to rescue William Penn from a debtors' prison. He was a member of the governor's council for twenty-six years, was speaker of the assembly in 1720; and mayor of Philadelphia in 1724. Logan had at one time been secretary to William Penn, was secretary of the province, a member of the governor's council, and mayor of Philadelphia in 1723. As representatives of the Penn interests and as creditors, both were opposed to any issue of paper currency. After paper money was first issued in Pennsylvania in 1723, Norris kept referring to it as "our rotten paper mony," "this Vile paper Currency," "this * * * paper Currency," "Vile Bills of Credit the contrivance & refuge of Bankrupts & designers," and "paper Currency (an abuse upon all Creditors)." [44] The governor of the province, Sir William Keith, supported Rawle, however, and helped to put the currency measure through the assembly.

In December, 1722, the governor wrote his superiors in England:

> I am to acquaint your Lordships that the people of this place are just now in a very great Ferment on Account that for some time past their usual Trade has stagnated for want of a sufficient currency of cash amongst themselves whereby to Exchange the produce of their Labour according to their accustomed Maner of Business;
>
> The Farmer brings his provision to Market but there is no Money to give for it, The ship Builder & Carpenter starve for want of Employment, and we sensibly feel that our usual Export decreases Apace, The Interest

[43] *Ibid.,* pp. 1663, 1464, 1465.

[44] *Letters of Isaac Norris, 1716 to 1731:* to John Askew, February 15, 1724, p. 369; to Noar, June 20, 1724, p. 381; to Ann Coaksley, July 30, 1724, p. 383; to Robert Price, October 31, 1724, p. 395; and to Mord Maddock, October 31, 1724, p. 399.

on Money is high, and the usurer grinds the Face of The poor so that Law suits multiply, our Gaols are full, and we are justly apprehensive of falling into debt, which we have Happily avoided Hitherto.[45]

Under these Circumstances, The clamor is universall for Paper Money, ...

The Example of our Neighboring Province New York, demonstrates, That paper creates a more Current and reddy sale of their product which is the very same with ours, ...

I observed that the Lawyers and a few Rich Usurors here are violent Bent on the opposeing the peoples Inclinations to paper Money, But both Merchant and Farmer cry out Incessantly for such a Quantity at least as will serve to Transact the necessary Business between them, ...[46]

In writing of this period at a much later date (1740), this same governor said:

The laborious, and most industrious Inhabitants of the small Province of Pennsylvania . . . . had successfully carried on all their Affairs without the Use of Paper Money, until the Year 1722, when by the late Increase [?] of their Shiping and foreign Trade, the City of Philadelphia labour'd under great Discouragement for want of a Currency; many of the labouring, but poorer Sort of Inhabitants, were daily leaving the Place, and transporting themselves and Families elsewhere; the Shop-keepers had no money to go to Market and the Farmer, or Planter's Crop was then reduced to the lowest Value; so that all the European Goods imported, as well as the Bread and Flower, or Country Produce, were bought up and engrossed at a low Price, by a Cabal of only four or five rich Men, who retail'd them again on Credit at what Rate they pleased, taking Advantage of the People's Necessities and Circumstances; by which Means they soon got the whole Country into their Debt, exacting Bonds of every Body at 8 per Cent. which was then the legal Interest.

This made such an universal Clamour all over the Province, that when the Assembly met, the latter End of the same Year, they hastened to prepare a Bill for establishing a Paper Currency. [47]

James Logan indicated the state of trade in Pennsylvania in May 1723, two months after the first paper-money act was passed but before the currency was actually issued, when he wrote:

. . . . These countries (this Province and Jersey) being drained of Money and by a general Decay of Trade that few buyers offer for land that are capable of making any tolerable Pay. . . . .

In Jersey Lands sell more Difficultly than with us. . . . .[48]

---

[45] The number of "expensive and Vexatious Law-suits" in Pennsylvania doubled from 1715 to 1722, when the number was "beyond what was usual or ever known in this Province before" (*Pennsylvania Archives* [8th Ser.], II, 1460, 1465).

[46] *British Board of Trade Papers*, Proprieties, Vol. XI, R42.

[47] Sir William Keith, *A Collection of Papers and Other Tracts Written Occasionally on Various Subjects* (London, 1740), p. 212.

[48] Logan to Amos Strettle, May 9, 1723, *Letter Book of James Logan*, p. 317.

In 1723 imports from England to Pennsylvania in pounds sterling were at the lowest point recorded between 1714 and 1774.[49]

Proposed remedies. — Other remedies besides the issue of paper money were proposed to the Colonial assembly as a means of relieving the colonists "from the Weightiest of their present Burdens and doleful Complaints." These were: to stop the hiring out of slaves who, working at reduced wages, prevented the employment of freemen; to make farm produce legal tender for payment of debts; to prohibit the export of gold and silver from the colony; to raise the official rating of coins by 25 per cent; to reduce the legal rate of interest from 8 to 6 per cent; and to call a debt moratorium. In fact, the 1723 legislature passed, along with the two acts for "emitting and making current" a total of 45,000 "Pounds of Paper Currency," other laws "for reducing the Interest of Money from Eight to Six per Cent," and "for respiting Executions upon certain Judgments of Courts in this Province." [50] Rawle had been the most active member of the assembly committee that drafted the first paper-money act, and he was one of the four men appointed to sign the currency issues.

Early in 1723 the governor of Pennsylvania told the legislature: "I daily perceive more and more that the People languish for want of some Currency to revive Trade and Business, which is wholly at a Stand; therefore I am of Opinion, that all the Dispatch imaginable ought to be given to the Paper Bill." [51] He pointed out that, because the paper-money issues in New York were "moderate for a Place of such large and extended Commerce, they continued of equal Value with their current Silver, until, in the Year 1717," when some depreciation took place because a large quantity was issued. He concluded from this that "to keep up the Credit of Bills [paper money], the Quantity must be moderate." [52]

PAPER-MONEY ISSUES OF 1723

On March 2, 1723, the assembly passed an act providing for a £15,000 issue of paper money to remedy "the extreme scarcity of money" because of which "the trade of this province is greatly lessened and obstructed." [53] Most of the £15,000 was to be lent at 5 per cent interest; the loans were to be secured by mortgages on land and houses and were to be paid back in eight annual instalments. No more than

---

[49] See Table I.
[50] *Statutes at Large of Pennsylvania from 1682 to 1801,* Vol. III.
[51] *Pennsylvania Archives* (8th Ser.), II, 1510.
[52] *Ibid.,* p. 1493.
[53] *Statutes at Large of Pennsylvania from 1682 to 1801,* III, 324.

£100 could be loaned to any one person, since these paper-money "bills of credit [were] chiefly intended for the benefit of the poor, industrious sort of people of this province, at an easy interest, to relieve them from the present difficulties they labor under." [54] When the loans were paid back, the paper money was to be destroyed. This currency was legal tender for all debts, and counterfeiters were to be punished by having both their "ears cut off," being whipped on the "bare back with thirty-one lashes well laid on," and fined or sold into servitude." [55]

The assembly of the province reported that the £15,000 in paper money

> being emitted, their Effect very sensibly appeared, in giving new Life to Business, and raising the Country, in some Measure, from its languishing State; but at the same time it was also manifest, that tho' the Method was effectual in its Kind, yet the Currency fell short in Quantity, and was in nowise proportioned to the Occasions of the People, nor sufficient to circulate the Bulk of our Trade; therefore the Legislature on December 12, 1723, being enabled by the first Experiment to form a more exact Judgment of what the circumstances of the Country and our Commerce would require, found it necessary to strike Thirty Thousand Pounds more, on the like Securities of real Estates, to be pledged in the same Manner [as in the first paper-money act.] [56]

Effects on business. — Within a very short time business recovery set in, and the "unhappy State of Affairs of this Province" changed to "the happy Prospect that this Province now affords." [57] The governor of Pennsylvania, in a book published somewhat later, wrote of these paper-money issues to overcome the existing business depression:

> It is inconceivable to think what a prodigious good Effect immediately ensued on all the Affairs of that Province; the Shiping from the West of England, Scotland, and Ireland, which just before used to be detain'd five, six, and sometimes nine Months in the Country, before they could get in the Debts due to them and load, were now dispatch'd in a Month or six Weeks at farthest. The poor middling People who had any Lands or Houses to pledge, borrow'd from the Loan-Office, and paid off their usurious Creditors; and to render them more easy for the future, as well as to bring Things nearer to Par, lawful Interest was at this Time reduced from eight

---

[54] *Ibid.,* p. 328.

[55] *Ibid.,* p. 331.

[56] *Pennsylvania Archives* (8th ser.), III, 1828 and 1829. Benjamin Franklin wrote of this action: "And it was not till they were convinced by experience of the utility of the measure, and the insufficiency of the sum, that they adventured to strike thirty thousand pounds more" (see *An Historical Review of the Constitution and Government of Pennsylvania, from Its Origin,* in *Works of Franklin,* ed. Jared Sparks London, 1759), III, 202.

[57] *Pennsylvania Archives* (8th ser.), III, 1829.

to six per Cent, by which means the Town was soon filled with People, and Business all over the Province increased at a great rate.[58]

The legislature also reported that "Trade revived" and "the Country began to feel a general Relief." In 1726 the assembly stated his "Representation" to the authorities in England:

> The whole Quantity that was struck thus in a very short Time emitted, and diffused into the Peoples Hands, the Face of our Affairs appeared entirely changed; Traders exerted themselves; the Produce of our Country came into Demand, and bore a Price, whereby the People were better enabled to pay the Proprietary's Quitrents, and answer other Demands; our City fill'd again with Inhabitants; Artificers found Employment; our British Trade increased; and Strangers, from the Encouragement of finding ready Pay, resorted to us; Ship-building was vigorously carried on; and both our Ship-wrights Yards, and our Port, were fill'd with Shipping; insomuch, that this Present Year, as appears from the List of Registers, double the Number of vessels have been built at *Philadelphia*, that had been in any Year before a Paper Currency: And by the Naval-Officer's Books, we find, that the Tons of Shipping cleared at the same Port in 1722, having amounted to no more than 3531; this Year there have been already cleared 6655 Tons, besides several large Vessels yet in Port, that are to sail before the Year expires.[59]

These figures for shipping are given in the table on page 126.[60]

When in 1725 the "decendants" of William Penn threatened to remove the governor of Pennsylvania, among other things, for "passing the Acts, which remitted a Paper Currency," the Colonial legislature wrote these "decendants," explaining how

> trade revived, ... the Value of our Country Product advanced, and the Ship-Wrights some of whom, before this Currency was struck, having left the Country for want of Work, and those that stay'd having little to do, are since returned, and come into full Employment at their Trade; so that many stately Vessels have been built, and more upon the Stocks, and several Iron-works are carried on; which, with divers other Instances of the Advantage this Currency has been to the Publick, as well as to those, who, both in City and Country, must have been ruined without it, we think may abundantly attone for this Part of the Governor's Conduct.[61]

According to Francis Rawle, "Numbers of Inhabitants whose Estates had laid dead, were furnish'd with Stock for Trade," by the paper-money

---

[58] Keith, *op. cit.,* pp. 213-214.

[59] *Pennsylvania Archives* (8th ser.), III, 1829.

[60] *Ibid.,* p. 1795. "Tonnage" means that of the vessel and not the tonnage shipped from Pennsylvania.

[61] *Ibid.,* II, 176.

Year Ending November 1	Number of Vessels	Tonnage
1719	128	4,514
1720	140	3,982
1721	111	3,711
1722	96	3,531
1723	99	3,942
1724	119	5,450
1725	140	6,655

Year Built	Number of Vessels Constructed	Number of Tons
1722	10	458
1723	13	507
1724	19	959

acts of 1723, "Which gave the quickest Push to Trade that has been known for divers Years before." [62]

Effects on foreign trade. — The figures for imports into Pennsylvania from England seem to support Rawle's assertion. From 1723 to 1724 such imports doubled in terms of British pounds sterling. In 1725 the total value of such imports into Pennsylvania was nearly three times the figure for 1723. Exports from Pennsylvania to England fail to show a similar increase. The figures are given in Table 1. The fact that imports into Pennsylvania from Britain increased almost 100 per cent from 1723 to 1724 at the same time that Pennsylvania's exports to Britain decreased over 50 per cent would seem to indicate that the economic recovery in Pennsylvania in 1724 came first in the domestic market rather than in the export market.

In Table 2 the imports of Pennsylvania from Great Britain are compared with the imports of the other British colonies in America from Great Britain. Not only are these import figures in terms of British pounds sterling but they are based on official values and not on market values. The method of computing them was to multiply the volume of

---

[62] *A Just Rebuke to a Dialogue betwixt Simon and Timothy, Shewing What's Therein To Be Found,* p. 5.

TABLE 1*

TRADE BETWEEN GREAT BRITAIN AND
PENNSYLVANIA IN BRITISH POUNDS
STERLING

Year	Imports of Pennsylvania	Exports of Pennsylvania
1720	24,532	7,929
1721	21,548	8,037
1722	26,397	6,882
1723	15,993	8,332
1724	30,325	4,057
1725	42,210	11,981
1726	57,635	5,960
1727	31,980	12,823
1728	37,479	15,231
1729	29,800	7,435
1730	48,592	10,582
1731	44,261	12,787
1732	41,699	8,525
1733	40,565	14,777
1734	54,392	20,217
1735	48,805	21,919
1736	61,514	20,786
1737	56,690	15,199
1738	61,450	11,919

* The figures in this table, and also those upon which Table 2 is based, have been taken from Sir Charles Whitworth, *State of the Trade of Great Britain in Its Imports and Exports Progressively from the Year 1697* (London, 1776), pp. 63, 65, 67, 69, 78. All figures are in British pounds sterling. The author says of them: "These Tables are compiled from the annual Accounts given in by the proper Officers to the House of Commons. They are therefore as authentic, and as accurate, as any that can be procured on the Subject. It must not, however, be disguised, that even these Accounts are not altogether to be depended on. Where Duties are to be paid, or Bounties received; there they are certainly accurate: But where no Duty is to be paid, no Bounty received; the Entries made at the Custom-house may perhaps, sometimes, exceed the real Value of Imports and Exports." But he points out that, if not always exactly accurate, these figures are relatively correct, since any tendency to overstate the value of items existed throughout the period after 1722, when "almost all Duties upon the Importation of raw Materials, or the Exportation of manufactured Goods, were taken off," and he adds that "there is no Reason to suppose that more unfair Entries have been made at any one, rather than at any other, Time, during this whole Period." Whitworth's figures correspond fairly closely with similar contemporary compilations (see *The Documentary History of the State of New York*, ed. E. B. O'Callaghan [Albany, 1850], I, 481).

TABLE 2

INDEXES OF COLONIAL IMPORTS FROM GREAT BRITAIN AND TOTAL
IMPORTS OF GREAT BRITAIN
(Average Yearly Imports 1715-19 = 100)

Year	Pennsyl-vania	New York	New England	Virginia and Maryland	Total Imports of Britain
1720	111.2	69.2	95.4	58.2	102.1
1721	97.7	93.9	84.8	66.9	96.7
1722	119.6	106.3	99.1	90.8	106.9
1723	72.5	98.1	130.7	65.1	109.1
1724	137.4	116.6	124.8	85.1	124.0
1725	191.7	130.7	149.5	102.9	118.9
1726	261.2	157.0	148.8	97.7	111.9
1727	144.9	124.8	138.7	101.4	114.0
1728	169.9	151.0	144.1	89.9	126.9
1729	135.1	119.8	119.3	57.2	126.4
1730	220.2	119.1	154.2	79.3	130.4
1731	200.6	122.3	135.9	90.0	117.2
1732	189.0	121.3	160.4	77.9	118.8
1733	183.8	121.1	136.7	97.8	134.4
1734	246.5	151.2	108.5	90.4	119.0
1735	221.4	148.7	140.1	116.4	136.8
1736	278.8	159.1	164.6	107.6	122.5
1737	256.9	232.8	165.9	111.1	118.6
1738	278.5	246.8	150.5	136.1	124.7

trade in each classification by the unit price in 1697, though for items not produced in 1697, like new fabrics and new kinds of articles, the current prices had to be used.[63] As has been pointed out, such a procedure gives results closely approximating a physical index of trade.

Because of the conclusions that are drawn from these statistics of British imports into Pennsylvania, it may be well to explain more fully the importance of such imports to the economy of Colonial Pennsylvania. If one makes allowance for the fact that British merchandise was usually marked up about 100 per cent above its English price by the Philadelphia merchants and also makes allowance for the difference in the exchange value of the British and Pennsylvania money (see Table 3), it would seem that the annual value of British imports into Pennsylvania from

[63] Bezanson, Gray, and Hussey, *op. cit.,* p. 264.

1724 to 1774 was more than twice as much as the total amount of Pennsylvania currency in circulation and was twice as much in value as were the total exports of wheat, flour, and bread from the port of Philadelphia in the years around 1730 and 1750.[64] On the same basis, the value in Pennsylvania of the imports from Great Britain amounted to about £3 per inhabitant around 1730.[65] With unskilled labor in Pennsylvania receiving two and one-half shillings a day, the per capita imports from Great Britain to Pennsylvania around 1730 were equivalent each year to about twenty-five days of unskilled labor.[66] From such figures it seems probable that imports from England represented at least one-fifth of the real income of the inhabitants of Pennsylvania.

The importance of British imports to domestic trade in Pennsylvania is further indicated by the following statement in a report in 1752 by a committee of the Pennsylvania assembly appointed to investigate, among other things, the "foreign and domestic Trade" of the colony: "Our domestic or Inland Trade is so connected with and dependent on our foreign Commerce, that it is difficult to distinguish, or obtain any separate Account of it." [67]

Conclusions from import figures. — A number of conclusions seem warranted from the figures in Table 2 for the imports of the various colonies from the mother-country, especially if one also takes into account similar figures for exports (not given in Table 2). First, the imports, the total foreign trade, and presumably domestic trade as well, increased in England and New England after 1721. Second, in 1723, when Pennsylvania first issued paper money, the business depression there was much more severe than in other colonies, while England and New England were not then suffering from a business recession. Third, in New York, where paper money was in circulation and where the pattern of production and commodity trade was very similar to that in Pennsylvania, the depression of business was much less severe than in Pennsylvania. Fourth, trade in Pennsylvania increased to a remarkable degree after December, 1723,

---

[64] *Pennsylvania Archives* (8th ser.), V, 3628-29.

[65] For population figures see n. 69. These foreign trade and population figures presumably do not cover exactly the same area. The figures for British imports into Pennsylvania probably include the imports into Delaware and into the southern part of New Jersey. The population figures for Pennsylvania may include Delaware (the three lower counties which had the same governor as Pennsylvania) but undoubtedly do not include the lower part of New Jersey. In 1723 one New Jersey writer estimated that one-fourth of the exports of New York and of Pennsylvania consisted of "thet Groath of New Jersey" (see *Archives of New Jersey*, V, 96).

[66] C. W. Macfarlane, "Pennsylvania Paper Currency," *Annals of the American Academy of Political and Social Science*, VIII (July, 1896), 126, and *British Board of Trade Papers, Proprieties*, Vol. XIV, T 25, dated November 23, 1739.

[67] *Pennsylvania Archives* (8th ser.), IV, 3519.

when the £30,000 currency act was passed, the imports into Pennsylvania from Great Britain having increased proportionately twice as much from 1723 to 1726 as in any other colony. One might have expected some increase in imports with the export of coin displaced by the paper money, to the extent that the export of coin did not represent a withdrawal of investments from Pennsylvania or a flight of capital. Every one of these four conclusions are supported by the contemporary writings which have already been quoted.

Some further conclusions can be drawn from these figures for the foreign trade of the colonies with Great Britain, which must have accounted for a considerable part of their total trade, as they were so dependent upon Great Britain for manufactured products. Imports into Pennsylvania increased rapidly after the additional currency issue of £30,000, authorized in September, 1729.[68] In fact, no other colony experienced such a large increase in British imports from one year to the next as did Pennsylvania following the two years of currency issues to overcome business depressions, in 1723 and in 1729. The total imports of Pennsylvania from Great Britain increased more rapidly during the two decades following the first issue of paper money there than did the imports of any other colony from Great Britain. This fact lends support to contemporary statements that the population of Pennsylvania increased very rapidly — about 50 per cent in the decade following the first issue of paper money.[69] Finally whereas the business recession in 1723 seems to have been confined primarily to Pennsylvania, Maryland, and Virginia, all the colonies seem to have suffered from a business recession in 1729.

Opinion in England and the colonies. — Early in 1726 the Lords of Trade and Plantations in England informed the Pennsylvania authorities that they were only restrained by "Tenderness for those Persons into whose Hands the Bills . . . . hav pass'd" from placing the paper-money acts enacted in Pennsylvania in 1723 "before His Majesty to be repeal'd" and promised to do just that "if any further Acts [were] pass'd for creating more Bills of Credit" to circulate as money.[70]

In the meantime, part of the loans made from the £45,000 of currency

---

[68] See Table 4 for a list of currency issues and the amounts outstanding at various dates.

[69] The governor, writing on March 15, 1731, to the British Board of Trade, stated: "The Inhabitants [of Pennsylvania] have been exceedingly encreased within these last ten years . . . . and 'tis believed within these ten years the Inhabitants have encreased above on half of what they were before." At that time he "guessed there may be about Forty five thousand Souls of Whites and four thousand Blacks" (see *British Board of Trade Papers, Proprieties,* Vol. XIII, S 34).

[70] *Pennsylvania Archives* (1st ser.), I, 186-87. The king had the right to veto any act of a Colonial legislature.

authorized in 1723 were repaid, so that by 1726 a sum of £6,110 thus repaid had been "totally destroyed" in accordance with the law.[71] This withdrawal of paper money from circulation "did greatly reduce the quantity of the currency," and the legislature, "being sensible of the great difficulties the merchants and people of Pennsylvania were reduced to in carrying on the trade and commerce of the province" and fearing that the "province would soon [be] reduced to the same Straits and Difficulties it had been under some Time before," passed another currency law on March 5, 1726.[72] This law provided that sums received in repayment of loans from January 1, 1725, to January 1, 1731, were to be reloaned so that a total sum of £38,890 would remain in circulation until 1731 (see Table 3).

This currency act of 1726 was passed before the letter of the Lords of Trade and Plantations was received in the colony, so the Pennsylvania assembly hastened to assure the lords "that this Currency has been so far from proving a Detriment, either to this Province or the British Trade, that it has been evidently beneficial to both," [73] and the new governor, Patrick Gordon, hoped that "their Lordships" would be reconciled to this 1726 act when they were

> duly apprized, that the Trade between Britain and this Province has been so far from suffering, that it has been manifestly encreased since the Establishment of that Currency here; and that more British Goods have been imported, more Ships built in this Place for their Merchants, than had been for many Years before. . . . .[74]

He wrote the lords that he had come to America "no wise prejudiced" in favor of paper money, since before embarking for Pennsylvania he had frequently heard in Britain "of the Disadvantage a Paper Currency had proved to some of his Majesty's Colonies abroad," but from the inquiries he had made in Pennsylvania he was "fully convinced of the Benefits this Province had received from those Bills of Credit" and he found "the general Inclination of the People of all Degrees to be the same in this Case." [75]

The currency experiment of 1723 in Pennsylvania was considered so successful that the legislature in New Jersey hastened to follow suit. The governor of New Jersey called the "Representatives together in General

[71] *Colonial Records,* IV, 362.
[72] *Statutes at Large of Pennsylvania,* IV, 197, and *Pennsylvania Archives* (8th ser.), III 1830.
[73] *Pennsylvania Archives*: (8th ser.), III, 1830.
[74] *Ibid.,* pp. 1789-90.
[75] *Ibid.,* p. 1832.

Assembly to provide Remedies for [the] many Hardships which His Majesty's good Subjects within this Colony, lie under, for want of a Currency of Money." In New Jersey, also, the number of "Law-Suits" had increased, and the inhabitants had sent "many Petitions" to the governor and the assembly for an issue of paper money or some other "Method for their Relief." [76] The general assembly met late in 1723. After "taking into their serious Consideration the Miserable Circumstances of the Inhabitants of the several Counties which they Represent, for want of a Medium of Trade or Currency of Money," the assembly passed on November 30, 1723, an act to issue £40,000 of paper money "on loan." They passed this act "being well Informed of the Relief which the Neighboring Provinces have found, in the like Case, by a Paper Currency, and hoping the like Effects from it, and finding no other Way to Remedy the Grievances aforesaid, of His Majesty's Subjects here." [77] Delaware also followed the example of Pennsylvania, issuing a considerable sum of paper money in 1724, which Rawle reports "reviv'd Trade, render'd Commerce and Dealing more easie and safe." [78]

Those who had opposed the issue of paper money, although admitting that it had afforded some temporary relief, thought for a time that the experiment would end disastrously. James Logan, for example, put the following words in the mouth of a character in a dialogue he wrote anonymously in reply to a pamphlet written by Francis Rawle:

> To instance first, the Paper-Currency; some say it has been advantagious, Relieved the Necessitous, and quickened Trade at home and abroad; and many of these are for more (for can we have too much of a good Thing?) Others conceive, that the Relief given to one, was by oppressing, if not defrauding another; That as to Trade, they allowed it to have at first View such an Appearance; but is a Flash and Deception. They doubt it will have such an effect as the Virginia Plant upon humane Bodies, create a false Joy, a Levalto in the Brain, but end in Sickness, Pain, and perhaps Death. These urge, That the Building of Vessels and other late Pushes in Trade are owing to the Apprehensions Men are under, who must receive their Dues in such a Specie as in Time would sink in Value, (according to Presidents) and were willing to lay it out in Vessels and Goods, while the Project was young, and before the Value or Prices altered; and conclude, That all will subside again, and for the future be governed by Proportion, and the Encouragement or Discouragement which may arise from Freights and Markets, &c. That as Foreign Goods rise in Disproportion to our Produce, as may reasonably be expected, and is in Part already seen, the Burden

---

[76] *Acts of the General Assembly of the Province of New Jersey* (1723), chap. lxxxvii.

[77] *Ibid.*

[78] *Ways and Means for the Inhabitants of Delaware To Become Rich* (Philadelphia, 1725), p. 6.

which at first seem'd to be thrown on others will fall upon the Planter and Tradesman.[79]

To this statement Rawle replied:

> .... he may see, if he'll please to open his Eyes, that Paper-Money will at this Time build Vessels, purchase Goods, and serve the other Uses of Money, as well as while the Project was young (as he terms it,) and the Planter and Tradesman in a concording Harmony will tell him, that Paper-Money reviv'd Trade, and freed them from great Difficulties. And I think I may place his Prediction of its Downfall amongst some others, that have not yet come to pass, and in all Probability never will.[80]

Although Logan reported in May, 1723, before the first paper money was put into circulation in Pennsylvania, that the colony was "now reduced to so low a Condition by being drained of Money and by a general Decay of Trade," [81] he reported in July, 1724, upon returning from a sojourn in England, that "Goods have sold briskly this year and at good value in paper Money." [82] In November, 1724, Logan wrote to his London agent:

> I am just out of Strowds [a heavy cloth used for blankets and coats] and very low in Duffells [a strong and very shaggy cloth] I never vented so many In a year before. The Traders talk with great Courage, but I know not what to make of it, only if they pay as they expect to do I shall have a large quantity of Peltry [to ship to England], Pray supply me however by all means as spedily as possible [with Strowds and Duffells].[83]

By the end of 1726 Logan admitted to the Penn family that paper money had been "really of Service to the Countrey." [84] In December of that year he wrote:

> Thou & others will admire [wonder] perhaps to find Coll. Gordon [the new Governor] give in so freely to our Paper Currency, but there must not be one word said against it here, and to speak the Truth, it has been of great Service to the Countrey.[85]

As will be indicated later, Isaac Norris thought in 1729 that John Penn, for political reasons, had better "comply with the time & present necessity" by permitting the passage of an act providing for an additional issue of £30,000 of paper money, which sum, he thought, "as our case stands may be advantageous." [86]

---

[79] *A Dialogue Shewing, What's Therein To Be Found* (Philadelphia, 1725), pp. 13 and 14.

[80] *A Just Rebuke to a Dialogue betwixt Simon and Timothy, Shewing What's Therein To Be Found,* pp. 11 and 12.

[81] Logan to Amos Strettle, May 9, 1723, *Letter Book,* p. 317.

[82] Logan to John Askew, July 30, 1724, *ibid.,* p. 343.

[83] Logan to John Askew, November 12, 1724, *ibid.,* p. 358.

[84] Logan to John Penn, December 12, 1726, *Logan Papers,* IV, 123.

[85] Logan to Joshua Gee, December 14, 1726, *ibid.,* p. 127.

[86] Norris to John Penn, April 30, 1729, *Letters,* 1716 to 1731, p. 525.

However, in 1723 Norris had been very alarmed at the turn of affairs in Pennsylvania. In that year he wrote:

> Through the decay of Trade and the forward humour of many People to run into Debt many have failed — and one knows not who to trust, And these Indescreet (and Some of them) Sluggish Idle people — have by Combination begun last year to throw out most of the Usual old Members [of the Assembly] and Chosen Such an Assembly as would find any Means to Ease them tho manifestly Unjust In order to it they have Raised and Established fifteen Thousand pound of paper bills to pass as Mony . . . . and this Mobbish people are again Combining for another assembly which will Raise more paper for Unless they can come at Something of less Vallue than they borrowed or became Indebted for their End is not answered. This is our Miserable Case — which will too probably terminate in the ruin or Great Suffering of all the frugal Industrious people who have Obtain'd any Substance. . . . .[87]

In December, 1723, Norris had written to James Logan that "the new Politicians are made to believe that the obnoxious men," the well-to-do traders, are the "Cause of our Poverty," and he added: "I told thee no Body Would be able to bound the Designers neither in Mode or Quantity" of paper money.[88] Norris later said that, if the issue of paper money had been "to help the Defect of Cash" by making "a small sum for the Conveniency of our home market & small payments, & we could prevent an Increase I should like it," but he thought that "the people would never cease" to demand more paper money and he believed that "a levelling principle was at the Bottom with the Crafty & designing." [89] He charged that "Lyes are their refuge — Privilege & power are to be strain'd till the strings break in order to Introduce a Change." [90]

In 1725 Logan gave the stock conservative argument that aid for the rich is the best way to help the poor, when he wrote in a pamphlet ridiculing a recent pamphlet by Rawle:

> And here I cannot but lament and wonder at the prevailing Politicks of late to cry out against Merchants and rich Men (alas we have too few) and at the same Time talk and bluster of promoting Trade and Navigation. Every Body that knows any Thing of the Matter, knows that these can never be carried on to general Benefit, without Men of good Stocks [funds], with Skill and Ability for the Purpose. . . . .
> These [well-to-do traders willing to take risks] are in the Sense I am speaking, Agents or Servants of a Country; if they thrive and reside in it, the Country has the Gain, and it will disperse.[91]

---

[87] Norris to Mord Maddock, September 23, 1723, *ibid.*, p. 338.
[86] Norris to James Logan, December 16, 1723, *ibid.*, p. 364.
[89] *Ibid.*, and Norris to John Penn, April 30, 1729, *ibid.*, pp 523 and 524.
[90] *Ibid.*
[91] *A Dialogue Shewing, What's Therein To Be Found*, pp. 32 and 33.

Norris was so afraid that the paper-money experiment in Pennsylvania would end in injustice, "attended with Gross anarchy & Confusion," that he warned Englishmen whose investments he was administering that their funds were in danger, and, on his own initiative, he liquidated the investments of some in order to return their funds to them in England.[92] Norris also began to send some of his own funds to England for investment as the "preservation of property [is] so much disregarded by Some (yet Selfish men) in power here." [93] Norris wrote to his London agent in connection with this flight of capital or transfer of funds abroad: "I would lodge a part of my Estate in such a manner that while the present Good Establishment in our Mother Country remains as I hope it Always will, for mine when we think or Speak of a Shilling may know what it means."[94]

Course of exchange rates. — Perhaps such "flight of capital" from Pennsylvania played a minor role in the rise of the exchange rate on England and helped to make paper money "the only Specie" in the colony. Table 3 indicates the amount of Pennsylvania currency necessary to buy £ 100 of English money in Philadelphia at various times.

The first issues of paper money in Pennsylvania were put into circulation at least by September, 1723 (the act was passed on March 2, 1723), when Norris reported that paper was the only money in the colony, gold and silver being sold as commodities "for Shipping off." [95] The exchange rate rose slightly between July and September, 1723. Some time after the second issue of £ 30,000 (authorized on December 12, 1723) Norris reported that it was "very Difficult to procure Bills" of exchange, though both Norris and Logan had made the same complaint in 1721 before any paper money had been issued.[96] In fact, the exchange rate was no higher in July, 1724, some time after the second issue of paper money, than it had been in 1721. Both Logan and Norris stated that gold and silver were entirely withdrawn from circulation after the second issue of paper money, though at the end of July, 1724, Logan stated that gold was then "so Scarce that my family in my absence have not received the value of £ 5 of it for every hundred pounds in paper." [97] Gold and silver continued to be imported into Pennsylvania; Norris stated in June, 1727, that the best

---

92 Norris to Mord Maddock, September 23, 1723, *Letters,* 1716 to 1730, p. 338; Norris to Anne Coakley, July 30, 1724, *ibid.,* p. 383; Norris to John Penn, April 30, 1729, *ibid.,* pp. 523 and 524.

93 Norris to John Askew, February 15, 1724, *ibid.,* p. 370.

94 *Ibid.*

95 Norris to Mord Maddock, September 23, 1723, *ibid.,* p. 338.

96 Norris to Ann Coaksley, July 30, 1724, *ibid.,* p. 383; Norris to John and Ann Clark, September 10, 1725, *ibid.,* p. 443; Norris to Charles Loyd, November 12, 1721, *ibid.,* p. 277; Logan to John Andrews, November 19, 1721, *ibid.,* p. 227.

97 Logan to John Askew, July 20, 1724, *ibid.,* p. 343; Norris to Ann Coaksley, September 23, 1723, *ibid.,* p. 337.

TABLE 3*

EXCHANGE RATE ON LONDON: NUMBER OF PENNSYLVANIA
POUNDS FOR £ 100 STERLING
(Silver par = 133 1/3)

Date or Period	Exchange Rate	Date or Period	Exchange Rate
November, 1721	143.0	October, 1725	153.33 and
November, 1722	137.5		155.33
July, 1723	137.5	May, October, and	150.0
September, 1723	143.0	December, 1727 . .	150.0
December, 1723	135.33 and	1728 . .	150.0
	136.33	1729 . .	151.7
July, 1724	143.0	1730 . .	153.1
September, October,	148.5 and	1731 . .	161.1
and November, 1724	149.5	1732 . .	165.0
First three quarters of	148.5 and	1733 . .	
1725	149.5		

* Sources: Logan to John Stork, November 14, 1721, *Letter Book, 1717 to
1731*, p. 222; Logan to John Andrews, November 19, 1721, *ibid.*, p. 227; Logan to
Sam Stork and to John Stork, November 9, 1722, *ibid.*, pp. 284 and 288; Logan to
Timothy Storbess, November 13, 1722, *ibid.*, p. 294; Logan to John Andrews, July 4,
1723, *ibid.*, p. 326; William Keith to British Board of Trade, *Proprieties*, Vol. XI,
R 47; Norris to Ann Coaksley, September 23, 1723, *Letters, 1716 to 1730*, p. 337;
Logan to John Askew, July 30, 1724, *ibid.*, p. 343; Norris to Richard Champion,
September 3, 1724, *ibid.*, p. 391; Norris to Robert Price, October 31, 1724, *ibid.*,
pp. 395 and 396; Logan to William and L. Aubry, November 9, 1724, *ibid.*, p. 357;
Archives of the State of New Jersey (1st ser.), pp. 154 and 155; A. Bezanson, R. D.
Gray, and M. Hussey, *Prices in Colonial Pennsylvania* (Philadelphia, 1935), p. 431,
for the years 1727-33.

way to acquire bills of exchange was "first to Endeavor to purchase Gold
or Silver as any happens to be Imported or can be procured at the Easiest
Exchange we can." [98] Various merchants stated that bills of exchange
could only be purchased with gold or silver and seldom, if ever, with
paper money.[99]

Currency issues. — Changes in the amounts of Pennsylvania currency
outstanding are indicated in Table 4. The dates given in the table are the
dates on which the currency acts were passed rather than the dates on
which the currency was actually put into circulation. The figures for the

---

[98] Norris to John Clark, June 3, 1727, *ibid.*, p. 491.

[99] Norris, *ibid.*, pp. 395, 396, 399, 452, and 491; Samuel Powel, Jr., to Nicholas
Witchell, October 16, 1728, *Letter Book*, p. 57 and to John Bell, *ibid.*, November 6,
1733.

total authorized issue really represent the difference between the amount of currency issued and the amount of currency retired and burnt each year. In August and September of each year, when repayments on loans were heavy, the full amount of money authorized was not in circulation, because some of the currency repaid remained for a short time in the hands of the loan-office commissioners. However, the commissioners soon reissued the sums paid as instalments on the principal of loans. A committee of the assembly reported in August, 1752, that "the yearly Quotas [repayments of principal] are, as fast as paid in, re-emitted to other Borrowers," for

> during many Years past, through the Smallness of the Sum to be from Time to Time re-emited, not only those admitted to borrow were obliged to be content with Small Proportions, but many who could give ample Security, have been delayed and disappointed. Even at this present Time, though Applications by failing of Success have been so much discouraged, we are informed there are no less than 1000 Appliers on the List, who wait their Turn to be supplied.[100]

The figures for the total authorized issue in 1724, 1725, and after 1755 may not be entirely accurate. They have been calculated from the annual audits and reports to the assembly, and in those reports the figures for the amounts of currency retired and burnt are on a fiscal-year basis (from August to August and, after 1764, from July to July). Therefore, the figures represent the amount of currency outstanding in the latter part of each year.

Changes in prices. — If one follows a curve indicating the changes in the price level from month to month in Pennsylvania in the 1720's, one finds that the movements of prices correspond very closely with changes in the quantity of money in circulation. An excellent index of the "average monthly wholesale prices of twenty commodities in Philadelphia" from 1720 to 1775 has recently been constructed by a group of economists at the University of Pennsylvania, based on a detailed study of prices in Colonial Pennsylvania.[101] The years 1741-45 are used as a base. This price index has a downward trend during 1720, 1721, and the first half of 1772. From July, 1722, to July, 1723, there was comparatively little change in the average of prices. The first paper-money issue of £15,000 was to be ready to loan out within two months after May 11, 1723; [102] the loans were quickly made, since there were not sufficient funds to satisfy all the would-be borrowers. From a low point of 84.7 in July, 1723, the index of prices rises to 92.3 in September and 95.0 in November of 1723. The notes for the next currency issue were to be "made and prepared be-

---
[100] *Pennsylvania Archives* (8th ser.), IV, 3519-20.
[101] Bezanson *et al., op. cit.,* p. 425.
[102] *Statutes at Large of Pennsylvania,* III, 324.

TABLE 4*

PENNSYLVANIA CURRENCY ISSUES AND AMOUNTS
OUTSTANDING PRIOR TO 1775

Date of Act	Amount of Issue (In Pounds)	Year	Total Authorized Issue (In Pounds)
March 2, 1723	15,000	1723	15,000
December 12, 1723	30,000	1724	44,915
		1725	38,915
March 5, 1726†		1726–29	38,890
May 10, 1729	30,000	1729–39	68,890
May 18, 1739	11,110	1739–46	80,000
		1746–49	85,000
		1750	84,500
June 24, 1746	5,000	1751	84,000
		1752	83,500
		1753	82,500
		1754	81,500
April 1, 1755	15,000‡	1755	96,000
January 1, 1756	55,000		
September 21, 1756	30,000	1756	177,510
March 10, 1757	45,000		
June 17, 1757	55,000	1757	263,899
April 22, 1758	100,000	1758	335,578
April 17, 1759	100,000	1759	407,884
April 12, 1760	100,000	1760	485,782
		1761	459,462
		1762	432,212
		1763	410,703
May 30, 1764	55,000	1764	456,000
		1765	432,235
		1766	408,571
May 20, 1767	20,000	1767	395,170
		1768	366,626
February 18, 1769	30,000	1769	367,474
		1770	343,503
March 9, 1771	15,000	1771	328,945
March 21, 1772	25,000	1772	319,971
February 26, 1773	162,000	1773	450,023
		1774	421,709

* Sources: Henry Phillips, *Historical Sketches of the Paper Currency of the American Colonies* (Roxbury Mass., 1865), pp. 37-45; *Pennsylvania Archives* (8th ser.), VII, 5649, 5650, 5785-86, 5929, 6053, 6231-39, 6266, 6428, 6564, and *ibid.*, VIII, 6711, 6888-89, 7016, 7138-39.

† Changing retirement of 1723 issues.

‡ Circulating bills.

fore the first day of the month March," 1724. From a low point of 88.4 in May, 1724, the price index rises to 98.9 in September, 1724, and to a peak of 115.7 in September, 1725. By 1726 the money in circulation had been reduced from £45,000 to £38,889, at which figure it remained until May, 1729. Since trade was expanding, prices tended to fall in 1727, 1728, and 1729 to a low of 95.1 for the index in May, 1729. In that month an additional issue of £30,000 was authorized, and the index of prices rose again to a peak of 107.1 in January, 1730. In Table 5 the yearly index of the wholesale price level in Philadelphia is compared with a recently constructed index for the cost of living in England. This table indicates that prices fell farther from 1720 to 1722 in England than in Philadelphia, but failed to rise as rapidly in England during the years 1723-26 as they did in Pennsylvania, where paper currency was then in circulation. Also, there was a downward movement in prices in Pennsylvania during the period from 1726 to 1729, when a reduced amount of currency was in circulation. The exchange rate on England also fell slightly, indicating a rise in the exchange value of Pennsylvania money. With the issue of paper

TABLE 5*

INDEXES OF WHOLESALE PRICES IN PHILADELPHIA
AND COST OF LIVING IN ENGLAND
(1720 = 100)

Year	Philadelphia	England
1720	100.0	100.0
1721	93.2	89.2
1722	96.4	84.3
1723	101.5	95.1
1724	109.1	97.1
1725	125.7	103.0
1726	126.1	98.0
1727	122.6	103.9
1728	115.6	109.9
1729	112.9	100.0
1730	115.9	87.3
1731	104.0	86.3
1732	102.3	79.4
1733	105.4	87.3
1734	108.1	89.2
1735	108.1	86.3

* Sources; Bezanson *et al, op. cit.,* converted from a 1741-45 base, and E. W. Gilboy, "Cost of Living and Real Wages in Eighteenth Century England," *Review of Economic Statistics,* August, 1936, converted from a 1700 base.

money in Pennsylvania in 1729, prices rose again, whereas they fell sharply in England from 1729 to 1730.

Indexes of the price of wheat and flour, then the most important exports of Pennsylvania, are given in Table 6. This table indicates that the price of wheat rose rapidly in Philadelphia from 1723 to 1724, while there was no rise in its price in Boston in terms of silver and no comparable rise in London, England. Monthly indexes for the price of wheat in Philadelphia show that the price began to rise in February, 1724, and reached a peak in April, 1725. The price of flour also rose sharply throughout 1724. Furthermore, the rise in the price of wheat and flour was relatively more rapid in Philadelphia from 1723 to 1726 than in Boston or London. Both wheat and flour declined in price in Philadelphia from 1725 or 1726 to 1728, a period when the currency in circulation was somewhat reduced in amount, yet in London both commodities rose sharply in price during that period. The prices of wheat and flour in Philadelphia in 1729 and 1730, after the £30,000 issue of currency in 1729, were relatively much higher than in Boston, and also than in London, where the prices of both commodities fell very sharply after 1728.

Logan reported that land values also rose with the issue of paper money. Whereas in 1723 he wanted his English landlord to reduce his rent, in 1724 he hastened to take out a three-year lease, as he explained to the landlord, "at the same Rent for tho Lands and Houses were much faln in value here before I went to England [in August, 1723] as I particularly wrote to thee, yet our Paper Money makes it up in some measure since the last Quantity was Struck and therefore I desire to make no further words about it." [103]

Conclusions on 1723 issues. — From the available statistics and the comments of contemporary writers, there can be little doubt that the currency issues of 1723 played an important part in the remarkable recovery of business in Pennsylvania from 1723 to 1726. Prices in Pennsylvania rose more rapidly from 1723 to 1726 than they did in England. Property values also recovered with the issues of paper money. The resulting rise in the price level relieved debtors, merchants, and producers, by helping to restore profit margins. Furthermore, loans of paper money at 5 per cent interest tended, for the time being, to lower the rate of interest in Pennsylvania, which had been at 8 per cent; and, as the assembly pointed out, the interest paid by the borrowers from the Pennsylvania Loan Office was sufficient to defray practically all the expenses of the Colonial government.

With regard to the colony's income from the loan office, Governor Gordon wrote to the British Board of Trade in March 1731:

---

[103] Logan to T. Story, October 25, 1724, *Letter Book,* p. 354.

TABLE 6*

INDEXES OF PRICES OF WHEAT AND FLOUR
(Price in 1720 = 100)

YEAR	WHEAT			FLOUR	
	Philadelphia	Boston†	London	Philadelphia	London
1720	100.0	100.0	100.0	100.0	100.0
1721	99.0	92.5	82.6	95.4	. . . .
1722	96.4	94.4	103.8	96.4	90.2
1723	88.6	90.0	101.6	95.0	83.3
1724	109.1	87.4	107.7	118.3	. . . .
1725	125.6	98.7	129.6	130.9	120.8
1726	124.0	105.5	110.6	135.1	97.5
1727	106.2	102.0	143.4	123.8	136.5
1728	110.1	92.0	142.0	108.2	120.8
1729	120.1	88.2	101.5	115.0	71.4
1730	119.5	94.4	87.5	124.9	83.8
1731	80.2	75.1	75.6	86.6	63.6
1732	87.7	83.4	80.2	88.2	64.8
1733	99.4	88.0	105.2	95.5	90.2
1734	115.3	83.4	108.5	113.5	95.2
1735	125.0	84.9	97.8	123.9	83.3

* Sources: Bezanson *et al., op. cit.,* p. 422; Ruth Crandall, "Wholesale Commodity Prices in Boston during the Eighteenth Century," *Review of Economic Statistics,* XVI, No. 6 (June, 1934), 121. The indexes of London prices are based on original figures taken from the Admiralty Accounts and Treasurers' and Contract Ledgers. The figures were supplied to the author by Elizabeth W. Gilboy, Committee on Research in the Social Sciences, Harvard University.
† Deflated by the price of silver in Boston.

By the Emission of a Paper Currency in this Province, an annual Interest arises thereon amounting to near three Thousand pounds this Currency which with a small Excise on Spirits not amounting to One thousand pounds, yearly raise together a Sufficiency to answer all the present Exigencies of this Government.[104]

The historian, Charles P. Keith, claims that

to this reduction of taxation to a minimum, merely some duties on a few imports, so that it was many years before another levy on land or wealth or poll tax was laid by the central government of Pennsylvania, is due the stride made by the colony in population and wealth.[105]

---

[104] *British Board of Trade Papers, Proprieties,* Vol. XIII, s34.
[105] *Chronicles of Pennsylvania from the English Revolution to the Peace of Aix-la-Chapelle, 1688 to 1748* (Philadelphia, 1917), II, 674.

Had Pennsylvania remained on the gold-and-silver coin standard, it seems likely that business there would not have revived much until a year later (1724-25) when the price of wheat began to rise rapidly in England and in Boston in terms of silver. Even then the business advance probably would have been much less rapid than it actually was, for prices rose considerably in Pennsylvania from 1724 to 1726, whereas in England they were about the same in 1726 as in 1724. Judging by the figures for Pennsylvania's trade with England and the statements of Colonial officials, the recovery in Pennsylvania in 1724 seems to have been a recovery of the domestic market stimulated by currency issues rather than a business revival resulting from an increased foreign demand for the exports of Pennsylvania.

The recovery of industry in Pennsylvania that followed the first issues of paper money seems to have been a "sound" recovery. Inflation and runaway speculation did not occur, as some "sound money" economists predict will happen under such circumstances. The recovery seems to have been as "natural" as it would have been had the colonists patiently waited for "natural forces" to start the wheels of industry again. It is, of course, rather difficult to bring on an extremely rapid rise in prices during a business depression, when much of the country's productive capacity is idle. The well-known inflations in history have occurred in connection with wars and not in connection with depressions.

PAPER-MONEY ISSUE OF 1729

Currency circulation in the colonies. — By a remarkable coincidence, none of the American colonies increased the amount of their currency in circulation during the years prior to 1729, except Rhode Island, where the currency was increased about £22,000 from 1726 to the middle of 1728. Even in Rhode Island the quantity of currency outstanding decreased from the middle of 1728 to the middle of 1733. From 1724 to 1729 the amount of paper money in circulation declined in New York, New Jersey, Delaware, Pennsylvania, South Carolina, Connecticut, and New Hampshire. In North Carolina the amount of currency outstanding remained fixed from 1722 to 1729, as it did in Pennsylvania from 1726 to 1729. The quantity of Massachusetts currency in circulation declined progressively after 1726, until in 1741 the amount in circulation was fully 50 per cent less than in 1726. The quantity of New Hampshire's currency in circulation declined over 20 per cent from 1727 to 1736, while the amount of Connecticut currency outstanding decreased almost 60 per cent between 1727 and 1730 and over 90 per cent between 1724 and 1736.[106] This marked reduction

---

[106] For data on the amount of currency in circulation in the different colonies see:

in the total amount of money in circulation in the American colonies from 1724, and especially from 1726, to the middle of 1729 is all the more significant in view of the fact that the population in the colonies was increasing rapidly at that time.

The only colonies to increase the amount of their currency in circulation in 1729 were Pennsylvania, Delaware, and North Carolina. New Jersey, Rhode Island, and Maryland followed next by making large new issues of currency in 1733.

At the same time that the quantity of currency in circulation was being reduced prior to the middle of 1729, so were Colonial purchases — at least of British goods. As Table 2 indicates, British imports into Pennsylvania, New York, and New England declined about 20 per cent from 1728 to 1729, and in Virginia and Maryland the decline was about 36 per cent. Indeed, imports from Great Britain to Virginia and Maryland even declined 11 per cent from 1727 to 1728. At this time Maryland and Virginia were the only colonies that were not on a paper-money standard.

In view of these facts, it is not surprising to find the Maryland legislature complaining in the middle of 1729 that "the Effects of the Scarcity of Gold and Silver in this Province, are very sensibly felt by the Inhabitants thereof." [107] In October, 1729, the governor of Maryland wrote:

> New York, Pennsylvania &c are vastly improved in foreign Trade, as well as home Manufactures, by a Paper Currency; it is that, in lieu of Specifik Coin, which seems, to give life, Expedition, and Ease to trade and Commerce . . . ., they [the above-mentioned colonies] are daily growing more and more populous, and are supposed to Increase as proportionably in Credit and riches; In Virginia and Maryland, the Case is much otherwise; . . . . For the people [of Maryland] are impatient for some kind of Relief in their Circumstances. [108]

---

for Connecticut, *British Board of Trade Papers, Proprieties,* Vol. XIV, T_{30}; for Delaware, *ibid.,* T_{25}; Massachusetts, A. McF. Davis, "Introduction" in *Colonial Currency Reprints, 1682-1751* (Publications of the Prince Society" [Boston, 1910]), pp. 69-70; New Hampshire, C. J. Bullock, *Essays on the Monetary History of the United States* (New York, 1900), pp. 215-25; North Carolina, *ibid.,* pp. 135-36, New York J. H. Hickox. *A History of the Bills of Credit or Paper Money Issued in New York* (Albany, 1866), pp. 22-27; New Jersey, *Documents Relating to the Colonial History of the State of New Jersey,* Vol. XV: *Journal of the Governor and Council, 1738-1748,* pp. 106-8; Rhode Island, E. R. Potter, "A Brief Account of Emissions of Paper Money Made by the Colony of Rhode Island" in *Historical Sketches of the Paper Currency of the American Colonies,* ed. Henry Phillips (Roxbury, Mass., 1865), p. 120; South Carolina, "An Account of the Rise and Progress of the Paper Bills of Credit of South Carolina. . . . ," *Statutes at Large of South Carolina,* IX (1849), 175-78.

[Ed. Note: Also see data in editor's introduction and sources cited there.]

[107] *Archives of Maryland,* XXXVI, 469.

[108] *Ibid.,* XXV, 602-3.

Although in the colonies other than Virginia and Maryland imports from Great Britain rose from 1727 to 1728 (the rise was 17 per cent for Pennsylvania), it may well be that the slump of 1729 actually began in most colonies in 1728. The Colonial merchants sent their orders for British goods some months before actual shipment of the goods from England, or they sold English merchandise in the colonies on consignment. Consequently, it took a considerable period of time for English exports to adjust to market conditions in the colonies. Statistics of English imports into a colony, therefore, reflect only with a substantial lag the actual business conditions in that colony.

Business conditions in Pennsylvania. — Early in 1728, trade in Pennsylvania again began to decline. An important Philadelphia merchant, Samuel Powel, Jr., wrote on January 1, 1728: "The pay here grows worse than when I Left Philadelphia [for a visit to England] and Goods Sell Lower." [109]

In February, 1728, the following statement on business conditions appeared in the *Pennsylvania Gazette:*

> Money here seems very scarce. Trade has been long in a deep Consumption, her Nerves relax'd, her Spirits languid, her Joints have grown so feeble, that she has had of late so terrible a Fall that she now lies bleeding in a very deplorable condition. 'Tis said several eminent Physicians have prescrib'd to restore her to her pristine Health, but in vain. But we are not without Hopes the President of the College will exert his utmost Skill, when 'twill not be doubted but she will recover her former Health Strength and Beauty.[110]

By April, 1728, the inhabitants in various sections of the colony were petitioning the Colonial legislature for an increase in the amount of paper money. For example, the legislature received a

> Petition of many of the Inhabitants of the City and County of Philadelphia, setting forth, that when the Bills of Credit passed in the greatest Plenty, the Trade of the Province increased, and our Produce kept up to a living Price; but since Part of the said Bills are sunk, the Trade begins to languish; and altho' the Quantity of the Bills, when emitted, might then be sufficient to circulate the Trade of this Province, yet the said Trade has, by the good effects thereof, been increased, as well as the Number of the People; and consequently the Trade must be reduced, the Manufactures lie on Hand, the Navigation discouraged, without a farther Addition to the Quantity of currency in circulation; therefore humbly pray, that a Bill may be brought for increasing the Sum to Sixty Thousand Pounds.[11]

---

[109] Samuel Powel to David Barclay, January 1, 1728, *Letter Book,* Vol. I: 1727-1739, p. 8. (MS at Historical Society of Pennsylvania.)
[110] *Pennsylvania Gazette,* No. IX, February 18, 1728.
[111] *Pennsylvania Archives* (8th ser.), III, 1876.

In May of 1728 Powel reported: "Our pay here is grown So Exceedingly bad that no business is to be done," [112] and in June he wrote to his agent in England: "Our pay is So very backward that it discourages me from being So largely Concerned [in purchasing merchandise] as I otherwise would with thee." [113] Apparently, business continued to decline throughout 1728 in Pennsylvania. In October of that year Powel wrote in three different letters to England:

> Since the pay is So bad that I am quite discouraged from adviseing thee to send any thing more this way (at least to me).[114]

> Pay here was hardly Ever So bad as now.[115]

> I wish thee knew as well as I do the difficulty that now Attends doing business here. The pay is grown So very bad by our being Exceedingly overdone with English Goods that if we Sell at 6 mo. Credit it is well if wee Can depend on being paid for them in 12 or 15 mo. and Sometimes it is much longer.[116]

In 1729 the business slump apparently became worse in Pennsylvania. In February, 1729, Powel wrote to a London agent: ". . . . but pay Comes in very Dully; I would have thee send no more Goods untill I write for them." [117] In April he reported: "Pay Grows worse with us Every day; I do not know what it will come to at last." [118] And in two letters in May he wrote: "Pay here is worse than Ever and our Town is Exceedingly Glutted with Goods." [119] ". . . . our Town never was so much Glutted with Goods as now and the pay grows worse." [120]

Currency legislation. — On May 10, 1729, a bill to issue an additional sum of £30,000 was passed in Pennsylvania, although the additional notes were not to be issued and put into circulation before September 15, 1729. This interval of four months between passage of the bill and issuance of the notes was to allow sufficient time for the act to receive the approval of the king. The paper-money act of 1729, like the acts of 1723, had occasioned considerable debate. Benjamin Franklin was one of the leading advocates of an additional issue of paper money at this time. He later wrote:

---

112 Powel to Nicholas Witchell, May 4, 1728, *Letter Book,* I, 24.

113 Powel to David Barclay, June 28, 1728, *ibid.,* p. 45.

114 Powel to Nicholas Witchell, October 16, 1728, *ibid.,* p. 57.

115 Powel to Robert Willan, October 4, 1728, *ibid.,* p. 48.

116 Powel to Jacob Wyam, October 16, 1728, *ibid.,* p. 58.

117 Powel to David Barclay, February 7, 1729, *ibid.,* p. 67.

118 Powel to John Askew, April 14, 1729, *ibid.,* p. 84.

119 Powel to John Askew, May 16, 1729, *ibid.,* p. 86.

120 Powel to David Barclay, May 16, 1729, *ibid.,* p. 88.

I was on the side of addition, being persuaded that the first small sum struck in 1723 had done much good by increasing the trade, employment, and number of inhabitants in the province, since I now saw all the old houses inhabited, and many new ones building; whereas I remembered well, when I first walked about the streets of Philadelphia [in 1723], eating my roll, I saw many of the houses in Walnut Street, between Second and Front Streets, with bills on their doors, "To be Let," and many likewise in Chestnut Street and other streets, which made me think the inhabitants of the city were, one after another, deserting it.

Our debate possessed me so fully of the subject, that I wrote and printed an anonymous pamphlet on it, entitled, *The Nature and Necessity of a Paper Currency*. It was well received by the common people in general; but the rich men disliked it, for it increased and strengthened the clamour for more money; and, they happening to have no writers among them that were able to answer it, their opposition slackened, and the point was carried by a majority in the House. My friends there, who considered I had been of some service, thought fit to reward me by employing in printing the money; a very profitable job, and a great help to me. This was another advantage gained by being able to write.[121]

Isaac Norris was one of the "rich men" to whom Franklin referred. A week before the 1729 currency act was finally passed, Norris wrote to John Penn:

> Paper Currency is now the whole bent, & the People are made to believe the Country is ruined without an increase; all their wants & necessities are to be relieved by it. They cannot nor will not See that the poorness of Marketts abroad occasions the Low price of our commoditys, & makes mony scarce.[122]

He told Penn that Governor Gordon was "Extremely Embarrassed" by the paper money act and did "all in his power" to oppose it, "the Extreamity of a flat Denial Excepted." Norris wrote that "after the best Endeavours to Lesson the sum, amend the form and gain so much time for Issuing as may in Degree pay Deference to Instructions & the Order from the [British] board of Trade, prudence led everybody" to agree to the act. Norris explained to Penn that despite "apprehensions, or the Ill Opinion I have had of paper currency in any Country, now we unhapily have it, & it hath thrown out of use & sight all the silver and Gold I cannot see it possible for us to do without it, ... untill trade may turn the ballance in our favour so as to procure specie to substitute in its room." He advised Penn to consider whether

---

[121] *Autobiography* (1895 ed.), pp. 129-31. Franklin printed all the paper money issued in Pennsylvania from 1729 to 1764 (see H. Phillips, "Sketch of Pennsylvania Paper Money," in *Historical Sketches of the American Paper Currency* [Roxbury, Mass., 1865], p. 18).

[122] Norris to John Penn, April 30, 1729, *Letter Book*, 1716-1730, pp. 523-24.

you also will not think it most prudent to comply with the times & present necessity, and we hope if a greater sum or further adition can be prevented the sum now proposed, as our case stands may be advantageous & the passing the Bill with your Concurrence take off your Enemys from one of the most formidable handles whereby to make head against your Interest.[123]

Governor Gordon had publicly declared many times that he was a true and sincere friend of the Pennsylvania currency, and two months before the passage of the act of 1729 he told the assembly:

> That there is Occasion for more of that Currency amongst us, I am fully persuaded; . . . .
> . . . . And as the whole Country seems unanimous in what is now before us, the Desire of an Addition to our Bills of Credit, and I have the Pleasure to observe, there is not one Person I advise with, who agrees not with me in the same real Inclinations to promote it; . . . .[124]

Upon passage of the act, the Pennsylvania assembly wrote as follows in a "Humble Address" to the Penn family:

> We the Representative of all the Freemen in this your Province, ... found ourselves obliged, by the loud and uncommon Cries of the whole Country, to take into Consideration the State of our Currency, and the universal Complaints of the Scarcity thereof amongst all Ranks of his Majesty's Subjects here: And it evidently appeared to us, that by the great Increase of the Inhabitants, the Bills of Credit, which some Years since were issued, being diffused into numerous Hands, fall very far short of being sufficient to answer the Ends of a Medium of Commerce for making the Requisite Payments in Business; by Reason whereof Trade seemed to be almost at a Stand, Manufactures were discouraged, and the whole Country languished. We therefore finding ourselves under a Necessity, in Discharge of the Trust reposed in us, for removing these heavy Pressures, to make a farther Provision of that Currency, by emitting the Sum of Thirty Thousand Pounds more, to be issued on Loan, as formerly, on a double Security of a clear Estate in Lands or Houses, at the annual Interest of Five per Cent. and to be wholly sunk in the Term of Sixteen Years.
> We are very sensible, may it please our Proprieties, of the strong Prejudices that have been taken up against this Sort of Currency. . . . . But if Experience be allowed to be the surest Instructor, it is now manifest, from indisputable Proof, after Six Years Trial of this Currency amongst us, that nothing has ever so much contributed to advance Trade, Navigation, the Price of Lands, and the general Interest of the whole Colony; for we may very justly say, that the Effects of it were no less visible amongst us, than those of a plentiful Shower of Rain to the Earth, after it had lain long parched and dried up for want of Moisture. Nor from that Experience

---

[123] *Ibid.*, p. 525.
[124] *Pennsylvania Archives* (8th ser.), III, 1933, 1935, 1963. See also the statement (*supra*) of the governor in favor of the Pennsylvania currency shortly after his arrival in the colony.

does it appear, that any one Inconveniency worth mentioning has ensued.[125]

The *Pennsylvania Gazette* commented on the passage of the paper-money act as follows:

> We have the agreeable News to acquaint our Country-Readers with, that our Right Honorable Governor has Graciously condescended to pass an Act for Thirty Thousand Pounds more of Paper-Currency, ...
>
> As this extraordinary Goodness of his Honour did more than ordinary affect the Publisher hereof [Samuel Keimer], even into Tears of Joy, so 'tis earnestly hop'd, (considering the Great Opposition made against Paper-Currency at home) it will fill every considered Person with the utmost Respect, Honour, Love and Obedience to Him, his Council, &c. and that all our Party-Feuds will henceforth vanish, and all our Strife be to love and assist one another; then while other Parts are under the Chastisement of Heaven, as several now are, we shall flourish under the Blessing of Providence, as formerly.
>
> 'Tis very remarkable and worth Observation by all, that during this late Scarcity of Money several Gentlemen of the Law have prevented any Actions being brought against honest Traders, (to their everlasting Honour be it spoken,) and that the Number of Writs on the Docket have been considerably less of late than in distant Times when Money was more Plenty.[126]

Business conditions following 1729 issue. — In September, 1729, the month when the lending of the new currency issue was to commence, Powel wrote to his agent in London:

> People are now grown So very backward in their payments that trade is hardly worth following and Indeed I Cannot advise thee to Send me any more goods unless thee will order thy remittances per the West Indies.[127]

But toward the end of the year Powel found that business conditions had improved in Pennsylvania. In November he wrote:

> . . . . If I could have foreseen the great alteration there has happened in the price of nails within this Six months I would have sent for a good parcell; they are now got to 9 *d* Currant and if no great Quantities come will not be under, but there is no Dependence on that.[128]

By January, 1730, Powel was still more optimistic and wrote to a London agent:

> If thee ships them [various commodities listed] I would not have thee miss the first opportunity for thy not Sending those I last ordered is a disappointment, they being much wanted here.[129]

---

[125] *Pennsylvania Archives* (8th ser.), III, 2477-78.
[126] *Pennsylvania Gazette,* No. XXI, May 15, 1729.
[127] Powel to John Askew, September 30, 1729, *Letter Book,* I, 104.
[128] Powel to Thomas Plumsted, November 8, 1729, *ibid.,* p. 111.
[129] Powel to Thomas Caney, January 8, 1730, *ibid.,* p. 132.

The revival of business late in 1729 and in 1730 is reflected in the figures for imports of British goods into Pennsylvania. From 1729 to 1730 such imports increased no less than 63 per cent — an increase far exceeding that in any other colony. The figures for New York, where there were no new currency issues at this time, even show a slight decrease (see Table 2).

The prosperity resulting from the currency issue of 1729, however, lasted only about a year. In 1730, Pennsylvania had "the greatest Crop that ever was raised" there, while at the same time there was then "no demand in Europe" for wheat, or likely to be any in the near future. [130] From August, 1730, to January, 1731, the price of wheat in Pennsylvania fell from 4 shillings to 2¼ shillings a bushel.[131] In a speech to the assembly in January, 1731, the governor said:

> . . . . It hath pleased God this last Year to Bless not only these Parts of America with a very plentiful Harvest, but also, as we hear, most of the Countries in Europe, which of Course has put a Stop to their Demand for our Produce; it therefore naturally follows, that our own Provision must be low. We ought however, as Plenty of the Earth has ever been held one of the greatest Blessings of Heaven, not only to acquiesce, but be humbly thankful for our present Affluence; yet as many may by this Means be pinched by a Stagnation of the Currency, which ever ensues in all Countries where their Produce is not in Demand, it may at this Time be incumbent on us to think of all possible Measures to recommend our Manufactures to a greater Degree Abroad, that when at Market they may find a readier Sale.[132]

Samuel Powel had said to a London agent in December, 1730: "Our place is so full of all kinds of goods & people pay so very bad that I cannot Encourage thee to Send any more at present." [133]

Undoubtedly, matters would have been worse in Pennsylvania, with the drop in the world-price of wheat and flour, had the additional £30,000 of currency not been issued in Pennsylvania. The currency issues helped to keep the prices of wheat and flour relatively higher there than abroad. Despite the remarkable rise in Pennsylvania's imports from Britain in 1730, Pennsylvania's imports did not fall off as sharply in 1731 as did New England's or the total imports of the mother-country (see Table 2). In fact, the imports of Pennsylvania held up at a remarkably high level during the period from 1730 to 1733, when the prices of wheat and flour were at such a low level throughout the world.

---

[130] See letter from Powel to Thomas Hyam, October 15, 1730, *ibid.,* p. 165.

[131] Bezanson *et al., op. cit.,* pp. 370-71.

[132] From speech of January 6, 1731 (*Pennsylvania Archives* [8th ser.], III, 2045).

[133] Powel to Thomas Foster, December 28, 1730, *Letter Book,* I, 178; see also Powel to Jacob Wyan, October 15, 1730, *ibid.,* p. 161.

Business conditions in other colonies. — Colonies producing the same products as Pennsylvania seem to have suffered as much as, if not more than, Pennsylvania did during this period. In a speech to the assembly in March, 1733, the governor of Pennsylvania said:

> I shall first observe that while Britain, our Mother country, ... fully enjoys the great Blessings of Peace and Plenty, yet divers of her Colonies find themselves distressed by the Lowness of the Markets for the Staple Commodities wherein their Trade consists; nor are we in this Case happier than the rest.[134]

At the same time (March, 1733), the governor of Maryland reported to the British Board of Trade on the "exceeding Poverty of the People" there, because the "Trade of the Province [had been] of late years greatly decay'd." [135] A year later (April, 1734) the governor of New York reported to the New York assembly that he had been studying the "causes of the decay of trade" there and "the discouragements it labors under," hoping to "find a remedy" that would "give life to the expiring hopes of your ship carpenters and other tradesmen, recall their unwilling resolution to depart the Province, and encourage others to come into it." [136] About the same time he reported to the authorities in London that the people of New Jersey "do labour under great hardships for want of Paper money." [137]

In the spring of 1737 and 1738 the governor of New York again complained about the "declining Trade" and that "with the decay of ship building Navigation and Trade; . . . . many people have left this Province, to go to Carolina Pensilvania and the several Charter Governments in New England; Whereby lands in the Country, and houses in town, are much fallen in their value and in their Rents." [138] A year earlier (February, 1736, and the fall of 1735) some merchants in Pennsylvania had complained that "Times" were "very dull," "Money very scarce and hard to be got in" and sales "very Slow and at a very low price." [139] One of them

---

[134] *Pennsylvania Archives* (8th ser.), III, 2165.

[135] *British Board of Trade Papers, Proprieties,* Vol. XIII, S_{38}. In August, 1731, he had said: ". . . . the Produce of their Tobacco, which for Several Years Past has been really so very low that it would not supply the Inhabitants with One half of the necessaries of Life" (*ibid.,* S^{23}).

[136] *Messages from the Governors, State of New York,* Vol. I: 1683-1776, ed. Charles Z. Lincoln (Albany, 1909), pp. 245-47.

[137] *New Jersey Archives* (1st ser.), V, 365.

[138] *Documents Relative to the Colonial History of the State of New York,* ed. E. B. O'Callaghan (Albany, 1855), VI, 112.

[139] See John Reynell, *Letter Book,* 1734-1737 (MS at Historical Society of Pennsylvania), pp. 11, 12, 14, 19, containing letters to Michael Lee Dicker, May 31, and September 15, 1735, and to Richard Deeble, May 31 and June 28, 1735. See also a letter from Samuel Powel, Jr., to John Bell, March 4, 1735, in Powel's *Letter Book,* I, 319.

claimed in 1735 that he had "Never found it soe Bad to Collect my Debts as this Year" and another said in 1736: "I have been more pinch'd for Money this Winter than ever I was in my Life." [140]

Observations on 1729 issue. — Though some of the Philadelphia merchants complained about the state of Pennsylvania's trade in their letters to London, one looks in vain for any complaints or petitions to the Pennsylvania assembly about the "decay of trade" or the "scarcity of money" during the decade following the currency issue of 1729. Furthermore, there are no complaints about the state of trade in Pennsylvania in the governor's reports to the British Board of Trade during that period as there are in the reports of the governors of other American colonies. Certainly, the figures for imports of British goods indicate that during the eight or ten years after 1728, the imports of Pennsylvania increased more rapidly than did the imports of the other American colonies or the mother-country (see Table 2). Furthermore, there is no statistical or other information indicating that the currency issue of 1729 was a detriment to trade in Pennsylvania. Benjamin Franklin wrote of Pennsylvania in the middle decades of the eighteenth century: "Abundance reigned . . . . and a more happy and prosperous population could not perhaps be found on this globe. In every home there was comfort. The people generally were highly moral." [141]

During the decade after 1729 no additional amounts of paper money were issued in Pennsylvania. In fact, Pennsylvania never had more than £ 85,000 of paper money in circulation at any time during the first half of the eighteenth century. Although there was some inducement to issue more in view of the fact that the interest receipts from the currency issues were so large that no taxes were levied for a number of years prior to 1750,[142] every addition to the currency in Pennsylvania during the first sixteen years of paper money was made solely for the purpose of combating a depression.

The merchants in London trading and exporting to the northern colonies in America, and especially in Pennsylvania, stated in a petition to the House of Commons in March, 1748, that the "moderate Quantity of Paper Bills" issued by Pennsylvania "in an advantageous Manner" had

greatly contributed not only to the Settling of that Colony, and to the Convenience of the People there, as a Medium in Dealings amongst themselves, but have also enabled them to send hither [to England] their Gold and

---

[140] Powel to John Bell, March 4, 1735, *Letter Book,* I, 319.

[141] Quoted from Franklin by Macfarlane, *op. cit.,* p. 70.

[142] W. R. Shepherd, *History of Proprietary Government in Pennsylvania* ("Columbia University Studies in History, Economics and Public Law," Vol. VI ([New York: Columbia University Press, 1896]), p. 427.

Silver, and thereby to enlarge their Trade with this Kingdom, and to take off much greater Quantities of Goods and Manufactures from hence than otherwise they could have done; and that said Paper Bills have not, as the Petitioners conceive, been injurious to any Person whatever.[143]

SUBSEQUENT CURRENCY HISTORY

By issues of paper money Pennsylvania had a more favorable price level during the fifty years following 1723 than the colony would have had without such currency issues. Chart I shows the price level in Philadelphia for each year from 1720 to 1774, along with the exchange rate in Pennsylvania between the Colonial currency and English money in London.[144] The reader will notice that the exchange rate on London had an upward trend from 1723 to 1747, which means that more and more Colonial currency had to be paid to acquire an English pound in London or

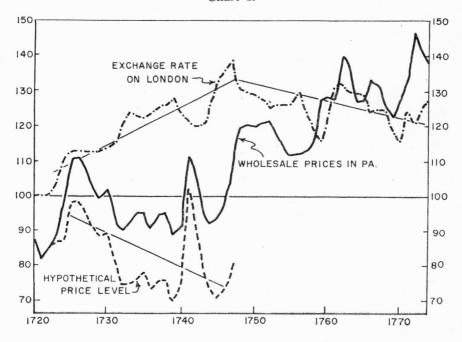

Chart I.

[143] *Journals of the House of Commons, from October 17, 1745, to November 22, 1750,* XXV, 806-7 and *New Jersey Archives* (1st ser.), VIII, 97.

[144] Figures for the price level and London exchange rate taken from Bezanson *et al., op. cit.,* pp. 431 and 433, and Table 3, p. 351.

to buy a bill of exchange payable in English pounds sterling. Despite this rise in the exchange rate on London, the trend of prices in Pennsylvania was practically horizontal.

The price level. — If Pennsylvania had not issued paper currency or the currency had not depreciated in terms of English coin, then the price level in the colony would undoubtedly have had a downward trend during this period, as was the case all over the world in countries on fixed silver and gold standards. If the exchange rate on London had been at par (100 on the chart), the price level in Pennsylvania up to 1747 would presumably have resembled the hypothetical price curve (the lowest curve on the chart) which was derived by dividing the price level by figures for the exchange rate on London. The colony's price level would without doubt have corresponded very closely to this hypothetical price curve, since Pennsylvania played such a small part in world-trade at that time.[145]

When a country's price level has a downward trend, business depressions are likely to be prolonged and periods of prosperity tend to be relatively short. That was the case, for example, in this country from 1865 to 1896 — from the end of the Civil War to Bryan's campaign for "free silver." By paper-money issues it would seem that Pennsylvania probably avoided the evil effects of prolonged depressions during the period from 1723 to 1746. After 1746, prices all over the world began to rise appreciably. The exchange rate on London from then on had a downward trend, which meant that Pennsylvania's currency was gradually appreciating in terms of English money. From this downward trend in the exchange on London one can conclude that the price level in Pennsylvania did not rise so rapidly after 1746 as it would have done had Pennsylvania never issued paper money but had continued to use only Spanish, Portuguese, and English coins at the same official rating. Therefore, a metallic monetary standard would have meant a more inflationary rise of prices in Pennsylvania after 1746 than actually did occur there on a paper money standard.

Perhaps if the French and Indian War had not intervened, the price level in Pennsylvania would have continued on a horizontal plane. Until 1746 the Quakers in Pennsylvania had prevented contributions to military

---

[145] The sharp rise in the exchange value of Pennsylvania currency late in 1740 and in 1741 (from $170 to $130 Pennsylvania currency for $100 sterling, with the prices of gold and silver falling in proportion) was explained by Governor George Thomas in March, 1741, as "Occasioned by the number of Governments Bills negotiated here for Paying, Victualling & Transporting the Troops, and by the Orders sent by the British Merchants for purchasing great Quantitys of Wheat to supply the want of it in Europe," and he thought that "so soon as these Demands shall cease, Exchange will probably rise again to 70 per Cent," or $170 Pennsylvania currency to $100 British sterling (*British Board of Trade Papers, Proprieties*, Vol. XV, T47).

campaigns against the French in Canada; [146] but in that year Pennsylvania, for the first time, issued paper money to help defray the expenses of an expedition against Canada. Until 1746 all paper money in Pennsylvania had been issued by loans and not by payments for Colonial expenditures. Even after this start with paper-money issues for war purposes, George Washington met defeat at Fort Necessity in 1754, and General Braddock suffered his severe defeat in 1755, without any financial aid from Pennsylvania. After Braddock's defeat, however, the Indians invaded frontier settlements in Pennsylvania and terrorized the inhabitants, so that the Colonial legislature soon approved a paper-money issue of £60,000 "for the king's use."

Between 1755 and 1760 a total sum of £485,000 in paper money was issued to aid in fighting the French and Indians, and all of it was to be redeemed from the proceeds of special taxes imposed at the time the currency was issued. Even with such provisions for redemption, there was as much as £485,782 of paper money in circulation in Pennsylvania by the middle of 1760. [147] This represented an increase of almost 500 per cent in the paper money of the colony within six years, but no objection was made by the Board of Trade in London as all the issues were "for the king's use." Prices in Pennsylvania did not rise in proportion to the increase in the supply of paper money because the demand or use for the paper money increased in several ways: some of the additional currency took the place of staple commodities which were still being used to some extent as money in Pennsylvania,[148] some of it was absorbed by other colonies where Pennsylvania's paper money was "eagerly sought for" either to hoard or as a medium of payments,[149] and some of it was absorbed by the increase of trade within the boundaries of Pennsylvania.

When the French and Indian War was over, Pennsylvania began to reduce the amount of paper money in circulation. A net sum of £25,000 was retired from 1760 to 1769,[150] which helped to bring about a 13 per cent decline in the price level from 1762 to 1769. This indicates that the colonists in Pennsylvania used restraint in issuing paper money and that, even in those days, a rise in prices caused by currency issues could be controlled. In fact, the price level in Pennsylvania was more stable during the fifty years following the first Colonial currency issue in 1723 than the American price level has been during any succeeding fifty-year period.

---

[146] In 1772 it was estimated that four-fifths of the people in Pennsylvania were Quakers (see *ibid.*, Vol. XI, R 7).

[147] See Table 4, p. 140.

[148] Macfarlane, *op. cit.*, p. 75.

[149] Phillips, *op. cit.*, p. 23.

[150] *Ibid.*, p. 25.

Opinions of Pennsylvania currency issues. — In August, 1752, a committee reporting to the Pennsylvania assembly on the "State of our Paper Currency" declared that, after "the first Experiment of Paper Money" in 1723, "experience demonstrate[d] more and more the Benefit arising from this Currency to the Province by the Encrease of Trade and People, and Improvement of Lands." The committee went on to explain:

> That in 1723, and for some Years before, the Trade of this Province languished for Want of a Medium; Building and Planting were discouraged, and the Inhabitants in City and Country rather diminished than encreased. This is not only consistent with the Knowledge of some of your Committee, who well remember the distressed Circumstances of the People at that Time, that many Tradesmen and others left the Country, and that a great Number of Houses were vacant and untenanted in the City: But the swift Declension of our Trade appears from the Customhouse Entries, ...
>
> From that Period [1721-23] the City and County have flourished and encreased in a most surprizing Manner. The Encrease of the City appears even to the Eye of every common Observer, the Number of new Buildings much exceeding the Old.[151]

Foreign-trade statistics indicate that between the two periods 1729-31 and 1749-51 there was a 428 per cent increase in British imports into Pennsylvania, a 118 per cent increase in Pennsylvania's exports to Great Britain, and a 169 per cent increase in the currency value of Pennsylvania's total exports of wheat, flour, bread, and flaxseed.[152] The increase in British imports into Pennsylvania from 1720-22 to 1749-51 was no less than 793 per cent.

After enjoying such a degree of success and prosperity on a paper-money standard, it is no wonder that the colonists in Pennsylvania complained loudly when the English parliament, after a report by the British Board of Trade, passed an act in September, 1764, prohibiting any American colony from issuing bills of credit (paper money) as legal tender for the payment of debts. Many years before the Board of Trade had taken the position that "tho' a Paper Currency may be advantageous to a Trading Colony," such a currency should not be permitted to exist in any colony unless it could be circulated without making it legal tender.[153] In its 1764 report, resulting from complaints by British merchants trading with Virginia and North Carolina, the board condemned all legal-tender currency issues as "absurd, unjust and impolitic." With mercantilistic bias

---

[151] *Pennsylvania Archives* (8th ser.), IV, 3515-16.

[152] Charles Whitworth, *State of the Trade of Great Britain in Its Imports and Exports Progressively from the Year 1627* (London, 1776), and *Pennsylvania Archives* (8th ser.), V, 3628-29. As has already been explained, the British foreign-trade statistics really represents a physical index of trade because the prices used then were official prices not affected by price changes.

[153] *New Jersey Archives*, IX, 36-37.

the board argued that paper money, "perhaps as unfit as anything can possibly be," tended to drive out gold and silver, "the materials fittest for" a medium of exchange. Statements were made to the board that "in the middle Colonies the publick faith has been preserved, and no inconvenience has been found to attend this practice; but on the contrary, that it has produced very beneficial Consequences."[154] The board, however, doubted the validity of such statements because the currency of the middle colonies had depreciated to some degree in terms of British pounds sterling. Even if the statements were true, they would, in the board's opinion, "be no argument in favour of a practice in its nature founded in fraud and injustice, which are stamped upon the Bills themselves, by compelling all persons to receive that as lawfull money which has no real intrinsic value in itself."[155]

In reply to the Board of Trade's report on Colonial currency, Benjamin Franklin wrote in 1764:

> On the whole, no method has hitherto been formed to establish a medium of trade, in lieu of money, equal, in all its advantages, to bills of credit, funded on sufficient taxes for discharging it, or on land security of double the value for repaying it at the end of the term, and in the mean time made a GENERAL LEGAL TENDER. The experience of now near half a century in the middle colonies, has convinced them of it among themselves, by the great increase of their settlements, numbers, buildings, improvements, agriculture, shipping, and commerce. And the same experience has satisfied the British merchants, who trade thither, that it has been greatly useful to them, and not in a single instance prejudicial.[156]

In the same year even stronger praise of Pennsylvania's experiment with paper money was expressed by Thomas Pownall, who before becoming a member of parliament, spent about a decade in the colonies as lieutenant-governor of New Jersey, governor of Massachusetts Bay, and governor of South Carolina. In his famous book on *Administration of the Colonies,* he wrote:

> I will recommend to the consideration of those who take a lead in business, a measure devised and administered by an American assembly — And I will venture to say that there never was a wiser or better measure; never one better calculated to serve the uses of our encreasing country; that there never was a measure more steadily pursued, or more faithfully executed, for forty years together; than the loan-office in Pennsylvania, formed and administered by the assembly of that province.[157]

---

[154] *Ibid.,* pp. 410-13.
[155] *Ibid.*
[156] Jared Sparks (ed.), *The Works of Benjamin Franklin* (Boston, 1840), II, 354.
[157] I (London, 1764), 188.

Of Pennsylvania's Colonial currency issues George Chalmers, who spent ten years in Maryland prior to the Revolutionary War, wrote in 1782 in his *Introduction to the History of the Revolt of the American Colonies*:

> The singular prosperity of the province [of Pennsylvania] may be attributed chiefly to the economical habits of the people and to the genius of their jurisprudence, partly to the prudent policy of promoting enterprise by feeding circulation with loans of paper money, gradual yet moderate.[158]

There seems to have been general agreement among contemporary writers that currency issues and the paper standard were managed very successfully in colonial Pennsylvania for over half a century after 1723.

---

[158] (Boston, 1845; suppressed in 1782), 158.

PART THREE
Pre-Civil War Economic Development

Contents

I.

EDITOR'S INTRODUCTION

Two of the seven pieces in this section deal with the issue of the economic welfare of the Young Republic during the difficult years of settlement and expansion in both the first quarter of the new century and on the eve of its presumed entrance into the modern age of western industrialism. The other five papers deal with traditional interpretations of the pattern of American economic development and the dynamic forces that affected its pace. In point of time, all the papers are most relevant for pre-Civil War interpretations of national development; but in point of fact, the implications are fundamental to issues of economic growth and development in the abstract and for the long-run. The articles are self-contained and require little introductory comment here. It should be pointed out that selections 6 and 7 were written especially for this volume.

Both Fogel and Fishlow are challenging long held generalizations about American economic development, and their work has stirred much controversy and criticism. The article by Fogel on the social savings of railroads is but a part of a much larger study. When this article was written the estimates were still in the provisional state, but they have since been revised downward, indicating that the social savings, though positive, were marginally small.[1] Fishlow's article and postscript is a direct challenge to a long held view of the direction of ante-bellum commodity trade movements that was first presented by Guy Callender, developed by Louis Schmidt, and then expounded by Douglas North. Fogel's initial discussion of the Fishlow paper was included in a longer paper by him giving an informed estimate of the condition of the field of economic history. It is reprinted here not only because it raises interesting substantive questions but also because it implies some insightful criteria for appraising the validity of work done in the New Economic History. Fogel's paper on 19th Century Interregional Trade extends the discussion of the issues raised by Fishlow's paper and Postscript. It also contains for the first time estimates of freight movements from New York to southern ports.

The paper by Gallman is one where the painstaking questioning and

---

[1] R. W. Fogel; *Railroads and American Economic Growth;* Johns Hopkins Press; Baltimore, Maryland, 1964.

reconstruction of original data of economic history is shown at its very best. Of more interest, however, is Gallman's scrutiny of the estimates of the 19th Century observers concerning by implication the relative income and wealth position achieved by the United States in the period preceding its modern industrialization. The point is worth noting, especially when one sees comparisons made at present with early American economic development and contemporary underdeveloped countries; compared to all other countries, possibly excepting England, America started its drive to industrialization from an income and product base far greater than any of today's countries can possibly hope to claim.

In order to provide partial continuity with the mainstream of American economic development and to create background material for these papers, the remaining sections of the introduction will deal with both the economic impact of the Revolutionary War and general explanations of pre-Civil War economic Development.

II.

The final words are yet to be written, if they ever can be, concerning the exceedingly interrelated causes of the American Revolutionary War. Certainly the influence of economic conditions was of great importance though far from determinative. The change in British Imperial policy emphasizing greater enforcement of economic controls over provincial economic life, and the severe economic contraction in the decade preceding the outbreak of the war were important and contributing factors to its cause. Historians will continue to debate the importance of these matters as against the social and political ideas that underlay most of our colonial history as primary causes of the conflict.

Similarly, the relative resources (both economic and otherwise) possessed by the colonies which affected their ability to wage war against an international military power are yet to be properly assessed by scholars. The internal readjustments that the war necessitated in the colonial economy were probably of far longer term importance than conventional historical scholarship now admits.

Although the Revolutionary War was not in any modern sense "total war," the total direct costs as a fraction of probable national output was great. It has been estimated that in specie value the direct costs incurred by the colonies of waging the military actions of the war totalled between $100 and $140 million. France was alleged to have spent $60 million in the United States, and possibly $250 million in all as a direct result of the Anglo-American conflict. The public debt of Great Britain increased about

$500 million during the course of the war. In all, then the direct financial cost incurred by the major participants was probably close to $1 billion.[2] Though losses due to physical destruction were small, these as well as the monetized value of human losses would properly be included in a total estimate of financial costs. And it is of equal, if not greater importance, to note that the loss of consumption goods necessitated by switching plant, equipment, and especially agricultural resources into wartime goods production constituted an indirect cost of the war which would be most difficult to measure.

Three questions of a long-term nature must be asked concerning the impact of the war on the course of American economic development. Did the war fundamentally alter the structure of the economy? Did the war create new blocs of resources that proved of critical value in our national development? Did the war facilitate the development of new economic institutions that were of determinative value to our long term economic development?

There is much evidence to suggest that the postwar national economy was but an extension of the colonial and wartime one. Indeed, the postwar depression was partially a cause of this since the colonies continued to accumulate a heavy import balance on current account with Great Britain but without the most favored nation treatment it enjoyed in the mercantilist framework, thus producing an inability to export goods and services in sufficient amounts to pay for imports. On the other hand, there is some merit to the view that the war accelerated the production of certain agricultural products and accentuated the pre-war slack in demand for others. Tobacco, rice and indigo exports fell appreciably during and after the war and wheat and flour exports, though not declining, did not grow at pre-war trend rates. Yet domestic output of grain products and domestic consumption did increase during and after the war. Moreover, the demand slack in southern staples may well have been an underlying dynamic element in the substitution of cotton for the prior staples of tobacco and rice as major earners of foreign exchange and domestic employment. One should also treat the massive income redistribution caused by the method of financing war spending (by issues of fiat money) as a structural shift caused by the war. (The wartime and postwar movement of prices shown in Chart III-I, suggest the scale on which such a redistribution might have occurred.) For in the postwar years, as Nettels has shown, incredibly sharp entrepreneurs in commercial centers in the east were left with substantial amounts of

[2] Wright, *Economic History of United States,* McGraw-Hill Book Co., New York 1949, page 189; Curtis Nettels, *Emergence of a National Economy,* Holt, Rinehart. and Winston, New York 1962, p. 20.

investible funds which they were quick to commit to other growth producing ventures.[3]

The distinguished historian of colonial America, Clarence Ver Steeg, has catalogued a number of items that suggest that the war created new blocs of resources of lasting significance to American national development.[4] He discusses these in some detail, and it is only in the interest of space that his contributions are condensed below. The following list of items were considered by Ver Steeg to be critical results of the impact of the war.

1. A shift of control of natural resources, most specifically mineral rights, from the sovereign to private entrepreneurs.

2. The release of land resources, *vide* the Land Ordinance of 1785, allowing the "institutionalizing" of American agricultural production.

Chart III-1

MEDIAN OF MONTHLY WHOLESALE PRICES OF 15
COMMODITIES IN PHILADELPHIA, 1770-1790
(1771-73 Monthly Average = 100)

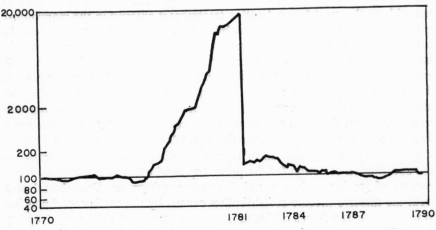

Source: Ann Bezanson, *Prices and Inflation in Penna.*

3. Opening of the China trade, a direct result of the loss of mercantilist protection. "What is significant is that the Asiatic trade introduced new

---

[3] Nettels, *Emergence of a National Economy*, p. 21-22. Confiscation of Loyalists' estates should also be considered in this same way.

[4] "The American Revolution Considered as an Economic Movement," in *The Huntington Library Quarterly*, XX; August 1957; pp. 361-372.

products, created new demands, and, in some respects, educated this country's merchants in new trading techniques." (p. 366)

4. The unification of the domestic market by reducing internal trade barriers.

5. The distasteful colonial experience with money and monetary institutions (lack of) exaggerated by the war made the population receptive to new financial institutions in the post war period.

6. An expansion of foreign capital inflows into America as a result of the war.

7. The economic, as distinguished from the social, implications of the abandonment of primogeniture and entail. ("To encourage a flexible land system. . . .")

One can only agree with Ver Steeg's comment that "Historians talk about American society with confidence, but they have never asked whether it contained within itself certain special characteristics that would decisively determine the course of economic life in the New Nation." (p. 372).

In any case, by 1790 what appeared as effects of the war were now being smothered by the pressing experience of the 1780's, culminating in the Constitution, important economic legislation of the Congress patterned after Federalist economic ideas, and the revival of domestic commerce. But the long-term prospects facing the Young Republic in the last decade of the century were very good, despite what some scholars (notably Douglas North) have concluded.[5] It is true that in 1790, American trade with Great Britain was less than it was before the war; it is true that our population of approximately four million (including 700,000 slaves) presented a domestic market of relatively small magnitude; and it is true that the probable prospects for our foreign trade in goods and services had been materially upset by the loss of mercantilist privileges. But it is equally true that our population of four million was sparse relative to our known resources, that the internal mechanisms of commerce, trade and agricultural settlement were drastically mollified by the Constitution and subsequent legislation, and that capital accumulation (domestic and net foreign inflows) was on the rise. Finally, the provincials had demonstrated that with limited resources they were capable of producing a society and an economy which had yielded a level of living surpassed only by England and France.

What is being suggested, therefore, is that far from looking bleak, the American economist of 1790 could well have found signs of significant encouragement. The basis for gloom in the outlook of certain scholars is

---

[5] See his *Economic Growth of the United States,* esp. pp. 18-20.

that some fundamentals of the colonial economy — international trade — extended beyond the decade following the war. This is, of course, true; but what is suggested here is that the ingredients for development were present in the America of 1790 and that if external events had not materialized to stimulate them, the dynamic internal forces would have done this. We no doubt would have followed an alternative development path, but we would not have remained a static or stagnant economy for long.

III.

Two interrelated events made the uncertainty of 1790 concerning the future growth of the American economy meaningless: the Napoleonic wars, and the development of high increases in productivity in agriculture and manufacturing stimulated by the new machine technology. These facts are well known by scholars. Callendar has documented the growth in American international trade in goods and services, the interrelated expansion of domestic farm production (especially in grains) and the resurgence of a lively re-export and shipping trade.[6] Douglas North has taken these elements of recovery and growth and fitted them to an interpretation of the dynamic ingredients of pre-Civil War economic development.[7] It is North's argument that the growth of the American economy was the result of market forces — prices, demand, technology, productive services — responding to new conditions of aggregate demand under competitive market conditions. The prime movers of the market mechanism in the years 1790 to 1860 were to be found in the income and employment generated by the export sector of the economy. The feedback from earnings in the carrying trade, i.e., exports of major raw materials such as cotton and grains, was felt in every sector of the country and produced structural changes in the allocation of productive investment and the distribution of income and employment.

There seems little doubt that North is correct in at least the main details of his argument. One can criticize his neglect of social and political institutions, since they may have conditioned the pace of our national development, but it is nevertheless true that the internal development of our industries and resources was solidly premised on the income and employment generated by the export sector of the economy. The statistical evidence of growth in output and international trade is amply presented in North's book as well as in certain tables in the *Historical Statistics* vol-

---

[6] See Callendar, *Economic History of United States,* p. 239.

[7] Douglas C. North, *Economic Growth of the United States, 1790-1860;* New York 1961. See also the excellent critique by S. Bruchey, and reply by North in *Explorations in Entrepreneurial History,* Second Series, I; Winter, 1964; pp. 145-163.

ume. Data alone, however, do not either support or refute; they must be put to a test in an analytical framework, and this is what North has done.

Chart III-II

CONSUMER PRICE INDEX, 1820-1860

(1851-59 = 100)

INDEX

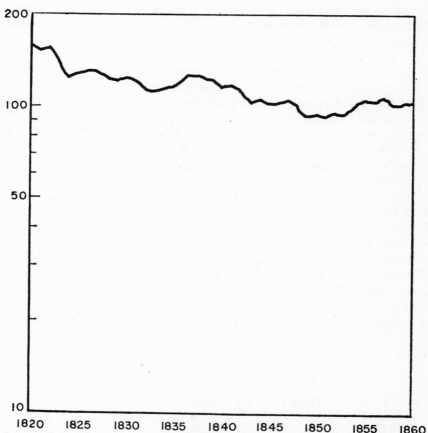

Source: Joint Economic Committee, *Historical and Comparative Rules of Production, Productivity and Prices*, Part II (1959), p. 39, Testimony of Ethel B. Hoover.

In retrospect one should not be startled by the nature of North's theoretical superstructure. For decades politicians have been exclaiming that America's economic growth is a tribute to the effectiveness and efficiency of a free market where entrepreneurs are free to make their own investment decisions with directions received from the impersonality of prices, profits, factor supplies and the like. Alfred Marshall, in *Industry and Trade* argued in much the same fashion when attempting to explain the long term economic development of England and the United States. Douglas North's argument is essentially a neoclassical one, and in viewing the facts of the American case one digs fruitlessly to find contrary explanations. The American economy, especially in the pre-Civil War decades, was a model of neoclassical economic growth where markets were freely competitive and the price system was truly responsive to changes in demand and factor supplies. Indeed, one is much impressed with the stability of domestic prices in the pre-1860 years as well as with their downward trend (Chart III-II). This is a statistic which lends considerable support to the notion that the transmission of the economic growth that was stimulated by the export sector and related satellite industries was being passed through to the consumer, a visible and outward evidence that the market system did function with considerable long-run effectiveness.

As may be gathered from the following article by Andreano, and from the sources cited there, no statistically acceptable series on national income and product exist for the years prior to 1839. One needs to have such a series to document the total growth of national product as well as to indicate the broad structural changes that took place in the origin and flow of income and product. Yet despite the nature of the controversy noted in the next Chapter, there are outward evidences of impressive vertical and horizontal extensions of the American economy in the decades before 1840: population and immigration figures, the growth of physical output of raw and semi-finished commodities, the buildup of certain forms of social overhead capital — canals, roads, ships, trains and the like — and the output of the export sector and related industries all show a marked

Table III-I

Commodity Output, 1839-1859

Year or End of Decade	Output (millions)	Population (thous.)	Output per capita	Output per worker
1839	$1,094	17,120	$64	$244
1844	1,374	20,182	68	—
1849	1,657	23,261	71	268
1854	2,317	27,386	85	—
1859	2,686	31,513	85	330

SOURCE: Robert Gallman, "Commodity Output, 1838-1899," in *Trends in the American Economy During the 19th Century* (Princeton, 1960), p. 16. NOTE: Commodity output is the sum of value added by agriculture, mining, manufacturing, and construction.

upward movement. After 1840, figures by Robert Gallman (represented here in an article related to his pioneering work on national income) can be used to indicate the overall drift of the entire economy. These are shown above.

Reduced to real per capita terms at average annual rates, the Gallman data show a growth rate in commodity output of just under 2% in the pre-1860 decades. These data, and the drift of argument in the Gallman paper printed here and in later papers by Goldsmith and Lebergott, are all related to one of the most intriguing issues now current in the discussions over how economic growth is started. More particularly, the issues raised by Rostow's book, *The Stages of Economic Growth,* a book which particularly concerned the American economy, need to be appraised in the light of Gallman's figures and others noted by the authors of papers printed in this section.

Rostow's argument is by now familiar to all, especially his statement of the so-called "take-off." Briefly stated, Rostow postulated three basic conditions (which implied many more, of course) by which a country passes through take-off.[8]

1. a doubling of the rate of productive investment as a fraction of national income or net national product. Rostow suggests a rate of movement from 5% or less to over 10%.
2. the development of one or more substantial manufacturing sectors with a high growth rate.
3. "The existence or quick emergence of a political, social and institutional framework which exploits the impulses to expansion in the modern sector and the potential external economy effects of the take-off and gives to growth an on-going character."[9]

The concept of take-off, as well as all of Rostow's work, has generated much criticism, and has been rather substantially challenged by the great authority of Simon Kuznets.[10] It is not necessary to discuss this here. Rather, Rostow's dating of the American take-off at 1843-1860 and the indications given by him as evidence for this change are the matters worthy of our attention. Rostow describes the American take-off as having occurred in a twofold manner: first, by the manufacturing and railroad development

---

[8] The literature bearing on Rostow's statements concerning the take-off in the American economy is large and only two of the most important contributions relative to American development need be noted here: Robert Fogel, *Railroads and American Economic Growth,* Chapter IV; and Douglas North's paper in W. W. Rostow ed., *The Economics of Take-off into Self-Sustained Growth;* New York 1963; pp. 44-62.

[9] W. W. Rostow, *The Stages of Economic Growth,* Cambridge University Press, 1960, pp. 39–40.

[10] See his essay in Rostow ed., *Economics of Take-Off,* pp. 22-43.

in the 1840's in the East, and second, by the great railway construction push in the Middle West during the 1850's. Rostow excludes the South as having participated in the take-off during this period, and limits the dating to only the North and West.

An entire chapter in Professor Fogel's book is devoted to an examination of the role played by railroad construction during the period singled out by Rostow as the American take-off. Fogel concludes that both the primary and secondary demands for inputs generated by railway construction were statistically very small, which casts considerable doubt on their ability to have led the alleged advance in capital investment and national output implied by Rostow's basic conditions. Fogel has also effectively questioned other possible positive evidence for Rostow's notion of a take-off, especially in the matter of structural change in the origin of output and in the variability of growth rates of manufacturing industries before and after 1840.[11] There is apparently little evidence to support Rostow's condition that the rate of productive investment doubled in less than two decades in the United States.

Nonetheless, despite the valid and empirically sound judgments about Rostow made by Fogel and Kuznets, it still seems probable that the secular rate of growth of the national product of the American economy made a significant upward break somewhere around the end of the third and the beginning of the fourth decade of the Century. Data presented by Gallman, Andreano, and elsewhere in this volume by Goldsmith and Lebergott, suggest that this was so; North also argues much the same thing in his book and the article cited earlier. What is the explanation? The answer seems to lie in causes of our national growth which are much more flexible in time and concept that can be admitted in the Rostovian framework. Economic change in America was a slowly cumulative thing and continued to gain momentum by the middle decade of the century. But its cause was deeper than a simple relationship between capital and output implied by the Rostow suggestions of take-off. In the American case, Rostow may be right but for the wrong reasons.

---

[11] See Fogel's *Railroads and American Economic Growth*, Chapter IV.

TRENDS AND VARIATIONS IN ECONOMIC WELFARE
IN THE UNITED STATES BEFORE THE CIVIL WAR

Ralph L. Andreano

I.

Much of the numerical data in this paper has been drawn from the studies conducted at the National Bureau of Economic Research and the published works of scholars associated with quantitative measurement in economic history. Historians not trained in the various intricacies of "Cliometrics" may find it difficult to challenge these findings and to incorporate them into the stream of more traditional institutional history. Real progress in the understanding of American economic history, however, depends as already noted, on a meshing of the work of the Cliometricians and that of the institutional historians. It is hoped that the interpretations of the data offered in the present paper will highlight both the shortcomings and advantages of quantitative and non-quantitative contributions to an understanding of 19th Century American economic history. The more immediate purpose of the paper is to examine trends in levels of living between 1800 and 1840, and between 1840 and 1860.

II.

Measuring and explaining living standards in any country both for sectors of the population and for regional areas is a subject pregnant with guesswork, and is likely to provoke vigorous disagreement. Quite properly, one may ask what is to be measured, explained and included in a "standard of living?" Even if agreement is possible, is it permissible to make interpersonal, interregional, or international comparisons of "standards of living" and still arrive at meaningful (and possibly policy-making) conclusions? Moreover, is it possible to equate "standard of living" with economic welfare? Specific answers to these questions are likely to satisfy few, and the best which can be hoped for is an understanding and reasonable appraisal of the shortcomings and advantages that undermine the alternative explanations. S. H. Frankel has argued persuasively that it is impossible to equate income with a given level of welfare in one country, based on its own set of social and cultural values, and with the level of welfare prevailing in another country having different sets of value structures. "It is a logical fallacy," he writes, "to regard the satisfaction or utility which (it is alleged) is 'yielded' by, or derived from, goods and services as 'income' in any meaningful sense, because the term 'income' is an accounting term and can only meaningfully express an accounting relation." [1]

There is merit in the point of view expressed by Frankel, but if one denies the possibility of making welfare comparisons of income and levels of living, then, in Colin Clark's words the door to "intellectual anarchy" is opened, and the result is description without analysis. [2] As illustrated in the passage quoted below, I. M. D. Little has argued that the danger of value judgments creeping into welfare comparisons is indeed great. But it is possible to isolate the area of comparisons that can clearly be accepted.

". . . if economists wait for someone to come along and give them a consistent set of value premises they would wait for ever. If we are to be able to make intelligent guesses about the kind of value premises that people might think reasonable, it is certain that we must study what kinds of things are relevant to people's happiness. . . . It is, however, important to remember that we can never conclude that something ought to be done, from the proposition that economic welfare has increased. The means of increasing economic welfare may decrease welfare in general." [3]

We are thus left with little choice. One must make welfare comparisons, yet always keep in mind that the reference point of such comparisons (whether it be "income" or a more general "standard of living" concept) must have some approximation to social and cultural values involved in the comparison. Otherwise, economic history becomes a penumbra of institutional description without evaluation.

In looking at changes in the level of living in the Pre-Civil War American economy, one therefore should not have inhibitions concerning welfare comparisons inside and outside the country. Certainly the Americans of that time had none; they were quick to make welfare judgments concerning their own progress as compared with that of the rest of civilized society. Adam Seybert, in his valuable statistical collection published in 1818, stated these feelings quite succinctly: "Where agriculture, the arts and manufacturing flourish; where domestic improvements have been en-

---

[1] S. H. Frankel, THE ECONOMIC IMPACT ON UNDER-DEVELOPED SOCIETIES. (Cambridge: HUP, 1953), 37.

[2] Clark, of course, makes welfare comparisons on a grand scale. See his THE CONDITIONS OF ECONOMIC PROGRESS. Third Edition (London: MacMillan and Company, 1957), esp. 16-17.

[3] I. M. D. Little, A CRITIQUE OF WELFARE ECONOMICS (London: Oxford University Paperback, 1961), 81-82.

couraged; where the more useful branches of education have been extensively cultivated; . . . there it is, that we can find the demonstrations of the prosperity and happiness of a people." [4]

III.

Granted the propriety of making welfare comparisons one is next faced with the need to choose the appropriate index and to decide whether or not the index is to be quantitative or qualitative. Terms such as "Standard of Living," "Level of Living," measurements of real per capita income, and other possible indexes are fraught with ambiguity. It may therefore be advisable to attach specific meaning to the respective terms, and briefly to assess their usefulness as indexes of welfare. The term *plane of living* is used to describe the list of all goods, services, and conditions *actually* consumed. *Level of living* is a term which describes the composite or aggregate of all items that constitute the *plane of living*. The *standard of living* is the list of goods, services, and conditions that one strives to attain. It is a concept of how one "ought" to be living.[5] The best of definitions are, of course, still imperfect. If one accepts the definition noted above, the issue of value and welfare judgments is still not solved. For example, if actual "levels of living" differ significantly among individuals, regions, or countries, is one with a lower "level" worse-off in terms of welfare? In a sense, any such comparison would place one "level" of living above another and establish it as a standard of measurement, and as an index of welfare. Perhaps this is unavoidable.

An index of welfare described by the concept "real per capita income" is perhaps the measure most widely used today. It is used interchangeably to denote both actual levels of living, and accepted and desirable standards of living. The measure is supposed to have virtues for such uses because it generally includes the income stream (incomes earned, subsidy and supplements, *ex* tax payments) deflated by changes in the purchasing power of money and by population growth.[6] Whether or not one can equate changes

---

[4] Adam Seybert, STATISTICAL ANNALS. (Philadelphia: Thomas Dobson and Sons, 1818), 1.

[5] See Willard Cochrane and Carolyn Shaw Bell, THE ECONOMICS OF CONSUMPTION (New York, McGraw-Hill, 1956), 17. The above definitions were implied in a United Nations report issued in 1954: "[The Committee] sought to clarify the terms 'standard of living,' 'level of living,' and related concepts, and recommended that in future discussions the expression 'level of living' be employed when reference is made to actual conditions of life, as contrasted with aspirations or ideas of what ought to be." U. N., *Report on International Definitions and Measurement of Standards and Levels of Living.* (New York, 1954), v.

[6] Use of the term in contemporary discussions of economic development of less developed areas is generally as a "Standard of living" in our terminology. See, Gerald M. Meier and Robert Baldwin, ECONOMIC DEVELOPMENT: THEORY, HISTORY AND POLICY. (New York: John Wiley and Sons, 1957), 4.

in real per capita income with changes in the "level of living," of course, depends on the completeness and content of the national income accounting upon which such estimates are based. If the original compilation of national income includes not only market transactions but non-market transactions and adjustments for payments in kind when deflating for purchasing power, average real per capita income will not exceed by far an index of the level of living. Yet for the presently underdeveloped countries or for the time period in American history considered here, national income estimates are little removed from guesswork, however ingenious such data may be.

To put substantive content into the term "level of living" and to appraise whether or not real per capita income is contained within the content of this welfare concept, three components must be considered and appraised. Let us call these components (1) social asset formation, (2) consumer asset formation, and (3) personal consumption of perishable goods and services.[7] Social asset formation would include those items which are supplements to personal income but are not always negotiable in market transactions: churches, health conditions, medical care, education, transportation facilities, etc. Consumer asset formation refers to those goods and services acquired with money income or non-marketable personal effort: insurance and savings, housing, and durable household and personal goods.[8] Perishable goods and services would include food, clothing, fuel, power, newspapers, etc.

IV.

The oldest approach to an index of either the level or standard of living was through family budget studies.[9] The studies of Ernst Engel and Le Play

---

[7] Arthur H. Cole, in a most suggestive article, has implied such a composite measure of national economic development. See his, "Durable Consumer Goods and American Economic Growth," QUARTERLY JOURNAL OF ECONOMICS, LXXVI, (August, 1962), 415-423.

[8] "The historian finds perfectly sound sense in the statisticians' designation of vacuum cleaners and automobiles, electric refrigerators, oil burners, outdoor grills, and a score of similar objects as appropriate specimens (of durable consumer goods), . . . but his mind is nearly overwhelmed when he thinks of the myriad of items which, in the evolution of our economy alone, have been logical antecedents of these household or at least family appurtenances. The citizen of our colonial era had his furniture and his rifle, his Bible and his chaise, while his wife was fortunate if she possessed iron pots in her kitchen, real "bed linen in her chest of drawers, and pewter utensils for her table. In fact, the heavy wool clothings of those decades were passed from father to son; it was surely quite 'durable.'" A. H. Cole, in *QJE*, LXXVI (August, 1962), 415-416.

[9] An excellent summary of the earliest budget studies in Europe and the U.S. after 1860 may be found in George Stigler, "The Early History of Empirical Studies of Consumer Behavior," JOURNAL OF POLITICAL ECONOMY, LXII (April, 1954),

in the middle of the 19th Century are well known. In Pre-Civil War America, however, the availability of budget studies is practically nil. Contemporary economists such as John Rae and Henry Carey discussed the role of consumption in determining a level of living, but few writers drew any welfare conclusions based on actual budgetary data. Edgar Martin's study of the STANDARD OF LIVING IN 1860 utilized family budgets published in contemporary newspapers and journals, and most of these (there were only a few in any case) fell in the period of the 1850's.[10] There are only two budgets for families living earlier than 1851 and only one of these is detailed enough to be used. Of course, none have sufficient information on consumer asset formation or allocable social assets for families. Indeed, there is little else in these budgets other than food, clothing, rent and fuel expenditures. Moreover, one can only guess as to their typicality for the entire population.

I have nevertheless, despite misgivings, given four of these budgets and a composite budget for over 300 families in 1875.

TABLE A

Comparison of Family Budgets in the United States, 1816-1875
[Percent of Total Budget Expenditures]

Category	1816-17 (1)	1851 (2)	1857 (3)	1875 (4)
Food	46.1%	41.2%	31.0% (a)	57.4%
Rent	28.1	29.0	41.5	16.7
Clothing	5.3	23.5	—	14.3
Fuel and Light	8.2(b)	5.3	16.9	6.7
Health and Education	0.8	—		1.0
Asset Formation	10.1(c)	—		—
Other	1.4(d)	—	10.6(e)	3.9
Totals	100.0%	100.0%	100.0%	100.0%

(a) includes liquor
(b) includes ice, household supplies, carfare, stationary and postage
(c) household furnishings and equipment, savings.
(d) church, charity, entertainment and recreation
(e) servants and pew rent

(1) Family of four said to be "professional" class. Chase G. Woodhouse, "The Standard of Living at a Professional Level, 1816-1817 and 1926-27," JOURNAL OF POLITICAL ECONOMY, XXXVII (October 1929), 556-557.

95-113. For an analysis of the work of Le Play, Carrol Wright, Ernst Engel and others also, see, Carle C. Zimmerman, CONSUMPTION AND STANDARDS OF LIVING. (New York: D. Van Nostrand, 1936), 354-376, 418-459.

[10] Edgar Martin, THE STANDARD OF LIVING IN 1860 (Chicago: University of Chicago Press, 1942), 294-5.

(2) Simple average of two budgets: one for a family of five, the other not specified. Both are said to be for "workingman's family." One is a weekly and the other is an annual budget. Martin, THE STANDARD OF LIVING IN 1860, 294; William Panschar, BAKING IN AMERICA, Vol. II, ECONOMIC DEVELOPMENT (Evanston: Northwestern University Press, 1956), 51.

(3) Family of four, "Typical Businessman" of New York with annual money income of $1500. Martin, THE STANDARD OF LIVING IN 1860, 395.

(4) Ethel Hoover's weights based on family budgets for 397 families in Massachusetts in 1875. See, her "Retail Prices After 1850," in TRENDS IN THE AMERICAN ECONOMY DURING THE NINETEENTH CENTURY, 183.

One budget given, supposedly of an "average New York businessman," must be dismissed; it contains no allotment for clothing, to say nothing of expenditures for health, education, or consumer asset formation. However, the three other budgets, with a 35-year interval between that of 1816 and the two for 1851, are of some interest. That for 1816-1817 is a rather detailed accounting, and by rearranging the items one can see that nearly four-fifths of the total budgeted expenditures were allocated for fuel, food, rent, clothing and light; the less satisfactory 1851 budgets required all of the budgeted expenditures for the same items. Personal capital formation — health, education, durable assets and savings — accounted for about one-fifth of the budget for 1816-1817, while no breakdown for the later year is available for such items. The proportions spent on food were roughly comparable in accounting method, and show a decline of about five percentage points between the 1816 and 1851 budgets. The composite budgets for 397 families in Massachusetts for 1875 shows a much higher allotment for food (57.4%) than any of the other budgets (except that for 1857), and lower relative expenditures for rent and fuel and light. The 1875 clothing figure was nearly three times that of the 1816-1817 budget.

It is difficult to draw any meaningful conclusions about trends in the level of living from these budgets, however interesting they may be. In the mid-19th Century, however, the use of family budgets for such purposes was widespread. In the Post-Civil War decades, budget studies in the United States multiplied considerably and the practice has continued to date. But the use made of these budgets is as a method of determining weights for computations of cost of living indexes.[11]

---

[11] Post-Civil War budget studies, pioneered by Carrol Wright, became gradually more inclusive than those shown in Table A. Data on health, nutrition, education and the like came to be included, and costing these budgets led to considerable activity among scholars to identify minimum standards of living. "The cost of such budgets," Dorothy Brady has written, "defined the 'poverty line,' which served to identify groups living in chronic want in the almost helpless struggle to obtain the

V.

Was the American of 1860 as "well-off" as the American of 1800? If one takes a time span of about a half-a-century at a clip, it is quite likely that on the basis of trends in real per capita income alone, this question could be answered in the affirmative. Raymond Goldsmith has calculated the trend of real per capita income for the United States for the years extending back to 1839. He estimates that real income per head has grown at an average annual rate of 1⅝% over the period. It would require evidence of grossly low living standards in the 18th Century to support the argument that real income was rising at a rate of even 1% for periods of 50 years or more before 1839. Goldsmith suggests an average rate of growth in per capita real income of about 1/2% per annum from the mid-18th Century to 1839.[12]

Mrs. Alice Hanson Jones, who has studied the level of living in Colonial America, has suggested that real income per head in 1760 was about 1/3 of the 1860 level. This is probably an underestimate for both dates, as Mrs. Jones recognizes, and the difference in income per head between 1760 and 1860 is probably closer to one-half.[13]

---

necessaries of life." See her "Scales of Living and Wage Earners' Budgets," in ANNALS OF THE AMERICAN ACADEMY OF POLITICAL AND SOCIAL SCIENCES, CCLXXIV (1951), 32-38. One of the pioneering studies of this type was Seebohm Rowntree's investigation of the standard of living in York. See his POVERTY: A STUDY IN TOWN LIFE (London: Macmillan and Company, 1901). For an analysis of Rowntree's work and other Post-Civil War budget studies see, Faith M. Williams and Carle C. Zimmerman, STUDIES OF FAMILY LIVING IN THE UNITED STATES AND OTHER COUNTRIES, United States Department of Agriculture, Misc. Publication 223 (Washington: GPO, 1935), esp. 2-68. Mrs. Hoover used as a basis for the weights in her Consumers Price Index, 1851 onward, the budgets noted in Table A. See, her "Retail Prices After 1850," in TRENDS IN THE AMERICAN ECONOMY DURING THE NINETEENTH CENTURY, STUDIES IN INCOME AND WEALTH, Vol. XXIV (Princeton: Princeton University Press, 1960), 183. Mrs. Hoover has extended her CPI index back to 1800. See her statement concerning the weights used for the index prior to 1850 in, Joint Economic Committee, HISTORICAL AND COMPARATIVE RATES OF PRODUCTION, PRODUCTIVITY AND PRICES (Washington: GPO, 1959), 401-402.

[12] Raymond Goldsmith, "National Product and Income: Long-Term Trends," in Joint Economic Committee, HISTORICAL AND COMPARATIVE RATES OF PRODUCTION, PRODUCTIVITY AND PRICES, (Washington: GPO, 1959), 278. [Reprinted in this volume.]

[13] Mrs. Jones offers a sobering word of caution: "The difficulty with generalizing for 1760 is that there was such a spread in living, from the self-sufficient backwoods, to the opulent southern plantation owner or Philadelphia merchant who lived richly on the finest imports from Europe. Also production was so much on a custom order basis. Homespun cloth was stout, food was better and more abundant than European working classes had, the Franklin stove had been invented, some housing was crude but some very elegant. Labor was scarce and indentured servants sometimes could rise in a few years to landowner status. There was no single currency and prices are

Working from quite different sources of data, it is Edgar Martin's hunch, admittedly unsupported, that the American of 1860 enjoyed a much higher level of living than the American of a century earlier. At the least, Martin concludes, the level of living in content and scale showed a marked rise between the beginning of the 1750's up to the eve of the Civil War.[14] There is even other qualitative evidence to support this view, and basic common sense notions of American history tell us that this interpretation must be the acceptable one. Harriet Martineau, Michael Chevalier, Alex De Tocqueville, and other observers of American life found little to comment upon except that Americans seemed to live so well.[15] Martineau, in commenting on pauperism in the states, wrote: "the pauperism of the United States is, to the observation of a stranger, nothing at all. . . . It is confined to the ports, emigrants making their way back into the country, the families of intemperate or disabled men, and unconnected women, who depend on their own exertions. The amount altogether is far from commensurate with the charity of the community. . . ." [16] Thus the answer to the question of whether or not the level of living of the average American increased during the century before the Civil War seems to be a resounding yes.

Yet the question cannot be dismissed so easily. As will be developed later, living standards not only increased during the 1850's as Martin has concluded, but it can be stated with confidence that the decade of the forties also witnessed an appreciable break in the possibilities and attainment of an increase in the structure and content of the level of living in

---

difficult to interpret. In transportation, education, health services, public services, availability of factory-produced goods, 1760 was certainly far below 1860. Perhaps in food, and even in clothing and housing 1760 might have had the edge in some ways." All statements in Letter to R. Andreano from Mrs. Homer (Alice Hanson) Jones, December 18, 1962.

[14] Edgar Martin, STANDARD OF LIVING IN 1860, 399. "That consumption in 1860 was on a higher level than it had been at the end of the Colonial period seems certain. Space does not permit any detailed examination of the factors leading to this rise. The whole period had been one of agricultural expansion and of improvement in both agricultural and industrial processes and equipment. At the same time, new facilities for transportation were making possible not only the gains from division of labor but the exchange of products between regions having different climates and resources. Capital, both business and personal, was accumulating, while the low unit costs resulting from mass production and abundant natural resources were making it possible for people to devote more and more of their income to the purchase of goods formerly regarded as luxuries. . . . There was little to impede this rise in the level of living, though the too rapid growth of some cities, partly the result of immigration, did tend to intensify the problem of providing adequate housing."

[15] Tocqueville, DEMOCRACY IN AMERICA, II (New York, 1954), 48-56.

[16] Harriet Martineau, SOCIETY IN AMERICA. Edited by Semour Lipset. (New York: Doubleday-Anchor, 1962), 317.

America. But doubt among economic historians concerning the trend of real per capita income for the period from 1800 to 1840 continues to persist despite evidence of the type cited above.

The only estimates of national income before 1840 are those of R. F. Martin, which have been available since 1939. Martin's data have been widely quoted and used by economic historians since that time, but apparently few who have cited his data were even dimly aware of the implications they contained.[17] Martin's estimates show a slight fall in real per capita income between 1799 and 1809, a substantially greater decline during the succeeding decade, and no decadal rise until 1839. In other words, the level of real per capita income in 1799 was not regained until 1849 and before turning up after 1839 had fallen, to a greater or lesser extent, for nearly three decades.[18] Was an American of 1799 "better off" than an American of 1809, 1819, and 1829? That is a primary issue raised by the Martin findings.

Şimon Kuznets, in a study published a decade ago, seriously questioned that income per capita could have declined in anything like the manner suggested by the Martin data. Kuznets argues that, assuming the same relative labor productivities in agriculture and manufacturing which prevailed in 1799, two structural changes in the economy — (1) an inter-industry shift of workers from the lower productivity sector, agriculture, to the higher productivity sector, manufacturing, and (2) an increase in the proportion of the population gainfully employed — would rule out any statistical likelihood of a decline in product or income per person in constant prices. With product per worker in agriculture in 1800 of .50, and in non-agricultural workers of 2.34, multiplied by the relative proportions of each to the total gainfully employed (at constant prices) one can see an increase in product per member of the labor force of 7.8% between 1799 and 1839. If one takes into account an estimated 10% increase in the labor force participation ratio, the overall gain in product per worker at constant prices would be 19%. Thus Kuznets says "this rise in per capita product in constant prices does not allow for any secular increase

---

[17] One need only pick any text in American economic history published since 1939 to verify this statement. In one of the best texts available, Harold F. Williamson, (ed.), GROWTH OF THE AMERICAN ECONOMY, Second Edition. (New York: Prentice-Hall, 1951), 329, the authors point out that the declines in real per capita income which show up from the Martin data "show very clearly the effects that wars and financial crises had on the country's growth." As will be noted elsewhere Douglas North's explanations of the Martin data is identical.

[18] R. F. Martin, NATIONAL INCOME IN THE UNITED STATES, 1799-1938. (New York: National Industrial Conference Board, 1939), 6, Table I.

in product per worker either in agriculture or in non-agricultural industries." [19]

One would think that the mere arithmetic of the *a priori* case presented
by Kuznets would relegate the Martin data to the limbo of beaten and bat-
tered economic historians. But the issue is still to be resolved, for within
the past two years several more scholars have joined the debate. William
Parker and Franklee Whartenby, in a searching critique of Martin's statistical methodology, while persuaded that Martin's data leave much to be
desired, are not fully convinced that history, or Kuznets, has upset the logic
of the conclusion. "The evidence appears to be too weak," they argue, "to
support Kuznets' inference that per capita real income followed a rising
trend from 1800 to 1840. The validity of his [Kuznets'] contention depends
upon the assumption of a constant or rising level of productivity in agriculture. . . . A small fall in agricultural productivity would have sufficed
to wipe out any such gains [i.e., a 19% increase in real product per capita."] [20]

The latest to be heard from is Douglas North in an article published in
1961.[21] North's contribution is a cyclical analysis of the period, drawn
largely from his own suggestive earlier work on the role of the foreign
trade sector in setting the pace of growth in national income in the United
tates prior to 1839.[22] His qualitative conclusion, however, is that "although Martin's methods will not stand scrutiny, his conclusion that per
capita real income was higher in 1799 than it was to be again for a half
century appears to be correct." [23]

Before one can adopt either the Martin data or the Kuznets stricture, a
judgment must be made as to whether or not real per capita income is a
reasonable approximation to the level of living as this term was defined

---

[19] Simon Kuznets, "National Income Estimates For the Period Prior to 1870,"
INCOME AND WEALTH OF THE UNITED STATES, TRENDS AND STRUC-
TURE, edited by Simon Kuznets. (Cambridge: Bowes and Bowes, 1952), 225-226.

[20] William Parker and Franklee Whartenby, "The Growth of Output Before 1840,"
in Conference on Research in Income and Wealth, TRENDS IN THE AMERICAN
ECONOMY IN THE NINETEENTH CENTURY. Studies in Income and Wealth,
Vol. XXIV (Princeton: Princeton University Press, 1960), 211.

[21] Douglas North, "Early National Income Estimates of the United States," in
Economic Development and Cultural Change, IX (April 1961), 387-396.

[22] Douglas North, THE ECONOMIC GROWTH OF THE UNITED STATES,
1790-1860. (New York: Prentice-Hall, 1961), esp. 24-35.

[23] North, "Early National Income Estimates," 387. The late Sumner Slichter,
extending productivity estimates for 1869 backward, came to the independent conclusion that the Martin data vastly understated the gains in per capita real product
realized before 1850. See, Sumner Slichter, ECONOMIC GROWTH IN THE
UNITED STATES: ITS HISTORY, PROBLEMS AND PROSPECTS, (Baton
Rouge: Louisiana State University Press, 1961), 48-51. For a more detailed analysis
of this debate and a suggested modification in the Kuznets position, see Appendix A
of this paper.

earlier. It is certain that the measure of real income per head is a *first* approximation, but is it sufficiently applicable to include changes in the level of living as evidenced by trends in consumer asset formation, social asset formation, and personal consumption of perishable goods and services? In addition, two other matters must be considered before we can accept the trend in real per capita income as a measure of economic welfare of the American population for this period: the distribution of income, and changes in the volume, structure, and duration of unemployment. Before attacking either the components of the level of living or the other adjustments, mention should be made of the high probability that the underlying data of the income estimates understates by a considerable amount the volume of goods and services accruing per head of population. For example, the original Martin data contained a gross estimate of "home manufactures," i.e., goods and services that did not enter organized market transactions, which actually originated in agriculture but which Martin assigned to the manufacturing sector. It is highly probable that this adjustment tended to understate income earned in agriculture. As Kuznets commented on this procedure, ". . . Persons among the gainfully occupied attached to agriculture may engage in other pursuits and thus derive income from other sources. . . . Further allowance should be made for income from work by farm residents in cities and for their receipts of property income from sources other than agriculture." [24] As will be noted later, in some cases income received in kind in the years before 1840 amounted to substantially high fractions of an individual worker's total real income. Thus, to the extent that real per capita income estimates cannot fully take account of the income supplements of this type, it is difficult to use the measure as an index of changing economic welfare.

This view is also supported by examination of trends in income distribution: *a priori*, if the distribution of personal income became *more* unequal, a decline in real per capita income would understate the decline in welfare. As already noted, there is no statistical data available on changes in the distribution of income between 1800 and 1840. Michael Chevalier found little to comment on in respect to the "condition of the richest merchant and that of a mechanic and a farmer." The difference, he suggested, "is merely in degree and not in kind." [25]

Stanley Lebergott has shown that non-farm real wages probably fell from 10-20% between 1800 and 1818, while farm real wages fell by less than

---

[24] Kuznets, "National Income Estimates Prior to 1870," 223.

[25] Michael Chevalier, SOCIETY, MANNERS AND POLITICS IN THE UNITED STATES. Edited by John W. Ward. (New York: Doubleday Anchor Book, 1961), 289. Elsewhere Chevalier does note, however, that in the later 1830's the gap between "merchant" and "mechanic" appeared to be widening. (p. 293).

5% for the same period. Between 1818 and 1830 the declines for non-farm were from 0-10% and for farm again less than 5%. In the succeeding decade, non-farm real wages rose from 10-20% and farm from 15-25%. This would seem to suggest that for the entire 1800-1840 period the burden of declining real wages was felt to a much greater extent by non-farm rather than farm workers, possibly pointing toward a widening of income distribution among the urban classes. With income generated in agriculture amounting to nearly two-thirds of the total for the economy, however, it would not be too far off the mark to suggest that movements of real wages in agriculture do not suggest any appreciable widening of personal income distribution as between non-urban income classes. Paul Trescott's estimates of transfer and subsidy payments to individuals and business firms show the greatest percentage increase between 1800 and 1820, the period in which real wages declined the most.[26] Lebergott also made an adjustment in his computations for certain income received in kind (payments for board, lodging, washing), although he was unable to adjust for goods received in kind (a common practice during this period). Such income supplements, as Lebergott suggests, "may have constituted a fairly stable real wage element. While the wage earner was thus guaranteed against any marked rise in his standard of living he was *pari passu* isolated from any marked decline." [27]

Data on unemployment before 1840 is also scanty but what is available suggests that the trend, structure, and duration of unemployment was not materially different from that in other ante-bellum periods. It has been estimated that although the economic decline of 1819 was one of the most severe in the United States with respect to manufacturing employment (Lebergott has estimated a reduction in manufacturing employment of about two-thirds of the work force in this sector), because the importance of manufacturing to the total economy was not relatively as great as in subsequent decades the volume of unemployment could not have exceeded 4% of the free white labor force.[28]

---

[26] The per capita figures for transfers and subsidy payments to individuals were: 1800, $15; 1810, $12½; 1820, $26; 1830, $14¾; 1840, $12½. Per capita figures for total subsidy and transfer payments to individuals and businesses for the same four decade points were: $24½, $26, $44½, $42, and $25. Computed from basic data in Paul Trescott, "United States Government and National Income, 1790-1860," in TRENDS IN THE AMERICAN ECONOMY DURING THE 19th CENTURY, 340.

[27] Stanley Lebergott, "Wage Trends, 1800-1900," in TRENDS IN THE AMERICAN ECONOMY DURING THE NINETEENTH CENTURY, 468. See Appendix B for an analysis of Lebergott's computations of real wages.

[28] See, Stanley Lebergott, in Joint Economic Committee, HISTORICAL AND COMPARATIVE RATES OF LABOR FORCE, EMPLOYMENT AND UNEMPLOYMENT (Washington: Government Printing Office, 1959), 582. [Reprinted in Part V.]

Thus, taking into account these details on income distribution and unemployment, it would appear that welfare judgments based on real per capita income data may not be too far out of line. An alternative approach to the level of living, i.e., examining social and consumer asset formation and personal consumption of perishable goods and services, should yield additional insights on the course of welfare during the controversial decades, 1800-1840. One of the most serious objections to real per capita income as a wholly satisfying index of changing welfare — inability to put a money value on goods and services produced and consumed outside the market economy — may be overcome with this alternative approach.

Social Asset Formation. There seems little doubt that the stock of social assets, sometimes called infrastructure or social overhead capital, more than kept pace with the rise in population between 1800 and 1840. Directly and indirectly such assets offered a return per head of population which cannot be accounted for by income estimates alone. Water systems in the urban areas, the proliferation of town and municipal buildings and agencies, town halls, church buildings, parks, public schools and the like, provided in greater or less extent supplements to personal income not easily measured. The combination of increased mileage of surface roads and canal buildings before 1840, for example, produced social benefits that most assuredly accrued to each head of population.[29] Concerning canals, Harvey Segal has written: "the social benefits of canals seem clearly to have exceeded their cost by a substantial margin. Had there been no canals, the expansion of industrial activity in the east would have been inhibited by reliance on a much narrower domestic market and by the high cost of foodstuffs produced on inferior land. . . ." [30] Richard Wade, in his fine study of western cities before 1830, documents the priorities given to social asset formation of all types at Pittsburgh, Cincinnatti, Louisville, Lexington, and St. Louis.[31] Further mention should be made of interurban transportation developments, improvements of navigation on the internal water-

---

[29] An estimate of total mileage of surfaced roads in the United States shows a fourfold increase between 1800 and 1810; 2½ fold rise for the next decade; and about a three fold increase for the 1820-1830 period. The overall increase was 2200% or at an average annual rate of 71%. Computed from data in Bureau of the Census, HISTORICAL STATISTICS OF THE UNITED STAES, 1789-1945. (Washington: Government Printing Office, 1949), 220.

[30] Carter Goodrich and others, CANALS AND AMERICAN ECONOMIC DEVELOPMENT. (New York: Columbia University Press, 1961), 247. Also see, Nathan Miller, THE ENTERPRISE OF A FREE PEOPLE: ASPECTS OF ECONOMIC DEVELOPMENT IN NEW YORK, 1792-1838. (Ithaca: Cornell University Press, 1962), 188, 263-264.

[31] Richard Wade, THE URBAN FRONTIER. (Cambridge: Harvard University Press, 1959), 72-100, 231-269.

ways and harbors, and the increase in public school building in New England, the middle Atlantic States, and parts of the newly emerging Western states.[32] Few Eastern cities, as well as those in more settled parts of the country, were without libraries that grew in numbers and size of collection between 1800 and 1840.[33]

In matters of health and medicine, already in 1815 Seybert could comment that yellow fever in Boston, New York, Baltimore, and Philadelphia had been unknown since 1803.[34] Crude death rates in urban and rural areas of the Northeast, middle Atlantic, and western states probably declined, although before 1840 this conclusion for the South slave and non-slave population is questionable.[35] Average life expectancy at birth probably increased some ten years, or about 30% between 1800 and 1840, and the proportion of dentists per 100,000 of population doubled over the same period.[36] Whether or not these direct results represented a "pay-off" or return on the accumulation and diffusion of social assets, it is difficult to claim with any degree of certainty; yet it is a plausible hypothesis consistent with this evidence, and not disproved by it.

---

[32] Chevalier, SOCIETY, MANNERS, AND POLITICS IN THE UNITED STATES, 219-261 contains an insightful analysis of the role of transportation and communications in improving the daily life of the American.

[33] See Louis B. Wright, CULTURE ON THE MOVING FRONTIER. (New York: Harper Torchbook, 1961), 101-117. In State and local histories of western states and cities is clear evidence of the growth of social assets that accrued per head of population. See, Logan Esarey, A HISTORY OF INDIANA FROM ITS EXPLORATION TO 1850. (Indianapolis: W. K. Stewart, 1915), esp. 254-289. Also see, Francis P. Weisenburger, THE HISTORY OF THE STATE OF OHIO, THE PASSING OF THE FRONTIER, 1825-1850, Vol. III, (Columbus: Ohio State Archaeological and Historical Society, 1941), esp. 144-210; Rev. Charles F. Goss, CINCINNATTI, THE QUEEN CITY, 1788-1912, I, (Chicago: S. J. Clarke, 1912), esp. 131-204. Frederick Jackson Turner also noted the importance of social asset formation to the level of living. See his, THE RISE OF THE NEW WEST, 1819-29. (New York: Collier Books, 1962), esp. 75-81.

[34] Seybert, STATISTICAL ANNALS, 48.

[35] See Seybert, STATISTICAL ANNALS, 50-51; Debow, STATISTICAL VIEW OF THE UNITED STATES, 104-105. There were, of course, other forms of disease which afflicted the populations of all regions, but the incidence of the most prevalent ones — cholera and various strains of influenza — seldom reached epidemic proportions. See A. H. Gale, EPIDEMIC DISEASES (London: Penguin Books, 1959), 66-71, 131-148. Yellow Fever in the southern states, of course, continued to persist and there were three large epidemics, 1847, 1853, and 1858. See Martha Carolyn Mitchell, "Health and the Medical Profession in the Lower South, 1845-1860," JOURNAL OF SOUTHERN HISTORY, X (November 1944), 426-427.

[36] Seybert, STATISTICAL ANNALS, 51; Louis J. Dublin and Alfred J. Lotka, LENGTH OF LIFE. (New York: Ronald Press, 1936), 44, 54, 65; HISTORICAL STATISTICS OF THE UNITED STATES, 1789-1945, 50; George Tucker, PROGRESS OF THE UNITED STATES IN POPULATION AND WEALTH IN FIFTY YEARS. (New York: Press of Hunt's Merchant Magazine, 1855), 63-68.

Consumer Asset Formation. Of equal significance per head of population as social asset accumulation and dispersion is the change that occurred in the scope, quality, and variety of goods and services that had longer-term consumption value and represented a marked change in one of the most important components of the level of living. It is not difficult to think of public land sales, for example, not only as a dynamic factor in the development process, but also as a conscious act of asset formation by individuals that contributed directly to one's level of living. It is surely difficult to put a "price tag" on the expectations of an individual in regard to his conception of ultimate happiness in the wilderness as distinguished from the more orderly life of the town and city. Yet such a benefit must have attached to individuals if one is to judge by the volume of personal land acquisitions transacted in the period between 1800-1840.[37] Similarly, acquisition of owner occupied residential dwellings, on the basis of qualitative evidence, increased between 1800 and 1840 in per capita terms.[38] Writing in the later 1830's about houses of "merchant and mechanic," Chevalier noted: "All have similar houses, built on a similar plan; only one has a front five or six feet wider, and is one or two stories higher; the arrangement of the rooms and the furniture are the same. All have carpets from the cellar to the garret, all sleep in large high-post bedsteads very much like the other . . .; only the carpets of the one are coarse and those of the other are fine, the bedstead of the rich is of mahogany and that of the mechanic of cherry or walnut."[39] Per capita assessed value in constant prices of real and

[37] There were, of course, wide fluctuations in year to year sales of public lands and the dating of these peaks by geographic region has been calculated by Douglas North and others. See his, GROWTH OF THE AMERICAN ECONOMY, 1790-1860, 74, 119, 120; Abramovitz, in HISTORICAL AND COMPARATIVE RATES OF PRODUCTION, PRODUCTIVITY, AND PRICES, 435, dated 1812, 1833 and 1852 as peaks in his calculation of average reference cycle standings.

[38] Housing assessed value was about $350 per capita in 1840. COMPENDIUM OF THE SIXTH CENSUS, 90-91. J. D. G. De Bow noted in 1850 that enumerating dwellings was required of the Census marshalls and this was done though the results were not compiled for the final census report. See, De Bow, STATISTICAL VIEW OF THE UNITED STATES: BEING A COMPENDIUM OF THE SEVENTH CENSUS. (Washington: Beverley Tucker, 1854), 47. The only data from which Abramovitz was able to build an average reference cycle standing showed a peak in urban building for 1836. See, HISTORICAL AND COMPARATIVE RATES OF PRODUCTION, PRODUCTIVITY, AND PRICES, 435.

[39] Chevalier, SOCIETY, MANNERS, AND POLITICS IN THE UNITED STATES, 289. Adam Seybert, in 1815, Noted: "the many large cities, towns, and villages . . . are monuments to the industry of the people. We have no authentic documents . . . whence to deduce the amount of the new property which has annually been created; that this addition must be immense, we conclude from the extent of the new lands, which are every year cleared and put into cultivation; from the roads and bridges, which are annually constructed, and the numerous buildings, which are daily erected for dwelling houses, workshops, and manufactories." STATISTICAL ANNALS, 4.

personal property rose 2½ fold between 1798-1838 and nearly an additional threefold in the next two decades.[40]

Possibilities concerning other forms of consumer asset formation can only be guessed at. Almost at random, two categories of consumption in personal households that were of a durable nature have been selected: earthenware and household furniture. Data for both items are totally inadequate except for the grossest type of generalization. Yet in constant prices between 1823-1840, the per capita share of claimed market valuation for earthenware increased from less than one cent to about six cents, and household furniture from less than three cents to nearly thirty-nine cents, or percentage increases respectively of approximately 500 and 1000.[41]

(See Table B.) Distribution, and presumably consumption, of pewter and silverware for household use, based on data for the predecessor companies of Reed and Barton, Silversmiths, also suggest that these items loomed larger in consumer asset formation than in the past. The domestic production and consumption of toys, games, hobby books, and other home-centered leisure and pleasure goods and activities probably increased two to three fold between 1800 and 1840.[41A] (See Table C.) [42]

Still another possibility for changing consumer asset formation concerns a disposition for partial deferment of present consumption of durable and non-durable goods for monetary assets. Growth in deposits in commercial banks is seen, as well as the acquisition of annuities, life insurance policies, and savings in the form of trust funds. In Massachusetts, where data is somewhat more accessible but nonetheless highly inadequate, evidence that many individuals preferred to hold their monetary assets in banking and insurance institutions surely is an indication of a wider diffusion of consumer asset structure. (See Tables D and E.)

Personal consumption of perishable goods and services. Judging from accounts of contemporary observers the variety, if not the quantity, of

---

[40] Computed from Tucker, PROGRESS OF THE UNITED STATES, 203; De Bow, STATISTICAL VIEW, 190. Hoover CPI used as deflator.

[41] The Lowell Manufacturing Company output of rugs and carpeting in 1832 amounted to nearly 10,000 square yards. See John Ewing and Nancy P. Norton, BROADLOOMS AND BUSINESSMEN, Harvard Studies in Business History, XVII (Cambridge: Harvard University Press, 1955), 26.

[41A] See Marshall and Inez McClintock, *Toys in America* (Washington: Public Affairs Press, 1961) 85-137. A brief survey of the list of American toy manufactures and the founding dates given at pages 449 to 464 shows a peak for the pre-1860 period in the 1830's.

[42] Louis Wright comments on the speed with which local potteries, silversmiths and furniture makers accompanied the development of towns and cities along the frontier before 1830. See his, CULTURE ON THE MOVING FRONTIER, 75-76. Carl Bridenbaugh's delightful and informative study, THE COLONIAL CRAFTSMAN (Chicago: University of Chicago Press, 1961) should also be consulted, esp. 65-96.

TABLE B.

CONSUMER ASSET FORMATION: HOUSEHOLD FURNITURE AND EARTHENWARE, 1823, 1840

1823	(1) Market Value	(3) Per Capita (constant prices)
Earthenware(a)	$ 107,273	$ 0.008
Household Furniture	374,964	0.027
1840	**(2)**	
Earthenware	$1,104,825	$ 0.56
Household Furniture	7,555,405	0.386

(1) Computed from DIGEST OF ACCOUNTS OF MANUFACTURING ESTABLISHMENTS IN THE UNITED STATES (Washington: Gales and Seaton, 1823).

(2) COMPENDIUM OF THE SIXTH CENSUS OF THE UNITED STATES, 1840. (Washington: Blair and Rives, 1841), 90-91.

(3) Population data from HISTORICAL STATISTICS OF THE UNITED STATES, 8. Hoover's CPI Index, 1851-59 base, used as deflator. See, HISTORICAL AND COMPARATIVE RATES OF PRODUCTION, PRODUCTIVITY AND PRICES, 397.

(a) Seybert, STATISTICAL ANNALS, 8, Reports earthenware manufacturers in 1810 with a claimed market value of $259,720 or about $0.002 per capita in constant prices.

TABLE C.

CONSUMER ASSET FORMATION:
SHIPMENTS OF SELECTED HOUSEHOLD PRODUCTS, 1830-34
by a New England Manufacturer

Item	Number	Shipped
Teapots	1830	1834
Lamps (pairs)	2,429	787
Sugar and Cream Sets	1,395	2,861
Coffeepots	870	129
Slop Bowls	760	62
Castor Frames	345	123
Tea Sets		410
Candlesticks		328
Ladles (dozens)		77
		21

SOURCE: Adapted from George Sweet Gibb, THE WHITESMITHS OF TAUNTON: A HISTORY OF REED AND BARTON, SILVERSMITHS, 1824-1943. Harvard Studies in Business History, VIII (Cambridge: Harvard University Press, 1946), 58.

TABLE D.

CONSUMER ASSET FORMATION:
HOLDINGS OF LIFE INSURANCE IN A
MASSACHUSETTS COMPANY
1824 - 1830

Year	Trust Deposits	Life Insurance	Annuities
1824	$ 370,677	$1,708	$14,872
1825	1,084,094	1,839	21,126
1826	1,802,122	1,806	26,272
1827	3,006,117	2,968	32,965
1828	3,596,202	3,608	37,912
1829	4,087,524	4,524	46,518
1830	4,865,254	4,469	63,284

SOURCE: Gerald T. White, A HISTORY OF THE MASSACHUSETTS HOS-
PITAL LIFE INSURANCE COMPANY (Cambridge: Harvard University
Press, 1955), 192, also see, 38-39.

TABLE E.

CONSUMER ASSET FORMATION:
YEAR-END BANK DEPOSITS
ALL MASSACHUSETTS BANKS, 1818 - 1830

1818	$1.8 (Millions)
1821	3.3
1824	3.3
1827	0.9
1830	1.4

SOURCE: Compiled from data in N. S. B. Gras, THE MASSACHUSETTS
FIRST NATIONAL BANK OF BOSTON, 1784-1934. HARVARD STUDIES
IN BUSINESS HISTORY, IV. (Cambridge: Harvard University Press, 1937),
601-623, 712-720.

domestic food consumption per head of population rose significantly during
the four decade interval, 1800-1840. One need not agree with Mrs. Trollope as to the quality of food preparation and the variety of diet, but,
writing in 1832, she observed:

"The ordinary mode of living is abundant, but not delicate. They consume an extraordinary quantity of bacon. Ham and beef-steaks appear
morning, noon, and night. In eating, they mix things together with the
strangest incongruity imaginable. I have seen eggs and oysters eaten together; the sempiternal ham with apple-sauce; beef-steak with stewed
peaches; and salt fish with onions. The bread is everywhere excellent, but
they rarely enjoy it themselves, as they insist upon eating horrible half-

baked hot rolls both morning and evening. The butter is tolerable; but they have seldom such cream as every little dairy produces in England; in fact, the cows are very roughly kept, compared with our's. Common vegetables are abundant and very fine. I never saw sea-cale, or cauliflowers, and either from the want of summer rain, or the want of care, the harvest of green vegetables is much sooner over than with us. They eat the Indian corn in a great variety of forms; sometimes it is dressed green, and eaten like peas; sometimes it is broken to pieces when dry, boiled plain, and brought to table like rice; this dish is called hominy. The flour of it is made into at least a dozen different sorts of cakes; but in my opinion all bad. This flour, mixed in the proportion of one-third, with fine wheat, makes by far the best bread I ever tasted.

"I never saw turbot, salmon, or fresh cod; but the rock and shad are excellent. There is a great want of skill in the composition of sauces; not only with fish, but with every thing. They use very few made dishes, and I never saw any that would be approved by our savants. They have an excellent wild duck, called the Canvass Back, which, if delicately served, would surpass the black cock; but the game is very inferior to our's; they have no hares, and I never saw a pheasant. They seldom indulge in second courses, with all their ingenious temptations to the eating a second dinner; but almost every table has its dessert, (invariably pronounced desart) which is placed on the table before the cloth is removed, and consists of pastry, preserved fruits, and creams. They are "extravagantly fond," to use their own phrase, of puddings, pies, and all kinds of "sweets," particularly the ladies; but are by no means such connoisseurs in soups and ragouts as the gastronomes of Europe. Almost every one drinks water at table, and by a strange contradiction, in the country where hard drinking is more prevalent than in any other, there is less wine taken at dinner; ladies rarely exceed one glass, and the great majority of females never take any." [43]

A more recent observation of food production admittedly less colorful than Mrs. Trollope's, suggests, however, that the output of American agriculture "increased at a rate sufficient to supply the more or less constant per capita requirements of a growing population and the pressing demands of foreign countries for cotton and tobacco." [44] On the basis of aggregate farm product output data, and not accounting for items consumed on farms, a selected cross section of major agricultural products (Table F) does not show any marked increase per head of population between 1800 and 1830 (in some cases there are slight declines), and only modest increases for the 1830-1840 decade. Probable per capita egg production was 6 dozen in 1800 and 1840, dairy products 5.0 lbs. in 1800 and 5.2 lbs. in 1840 (an increase of less than 5%), and fruits, 2 bushels in 1800 and 2.6

---

[43] Mrs. Frances Trollope, DOMESTIC MANNERS OF THE AMERICANS, Edited by Donald Smalley. (New York: Vintage Book, 1960), 297-298.

[44] Marvin Towne and Wayne Rasmussen, "Farm Gross Product and Gross Investment," in TRENDS IN THE AMERICAN ECONOMY DURING THE NINETEENTH CENTURY, 258.

bushels in 1840 (an increase of 30%). If production per head approximates the trend in consumption per head, it would be difficult on the basis of these data alone to assert that the food component of the level of living increased over the four decades. At best the data indicate no substantial decline. However, by the more inclusive composition of the level of living used here, evidence of changes in per head food consumption can only be considered as a first approximation to changes in the level of living. (The data of Table F, as pointed out in Appendix A, may cast some doubt about the possibility that productivity per worker in agriculture could have fallen in magnitude sufficient to overcome the Kuznets results.)

TABLE F.

PROBABLE PER CAPITA PRODUCTION OF SELECTED AGRICULTURE PRODUCTS

Item	1800	1810	1820	1830	1840
Cattle and Calves (lbs.)	10	15	15	13	15
Egg (Dozens)	6.0	5.9	6.0	5.9	6.0
Dairy Products (lbs.)	5.0	5.2	5.2	5.2	5.2
Irish Potatoes (bu.)	3.1	3.1	3.1	3.1	3.2
Peas and Beans (bu.)	2.4	2.4	2.4	2.3	2.9
Fruits (bu.)	2.0	2.0	2.0	2.0	2.6

SOURCE: Computed from, Towne and Rasmussen, "Farm Gross Product and Gross Investment," in TRENDS IN THE AMERICAN ECONOMY DURING THE 19th CENTURY, 283, 288, 289, 303, 305. Population data from HISTORICAL STATISTICS OF THE UNITED STATES, 8.

Data on personal consumption of tea, coffee, and wine, show a definite rise between 1808 and 1846 (coffee consumption per capita from 2 1/2 to 5 2/3 lbs., tea from 1/2 to 4/5 lbs., and wine from 1/4 gallon to 1/3 gallon), yet it would be foolhardy to suggest that these alone indicate a rise in the level of living. (See Table G.) Such an interpretation is plausible but many would rather interpret such data as indicating a shift in consumer preference patterns.

VI.

For the two decades after 1839-40 there can be little doubt that the economic welfare of the American population was on a rising trend. A multitude of welfare indexes can be used to verify this claim. Robert Gallman's estimates of commodity production, and the reports of contemporary statisticians such as George Tucker, Ezra Seaman, and J. D. DeBow, all show rising trends in national affluence for the two decades before the Civil War. This is hardly surprising, for all the scholars who have studied

TABLE G.

PROBABLE ANNUAL PER CAPITA CONSUMPTION OF TEA, COFFEE, WINE, SUGAR 1808 - 1840

		1808 - 1812	1836 - 1840
(1)	Coffee — Total Consumption (Annual Average)	16,158,000 (lbs.)	96,274,000 (lbs.)
	Per Capita Consumption	2 1/2 (lbs.)	5 2/3 (lbs.)
(2)	Tea — Total Consumption (Annual Average)	3,445,932 (lbs.)	14,591,000 (lbs.)
	Per Capita Consumption	1/2 (lbs.)	4/5 (lbs.)
(3)	Wine — Total Consumption	1,737,002 (gallons)	5,422,000 (gallons)
	Per Capita Consumption	1/4 (gallon)	1/3 (gallon)
(4)	Sugar — Total Consumption	55,000,000 (lbs.)	121,000,000 (lbs.)
	Per Capita Consumption	7 3/5 (lbs.)	7.0 (lbs.)

SOURCES: Compiled From Basic Data in Tucker, PROGRESS OF WEALTH IN THE UNITED STATES, 205 and HISTORICAL STATISTICS OF THE UNITED STATES, 549.

this period, and especially the Cliometricians, have claimed it as a watershed of economic development, a break with the agrarian past and the beginnings of self generated industrialization in the United States. Walt Rostow's much maligned study, THE STAGES OF GROWTH, calls this the period of the "take-off," as already noted, while others, such as Raymond Goldsmith, Moses Abramovitz, Robert Gallman, and most importantly the contemporary chroniclers, refer to these decades as turning points in American economic development.[45] Raymond Goldsmith's statement is worth quoting: "There . . . must have occurred a fairly sharp break in the trend of real national product per head sometime before 1839. Exactly when this break occurred we cannot yet say, on the basis of the statistical data available. I would hazard a guess however, which may shock scrupulous economic historians, that the break occurred not very long before 1839 and that it reflects both the transition of the United

---

[45] See W. W. Rostow, THE STAGES OF GROWTH (Cambridge: Cambridge University Press, 1960), 38 and Douglas North, *Economic Growth in the United States*, 204-205. Abramovitz has calculated average reference cycle standings for some 22 leading series that show, for the most part, a full cycle long swing of 18 years between troughs centered at 1840. See, his "Long Swings in United States Economic Growth," in Joint Economic Committee, HISTORICAL AND COMPARATIVE RATES OF PRODUCTION, PRODUCTIVITY AND PRICES, Tables 2, 3, p. 435. [Reprinted in Part V.]

States from a predominately agricultural to a more and more industrial country and the advent of the railroads." [46]

To judge whether or not this rising trend in real per capita income also included an increase of similar magnitude in the level of living is comparatively easier than for the 1800-1840 period. It should be pointed out, however, that if one accepts the concept of a "sharp break" in the trends of real income per head, this also implies that prior periods could not have experienced similarly high rates of growth. Perhaps the original judgment of R. F. Martin of falling real per capita income for the first two decades of the century is much closer to the qualitative if not the statistical mark. Certainly the acceptance of the "sharp-break" hypothesis weakens the Kuznets claim for the contrary result. Perhaps the statisticians and cliometricians need assistance at this juncture from the more conventional historian.

Few who have studied social change in detail and depth have found evidence which can clearly demonstrate the strategic importance of one short period of years over another. Social and economic change is gradual and evolutionary, and what may apppear as a "sharp-break" is but a culmination of a series of less noticeable and more broadly gauged advances in society. Certainly in the United States during the 1800-1840 period an accumulation of forces was propelling the social and economic life of Americans forward, even if the pace was not statistically spectacular. From our reference point, the level of living in 1840, the welfare of the American population, was decidedly different and undoubtedly improved in relative terms from what prevailed during the first years of the century. What occurred after 1839 only served to highlight the progress which had been made. Indeed it may not be unwise to think of the two decades before the Civil War as the "pay-off" rather than the "take-off" period of American development.

With these general observations in mind, it is quite easy to document the improvement and changes in economic welfare between 1840 and 1860. Per capita real income probably rose at an average annual compound rate of just under 2%. Real wages of farm and non-farm workers rose significantly. While the form of social asset formation changed — railroads, for example, rather than canals and roads in the earlier period, represented the most important structural change — its breadth of coverage and relative return per head of population put the American of 1860 at a higher level of living than 20 years earlier. Public facilities in the urban areas, of which there were more and of larger size than ever before, improved. Asset formation by consumers broadened and increased. My own leading indicator used

---

[46] In "National Product and Income: Long-Term Trends," HISTORICAL AND COMPARATIVE RATES, 278. [Reprinted in Part V.]

here, the per capita share of claimed market value of household furniture in constant prices, rose from about 38 cents in 1840 to 71 cents on the eve of the war. Other consumer durables, some previously unavailable and others formerly limited in supply, were part of personal asset formation: sewing machines, watches, other forms of household and personal durables, became widely diffused. Consumption of perishables increased and broadened in scope. Between 1839 and 1860 leading indicators such as coffee consumption rose one and one-half fold, and consumption of tea and sugar nearly threefold. (See Table H.)

An extremely interesting estimate by the remarkable Ezra Seaman (as adjusted by Gallman) of the composition of commodities flowing into consumption for 1839 shows perishables (food and kindred products) accounting for 73% of the total value, and 27% for durables, semi-durables (dry goods, home furnishings, furniture, appliances, and utensils. Stated alternatively, as per Gallman's calculations, in 1839 about 62% of net national product in current prices was accounted for by commodities flowing to consumers, about 29 percent for services flowing to consumers, and some 9% representing net investment.[47]

Changes in the distribution of personal income and the frequency and duration of unemployment must be balanced aganst the rising trend in the level of living suggested by such leading indicators. Starting with the very severe business recession of 1837, four other sharp declines in the level of economic activity which produced short-period increases in the rate of unemployment can be distinguished. Ranked by the percentage increase in relief load in Massachusetts and New York, the order of severity for the five downturns was as follows: 1837, plus 102%; 1849-50, plus 60%; 1856-57, plus 30%; 1843-44, plus 15%; 1840-41, minus 6%. Lebergott has estimated for the 1856-57 decline an unemployment rate for the total labor force of 5-6%.[48] Thus, to the extent that the interindustry shift from agricultural to non-agricultural employment increased, the frequence of unemployment in the years after 1839 tended to blur, at least for short periods, the over-all advance in the level of living.

Changes in the distribution of personal income may have also helped to aggravate somewhat, at least for some important income classes, the short period infrequency of employment. However, Edward Budd's study of factor shares shows labor income as a rising fraction of total factor income after 1850, so that any change in the distribution of income

---

[47] As Gallman points out, the Seaman data are remarkably usable and reasonably close to those arrived at by alternative means. See Robert Gallman, Selection 2.

[48] All data from Lebergott, HISTORICAL AND COMPARATIVE RATES OF LABOR FORCE, 582-585. [Reprinted in Part V.]

TABLE H.

INDICATORS OF CHANGES IN THE COMPONENTS OF THE LEVEL OF LIVING, 1839 - 1860

Indicator	1839-40	1849-50	1859-60
(1) Real Per Capita Income (Martin)	$198	$235	$296
(2) Real Per Capita Income (King)	—	$214	$235
(3) Per Capita Commodity Production (Gallman)	$ 64	$ 71	$ 85
(4) Real Wages (Percentage Change)			
(4.1) Farm Workers	+15 to 25%	+5%	+15 to 25%
(4.2) Non-Farm Workers	—10 to 20%	—5%	+ 0 to 10%
(5) Social Asset Formation			
(5.1) Railroad Construction Costs, per capita, real terms	$2 1/5	$8 2/5	$15 2/5
(5.2) Canal Investment, real per capita	$6 1/3	$ 1/4	$ 1/3
(5.3) Fixed Capital per capita	$14 2/5	$16 4/5	$23 1/3
(5.4) Physicians, Per 100,000 pop.	—	176	175
(6) Consumer Asset Formation			
(6.1) Household Furniture - per capita of market value, constant prices	$ .38	$ .74	$ .71
(6.2) Per Capita, assessed real and personal property, constant prices	—	$323	$512
(6.3) Bank Deposits per capita, constant prices	$7	$6 2/3	$10
(6.4) Insurance and annuities, Mass. Hospital and Life	$94,800	$104,200	$100,500
(6.5) School Enrollments all ages, per 100 of population	10	47.2	50.6
(7) Consumption of Perishable Goods			
(7.1) Annual Per capita Coffee Cons.	5 2/3 (lbs.)	7 1/10 (lbs.)	8 1/2 (lbs.)
(7.2) Annual Per capita Tea Cons.	1/2 (lbs.)	1 1/2 (lbs.)	1 1/5 (lbs.)
(7.3) Annual Per capita Sugar Cons.	7.0 (lbs.)	11.0 (lbs.)	20.0 (lbs.)
(7.4) Farm Gross Output, per capita constant prices	$71	$70	$68

TABLE H. CONTINUED

Sources and Notes:

(1) From R. F. Martin, NATIONAL INCOME IN THE UNITED STATES, Table I, 6. 1926 Prices.

(2) W. I. King, THE WEALTH AND INCOME OF THE PEOPLE OF THE UNITED STATES (New York: Macmillan and Company, 1915), Table 22, 138. 1929 prices.

(3) Robert Gallman, "Commodity Output, 1839 - 1899," in TRENDS IN THE AMERICAN ECONOMY DURING THE 19th CENTURY, Table I, 16. Absolute Figures.

(4) Lebergott, "Wage Trends, 1800 - 1900," in TRENDS IN THE AMERICAN ECONOMY DURING 19th CENTURY, 493.

(5.1) Computed From E. R. Wicker, "Railroad Investment Before the Civil War," in TRENDS, 516. Data are from Poor's; Deflated by Hoover CPI, 1851-59 Base.

(5.2) Computed From Jerome Cranmer, "Canal Investment, 1815-1860," in TRENDS, 555-556. Deflated by Hoover CPI.

(5.3) 1879 Prices, Includes manufactured producer's durables, farm improvements, construction computed from data in Gallman, "Commodity Output, 1839 - 1899," in TRENDS, 37.

(5.4) HISTORICAL STATISTICS OF THE UNITED STATES, 213.

(6.1) Table B. Tucker, PROGRESS OF WEALTH, 168; Kennedy, PRELIMINARY REPORT, 8th Census, 186. Deflated by Hoover CPI.

(6.2) Tucker, PROGRESS OF WEALTH, 203; DeBow, STATISTICAL VIEW, 190; Kennedy, PRELIMINARY REPORT OF 8th CENSUS, 194. Deflated by Hoover CPI.

(6.3) HISTORICAL STATISTICS OF UNITED STATES, 625, Deflated by Hoover CPI.

(6.4) Absolute Values, White, HISTORY OF MASSACHUSETTS HOSPITAL LIFE INSURANCE COMPANY, 192-93.

(6.5) HISTORICAL STATISTICS OF THE UNITED STATES, 213; 1840 Figure estimated from DeBow, STATISTICAL VIEW, 150.

(7.1) From import Data in HISTORICAL STATISTICS OF UNITED STATES, 549.

(7.2) From import Data in HISTORICAL STATISTICS OF UNITED STATES, 549.

(7.3) From import Data in HISTORICAL STATISTICS OF UNITED STATES, 549.

(7.4) Computed From Data in Towne and Rasmussen, "Farm Gross Product and Investment," in TRENDS, 266. Includes value of improvements and home manufactures. Deflated by Hoover CPI.

by broad income classes probably was not at the expense of labor.[49] But it is quite clear that both during and after the Civil War a substantial redistribution of income from workers to entrepreneurs occurred, although whether or not this was a purely war-induced development or was a trend already underway, one can only speculate about.[50]

One possible approach to the prevailing distribution of income available for 1852 is a frequency distribution of assessed real estate and personal property values held by whites and free negroes in counties in seven states. The states were Kentucky, Michigan, Pennsylvania, Rhode Island, South Carolina, Louisiana, and Ohio. All county population to total state population amounted to 6%, and the total enumerated to total county population was a little above 5%. These data show that of the 23,000 plus persons ranked by class intervals, 85% claimed real estate and property holdings valued at less than $5,000, an additional 7% fell in the $5,000 to $10,000 interval, 6% between $10,000 and $50,000, and the remaining 2% was distributed from $50,000 to $1,000,000. One person fell in the $500,000 to $1,000,000 class (see Table I). What these data may suggest about personal income distribution I am not prepared to guess. It does not seem too far fetched to suggest, however, that this sampling of states covering the major economic and geographic regions of the country could well conform to an actual distribution of income class of persons. Of course this must be taken only as a very guarded and cautious statement, for it is not possible to know how the population size conformed in details to the national population. As a gross impression, however, the data suggest a slight skewness in distribution, but whether or not this represented greater inequality than in previous periods cannot be said. Edgar Martin claimed that in the 1860's only about 1% of the population of New York City received annual incomes of $842 or more.[51]

However one wishes to weigh the importance of possible changes in

---

[49] In, "Factor Shares, 1850-1910," in TRENDS IN THE AMERICAN ECONOMY, 375. There were perhaps a dozen "millionaires" in New York City in the mid-1840's. Absolutely, the income gap probably widened between 1790 and 1860 but it is difficult to suggest that the gap also grew in relative terms. See *Wealth and Biography of the Wealthy Citizens of New York City* (New York, 1845).

[50] See Rufus S. Tucker, "The Distribution of Income Among Taxpayers in the United States, 1863-1935," QUARTERLY JOURNAL OF ECONOMICS, LII (1938), 585. For Wesley Mitchell's observations on this point see his "Production and Consumption of Wealth," in Ralph Andreano (ed.) THE ECONOMIC IMPACT OF THE AMERICAN CIVIL WAR (Cambridge: Schenkman Publishing Company, 1962), 3-10. A different and more sober review of the Mitchell data can be found in Reuben A. Kessel and Armen A. Alchian, "Real Wages in the North During the Civil War; Mitchell's Data Reinterpreted," *Journal of Law and Economics,* II (Oct. 1959).

[51] Martin, THE STANDARD OF LIVING IN 1860, 393.

the distribution of income and in the frequency of unemployment, the general trend in the overall components of the level of living appeared to increase appreciably during the two decades before the war. Edgar Martin certainly concluded so for the decade of the 1850's, and there is little evidence either qualitative or quantitative to suggest an alternative conclusion. There is yet a piece missing from this broad and general picture. We have treated economic welfare and America as if both were homogenous entities, and this is clearly not the case for there were variations by region, by broad social classes, and in relation to other countries.

TABLE 1

FREQUENCY DISTRIBUTION OF ASSESSED REAL ESTATE AND PROPERTY HOLDINGS OF WHITES AND FREE NEGROES, SELECTED COUNTIES IN SEVEN STATES, 1852

Interval	Number of Persons	% of Total
Under $1,000	10,331	44%
$1,000 — $5,000	9,585	41%
$5,000 — $10,000	1,777	7%
$10,000 — $50,000	1,428	6%
$50,000 — $100,000	159	2%
$100,000 — $500,000	44	.2%
$500,000 — $1,000,000	1	.05%
Total	23,325	

NOTES: All county population as proportion of total state was 6%; enumerated as proportion of total county was 5 + %.

States and respective counties were:
Kentucky: Franklin; *Michigan*: Allegan, Barry, Berrien, Branch; *Pennsylvania*: Pike, Potter; *Rhode Island:* Bristol, Kent, Washington; *South Carolina:* Abbeville, Anderson, Barnwell, Beaufort, Charleston, Marion, Marlboro; *Louisiana:* East Felicianna, Plaquemines, Point Coupee, Rapides, Ouachitaffi; *Ohio:* Erie.

SOURCE: Compiled from Basic Data in DeBow, STATISTICAL VIEW, 191, 237, 243, 255, 285, 296, 302

VII.

Many foreign observers of American life in the pre-Civil War decades commented on its remarkable homogeneity and how it had been formed out of such diverse ethnic backgrounds. To be sure, to an outside observer the American scene appeared to lack the strict class lines of the Old Country. Moreover, the dynamic ethos of progress which Americans possessed in abundance tended to mask social and economic differences and to give the appearance of a society in which the ease of social and economic mobility and the uniformity of traditional values were more apparent than the differences. The dimension of diversity is surely one which needs more research, for scholars know little enough about it.

In regard to the level of living, it is quite clear that the diversities by region and income and social class were widespread, even though the average trend of the level of the living for the entire country was a rising one. There were differences in real per capita income, in the per head return on social assets, on the composition of consumer assets, and in diet, nutrition, food consumption and the like, that persisted in the United States before the Civil War. (Some of these differences, of course, are still with us.) It is not possible to explore in detail the sources or all the possibilities of these differences; rather, I can only hope to suggest a few cases.

Regional variations in real per capita income. Fortunately for the two decades before the war we have the personal income estimates of Richard Easterlin. His estimates are based on contemporary writers like Ezra Seaman, and they conform quite closely to an index of welfare with the components suggested earlier. Easterlin's data show that by per capita personal income in 1840 and 1860, the "richest" area of the country was the Northeast (Maine, Vermont, New Hampshire, Connecticut, Rhode Island, New York, Pennsylvania and New Jersey). The Northeastern states were followed by the South (Maryland, Delaware, West Virginia, Washington, D. C., Virginia, North Carolina, South Carolina, Georgia, Florida, Kentucky, Tennessee, Mississippi, and Alabama) and by the North Central States (Ohio, Indiana, Illinois, Michigan, Wisconsin, Missouri, Iowa, Minnesota, North Dakota, South Dakota, Nebraska, Kansas). What is more interesting is the proportion of each area in relation to the national average and the rate of change by area between 1840 and 1860. Taken as a percentage of total United States average, per capita personal income rose from 135% to 139% for the Northeast. In the North Central states there was no change between decades at 68%, and for the South there was a decline from 76% to 72% of the United States average. The Northeastern region thus shows a rising level of relative per capita income and the South a declining one. As Easterlin commented: "This conclusion implies a relative deterioration in the income position not only of the total Southern population but of the favored white population as well." [52] It should be remembered that this comparison is in *relative* and not *absolute* per capita income; most probably the absolute level of per

---

[52]Easterlin, in Seymour Harris (ed.), AMERICAN ECONOMIC HISTORY, 530.

capita income rose appreciably in the South during the two decades. Yet compared to overall income growth the area was lagging behind the other parts of the country. (See Table J).

While real per capita income in this instance is a fairly accurate approximation to variations in the level of living, any other ranking based on consumer and social asset formation and consumption of perishables per head tends to confirm the drift of Easterlin's findings. Indicators of investment per capita in social assets such as railroads, education and the like show New England, Middle Atlantic, and the North Central states outstripping the South.[53] In matters of health, for example, even aside from the crippling epidemics of cholera and yellow fever which invaded the southland with regularity between 1840 and 1860, crude death rates rose between 1850 and 1860 for most of the slaveholding South (specifically, Alabama, Florida, Louisiana, Mississippi, South Carolina, Tennessee, Texas, and Virginia), while they declined in nearly every other region.[54] Other assets of consumers and society — per head banking deposits and insurance holdings, housing and household durables — also compared unfavorably for the South.

Variations in the Level of Living by Social Classes. Within this broad pattern of regional income per head must also be added a word or two concerning social classes. Was the urban worker of New England as "well-off" as the urban or rural white wage earner of the South? of the West? Did the level of living of the slave population fall or rise between 1800 and 1860? Did the welfare of the free negro compare favorably with the free whites? One can only suggest certain possibilities to these questions for the research gap is enormous.

Slaves. In regard to the level of living of the slaves, one is faced with a morass of conflicting evidence. U. B. Phillips felt that the economic interest of the slaveholder demanded that he maintain slaves at some minimum level of living, and that this level did not materially change in the half-century before the war.[55] Kenneth Stampp and the work of Herbert Aptheker suggest that such a minimum level of living was not uniform and that it was well below what might be considered "biological subsist-

---

[53] See Kennedy, PRELIMINARY REPORT ON THE 8th CENSUS, 22-23; EIGHT CENSUS OF THE UNITED STATES, MORTALITY AND MISCELLANEOUS STATISTICS (1860), 502-504; DeBow, STATISTICAL VIEW, 152-153.

[54] EIGHT CENSUS OF THE UNITED STATES, MORTALITY AND MISCELLANEOUS STATISTICS, (1860), 503. Also see Mitchell, "Health and the Medical Profession in the Lower South, 1845-1860," in JOURNAL OF SOUTHERN HISTORY, X (November 1944), 427-429.

[55] see his LIFE AND LABOR IN THE OLD SOUTH (Boston: Little, Brown, 1929, 197).

TABLE J

REGIONAL TRENDS IN POPULATION AND PERSONAL INCOME, 1840 - 1860

Region	% Distribution of Total U.S. Pop.		% Distribution of Personal Income		Per Capita Personal Income as % of Total U.S. Average	
	1840	1860	1840	1860	1840	1860
United States	100%	100%	100%	100%	100%	100%
Northeast	43	36	58	50	135	139
New England	13	10	17	14	132	143
Mid. Atl.	30	26	41	36	136	137
North Central	20	29	13	20	68	68
ENC	17	22	12	15	67	69
WNC	2	7	2	4	75	66
South	37	33	14	9	76	72
S. Atl.	20	14	14	9	70	65
E. S. Cent.	15	13	11	9	73	68
W. S. C.	3	6	4	8	144	115
West	—	2	—	4	—	—

SOURCE: Richard Easterlin, "Regional Income Trends, 1840 - 1950," in AMERICAN ECONOMIC HISTORY, Seymour Harris (ed.) (New York: McGraw-Hill, 1961), 528, 535. Also see Easterlin, "Interregional Income Differences" in TRENDS IN THE AMERICAN ECONOMY, Appendix D, Tables D-1, D-2, pp. 36-137.

NOTES: *Northeast*: Maine, Vermont, New Hampshire, Massachusetts, Connecticut, Rhode Island (New England); New York, Pennsylvania, New Jersey (Middle Atlantic). *North Central*: Ohio, Indiana, Illinois, Michigan, Wisconsin (East North Central); Missouri, Iowa, Minnesota, North Dakota, South Dakota, Nebraska, Kansas (West NC). *South*: Maryland, Delaware, West Virginia, Washington, D. C., Virginia, North Carolina, South Carolina, Georgia, Florida (S. Atlantic); Kentucky, Tennessee, Mississippi, Alabama, (East S. Central); Oklahoma, Arkansas, Louisiana, Texas (West South Central). *West*: all others.

ence." Aptheker suggests that the level deteriorated as one approached 1860.[56] In relation to other classes of population in the South it is clear that the level of living of the slaves deteriorated relatively in the decades before the war, and that the existence of a much more highly stratified social structure in the south provided variations in living standards much greater than in other regions. As Harriet Martineau noted: "What is life in the slave states, in respect of work? There are two classes, the servile and the imperious, between whom there is a great gulf fixed." [57]

Free negroes. The free negroes, of whom there were nearly half a million in 1860, undoubtedly fared better than the slave population. But even their lot was below that of a free white and possibly even a free white non-slaveholder in the South. McMaster has chronicled the fate of the free negroes in the Middle Atlantic states during the 1820's, and comparison of other data on asset formation and income potential gives no cause to suspect that this level rose materially in the intervening decades.[58] A sampling of occupations listed for free negroes in 1850 for Connecticut, Louisiana, and New York shows that in both regions the overwhelming proportions of those free negroes holding jobs was in the categories of "general laborer," waiters, and "sweeps." [59]

Entrepreneurial class. The planter, the commercial farmer, the hotel-keeper, the merchant, and the industrial businessmen formed a class in American life clearly distinguished from all others. The ability to organize resources, to undertake risky ventures, and to make and respond to market opportunities was a classic feature of American life during the pre-war decades, and in a sense "every man was an entrepreneur."[60] But this is one area in which we know very little concerning variations in levels of living. For one thing, it is difficult to know even a little bit concerning

[56] Kenneth Stampp, THE PECULIAR INSTITUTION. (New York: Alfred A. Knopf, 1956), 280-281, 284-285; Herbert Aptheker, NEGRO SLAVE REVOLTS IN THE SOUTH, 1626-1860. (New York: International Publishers, 1939), 6-8, 54-59.

[57] Martineau, SOCIETY IN AMERICA, 217. In 1860, slaves comprised about 20% of the total population of the major cities of the South. Richard Wade has suggested that the level of living of the Urban slave was probably relatively and absolutely higher than that of the country slave. See his *Slavery in the Cities,* (Chicago: 1964), esp. Chapter 5.

[58] John Bach MacMaster, HISTORY OF THE PEOPLE OF THE UNITED STATES. 7 vols. (New York: Appleton and Sons, 1901), IV, 558-559; DeBow, STATISTICAL VIEW, 66-67, 80-81.

[59] Debow, STATISTICAL VIEW, 80-81. A touching account of a sensitive free negro girl and the difficulties of life she encountered is, THE JOURNAL OF CHARLOTTE L. FORTEN: A FREE NEGRO IN THE SLAVE ERA. Edited by Ray Billington (New York: Collier Books, 1961), esp. 82-101.

[60] The definitive work suggestive of many new lines of research on this topic is Arthur H. Cole, BUSINESS ENTERPRISE IN ITS SOCIAL SETTING. (Cambridge: Harvard University Press, 1959), esp. 6-7, 114-115.

variations in entrepreneurial income. One can only suggest certain broad extremes: the southern planter, on the average, undoubtedly had a higher level of living than most other entrepreneurial elements in the South, but he was probably not the equal of the successful New York and Boston merchants and industrialists.[61] Easterlin's calculations of property income per capita by region generally confirms this.[62] For generalization beyond this one needs to know much more about living habits, consumer behavior, and per capita variation in entrepreneurial income. This is an area which is begging for new and interpretative research.

Wage-earners. Variations in levels of living among and between different classes, skills, and regional locations of wage-earners is also a subject about which only a few broad generalizations can be made. One can only suggest that the differentials that existed, say as those evidenced by money wage rates, were based on relative skills, sex, the comparative organization of the labor market, and the relative state of development of a particular region.[63] As a gross generalization it might be argued that except for greater susceptibility to loss of employment because of the business cycle, the average urban common wage-earner was "better-off" by 1860 than his counterpart in rural areas. On the other hand, he was not as well off compared to skilled workman in any region of the country.[64] It is certain, however, that the lines of labor mobility between skills and regions, even in the South, was far greater by 1860 than at any other previous time. Indeed it was this very aspect which most foreign observers associated with higher levels of living for American workers.[65] But much more research is necessary on consumer asset formation by various types of wage-earners, on variations and similarities in other components of the level of living, and on the degree of social and economic mobility between skills. Similarly, work is also needed on the levels of living faced by immigrants.[66]

---

[61] See Alfred Conrad and John R. Meyer, "The Economics of Slavery in the Ante-Bellum South," in JOURNAL OF POLITICAL ECONOMY, LXVI (April, 1958), 95-122 and Appendixes. Anna Jacobson Schwartz, "Gross Dividend and Interest Payments by Corporations in the 19th Century," in TRENDS IN THE AMERICAN ECONOMY, 407-448.

[62] Easterlin, "Interregional Income Differences," in TRENDS IN THE AMERICAN ECONOMY, esp. 91.

[63] See Lebergott, "Wage Trends, 1800-1900," in TRENDS IN THE AMERICAN ECONOMY, 450-461.

[64] See John R. Commons, et. al, A HISTORY OF LABOUR IN THE UNITED STATES (New York: MacMillan Company, 1926), I, 155, 158-159, 170-171, 182, 303.

[65] See, for example, Chevalier, SOCIETY, MANNERS, AND POLITICS IN THE UNITED STATES, 267.

[66] Chevalier, SOCIETY, MANNERS AND POLITICS, 331, has an interesting discussion of an Irish immigrant as he fared in New York compared with the old country, circa 1837.

Oscar Handlin's work on the levels of living among New York City immigrants in the pre-war decades shows their greater susceptibility to unemployment, higher crude death rates than other white groups, and the restrictions on social and labor mobility faced by most immigrant groups, particularly those who were unskilled. This would suggest that the "level of living" for New York City immigrants, mainly the Irish, was probably only slightly above the "biological subsistence minimum." Even so, such immigrants were probably "better-off" than they had been in the old country.[66a]

International income comparisons. Against the broad variations in the level of living within the United States, it is quite clear that compared with other industrialized nations in the two decades before the Civil War the average American was much "better-off." Edgar Martin certainly concluded so, and nearly all foreign observers of American life made similar judgments.[67] Parallel evidence based on growth rates in real per capita income suggest the validity of this conclusion. Simon Kuznets' study of long-term growth rates projected back into the pre-war decades, show that real per capita output and income in the United States, certainly by 1860 and possibly earlier, must have exceeded the levels of other industrialized nations.[68] Ezra Seaman estimated domestic product per head in 1840 at $60 in the United States, at $47 (in terms of United States dollars) in France, $60 in Holland and Belgium, and $84 in England and Wales. As Gallman, who has worked with the Seaman data, has commented, "since the levels of living of the advanced nations of today are . . . the results of growth over the last 100 years, the United States of 1839 must have been, indeed, one of the wealthiest nations of the world."[69] Raymond Goldsmith has also concluded that possibly as early as 1830, but no later than 1860, income per head in the United States was already equal to that

---

[66a] See Oscar Handlin, *The Newcomers: Negroes and Puerto Ricans in a Changing Metropolis.* (New York: Doubleday Anchor Book, 1962) esp. 12-15.

[67] Martin, THE STANDARD OF LIVING IN 1860, 401. See, Chavalier, SOCIETY, MANNERS AND POLITICS IN THE UNITED STATES, 266-281 for a brilliant qualitative comparison of the economic welfare and outlook of the American with that of the European.

[68] Simon Kuznets, "Quantitative Aspects of the Economic Growth of Nations: Levels and Variabilities of Rates of Growth," I, ECONOMIC DEVELOPMENT AND CULTURAL CHANGE, (October, 1956), Sumner Slichter, ECONOMIC GROWTH IN THE UNITED STATES, 46-47, has taken Kuznets' data and projected it back to the time of Columbus and Charlemagne to suggest long-term growth rate possibilities. "An increase of only one-fourth of one percent a year would have meant that at about the time of Christ output per worker would have been only about $7.70 a year, and at about the time of Pericles only $3.60 a year."

[69] in ECONOMIC DEVELOPMENT AND CULTURAL CHANGE, 399. Seaman data quoted there also.

of Britain.[70] While one must take such income comparisons with care, it does seem that by 1860, per head of population, the American was "better-off" than his counterpart anywhere else in the industrialized world. Moreover, income per head at this time before the big push in industrialization shows that the United States as compared with underdeveloped countries of today started from a far better welfare position. This certainly suggests that one must be quite guarded in making comparisons (especially for policy purposes) of America as an underdeveloped nation and to those parts of the world today which have per capita income levels considerably less than what Americans had in the 1840's.

VIII.

This paper has dealt with only the broadest trends in levels of living in the United States. While there is some disagreement, the trend in the level of living in the United States appears to have increased, at least somewhat, between 1800 and 1840; after 1840 and for the next two decades the level of living appears to have increased at accelerating speeds. While there were variations in levels of living based on income class, social groups, or region, the nation as a whole, certainly by 1860, was the richest in the world. In the per head return of social assets, in the composition of common assets, and in the bundle of personnel consumption perishable goods and services, the average American of 1860 was "better off" than his counterpart in 1840, and that of 1840 "better-off" than the average American of 1800.

Appendix A

The relevance of Douglas North's support for the Martin position must be seriously questioned. It is not self-evident that a clear trend of output and income per capita over the course of four decades can be reversed by cyclical activity unless such business declines were unusually severe and long-lasting; then, of course, the use of the term cyclical, and not secular, decline becomes questionable. The *a priori* Kuznets case rests on (1) an estimated interindustry shift and (2) an increase in the labor force participation ratio. North's argument does not suggest that declines in the level of economic activity either reversed the interindustry shift or dampened the rising trend of the labor force participation ratio. Nor does North suggest another possible explanation in support of Martin's findings that declines in the level of economic activity resulted in a reduction in the trend rates of per worker productivity in manufacturing.

---

[70] HISTORICAL AND COMPARATIVE RATES OF PRODUCTION, 278-279. [Reprint in Part II].

Parker and Whartenby have suggested that a relatively small decrease in agricultural productivity from the constant or rising levels assumed by Kuznets, would be sufficient to "wipe-out" the projected 19% increase in product per worker in constant prices. Douglas North, however, seriously questions this possibility and calculates a decline in agricultural productivity of the magnitude of 50% to erase both the interindustry and labor force participation ratio shifts. This is undoubtedly correct.

None of these scholars, however, has suggested two other possibilities as a way of upsetting the Kuznets *a priori* case: constancy in the labor force participation ratio; a different population base. Even with no change in the labor force participation ratio of .29, assuming constant productivity, there still would have been an increase in worker product of about 9.2% as a result of interindustry shifts.[1] Similarly, taking as a population base "total residing in the United States" instead of "Total Continental United States," only alters the rise in the participation ratio slightly. Calculations with this population base are shown in Table I - A.

The rise in the participation ratio is about 1 1/2 percentage points smaller than that calculated by Kuznets; from .286 in 1800 to .310 in 1840, or a rise of about 8 3/4%. In constant prices, and assuming the same productivity relatives as Kuznets, and the same interindustry shift of workers, this change in the labor force participation ratio would yield an increase of about 12% in output per member of the total labor force. Instead of a 50% decrease in agricultural productivity necessary to wipe out the per worker gain in real output, with this small change in the participation ratio only a decline of about 1/5 would be required. William Parker's preliminary studies of agricultural productivity, however, show a rise in output per man hour in corn production of 18% between 1800 and 1840, and of 46 percent in cotton production for the same years. It would take a change of about one-tenth in the labor force participation ratio coupled with a decrease of about 1/5 to 1/4 in agricultural productivity before the Kuznets *a priori* case can be seriously questioned. A 10% drop in non-agricultural productivity, though unlikely, would be sufficient to reduce the product per member of the work force (with the Kuznets labor participation ratio of .29 and .32) to only an increase of about 9%; with the alternative ratio of Table I - A the increase would still be of about the same percentage magnitude. Towne and Rasmussen show a 10% decline in gross farm product (including improvements and home manufactures) per worker in agriculture in constant prices between 1800 and 1820, of about 8% between 1800 and 1830, and no decline as between 1800 and

---

[1] Slichter seemed to be suspicious about the magnitude of the rise in the labor force participation ratio calculated by Kuznets. He does not offer any alternatives, however. See, Slichter, ECONOMIC GROWTH IN THE UNITED STATES, 48 n9.

1820.[2] This would seem to rule out the possibility for finding productivity declines of the magnitude required to wipe out the Kuznets case.

A rather weak piece of inferential evidence which would tend to disqualify the Kuznets general case is Goldsmith's assertion; and that is all it is, that a growth rate of about 1/2 percent per annum in real per capita income was probably characteristic of the 50 year period prior to 1839. In a sense, this would lend credence to the fact that real per capita income could have fallen between 1800 and 1829. Trescott's calculations of subsidy and transfer payments, however, show substantial increases between 1800 and 1830, and this would probably diminish the importance of the Goldsmith point. (See Table II - A.)

TABLE I - A

Year	Total Population (Kuznets) 1.	Total Population (other) 2.	Gainfully Occupied (Kuznets) 3.	Labor Force Participation Ratio Kuznets 4.	Other 5.
1800	5,308 (Thous.)	5,297 (Thous.)	1,523 (Thous.)	0.29%	0.286%
1810	7,240	7,224	2,107	0.129	0.291
1820	9,638	9,618	2,881	0.30	0.309
1830	12,866	12,901	3,932	0.31	0.312
1840	17,069	17,120	5,420	0.32	0.310

SOURCE: 1, 3, 4, Kuznets, "National Income Estimates Prior to 1870," 225
2, HISTORICAL STATISTICS OF THE UNITED STATES, 7.

TABLE II - A

Per Capita Subsidy and Transfer Payments, 1800 - 1840

Year	Current Prices (1)	Constant Prices (2)
1800	$24 1/2	$13
1810	26	14 2/5
1820	44 1/2	27 4/5
1830	42	34
1840	25	21 4/5

(1) Computed from Basic Data in Trescott "United States Government and National Income, 1790-1860," in TRENDS IN THE AMERICAN ECONOMY DURING THE 19th CENTURY, 340.

(2) Hoover's CPI, 1851-59 base, was used to deflate money values. See Hoover, HISTORICAL AND COMPARATIVE RATES OF PRODUCTION, PRODUCTIVITY, AND PRICES, 397.

---

[2] Computed from Towne and Rasmussen "Farm Gross Product and Gross Investment," in TRENDS IN THE AMERICAN ECONOMY DURING THE 19th CENTURY, 266.

APPENDIX B

Lebergott's estimates of real wages for the period before 1850 were based on wholesale prices whereas retail prices would be a better approximation. Lebergott does suggest, however, that possibly as much as one-half of the worker's real income before 1840 was unaffected by market transactions. To the extent that this was true use of either wholesale or retail prices as the deflator of money wages would seriously overestimate declines in real wages and underestimate increases. In Table I - B, nevertheless, I have made adjustments in the point changes for retail prices based on Ethel Hoover's preliminary Consumers Price Index. The main modification which this shows is one of degree and magnitude: between 1800-1818 money wages fell faster than retail prices, while wholesale prices showed an appreciable increase. Thus the fall in real wages both for farm and non-farm, especially the latter, would tend to be somewhat overstated as to magnitude. Between 1818-1830 retail prices fell faster than wholesale prices and considerably faster and deeper than money wages for farm and non-farm workers. Thus the decline in real wages would again tend to be overestimated on the basis of wholesale prices. For 1830-1840 using retail prices makes no appreciable difference. These data should be appraised in connection with data in Table II - A of Appendix A.

TABLE I - B

TRENDS IN WAGES AND PRICES, 1800 - 1840
(percentage changes between dates)

Year	Money Wages		Prices	
	Non-Farm (1)	Farm	Wholesale (2)	Retail (3)
1800 - 1818	—10 to 20	— 5 to 10	+10 to 15	— 8
1818 - 1830	a	— 5 to 10	—40	—70
1830 - 1840	+10 to 20	+15 to 25	a	a

a   increase or decrease less than 5%

(1)   From Stanley Lebergott, "Wage Trends, 1800-1900," in TRENDS IN THE AMERICAN ECONOMY DURING THE NINETEENTH CENTURY, 493.

(2)   Warren and Pearson Index, from HISTORICAL STATISTICS OF THE UNITED STATES, 116.

(3)   Ethel Hoover, in Joint Economic Committee, HISTORICAL AND COMPARATIVE RATES OF PRODUCTION, PRODUCTIVITY, AND PRICES, 397. Hoover's index is based on retail prices.

ESTIMATES OF AMERICAN NATIONAL PRODUCT MADE BEFORE THE CIVIL WAR*

ROBERT E. GALLMAN†

The two decades before the Civil War were crucial in American economic development.[1] They call for intensive study. Yet the quantitative framework for economic investigations is inadequate. Students of the period have made some use of the modern estimates of pre-war national product, but these estimates are unreliable and incomplete.[2] On the other hand, the work of the pre-Civil War estimators has received very little attention. No one has published a complete account and appraisal of this work, and few have used it.[3] This is surprising, in view of the number of pre-war estimates that even a casual inspection suggests are promising. Tucker made two (1839, 1849), Burke, two (1847, 1848), and Seaman, four (two for 1839 and one for 1849 and 1859).[4] All rest, mainly, on

---

* Fittingly, Simon Kuznets drew these estimates to my attention.

† Robert E. Gallman is Professor of Economics at the University of North Carolina.

[1] For example, see W. W. Rostow, *The Stages of Economic Growth* (Cambridge, 1960), p. 38.

[2] See Simon Kuznets, "Long-Term Changes in the National Income of the United States of America Since 1870," in *Income and Wealth of the United States, Trends and Structure* (Baltimore, 1952), Appendix, pp. 221-241, and William N. Parker and Franklee Whartenby, "The Growth of Output Before 1840," in Conference on Research in Income and Wealth, *Trends in the American Economy in the Nineteenth Century* (Studies in Income and Wealth, Vol. XXIV) (Princeton, 1960). For reliable estimates of rates of change of G. N. P., 1839-1879, see the testimony of Raymond Goldsmith in United States Congress, Joint Economic Committee, *Employment, Growth, and Price Levels, Hearings* (86th Congress, 1st Session), Part II (Washington, 1959), p. 271, and Robert E. Gallman, "Commodity Output, 1839-1899," in Conference on Research in Income and Wealth, *op. cit.* The G. N. P. estimates underlying these rates have not been published.

[3] But see Parker and Whartenby, *op. cit.;* Gallman, *op. cit.;* Paul Studenski, *The Income of Nations* (New York, 1958), pp. 129-132; and Richard A. Easterlin, "Interregional Differences in Per Capita Income, Population, and Total Income, 1840-1950," in Conference on Research in Income and Wealth, *op. cit.*

[4] George Tucker, *Progress of the United States in Population and Wealth* (New York, 1855). (This essay was previously published in *Hunt's Merchant's Magazine*, IX (1843). Reports of the Commissioner of Patents (Edmund Burke), United States Congress, *H. R. Ex. Doc. 54* (30th Congress, 1st Session), pp. 558-561, and United States Congress, *H. R. Ex. Doc. 59* (30th Congress, 2nd Session), pp. 719-726. Ezra C. Seaman, *Essays on the Progress of Nations* (Detroit and New York, 1846); *Supplement No. I* (to the Essays . . .) (New York, 1847); *Supplement No. II* (New

census data which are quite good.[5] Seven are composed of net product estimates for industrial sectors and cover the commodity producing sectors, trade, transportation, finance (five), real estate (two), and the professions (two). (We will refer to these as "domestic product" estimates, although the term is not quite appropriate.) The eighth is a net national product estimate, built up from final product flows. In the main, the estimators described their techniques carefully and provided abundant details.

As part of a project directed toward the construction of new estimates we reviewed the work of these men, tested it, and concluded that it is valuable. This paper is concerned with the broad features of pre-war development which their estimates describe. We do not have the space to make a full defense of all of our appraisals of their findings, but these appraisals rest, in large measure, on work described in another paper.[6]

Seaman, an indefatigible quantitative worker, produced other estimates which should be noticed in passing. He worked out national income for 1866 from income tax data and gave the size distribution of income. The aggregate holds up under the limited testing we have given it.[7] He also published unsupported figures for domestic product for an unidentified year before 1800, 1847, and 1869. The last is probably quite accurate.[8] We will have occasion to refer, below, to both the 1866 and the 1869 estimates.

Domestic Product

Seaman and Tucker began with census data and worked toward sector net products. They intended to make unduplicated aggregates and very nearly succeeded. When minor conceptual differences are resolved and

---

York and Detroit, 1848); Second Edition (New York, 1852); *The American System of Government* (New York, 1870). The present paper depends mainly on the 1852 edition of the *Essays* . . . and *The American System of Government*. See, also, the Report of Secretary of the Treasury R. J. Walker, United States Congress, *Sen. Doc. 444* (29th Congress, 1st Session), p. 39.

[5] Gallman, *op. cit.*

[6] *Ibid.*

[7] Extrapolating the estimate to 1869 on Frickey's production index (Edwin Frickey, *Production in the United States, 1860-1914* [Cambridge, Mass., 1947], p. 127) and the Warren and Pearson "all commodities" wholesale price index (*Historical Statistics* [1960], Series E-1) yields a result almost identical to Kuznets' Variant I net national product estimate and slightly below the Variant III estimate (Simon Kuznets, *Capital in the American Economy: Its Formation and Financing,* to be published). Substituting general or consumer price indexes for the Warren and Pearson index (*Historical Statistics* [1949], Series L-1 and [1960], Series E-148, 157, 158) produces results which fall within ten percent of Kuznets' estimates.

[8] See footnote 11.

one or two obvious errors are corrected (Table 1, Panel B) there remain three important differences between the two: Tucker's figures for farm prices and the value of animal products are higher than Seaman's, while Seaman's service estimates are higher than Tucker's. Seaman's price data and service estimates are far better than Tucker's, but his animal products estimates are not.[9] His figures for services may also be too low (see below). Were we to correct these components, the new Seaman aggregates would lie between the limits set by the Seaman and Tucker estimates in Panels B and C of Table 1, and nearer the upper limits. They would also be quite accurate.

Burke extrapolated the 1839 census returns to 1847 and 1848. Most of the important agricultural extrapolations are sound.[10] His agricultural prices are supposed to be from New York, but, in fact, are roughly consistent with Seaman's average prices on farms. The estimates for manufacturing are probably low; for services, low by Seaman's standards and high by Tucker's; for animal products, low by Tucker's standards and high by Seaman's. In their original form they involve much double counting, all of which is eliminated from the figures in Panel B of Table 1.

With this background, we can try to place the level of pre-war product in a broad comparative framework. In prices of 1879, domestic product per head in 1839 ran between $70 and $80 (Panel C, Table 1). Domestic product, as defined by Seaman and Tucker, apparently accounted for between 85% and 95% of net national product, in current prices.[11] Assuming the same relationship between constant price magnitudes, net national product per head in 1879 prices ran between $75 and $95. Such evidence as we have suggests that constant price domestic product might have accounted for a smaller share of national product than we have assumed and that, therefore, our estimates of national product per head are conservative.[12] In any case, they are about half the value of Kuznets' current price estimate for the decade 1874-1883.[13] Kuznets' constant price estimate for the same decade runs about 30% of his constant price estimate for 1950-54. Consequently, per capita product in 1839 must have been

---

[9] Gallman, *op. cit.* See, also, the discussion of the service estimates.

[10] Gallman, "A Note on the Patent Office Crop Estimates of the 1840's," manuscript.

[11] Based on comparisons of Seaman's domestic product estimates for 1839 and 1869 with national income or net national product taken from Kuznets or derived from Seaman's work (see footnote 7 and Table 5).

[12] See footnote 43.

[13] Simon Kuznets, "Quantitative Aspects of the Economic Growth of Nations," Part I, *Economic Development and Cultural Change*, V, 1 (1956), 82 — net national product divided by population. The results described in this paragraph would have been about the same had we used Kuznets' annual estimates for 1879 and one of the years of the early 1950's (*Capital in the American Economy . . . , op. cit.*).

between one-sixth and one-seventh (and nearer one-sixth, for reasons given above) of per capita product 110 years later. Now according to Kuznets, about two-thirds of the world's population lived, in 1949, in regions where per capita product was considerably less than one-seventh of the United States level.[14] The results of comparisons such as these are subject to familiar qualifications. Nonetheless, it is quite clear that the United States was not a poor country in 1839, even by modern standards.

Table 1. *Domestic Product in the United States, 1839-1859*

Panel A: Original Estimates, Current Prices (mil. $)[a]

	1839	1847	1848	1849	1859
Tucker	1,063			1,986	
Burke		1,739	2,049		
Seaman	1,040			1,485	2,630

Panel B: Adjusted Estimates, Current Prices (mil. $)[b]

	1839	1847	1848	1849	1859
Tucker	1,067			1,835	
Burke		1,497	1,557		
Seaman	995			1,514	2,705

Panel C: Adjusted Estimates, 1879 Prices (mil. $)[c]

	1839	1847	1848	1849	1859
Tucker	1,389			2,141	
Burke		1,701	1,852		
Seaman	1,222			1,750	2,768

Panel D: Adjusted Estimates, 1879 Prices, Per Capita ($)[d]

	1839	1847	1848	1849	1859
Tucker	81			92	
Burke		77	82		
Seaman	72			76	88

a. Tucker, *Progress of the United States . . .* , *op. cit.*, p. 195 and App., p. 66. Burke, 30th Congress, 1st Session, *H. R. Ex. Doc. 54*, p. 561, and 30th Congress, 2nd Session, *H. R. Ex. Doc. 59*, p. 726. Seaman, *American System of Government, op. cit.*, p. 229. The 1849 estimate is corrected for what is apparently an error in the transcription of the agricultural estimate. See Seaman, *Essays . . .* , *op. cit.*, 1852 ed., pp. 626, 628.The years are census years (e.g., June 1, 1839-May 31, 1840). (For fuller citation of these sources, see footnote 4.)

b. Estimates of Panel A adjusted to achieve, so far as possible, conceptual comparability among the estimates of different workers and comparability of both concept and technique among and within the estimates of individual workers. Items included in most estimates were added to those estimates from which they were missing. Items missing from most estimates were eliminated from those in which they were included. Thus estimates for all service sectors, other than trade, transportation, and finance, are omitted from Panel B. All estimates are gross of depreciation. Tucker's obviously erroneous ratio of value added to value of output for industry was corrected. Further details will be supplied by the author on request.

c. Estimates of Panel B deflated, by sectors, by use of the price indexes in Gallman, "Commodity Output . . ." *op cit.* and the various Warren and Pearson indexes in

[14] Kuznets, "Quantitative Aspects. . . ," *op. cit.*, pp. 17, 24.

Since the levels of living of the advanced nations today are, in large measure, the results of growth over the last 100 years, the United States of 1839 must have been, indeed, one of the wealthiest nations of the world. Seaman recognized this. He estimated that domestic product per head around 1840 (United States dollars) came to $47 in France, $60 in Holland and Belgium, $84 in England and Wales, and about $60 in the United States.[15] He gave details which show that the foreign estimates are conceptually the same as the American estimate. The foreign data were not complete and Seaman had to piece them out with inferences from the American data. Still, Seaman's evidence may have some value, at least for establishing relative levels of product per head around 1840. For example, Seaman made his French estimate by weighting outputs with American prices. According to Gilbert, French product per head, weighted with American prices, came to about 55% of American product per head in both 1950 and 1955.[16] Apparently, French real product per head around 1840 was something under one-quarter real product per head in 1949-53.[17] We can infer, then, that French real product per head around 1840 amounted to about one-eighth of American real product per head in the early 1950's, or roughly 20% less than American real product per head in 1839. This is the relationship Seaman shows between per capita products in current prices. Perhaps this is no more than an interesting coincidence. But there is a presumption that Seaman's foreign estimates bear further investigation.

We turn next to rates of change calculated from Seaman's and Tucker's work (Table 2). These rates have to be handled very carefully. They were calculated from data referring to single years which may be affected by transient phenomena. Several shortcomings of the estimates (e. g., the deflation of the service sectors) which were of little consequence to the results of the preceding analysis have more importance here.

Historical Statistics (1960), p. 115. The Warren and Pearson indexes were used mainly as extrapolators. However, the service sectors (mainly trade) were deflated by the Warren and Pearson "all commodities index," shifted to the base 1879 (census year). The weights of this index represent "the importance of the priced commodities in the total trade of the United States," *ibid.*, p. 103.

d. Estimates of Panel C divided by population figures in Table A-20, *Historical Statistics* (1960), p. 8. Population figures for 1847 and 1848 were derived by interpolating figures in Table A-20 on data in Table A-1, p. 7.

[15] *Supplement II, op. cit.*, p. 124, and *Essays . . .* (1852), *op. cit.*, pp. 445 and 462. See, also, Table 1.

[16] Milton Gilbert and Associates, *Comparative National Products and Price Levels* (Paris, 1958), p. 23.

[17] Kuznets, "Quantitative Aspects. . . ," *op. cit.*, p. 59 — mean of the annual average of 1831-40 and 1841-50 taken to stand for 1840.

Table 2. *Rates of Change of Domestic Product and Domestic Product per Capita, United States, 1839-1859, Adjusted Estimates in Prices of 1879*[a]

	Domestic Product		Domestic Product per Capita	
	1839-1849	1849-1859	1839-1849	1849-1859
Tucker	54%	——	13.4%	——
Seaman	43%	58%	5.4%	16.6%

a. Calculated from data in Table 1, Panels C and D.

The transient factors affecting the data are these: 1839 and 1860 were at business cycle peaks, while 1848 and 1858 were at troughs.[18] But the peaks (especially the former) were probably not high. Both followed major peaks (1836, 1856), which were at the summits of long upswings.[19] Both were weakened by long downswings from these summits. On balance, the rates of change shown in Table 2 are probably not unduly distorted by the effects of transient phenomena.

The rates of change calculated from the Seaman and Tucker series are quite far apart, but this fact is unimportant when the rates are set against the background of subsequent American experience. Since the Seaman and Tucker estimates cover most of net national product, rates calculated from them probably reflect, fairly accurately, the growth of net national product. According to Kuznets, net national product increased by about 55% per decade, between 1869 and 1908, and under 30% per decade, during the 20th century. Decade rates ranged between 35% and 88%, in the earlier period, and 4% and 50%, in the later.[20] The pace of development before the war, then, was apparently as rapid as after it, and more rapid than during the 20th century. The rates of growth before the war and in the three decades before 1900 are among the highest on record.[21] On the other hand, the pre-war rates of change of product per capita are lower than most of the post-war 19th century rates and do not even reach the levels of the highest 20th century rates. Records of other countries show frequent examples of higher rates.[22] Allowing reasonable margins for error in the pre-war estimates, these findings seem quite firm. Appending Seaman's and Tucker's evidence to Kuznets', then, we get a picture of a country in which population and aggregate product grew at excep-

---

[18] *Historical Statistics* (1949), p. 320.

[19] *Ibid.*, and *Thirty-ninth Annual Report, National Bureau of Economic Research* (New York, 1959), p. 25.

[20] Kuznets, "Quantitative Aspects . . . ," *op. cit.*, pp. 40, 84.

[21] *Ibid.*, pp. 10, 13, 38-40.

[22] *Ibid.*

tionally high rates, over the 19th century, and in which the rate of advance of product per head rose from initially moderate levels.

Table 3 contains sector distributions of domestic product. The fishing, forest, manufacturing, mining, and construction sectors are joined together because we cannot separate them without doing violence to the estimates, although it would be desirable to group the first two with agriculture. In any case, the fishing and forest industries were of relatively minor significance, throughout.

Comparing Panels A and B one can see that the adjustments we made to the series changed the sector distributions very little. Deflation also had little effect. One fact stands out clearly, whether one looks at Panel A, Panel B, or Panel C, the work of Seaman, Tucker, or Burke. The share of agriculture is very large when compared with the shares of the other sectors. It is also very large when compared with the shares of agriculture in the products of all but the poorest countries of the world today.[23] But we know that the United States was relatively rich, at this time. These findings dramatize the familiar fact that cross section data and historical data are imperfect substitutes for one another in the study of development. The United States began the process of industrialization when far richer than the nonindustrialized nations of the world today.[24]

Seaman's and Tucker's series clearly show a process of industrialization. In the Seaman adjusted current price series the share of agriculture falls by a fifth, between 1839 and 1859, while the share of industry increases by half. But the current price data understate the real change. Seaman and Tucker both weighted agricultural output in 1839 with prices for the early 1840's, while they used 1839 prices, in the main, to weight the other sectors. Prices fell sharply after 1839. Consequently, the current price data for that year understate the importance of agriculture. In deflating, we corrected for this, as well as for the effects of changes in relative prices from one year to the next. The constant price data, therefore, show a more pronounced structural shift, the share of agriculture falling by one-third, between 1839 and 1859, and the share of industry doubling. According to Seaman, these structural changes took place mainly between 1839 and 1849. Interestingly, Seaman's series implies a lower rate of change of domestic product per capita during this decade than during the one that follows (Table 2), a finding which is not entirely surprising.[25] But the data are not free of the effects of transient phenomena and they are not so

---

[23] Simon Kuznets, "Quantitative Aspects of the Economic Growth of Nations," Part II, *Economic Development and Cultural Change,* Supplement to V, 4 (1957), 8, 10, 62-65.

[24] Kuznets comes to the same conclusion. "Quantitative Aspects. . . ," Part I, *op. cit.,* p. 25.

strong that we can place heavy reliance on either the timing of structural changes which they describe or on the relative sizes of the rates of change of the two decades.

The shares of product the three estimators attribute to services are not at all alike. Burke and Tucker may have intended to count only the returns to property. In any case, their estimates were made from capital stock figures and estimated rates of return. But Seaman's method was far more elaborate. He made a detailed estimate for trade and transportation in 1839 and then carried it forward at rates derived from various series reflecting changes in internal and foreign commerce. Apparently the extrapolation made no allowance for changing transportation rates or distribution margins. The finance estimates were added in the last revision and no explanation of the concept, data, and estimating techniques involved was offered. But the trade and transportation estimates were the important ones and the work for 1839 demands careful consideration.

Seaman estimated value added by trade and transportation in two ways. First, he traced flows of goods through distribution and multiplied the values of flows by markups. He added estimates for value added by transportation, presumably based on data salted throughout his book, and subtracted depreciation. Second, he took the capital and employment returns for these sectors from the census, corrected them, and applied estimated rates of return and compensation. The two procedures led to identical results.[26]

The first technique is similar to one used by Barger to get value added by distribution from 1869 to the present and, consequently, we can test part of Seaman's work against Barger's.[27] As noted earlier, Seaman estimated domestic product for 1869, although he gave no sector details. Barger's figure for value added by distribution is equal to about 25% of the value of that estimate.[28] Apparently the trade sector did not account for an unusually large share of product in 1869, since Barger's series represents a gently rising share of the value of commodity output plus

---

[25] See Phyllis Deane's findings with respect to British industrialization. "The Industrial Revolution and Economic Growth: The Evidence of Early British National Income Estimates," *Economic Development and Cultural Change*, V, 2 (1957), 167. But the circumstances surrounding British and American industrialization were so different that Miss Deane's evidence may not be relevant to the American case. See, also, Rostow, *op. cit.*, p. 40.

[26] Seaman, *Essays . . .* (1852), *op. cit.*, pp. 458-9.

[27] Harold Barger, *Distribution's Place in the American Economy since 1869* (Princeton, 1955).

[28] *Ibid.*, p. 70, and Seaman, *The American System of Government*, *op. cit.*, p. 229 — domestic product in gold prices multiplied by Seaman's currency price of gold, p. 230.

Table 3. *Shares of Industrial Sectors in American Domestic Product,*
1839–1859ᵃ

Panel A: Original Estimates in Current Prices

	1839		1847	1848	1849		1859
	Seaman	Tucker	Burke	Burke	Seaman	Tucker	Seaman
Agriculture	56%	62%	68%	73%	46%	59%	48%
Industryᵇ	26	29	22	19	34	33	32
Servicesᶜ	18	9	10	8	20	8	20

Panel B: Adjusted Estimates in Current Prices

Agriculture	57%	70%	59%	60%	47%	62%	46%
Industryᵇ	22	21	26	25	32	27	33
Servicesᶜ	21	9	15	15	21	11	21

Panel C: Adjusted Estimates in 1879 Prices

Agriculture	67%	80%	63%	65%	48%	65%	45%
Industryᵇ	17	14	22	20	31	26	35
Servicesᶜ	16	6	15	15	21	9	20

ᵃ· See source notes to Table 1.

ᵇ· Manufacturing, mining, construction, fishing, and forest industries (less firewood which is included with agriculture).

ᶜ· Trade, transportation, and finance.

value added by trade to the end of the century.[29] Now in 1839, according to Seaman, the share of internal trade in domestic product ran to only 12% or 13%.

The level of value added by trade depends upon the value of goods traded, the trade markups, and the composition of the value of goods traded (since this determines the weights given the various markups). The *share* of value added by trade in domestic product depends upon the last two factors and upon the *share* in domestic product of the value of goods traded. Now Seaman's flow estimate (value of goods traded) runs something over half the value of his domestic product estimate, in 1839, while Barger's flow estimate is something under half the value of Seaman's domestic product estimate for 1869.[30] These relationships fall roughly into line with what the subsequent historical record shows. That is, Barger's flow estimates (current prices) probably account for roughly half of domestic product (Seaman concept) from 1869 to at least 1919, with the share declining slightly, over time.[31] More important, for present purposes, the findings indicate that the sharp increase in the relative importance of

---

[29] Barger, *op. cit.,* p. 38.

[30] *Ibid.,* p. 70, "amount sold through retail stores," and Seaman, *The American System of Government, op. cit.*

[31] Compare Barger, *op. cit.,* "amount sold through retail stores," (p. 70) with the sum of value added by distribution (p. 70, lines 3, 7, 9) and the value of commodity

trade between 1839 and 1869, shown by the Seaman and Barger estimates, is not due to a relatively rapid advance in the value of goods through distribution. And apparently it is the former factor which is the more important. Weighting Seaman's flows with Barger's markups yields a value added estimate, for 1839, which runs just under 22% of domestic product, a percentage only slightly lower than the one calculated for 1869 from Barger's trade estimate and Seaman's domestic product figure.

Barger has found that markups have risen gradually over the long run, so that the fact of a rise between 1839 and 1869 is not inconsistent with the long term record which we already have. But the magnitude of the rise does not fit in with Barger's evidence for the period after 1869. If we extrapolate Barger's markups to 1839 and use them to weight Seaman's flows we get a value added estimate which is almost half again as large as Seaman's.

Why were Seaman's markups so low? We have been treating Seaman's estimate for internal trade as a gross value added estimate, which would seem to be justified by Seaman's use of the device of the markup. But this interpretation requires that we assume that wealth income, on the other side of the accounts, is gross of various payments out of the sector (e. g. , expenditures for rents, interest, supplies, etc.). It may be, however, that Seaman was attempting to estimate income originating and that his markups were put at levels which would lead to an estimate consistent with that based on the labor and capital figures; i. e. , that the markups are net of various expenses which do not enter into income originating. He did not have to do this to reach an unduplicated aggregate for all sectors. The expenses in question would be, mainly, payments to sectors omitted from Seaman's aggregate. But Seaman may not have recognized this, or (more likely) he may not have appreciated the distinction between gross value added and income originating. In any case, it is interesting that Barger's estimate of net income originating in trade for 1869 runs just under 11% of Seaman's domestic product estimate.[32] Seaman's figures for trade, which, we have seen, accounts for 12% or 13% of domestic product in 1839, is gross of depreciation. The form of Seaman's service estimate makes it impossible to allocate depreciation for the service sector between trade and nontrade components. But it is unlikely that the deduction of depreciation would reduce the share of the trade sector in domestic product to less than 11%.[33] Interpreted as an income originating estimate, then, Seaman's figure gives the trade sector about the same relative importance, in 1839,

output, William Howard Shaw, *Value of Commodity Output since 1869* (New York, 1947), pp. 62-65.

[32] Historical Statistics (1960), Series T-1, 2, and Seaman, *The American System of Government, op. cit.*

[33] Seaman, *Essays* . . . (1852), *op. cit.,* pp. 458-9.

as it enjoyed in 1869. Interpreted as a gross value added estimate, it pictures trade as relatively less important in 1839 than after the war, as noted above. However, as we have seen, if the 1839 estimate does represent gross value added, it is surely too low. The evidence suggests that if the share of the trade sector in domestic product did increase after 1839, the increase was moderate. The major component of the service sector is understated, then, relative to the commodity sector estimates, which are reasonably accurate statements of gross value added.[34] If the other service components are understated to about the same degree, the share of the service sector in domestic product in 1839 (current prices) probably amounted to nearer 30%, than to the 20% or so given by Seaman (Table 3, Panels A and B). If the service shares in Table 3 are too low, the shares of the other sectors are too high. Nonetheless, the broad conclusions reached above, with respect to the other sectors, remains secure.

The deflator for the service sector leaves something to be desired. At best, it represents only trade. The prices of services rendered are represented by the prices of goods sold. A rise in markups is always interpreted as a rise in product, therefore. Furthermore, the weighting scheme produced may not be appropriate, since no account is taken of the fact that markups differ from one line of goods to another. For these reasons, the constant price data add little to what the current price data have to show us.

National Product

We turn now to Seaman's estimates from the final product side for 1839. We begin with the component for which Seaman gives the clearest and most detailed information, the value of commodities flowing to consumers.

As in the case of the domestic product estimate the basic source of data available to Seaman was the census. But census data were manipulated in different ways and different gaps in census coverage had to be filled. One finds that the two sides of the accounts are not entirely consistent. For example, it is possible that Seaman intended to estimate the average annual flow over the three years centered on 1840, rather than the flow for 1839.[35] Each side includes some items apparently left off the other. Not all of value added by internal trade is accounted for in the flow of goods to consumers. But these inconsistencies are not of a very serious

---

[34] But see the discussion at the beginning of this section relative to Seaman's agricultural estimates.

[35] Seaman, *Essays* . . . (1852), *op. cit.,* pp. 279, 280, 284. But see, also, pp. 275, 277, 278. Prices used to weight agricultural commodities are again averages for the early years of the 1840's.

nature. Were they all rectified the broad picture of the level and sector division of domestic product, sketched in the preceding section, would remain unchanged. We can concentrate here on the composition of the flow of commodities. Adjustments to the estimates which seem called for can be taken up below.

Table 4, Panel A, contains statements of the composition of the value of the flow of commodities into consumption in 1839, 1869, 1879, and 1899. The first statement is based on the work of Seaman, of course; the last three, on the work of Shaw (see the notes to the table). Shaw's classification is followed, with certain concessions to Seaman. Several items of consumption had to be left out of the table to make the estimates of Seaman and Shaw comparable. Firewood, accounting for about 5% of the value of all commodities flowing into consumption in 1839, is the most important perishable missing. The durables omitted accounted for about half the value of that class of commodities flowing into consumption, and about 5% of the value of all commodities flowing into consumption in 1899. So far as possible, Seaman's estimates have been expressed in producers' prices or prices at port of entry, to make them comparable to Shaw's. However, several of the items in the food and kindred products class are valued in consumers' prices.

According to the data of Panel A the shares of perishables, semi-durables, and durables in the value of commodities flowing into consumption changed very little over the period 1839-1899. The composition of semi-durables changed somewhat, the share of shoes rising and the share of dry goods etc. falling. Within the perishables group there were moderate shifts in the relative importance of the various items represented, all of which seem plausible enough. Were distribution entirely eliminated from the 1839 estimate and were firewood added to all of the fuel and lighting estimates it seems fairly certain that we would have a picture of even greater stability of the structure of the perishables class. These adjustments cannot be made. However, there are more important adjustments which seem called for and which can be made.

Seaman's estimate of the value of animal products is consistent with his estimate on the domestic product side, and we have already seen that that is too low. Seaman also probably misinterpreted the census leather returns and made an estimate of the value of shoes which is too low.[36] The error is quite minor, when one is concerned with the aggregate flow of commodities, but it does distort the composition of the semi-durable class. Furthermore, Shaw's estimates of the value of animal products for 1869, 1879, and 1889 are also too low.[37] The error in 1869 is fairly serious, in

---

[36] Gallman, "Commodity Output . . . ," *op. cit.*
[37] *Ibid.*

1879 less serious, and 1889 not at all serious. Finally, the data of Panel A rest on current price estimates. More interesting would be distributions resting on constant price estimates.

Panel B contains distributions of value among the major components of the flow of commodities, adjusted (crudely, it should be noted) for the underestimates noted above, while Panel C contains distributions of constant price estimates. The picture which emerges from Panel C is one of a long term, moderate decline in the relative importance of perishables as against semi-durables. This decline might have been even more moderate if we had been able to include some of the minor components of the perishables class in Panel C and if we had been able to eliminate the value of all distribution from the estimates underlying the figures for 1839. Within the semi-durables class there is long term structural stability.

The data of Table 4 have to do with the product of farms and business enterprises, less exports and plus imports.[38] In 1839 home production must have been an important contributor to commodity output and between 1839 and 1899 the importance of this sector must have declined. How far would the findings of Table 4 be modified were we to include in our measures the product of home manufacturing? The question cannot be answered with complete satisfaction. However, Seaman does have estimates of value added to the production of textiles and clothing by home manufacturing and we can see, therefore, how far the composition of the flow of commodities in 1839 is altered when we include in our product measure the home manufacturing of textile products. No doubt the importance of home manufacturing to the output of textile products was greater than to any other broad class of production, in 1839. A substantial amount of cloth production and most clothing production must have gone on in the home. Furthermore, the ratio of value added by cloth and clothing production to the value of output of cloth and clothing is very large, whereas, for example, the ratio of value added by food processing (another important home industry) to the value of output of food is generally quite low. In any case, if we add Seaman's estimate (deflated) to the data underlying the 1839 figures in Panel C and calculate new percentages we find that the share of perishables in the aggregate comes to 67%, while the share of semi-durables amounts to 33%. Within the semi-durables group dry goods etc. accounts for 82% of the total while shoes accounts for 18%. That is, the composition of the flow is altered markedly and becomes roughly the same as the composition of the flow in 1899, a year when home manufacturing must have been a far less important source of commodity production. Presumably, then, a considerable part of the limited

---

[38] Shaw, *op. cit.,* pp. 80, 101-104. Some of Seaman's estimates may include value added by home manufacturing.

Table 4. *Composition of the Value of Commodities Flowing into
Consumption, United States, 1839–1899*[a]
(percent)

Panel A: Original Estimates in Current Prices

		1839	1869	1878	1889	1899
1.	*Perishable*	67	66	68	68	69
	(a) Food and Kindred Products	92	87	84	83	83
	(b) Tobacco Products	2	5	6	7	7
	(c) Soap	2	1[b]	1[b]	1[b]	1[b]
	(d) Magazines, Books, etc.	1	3	4	4	4
	(e) Fuel and Lighting (less firewood)	3	5	5	5	5
	(f) Totals	100	100	100	100	100
2.	*Semi-Durables*	31	29	29	27	27
	(a) Dry Goods, Notions, Clothing, Home Furnishings	87[c]	73[d]	79[d]	80[d]	80[d]
	(b) Shoes	13	27	21	20	20
	(c) Totals	100	100	100	100	100
3.	*Durables* - Furniture, Appliances and Utensils	2	4[e]	4[e]	4[e]	4[e]
4.	*Totals*	100	99	101	99	100

Panel B: Adjusted Estimates in Current Prices

		1839	1869	1878	1889	1899
1.	*Perishables* - Food and Kindred Products	69	76	70	67	68
2.	*Semi-Durables*	31	24	31	33	32
	(a) Dry Goods, etc.	84[c]	73[d]	79[d]	80[d]	80[d]
	(b) Shoes	16	27	31	20	20
3.	*Totals*	100	100	100	100	100

Panel C: Adjusted Estimates in Prices of 1879

		1839	1869	1878	1889	1899
1.	*Perishables* - Food and Kindred Products	73	74	70	66	68
2.	*Semi-Durables*	27	26	31	34	34
	(a) Dry Goods, etc.	77[c]	68[d]	79[d]	78[d]	79[d]
	(b) Shoes	23	32	21	22	21
	(c) Totals	100	100	100	100	100
3.	*Totals*	100	100	101	100	100

a. Panel A: Derived from William Howard Shaw, *Value of Commodity Output since 1869* (New York, 1947), pp. 30-43, and Seaman, *Progress of Nations . . .* (1852), *op. cit.*, pp. 274-284. Panel B: Derived from data underlying Panel A, adjusted by use of data in Gallman, "Commodity Output" . . . ," *op. cit.*, Panel C: Derived from data underlying Panel B deflated by use of price indexes E-3, 4, and 5, *Historical Statistics* (1960).

b. Production.

c. Textiles, clothing (except shoes), hats, rugs and carpets.

d. Shaw's items 6, 7, 9, 14a, 14b.

e. Shaw's items 12, 13a, 15.

structural change over time shown in Panel C must reflect changes in the units of organization of production, rather than changes in the composition of the value of commodities flowing into consumption.

These findings are not totally unexpected. We have been dealing with fairly broad groupings, representing (mainly) food, on the one hand, and clothing, on the other. We know that the United States was already quite rich, by 1839. One would not expect a comprehensive measure to show major shifts between these broad classes, then. However, within these groups there were, no doubt, some important compositional changes. Preliminary work suggests that the share of meat products in food and kindred products (current prices, adjusted estimate) declined from 1839 to 1899, while the shares of dairy products and eggs and (less certain) fruits and vegetables increased. But comparisons of Shaw's and Seaman's work below the minor group level are not easily and simply carried out and they are best left to another occasion.

In the 1852 edition (page 284) Seaman follows his consumption and capital accumulation estimates with the statement:

> Almost all industry is in some sense productive; but none is generally ranked by political economists as productive, however useful it may be, except such as produces material products, or adds value to them by transportation, and sale, which is a sort of quasi-productive industry. Hence we exclude from the rank of productive industry, housekeeping, the labor of domestic servants, all professional business, teaching of all kinds, all matters of pleasure and amusement, official labor, military service, and the administration of justice.

He goes on to say, however, that the value of these services probably amounted to between $150-200 million. Presumably this estimate includes the value of housewives' services and excludes rents of residences. The manner in which it was made, the fact that no data were elicited to support it, and the fact that it figures not at all in subsequent analysis in the book suggests that it was more offhand than any other estimate Seaman made.

In the 1846 edition (page 305) Seaman makes a similar estimate, but covering a somewhat different assortment of services. In the body of his estimates he places the value of rents of residences (including imputed rents, apparently) at about $90 million. He goes on to say that the value of ". . . ordinary domestic labour, medical and other professional services, education, religious instruction, books, newspapers, amusements, and . . . the expenses of government and the administration of justice . . ." ran around $21 per head, apparently of the free population and house servants. Seaman rounds the number of this population to 15 million, which would bring the service estimate to $315 million. Deducting the value of books and newspapers, given in the 1852 edition (page 282), leaves $310 million for services, other than the services of residences, and $400 million for all services. Apparently the value of housewives' services is not included. What made Seaman increase the coverage and reduce the value of his estimate between 1846 and 1852 is not known.

There is a check on part of the estimate. In the 1852 edition Seaman put down the value of residences (including yards, trees, and outhouses) at about $1 billion, which means that the rents of residences ran 9% of their value. According to Kuznets, rents ran between 9% and 14% of the value of residential property and averaged about 10%, during the latter part of the 19th century and the early decades of the 20th.[39] There was no long term tendency for the ratio to rise or fall. If one can extrapolate Kuznets' work, Seaman's estimates of the value of property and the value of rents are at least consistent with one another. Kuznets' work also shows that rents amounted to about half the value of services and that there was no strong tendency for this relationship to change before the First World War.[40] Extrapolating from Kuznets again, the value of services other than the services of dwellings should have amounted to roughly $90 million, in 1839. This, of course, is far below either of Seaman's estimates, but in view of the fact that the estimate published in 1852 includes the value of the services of housewives, while the extrapolation does not, the discrepancy between the figures may be entirely reasonable.[41] To take some liberties with Seaman, we might set his estimates of the value of services (less housewives' services) at $180-400 million. The question whether the range between these figures is so wide as to foreclose the possibility of meaningful conclusions regarding services can be deferred until the estimates are set within the context of national product.

The census of 1839 returned capital invested in various economic sectors and Seaman applied estimated rates of change to derive average annual net investment for the years 1839-1841. He made no real attempt to defend the estimated rates. The basic stock figures must be regarded, *a priori*, as of dubious quality, since the census organization apparently made no effort to define the term "capital." In places Seaman seems to view the figures as returns of fixed capital, whereas in other places he seems to believe that they include inventories. It is fairly clear, however, that the returns for trade must have included inventories and Seaman was surely aware of this.[42] He also explicitly included changes in the value of animal inventories in his net investment figures.

---

[39] Simon Kuznets, *National Product Since 1869* (New York, 1946), pp. 144, 201, 202. But note that the rental estimates are annual averages for decades.

[40] *Ibid.*, p. 144.

[41] Seaman's concept of government product apparently differs from Kuznets' but the quantitative significance of this deviation is slight.

[42] His data imply an average of $4,000 of capital per retail store, which is certainly too high, if taken to refer to buildings and equipment, alone. *Essays . . .* (1852), *op. cit.*, p. 459.

The census returned no capital stock figures for agriculture, transportation, the public sector, religious organizations, and residences. Seaman supplied investment estimates in each case, but the bases on which they rest are often not clear. The terminology used suggests that some of these estimates refer to gross investment. The estimate for railroads, canals, and waterworks is net of foreign debts accumulated in their construction. No other account is taken of changes in claims against foreigners.

To summarize, Seaman's investment estimates rest on fairly insecure bases and go undefended, in the main. They are probably mainly net investment estimates, but some components may be gross. Changes in claims against foreigners are not fully represented and changes in the value of inventories may not be fully represented. On balance, it is probably fair to say that the aggregate estimate is somewhat larger than a net investment estimate, but closer to a net than to a gross estimate.

Table 5 contains distributions of net national product made up from the work of Seaman and Kuznets and covering 1839 and the decades following the war. Seaman's low service estimate is incorporated in the figures on which the Variant A distribution for 1839 rests, while the high service estimate is included in the estimates on which the Variant B distribution rests. The conclusions one draws from the table with respect to structural changes between 1839 and the post-war years depend entirely on the variant for 1839 in which he reposes confidence. The structure of Variant B is similar to the structure of product after the war. The share of net investment in product is slightly smaller, while the shares of the other two components are slightly larger. But relying on Variant A, one finds that the shares of services and commodities flowing to consumers changed dramatically, betwen 1839 and the post-war years, while the share of net investment changed but slightly. As we have seen, Kuznets' evidence suggests that Variant A is the better estimate. Indeed, no conceivable extrapolation of services from Kuznets' work which makes use of Seaman's rent or residential property estimates would produce a distribution of product which would differ markedly from the Variant A distribution.

If we accept the Variant A distribution, the question immediately arises as to whether the difference between the share of net investment in 1839 and the post-war years represents a real and long term change over time. The number of percentage points separating the 1839 and post-war shares is not great. But Seaman's investment estimate is less net than the post-war estimates, as we have seen. Furthermore, net national product is understated in 1839, since distribution is inadequately represented in the flow of commodities to consumers. For both of these reasons, the 1839 investment proportion is overstated. On the other hand, the investment proportion is sensitive to business conditions. While the three year average represented in the 1839 investment figure (1839-1841) relates to a peak business cycle year and the two following it, these years do lie on the down side of a long swing peak, as noted earlier. Investment may have been unusually depressed and, therefore, we may not be justified in resting conclusions concerning long term developments on figures for this period. Finally, we are really interested not in the current price investment proportion, but in the constant price proportion. At a guess, the share of investment might very well be higher if national product in 1839 were expressed in post-war prices. The share of services might also be higher but, again at a guess, it is unlikely that it would be as high as after the war.[43] But all of these speculations rest, it should be remembered, on very insecure data. At best we can say, with some confidence, that the shares of the value of commodities and services in current price national product changed significantly. Further work with Seaman's estimates may eventually permit additional conclusions.

Table 5. *Composition of Net National Product, Current Prices, United States, 1839 - 1898*[a]

	1839 A	1839 B	1869-78	1879-88	1889-98
1. Commodities flowing to consumers	73.5%	61.7%	61.5%	59.8%	57.6%
2. Service flowing to consumers	15.7	29.2	26.9	27.7	28.7
3. Net investment	10.9	9.1	11.6	12.4	13.7
4. Totals	100.1	100.0	100.0	99.9	100.0

a. 1839: See text. The adjustments described in the notes to Panel B of Table 4 are incorporated in the estimates underlying these shares.
   1869-1898: Derived from data in Simon Kuznets, *Capital in the American Economy*, op. cit. Kuznets' figures rest on Shaw's estimates and, therefore, they have been adjusted in the manner described in the notes to Panel B of Table 4.

Concluding Remarks

The work of the pre-Civil War estimators holds up well enough under various tests to be useful to estimators of pre-war national product. As they stand, the estimates picture a wealthy agricultural nation embarking on industrialization. Aggregate product and population are growing rapidly, but product per head is advancing at only a moderate pace. The

---

[43] Compare the movements of the components of the Hoover consumer price index between 1851 and 1880 (*Historical Statistics* [1960], Series E-148-156). See, also, the price indexes in Gallman, "Commodity Output . . . ," *op. cit.*

composition of the flow of commodities into consumption is not much different from the post-war composition, if one looks only at the major components. Within these components there are probably important differences, however. The share of commodities flowing to consumers in national product (current prices) is larger than after the war, while the share of services is smaller. The investment proportion may also be smaller.

ANTEBELLUM INTERREGIONAL TRADE RECONSIDERED*

ALBERT FISHLOW ‡

Like Gaul, the antebellum United States was divided into three regions: North, South, and West. Unlike Caesar, however, economic historians have been more concerned with the opportunities thus afforded for regional specialization than the varying warlike characteristics of the populace. From their investigations has arisen one of the abiding generalizations of the structure of the pre-Civil War economy: an industrial North, an agricultural West, and a staple South — all extensively interdependent. This view was summarized by Louis Schmidt in 1939 and has been again brought into prominence by Douglas C. North just recently.

> The rise of internal commerce after 1815 made possible a territorial division of labor between the three great sections of the Union — the West, the South, and the East. . . . The South was thereby enabled to devote itself in particular to the production of a few plantation staples constituting a large and growing surplus for the foreign markets and depending on the West for a large part of its food supply and in the East for the bulk of its manufactured goods and very largely for the conduct of its commerce and banking. . . . The West became a surplus grain- and live-stock-producing kingdom, supplying the growing deficits of the South and the East.[1]

It is this position I wish to reconsider in this paper. Specifically, I shall hold that the trade between the West and South was always of limited importance to both regions: the South was neither a major market for western produce nor in dire need of imported foodstuffs. Thus to paraphrase (and negate) the comment of Guy Callender more than half a century ago the commerce between different agricultural communities in America has played a less important role in our economic history than has recently been argued. Rather, the rapidly growing commerce between East and West played that significant role. In the second part of the paper, with the assistance of a set of interregional trade estimates, I shall show that there was indeed a relative expansion both in regional exports and in their domestic consumption. Interregional exchange was a prominent feature of

* I wish to express my appreciation to the National Bureau of Economic Research for assistance in preparing this article during my stay there. A fuller discussion of some of these points may be found in Chap. VII of my *Railroads and the Trans-*

American antebellum development, but not as a result of interdependence among all regions.

For much of the period from 1815 to 1860 New Orleans was the great shipping point for the produce of the interior. The growing volume of receipts at New Orleans, far overshadowing the value of tonnage from the western states arriving at tidewater by the Erie Canal, testifies to that. Unfortunately, however, the produce finding its way to the Crescent City included much beside western exports, as many have recognized in passing. I wonder whether this limitation has been sufficiently appreciated. As early as the 1820's, receipts of cotton, tobacco, sugar and molasses amount to more than half the total value of imports; by the 1850's, these southern commodities made up some three-fourths of the total.[2] For the time when New Orleans was a depository for western products almost exclusively we must go back before the spread of the cotton culture to the western South in the latter 1810's. Thereafter, the trade between the West and the South is most certainly not "recorded in receipts at New Orleans."

This is not to deny that western products did follow the winding course of the Mississippi to New Orleans in significant amounts for much of the period. As late as 1849, it has been estimated that some 40 percent of the western exports of corn, a third of the flour, three-fourths of the salt meat, and two-thirds of the whiskey all were shipped to that southern gateway.[3] Very little was retained for consumption within the South, however. Most was shipped on to northern cities or foreign ports. Table I shows the extent of this re-export. Not until the very end of the period were more than half of the principal imports of foodstuffs consumed within the South, including shipments to other southern cities. By then the failure of receipts to keep pace with the rapidly growing export potential of the West meant that consumption of western imports was not notably above the levels established a decade earlier.

Although Table I does not go back before 1842, there is no reason to believe that the trend described by it was broken then. We would expect New Orleans to be even more important for its re-export functions the

---

formation of the Ante Bellum Economy (forthcoming). I hope to amplify the contents of the technical appendix and to publish them with further analysis in the near future.

‡ Albert Fishlow is Assoc. Prof. of Economics at the Univ. of Calif. (Berkeley).

[1] Louis B. Schmidt, "Internal Commerce and the Development of a National Economy Before 1860," *J.P.E.*, 1939, p. 811. Cited by Douglas C. North, *The Economic Growth of the United States, 1790 to 1860* (Prentice-Hall, 1961), p. 103.

[2] For the 1850's, U.S. Treasury Department, Bureau of Statistics, *Report on Internal Commerce for 1887* (Washington, 1888), p. 209. For the earlier period I have estimated the value of cotton, tobacco, sugar, and molasses receipts and compared these with total receipts given in the *Report*, p. 191 (see Table VII-4, *Railroads*).

[3] See Table 2 *infra*.

TABLE 1—RECEIPTS AND RE-EXPORTS OF WESTERN FOODSTUFFS AT NEW ORLEANS

Year Ending August 31	Flour (bbls.)	Corn (sacks)	Pork (bbls.)	Bacon (hhds.)	Beef (bbls.)	Lard (kegs)	Whiskey (bbls.)	Value ($000's)
1842-45*								
Receipts†	491,836	490,169	333,232	30,856	36,023	654,063	81,537	$ 8,275
Exports‡	245,542	189,573	244,115	8,012	19,835	575,974	7,274	4,823
Consumption	246,294	300,596	89,117	22,844	16,188	78,089	74,263	$ 3,452
Ratio of consumption to receipts	.50	.61	.27	.74	.45	.12	.91	.42
1846-49								
Receipts†	1,043,949	1,887,984	507,219	57,760	78,393	1,204,501	126,005	$20,824
Exports‡	726,399	1,446,457	308,492	25,303	49,417	1,064,975	15,948	13,830
Consumption	317,550	441,527	198,727	32,457	28,976	139,526	110,057	$ 6,994
Ratio of consumption to receipts	.30	.23	.39	.56	.37	.12	.87	.34
1850-53								
Receipts†	817,244	1,306,799	441,235	87,378	69,446	1,005,985	140,090	$22,211
Exports‡	304,836	496,277	234,578	30,232	49,624	910,169	8,970	10,803
Consumption	512,408	810,522	206,657	57,146	19,822	95,816	131,120	$11,408
Ratio of consumption to receipts	.63	.62	.47	.65	.29	.10	.94	.51
1854-57								
Receipts†	989,735	1,588,001	325,243	67,658	48,433	702,801	141,424	$26,300
Exports‡	529,863	820,267	139,447	16,127	28,340	724,726	7,179	13,053
Consumption	459,872	767,734	185,796	51,531	20,093	−21,925	134,245	$13,247
Ratio of consumption to receipts	.46	.48	.57	.76	.41	−.03	.95	.50
1858-61								
Receipts†	1,149,695	1,820,616	275,246	63,910	42,287	448,381	139,129	$24,984
Exports‡	425,542	410,004	39,543	4,907	15,051	405,351	4,425	6,873
Consumption	724,153	1,410,612	235,703	59,003	27,236	43,030	134,704	$18,111
Ratio of consumption to receipts	.63	.77	.86	.92	.64	.10	.97	.72

SOURCE: *Hunt's Merchants' Magazine*, 1842, pp. 391-92; 1844, pp. 419-21; 1845, pp. 370-72; 1846, pp. 406-09; 1847, pp. 413-14; 1848, pp. 511-16; 1849, pp. 554-56; 1850, pp. 536-37; 1851, pp. 602-05; 1852, pp. 489-92; 1853, pp. 624-29; 1854, pp. 475-77; 1855, pp. 601-04; 1856, p. 474 and New Orleans *Price Current*, Sept. 1, 1856; 1857, pp. 603-07; New Orleans *Price Current*, Sept. 1, 1858, and Aug. 31, 1861; *DeBow's Rev*, 1860, p. 521.
*The year 1843 is not included.
†Calculated in homogeneous physical units by dividing total receipts of product by price of physical unit.
‡Foreign exports plus coastwise shipments to Boston, New York, Philadelphia, and Baltimore. Unspecified coastwise shipments were credited to southern ports.

further back we go in time because there was no access to the Erie Canal from the already relatively densely settled Ohio Valley until 1833. There are indications suggesting that this was so. Information upon total receipts at New Orleans and total exports, foreign and coastwise, is available for two earlier years, 1837 and 1833. In the former the exports actually exceeded receipts, while in the latter the difference is only slightly positive. This signifies little consumption at New Orleans, and because coastwise trade with other southern cities was limited until the 1850's, affirms the same for total imports of western produce. In any event, total receipts of western produce at New Orleans were very much smaller before the early 1840's — less than half as much in 1836-40 than 1841-45; so consumption necessarily would have been limited even if all foodstuffs were retained.[4]

The significance of the Mississippi to the West therefore was only secondarily as a route to the South. Rather it was a means of reaching eastern and foreign ports, and especially the former; until the later 1850's, twice as much was re-exported to northern cities as to other nations. Laments for the decline of New Orleans as a site of western receipts did not blame declining southern appetites, but, properly, focused on the rapid construction of rail feeders that narrowed the economic hinterland of New Orleans. Nowhere was the shift more obvious than in the Ohio Valley. The proportion of flour flowing eastward or northward from Cincinnati increased from 3 percent in the early 1850's to 90 percent in 1860; similarly for pork, there was a shift from 7 percent to 42 percent.[5] Table 1 shows the combined effects of these shifting loyalties and the more rapid growth of that part of the West tributary to the Lakes: almost twice as much flour, eight times as much as pork and bacon, twice as much lard, and three times as much of both corn and beef were exported from New Orleans in 1846-49 than in 1858-61.

These more refined consumption data permit us now to re-examine the trade in foodstuffs between West and South from the standpoint of its relative importance to each region. For the West this means the relative importance of the southern as opposed to the eastern and foreign markets; for the South it means a comparison of the imports of western commodities

---

[4] *Report on the Internal Commerce for 1887*, pp. 199, 215, 285 ff., 377; Thomas S. Berry, *Western Prices Before 1861* (Harvard Univ. Press, 1943), p. 581. Source difficulties aside, one reason why it is not easy to go back before 1842 is the lack of dollar values and specific prices to enable conversion of receipts and exports to homogeneous units. This means an arduous task of reconciling different scales of measurement, as well as lack of weighted annual prices.

[5] Berry, *Western Prices*, p. 91; Israel Andrews, *Trade and Commerce of the British North American Colonies*, House Executive Document No. 136, 32nd Cong., 2nd Sess., p. 711.

TABLE 2—THE IMPORTANCE OF THE SOUTHERN MARKET TO THE WEST
(Percent)

Commodity	Proportion of Western Exports Shipped Via New Orleans						Proportion of Receipts of Western Produce at New Orleans Consumed in the South					
	1839*	1844	1849	1853	1857	1860	1842*	1844	1849	1853	1857	1860
Flour	53	30	31	27	34	22	42	50	30	60	41	86
Meat products ...	51	63	50	38	28	24	41	31	34	62	69	95
Corn	98	90	39	37	32	19	46	70	21	44	65	91
Whiskey	96	95	67	53	48	40	80	95	89	90	93	98
Total foodstuffs ..	49	44	40	31	27	17	37	38	29	52	52	85

Commodity	Proportion of Western Exports Consumed in the South						Proportion of Western Exports Re-exported Via New Orleans					
	1839*	1844	1849	1853	1857	1860	1842*	1844	1849	1853	1857	1860
Flour	22	16	9	14	14	19	31	15	22	13	20	3
Meat products ...	21	19	17	24	19	23	30	44	33	14	9	1
Corn	45	63	8	16	21	17	53	27	31	21	11	2
Whiskey	77	90	60	48	45	39	19	5	7	5	3	1
Total foodstuffs ..	18	17	12	16	14	14	31	27	28	15	13	3

*Years ending circa August 31, but not exactly in the case of eastern exports. Note that the 1842 consumption proportions have been applied to 1839.

SOURCE: Proportion of Western Exports shipped via New Orleans: A. L. Kohlmeier, *The Old Northwest as the Keystone of the Arch of American Federal Union* (Principia Press, 1938), pp. 33, 52-53, 83-85, 116-17, 146-48, 191-93, 248-49. Meat products include livestock (estimated for 1839-53). In certain instances there are small inconsistencies between the next descriptions and the summary chart. These have been decided as best possible; they do not affect the results. Total foodstuffs include wheat, which is not shown separately. The proportion is determined from total values as obtained with western prices. See the Technical Appendix (obtainable from the author) for more detail.

Proportion of New Orleans Receipts Consumed in the South: Table 1. Meat products are the weighted sum of bacon, pork, and beef. Total foodstuffs include lard and whiskey, but exclude wheat. This slight incomparability with panel 1 does not influence the findings.

Proportion of Western Exports Consumed in the South: Panel 1 times panel 2.

Proportion of Western Exports Re-exported via New Orleans: Panel 1 minus panel 3.

with the volume of southern production. Table 2, drawing upon the estimates of total western exports of A. L. Kohlmeier, satisfies the first requirement. It demonstrates convincingly the limited extent of the southern market. In total value, less than a fifth of western products were consumed in the South throughout. Only a rising trend of salt meat consumption kept the record as good as this, and here the border states were responsible. In 1853, Louisville contributed a fifth of the pork and bacon received at New Orleans; in 1860 its share had increased to a third.[6]

If relatively unimportant to the West, the imports were truly minute compared with the production of foodstuffs within the South itself. The 1842 corn consumption of 241,049 sacks (= 2 bushels each) is far less than 1 percent of the 1839 southern crop of 225 million bushels; the corresponding ratios for the census years 1850 and 1860 increase to be sure, but reach a maximum in the latter year of only 9 percent! For wheat the situation is not greatly dissimilar. Wheat imports (principally in the form of flour reckoned as five bushels per barrel), amounted to 960,000 bushels in 1842, 2,600,000 in 1850, and 4,250,000 in 1860. Output was 25 million bushels in 1839, 20 million in 1849, and 38 million in 1859. At best, due to the poor crop of 1849, imports aggregate 13 percent of the total. Note that although imports increased rapidly between 1850 and 1860, local production increased still more rapidly; so the South was less dependent at the end of the decade than at its beginning. Despite the simultaneous boom in cotton, the share of the South in national wheat output actually increased over this interval. Not surprisingly, the relative importance of meat products is more akin to the self-sufficiency in corn. The 1850 census credits to the southern states a product of almost $49 million in slaughtered animals — an estimate that must be raised to $119 million to compensate for understatement. Imports of pork, bacon, and beef aggregated only $3.6 million in the comparable year 1850. In 1860, the ratio of imports, similarly calculated, climbed to the 5 percent mark.[7]

The independence of the South evinces itself even more clearly when contrasted to the role western imports played in satisfying eastern deficiencies. As early as 1849 the 7.5 million equivalent bushels of wheat retained in the East augmented local production by 20 percent. By 1860

---

[6] Kohlmeier, *Old Northwest*, pp. 118, 202.

[7] These census data for the South exclude Delaware, Maryland, and Missouri. The relationship between reported value of slaughtered meat products and actual value is taken from the ratio of the national census totals to the aggregates reported in Robert E. Gallman, "Commodity Output, 1839-1899," *Trends in the American Economy in the Nineteenth Century* (Princeton Univ. Press. 1960), p. 46. Although the comparisons here have been made in terms of single years, the reader can quickly satisfy himself from the annual averages of Table 1 that the use of a longer interval near the census dates reinforces the conclusions if it affects them at all.

the imports exceeded actual output by 20 percent; that is, imports accounted for 53 percent of consumption. In corn and meat products, the East moved from self-sufficiency in the former and imports of a little more than 7 percent in the latter to deficits of 20 percent in both products. Growing eastern demands furnished the wherewithal for western expansion; in turn, that region became dependent upon the abundance brought forth upon the lands across the Alleghenies.[8]

One possibility remains to refute these contentions: that would be a substantial flow of western produce directly to southern sites, and by-passing New Orleans. Such a circumstance is doubtful. The shipments from Cincinnati to down river ports other than New Orleans do not appear to be of any significance. During the years 1848-50, less than 1 percent of the provisions shipped from that city to New Orleans were destined to these other ports; of corn the ratio is 10 percent, but Cincinnati was not the leading southern forwarder; of flour, another growing export of St. Louis, the proportion is about 20 percent on average. At the other side of the transaction, receipts at different southern cities appear limited. Shipments up the Cumberland and Tennessee rivers "supplied a local market in Western Kentucky and were comparatively limited in quantity." The shipment of 297,119 pounds of meat from Vicksburg to Jackson in 1850 is no more than .1 percent of the receipts at New Orleans in the same year. Distribution by rail from Mississippi River points to the interior South likewise is doubtful. The Memphis and Charleston Railroad carried only 4,000 tons of all varieties eastward to the latter city in 1860 — too small to count.[9]

Routes to the South other than the Mississippi and the limited channels enumerated above were virtually nonexistent before the war. There was no through connection at all between western and southern railroads and the tortuousness of many transshipments would soon cause exorbitant expense. The underlying economics also make shipment via New Orleans far more probable. Not only was that city a major distribution point, but the limited back haulage would make for low rates upstream. Logic seems to have its counterpart in fact. The *Internal Commerce Report* for 1887

---

[8]Eastern consumption was calculated as the sum of direct exports to the East as estimated by Kohlmeier, plus re-export to northern cities from New Orleans, minus shipments abroad from eastern ports. For 1860 these last could be obtained directly from the Report on Commerce and Navigation for that year; for 1849 they were estimated as national exports less known exports from New Orleans.

[9] *Hunt's Merchants' Magazine*, XXIII (1850), p. 542; Kohlmeier, *The Old Northwest*, p. 202; John H. Moore, *Agriculture in Ante Bellum Mississippi* (Bookman Associates, 1958), p. 111; *American Railroad Journal*, 1860, pp. 840-41 (the through receipts of the Memphis and Charleston were converted to tonnage on the assumption of a 3-4 cent ton-mile rate and a length of road of 271 miles).

remarks: "There was no trade between the Western cities and the Southern plantations, very little even with the towns; it all paid tribute to New Orleans. . . . Of these shipments upstream over 75 percent . . . were articles which had previously been sent downstream."[10] If the border states of Kentucky and Tennessee be regarded as part of the West rather than the South, some further trade undoubtedly occurred that is not reckoned in here, particularly in livestock. But it is hardly clear that such a treatment is more appropriate: in their commitment to slavery, size of farms, ethnic character of population, and indeed, in the case of Tennessee its considerable production of cotton, these states were part of the South. Note again, therefore, that our trade figures from the West actually overstate consumption of western foodstuffs because they include the downriver shipments from Louisville.

Despite this, the clear picture that has emerged is one of tenuous linkage between the two regions. To the West, the South was a minor matter for its own demands. And as early as 1839, more western products were shipped directly eastward than re-exported via New Orleans. Table 2 records the re-export trade in its fourth panel. After 1849 it dwindles rapidly and becomes insignificant by 1860. By then New Orleans was far from the central pivot it had been in the 1810's. On the other side, the southern states were far from dependent upon the agricultural largess of the West for their needs. The greater than average per capita production of corn, peas, and beans in the South supports this observation; so, too, do the larger cattle and swine inventories. The southern social structure, with its large numbers of land-owners with few slaves or none at all, also may be invoked. It is suggestive of an economic organization with both widespread self-sufficiency and local sale of foodstuffs to nearby plantations. In conclusion, one may contrast the strength of this case for little southern consumption of western produce with the virtual absence of affirmative evidence for the conventional wisdom of a close interconnection.[11]

Antebellum Trade More Generally

Another perspective from which to view this West-South trade is the context of the other interregional flows. I have set out some estimates of

---

[10] P. 205.

[11] There has never been unanimous acceptance of substantial interdependence between West and South. Among the prominent dissenters is Isaac Lippincott in his excellent, but neglected, "Internal Trade of the United States, 1700-1860," *Washington University Studies*, IV, Part II, No. 1 (1916). See too the reviews of North's *Growth of the United States* by Richard Easterlin in the *J. of Econ. Hist.*, 1962, p. 125. George Rogers Taylor, in *The Transportation Revolution* (Rinehart, 1951),

these for various years from 1839 through 1860 in Table 3. Their derivation is described fully in a technical appendix available from the author upon request. Briefly, I may indicate here the nature of these estimates. The trade flows to the West and from West to East directly are obtained by valuing Kohlmeier's shipments to specific commodities, and adjusting for undercoverage; eastern consumption of western products counts in imports via New Orleans and subtracts foreign exports. The flow from West to South is made up of all receipts at New Orleans less imports of cotton, sugar, molasses, and tobacco with consumption determined by the proportion of the selected products of Table 1 retained in the South.[12] The flow from North to South is derived by subtracting the trade from the West to the South from estimated total southern import capacity; the South-North exchange is also a residual.

One important limitation of these data should be noted. The flows for the most part exclude full distribution mark-ups since they are valued at the wholesale prices of the region of origin. This procedure has been adopted since the regional allocation of expenditures for freight, insurance, banking, and other services is largely unknown. A measure of the maximum understatement of commerce is given by the extent of interregional price disparity. Sample calculations for both 1839 and 1860 for the West-East trade point to a weighted average differential of 20 percent. Similar calculations for the South-West exchange show a somewhat smaller variation of perhaps 15 percent, depending upon whether southern or western prices are used to value western imports. The trade data of Table 3 are too small by the proportion of this differential accounted for by extra-regional payments.

Despite this restriction and the uncertainties in the attempt — due in part to the unsatisfactory nature of some of Kohlmeier's estimates, in part to the variation in quoted prices even within the same region, and in part to the necessity of valuing "merchandise" by the ton — those figures do suggest an order of magnitude that is probably closer to the truth than the variety of other similar figures that are current.[13] Kohlmeier's estimate

---

comments on the role of New Orleans as a forwarder and the decline of the function, but does not discuss southern consumption explicitly.

[12] This yields an upper bound for southern receipts from the West since residual receipts include hemp from Kentucky, etc. A comparison with the same method used for the East, and the same escalation factor for undercoverage, gives smaller imports in every year. The two estimates are quite close absolutely, however, See the Appendix.

[13] One test of the data is the apparent sense they make with regard to capital inflows to the West (for this region since both imports and exports are derived independently the comparison is meaningful). Table 3 shows the West as a capital importer in 1853 and 1857, as an exporter in 1844 and 1849, and in approximate balance in 1839 and 1860. The first set of years coincide with rapid western expansion, the 1840's with less frenetic extension onto new lands, less railroad and canal construction, etc.

TABLE 3

INTERNATIONAL MERCHANDISE TRADE FLOWS*
(Millions of Current Dollars)

YEAR	ORIGINATING REGION	NORTH	WEST	SOUTH
1839	North	—	19.7	85.6
	West	11.8 7.1	— —	14.9 5.5
	South	39.7 15.1	6.3 2.2	— —
1844	North	—	25.2	73.2
	West	20.1 14.5	— —	19.9 7.6
	South	32.4 11.6	6.2 3.5	— —
1849	North	—	41.4	80.0
	West	36.8 24.2	— —	36.1 10.5
	South	32.0 18.9	8.1 4.8	— —
1853	North	—	94.5	147.1
	West	63.2 47.9	— —	36.9 19.2
	South	61.9 33.0	17.2 11.9	— —
1857	North	—	163.1	165.7
	West	96.9 45.8	— —	49.1 25.5
	South	71.1 38.0	13.2 5.5	— —
1860	North	—	164.3	213.8
	West	146.5 107.6	— —	42.8 36.4
	South	69.4 44.6	20.3 13.6	— —

*Uppermost figure refers to gross flow whether for consumption or re-export; bottom figure is estimated consumption. In the case of the South-North entry this is limited to northern purchases of southern cotton, and molasses.

SOURCE: See Appendix (obtainable from the author), Tables A-10, A-11.

for western trade in 1844, as quoted from the *Congressional Globe,* is $120 million for imports and $115 million for exports. Yet in that same year the Erie Canal valuations for western shipments, which we have used in our derivations, were, respectively, $14.8 million and $15.9 million, and that artery carried something like half the exports and even more of the imports, according to Kohlmeier's own estimates. The East-West figures also go beyond the calculations contained in *Statistics of Foreign and Domestic Commerce* wherein both through and way tonnage — much of the latter consisting of local coal destined for eastern seaports — are valued at generous prices to reach what appears to be a rather high value. Similarly, these flows between North and South are an improvement over Kettell's unfounded conjectures of 1860.[14] His total imports into the South are as great as $462 million whereas the maximum value of cotton, tobacco, rice, and naval stores exports before the Civil War was never more than $275 million, against which must be reckoned direct foreign imports of some $35 million and imports from the West of almost equivalent size.[15]

The data of Table 3 fix the West-South traffic as one of limited scope. Whether we use gross flows or net consumption, the trade always ranks at the lower end of the spectrum. In its meager rate of growth it stands in sharp contrast to the increasing exchange between West and North. Where consumption of western produce by North and South was at approximate parity in 1839, the former was absorbing three times as much by 1860. Gross flows diverge most sharply in the decade of the 1850's as the extension of direct and more efficient East-West transport routes drew the commerce that had once been transshipped from New Orleans. The reciprocal flows inward to the West show the same asymmetrical development. From the earliest, high-valued merchandise was able to bear the cost of transportation and entered from the East, leaving for the South the distribution of assorted groceries and locally produced sugar and molasses. Thus in 1839 the West already depended more heavily upon the East than

---

[14] Kohlmeier, *Old Northwest,* pp. 56-57; *Statistics of Foreign and Domestic Commerce,* Senate Exec. Doc. No. 55, 38th Cong., 1st Sess., pp. 129, 181; Thomas P. Kettell, *Southern Wealth and Northern Profits* (New York, 1860), p. 75.

[15] The derivation of these sums is shown in the calculations in the appendix. My imports are understated since exports are valued f.o.b. and hence exclude some of the revenues. If these additional receipts bought imports of services, my import capacity would approximate merchandise imports. These still fall far short of Kettell. I would point out in this connection that such services neither are as large nor was the South as dependent upon the North as is sometime suggested. Commission rates for cotton were low and ocean transport costs a small proportion of value. On the second point, little of the cotton crop was re-exported through northern ports (5-8 percent in the late 1850's), many of the charges for pressing, storage, drayage, etc., were local, and there was as rapid growth of southern banking in the 1850's as nationally, measured by loans and discounts outstanding.

the South for its imports. By 1860 the advantage had grown enormously; almost ten times as much of western purchases came from the East than upriver. However one reads the record, the tale is straightforward: an initially narrow commerce between the West and the South that failed to keep pace with the rapid expansion in western agricultural bounty and which was supplanted by a total exchange between East and West that ranked first by 1860.

This is not to gainsay the continuing trade between North and South. Over most of the antebellum period the coastwise trade was the most important artery of interregional commerce. Certainly until the mid-fifties the southern market was the largest that faced the North. Yet it is one about which we know perhaps least. Often it is assumed that the South possessed a higher propensity to consume foreign imports, obviously blunting the impact of its demands upon domestic development of manufactures. Yet the sheer size of the market must have given it a key role in American industrialization prior to the 1850's. Philadelphia in particular among the northern cities seems to have cultivated that territory for its rapidly increasing output of machinery.

Table 3 does more than garb these specific flows with greater statistical precision. It enables us for the first time to examine in quantitative terms the role of interregional trade in antebellum development. Adherents to the tenet that it is the domestic market that counts can take heart from the results. Even if we suppose northern distribution of imported merchandise accounts for a fourth of its shipments to other regions, domestic consumption of the produce of other regions exceeds foreign exports in every year. More significant still is the obvious relative growth in the domestic market during a period of accelerated income advance. Exports to other regions increase from $109 million in 1839 to $480 million in 1860; exports to other countries from $102 million to $316 million.[16] The regional variation is of interest. The North always fared better in exports to other regions than abroad; conversely the South depended more upon old England than New England for sales of its great staple. The West moves from a southern to a northern stance: in 1839 foreign coun-

---

[16] The total consumption of domestic produce of other regions is the sum of the bottom entries of Table 3 plus three-fourths the flow of eastern merchandise to other regions. Western imports of salt and iron from the East are treated as of domestic origin while coffee and sugar are treated entirely as foreign; all trade from North to South is treated as merchandise. Since the ratio of imports of manufactures to census value of eastern domestic production (minus the two important processing industries of sawing and milling) is less than .2 in 1849 and 1859, the adjustment is not likely to overstate the domestic market. For exports and imports by class, see North, *Economic Growth*, pp. 284, 288, and for detail on western imports from the East see the Appendix (obtainable from the author).

tries afford a slightly better market for its foodstuffs than the still pre-dominantly agricultural East and plantation South; by 1860, domestic consumption exceeds exports by a substantial margin.[17]

Export base proponents also can find much to their taste. The sum of the exports to other regions and abroad increases in importance between 1839 and 1860. Relative to gross national product in the former year they are 13 percent; in the latter 19 percent. Over this period their potential influence was therefore considerably enhanced. Again, the specific regional patterns deserve mention. Southern exports increased only slightly, from 23 percent to 29 percent of income. The West's dependence upon an external market radically altered from less than 13 percent to 23 percent of its product. The northern export percentage moved intermediately from 10 to 15. The region displaying the greatest increase in income and popu-lation, the West, also had the stimulus of the most rapidly growing external market, exactly as export base theory would predict.[18]

Final Comment

Full exploration of these intriguing suggestions is beyond the scope of this paper. But before the analysis of the role of interregional trade in American antebellum development can press home, further advances in two directions will be required. Refinement and extension of the basic trade estimates is an essential step; a promising possibility is a com-plementary approach from the side of regional consumption requirements. Equally urgent is modification of the export base theory to render it more amenable to empirical test. At present it does not completely satisfy this criterion.

Such a restatement can draw upon some of the preliminary findings

---

[17] These comparisons consist of the sum of consumption of western products by North and South as given in Table 3 and the national exports of breadstuffs and provisions, amounting in millions of dollars as follows: 1839, $14.1; 1844, $18.0; 1849, $38.2; 1853, $33.0; 1857, $74.7; 1860, $45.3.

[18] The current dollar gross national product estimates are those of Robert E. Gallman in "Gross National Product in the United States, 1834-1909," to be pub-lished in Volume 29 of *Studies in Income and Wealth*. They were converted to regional values for 1840 and 1860 by the use of Richard A. Easterlin's regional relatives for the two dates as given in Seymour Harris, ed., *American Economic History* (McGraw-Hill, 1961), p. 528. Western exports are approximated by the sum of domestic consumption in South and North plus foreign exports of breadstuffs and provisions; southern exports are made up of sales of cotton, tobacco, rice, sugar, naval stores, and molasses (see Appendix, Table A-7); northern exports to other regions are estimated as in fn. 17 to which are added national exports of manufac-tures and semimanufactures. For both North and West the results are not exact, but they should be close to the correct magnitudes.

reached here. The transition of the West from reliance on a foreign to a domestic market, in contrast to continued southern dependence on overseas markets, suggests that differences in destination of exports may play a greater role than has been recognized. Exports to another region may be more stable and less subject to competition than sales on a world market; regional interdependence may also bring with it a greater reciprocal inflow of labor, capital, and institutional influences. Whatever the merit of this speculation, the approach must certainly come to grips with our central result: the small, and lessening, linkage between the West and the South. Interregional interdependence there was before the Civil War, but increasingly exclusive of the South, a circumstance not unrelated, one might add, to the decision for Confederacy by the South, and that for Union by the West.

A Provisional View of the "New Economic History"

ROBERT W. FOGEL*

Professor Fishlow's computations are based on the assumption that virtually all trade from the West to the South took place through New Orleans. This single-route model of West-South trade affects the computation of the numbers in three of the six cells shown in each of the six yearly matrices of interregional trade flows presented in his third table. As a consequence of limiting himself to the New Orleans data in determining the extent of West-South trade, Fishlow concludes that western commodities consumed in the South were a relatively unimportant and a declining share of the shipments from the West during the decades leading up to the Civil War.

Available evidence suggests that Fishlow's findings may be the result of an incorrect specification of antebellum interregional trade routes. It seems likely that during the 1850's a sizable share of western products was shipped to the South via the North Atlantic port cities of New York, Philadelphia, and Baltimore. In the comments that follow I want to focus particular attention on routes of trade between the West and the South Atlantic States of Virginia, North Carolina, South Carolina, and Georgia.

The earliest report readily available to me on the magnitude of the shipments along competing routes from the West to the south Atlantic states refers to the post-Civil War period. According to data collected by the Southern Railway and Steamship Association for the year 1881-82; the overwhelming proportion of southern bound western goods reached the major South Atlantic cities by way of New York and Baltimore rather than by direct rail connection with the West. In that year direct shipments from Chicago to Charleston, South Carolina, came to 4,511 tons; but more than three times that amount was shipped to Charleston through

* Robert W. Fogel is Professor of Economics at the University of Chicago.

Professor Fogel's comments reprinted here were part of a longer and more methodological discussion of a series of papers on the "New Economic History," given at the annual meeting of the American Economic Association in 1963, and cited in Part One of the present volume. The present excerpts from Professor Fogel's longer paper were selected for reprinting because they highlighted an important substantive question in the interpretation of American economic history and therefore fit neatly into the analytical problems raised by Professor Fishlow's paper.

the ports of New York and Baltimore. The ratio on goods sent from Chicago to Savannah was nearly two to one in favor of the northern trunk-line and coastal route.[1] The report of the Southern Railway and Steamship Association leaves little doubt that this indirect route to the south Atlantic states enjoyed a cost advantage that enabled it to dominate — at least in the two decades following the Civil War — all other alternatives:[2]

> In making through rates from Chicago to Southern coast points, we take as our basis the trunk lines' rates in effect from Chicago to Baltimore, plus the steamships' rates from Baltimore to Charleston and Savannah; and the totals thus made have been for years, and will probably continue to be, lower than any per mile rate used by the all-rail lines from the West to interior Southern points, as Atlanta, Macon, Augusta, &c. The all-rail lines have therefore to adopt the lowest total produced by combination of trunk-line rates plus steamer rates, adding thereto only a sufficient amount to cover the cost of insurance and allowance for the greater amount of time consumed in transportation by rail and water lines. Southern port rates having thus been arrived at, the rates to Augusta, Macon, Atlanta, &c., have to be made competitive with the Southern port rate, otherwise the business of interior points would be diverted entirely to the coast.

What is most interesting about the Association's statement is the absence of any reference on shipments through New Orleans as a factor in establishing rates from the West to South Atlantic cities. Was this pre-emption of the supremacy of the route on which Fishlow places so much emphasis a phenomenon of the post-Civil War period or did it take place in the antebellum era? Data on relative prices suggest that the usurpation was probably fairly complete by 1850, if not sooner. Table 1 shows that while New Orleans enjoyed a price advantage over New York on four basic commodities in the early 1830's, by 1850 prices were lower in New York on two of the four original items as well as on corn. The movement against New Orleans continued through the decade, and by 1859 wholesale prices at New York were from 2 to 39 percent below New Orleans prices on all five commodities.

Consequently, even if transportation costs between the south Atlantic ports and New York in the late fifties were the same as those between the South Atlantic ports and New Orleans, it would have paid for southern merchants to have purchased in the North. Yet several factors suggest that shipping costs favored the northern alternative. One factor is distance.

---

[1] Charles A. Sindall, "Development of the Traffic Between the Southern States and the Northern and Northwestern States," U. S. Treasury Department, *Report on the Internal Commerce of the United States, 1886* (Washington: GPO, 1886), Tables 4 and 6.

[2] *Ibid.*, p. 683.

TABLE 1

WHOLESALE PRICES OF SELECTED COMMODITIES AT NEW YORK AND
NEW ORLEANS

(In Dollars Per Unit)

Commodity and Unit	1 New York	2 New Orleans	3 Premium at New York	4 Column 1 as a Percent of Column 2
		1834		
Flour (barrel)	4.98	4.64	0.34	107
Mess beef (barrel) ...	9.57	9.29	0.28	103
Mess pork (barrel) ...	14.29	12.64	1.65	113
Lard (pound)	0.079	0.069	0.01	114
		1850		
Flour (barrel)	5.51	5.05	0.46	109
Corn (bushel)	0.630	0.647	—0.02	97
Mess beef (barrel) ...	8.29	11.43	—3.14	73
Mess pork (barrel) ...	10.70	10.71	—0.01	100
Lard (pound)	0.0642	0.0638	0.0004	101
		1859		
Flour (barrel)	5.12	5.54	—0.42	92
Corn (bushel)	0.863	0.970	—0.11	89
Mess beef (barrel) ...	8.84	14.46	—5.62	61
Mess pork (barrel) ...	16.49	16.80	—0.31	98
Lard (pound)	0.108	0.114	—0.006	95

SOURCE: Arthur Harrison Cole, *Wholesale Commodity Prices in the United States 1700–1861, Statistical Supplement* (Harvard Univ. Press, 1938).

New York's advantage over New Orleans is 417 miles in the case of Savannah, Georgia; 531 miles in the case of Charleston, S. C.; 717 miles in the case of Wilmington, N. C.; and 1,205 miles in case of Norfolk, Virginia (see Table 2). Second, even in the 1830's when New Orleans enjoyed a slender price advantage over the northern port cities on mess beef, Charleston, S. C., appears to have made its primary purchases on this item in the North. In every year of the decade the price series at Charleston listed in Cole's compendium is described as "Boston mess." Similarly the description of the Charleston pork series in 1836 is "New York mess, March-December," although the average New York price

TABLE 2

DISTANCES BETWEEN SELECTED PORTS
(In Nautical Miles)

	New Orleans	New York	Baltimore	Phila-delphia	Boston
Savannah, Georgia ..	1,122	705	625	672	944
Charleston, S.C.	1,163	632	552	599	871
Wilmington, N.C. ...	1,279	562	482	529	801
Norfolk, Virginia ...	1,499	294	172	257	567

SOURCE: U.S. Coast and Geodetic Survey, *Distances Between United States Ports*, Serial No. 444 (Washington: GPO, 1938).

exceeded the New Orleans average by from $0.50 to $2.25 per barrel in four of the last ten months of the year.[3] Third, export prices on flour and pork shipped from Atlantic and Gulf ports show a generally rising level of prices as one proceeds down the coast from Baltimore to Key West, after which the prices fall off (see Table 3).

Relative prices thus suggest that if, in 1860, the South Atlantic States incurred deficits in the production of foods that the West produced for export, these states would have made their purchases primarily in the markets of Boston, New York, Philadelphia, and Balitmore. The question then becomes, "How large might the deficits have been?"

Some notion of the magnitudes that might have prevailed can be obtained by utilizing an approach that Professor Fishlow mentioned but did not pursue: estimation of the deficit from production and consumption data. Following Gallman's method of basing estimates of annual meat production on the June 1 stock of animals, and adopting Fishlow's assumption of contant average slaughter weights, it is possible to compute national disappearance figures of beef for both 1840 and 1860.[4] Given the constant average slaughter weight of cattle,[5] it appears that for the nation as a whole, consumption declined by 7 percent between the two dates. If one assumes that the South Atlantic States were self-sufficient in 1840 and that per capita consumption in the region declined at the same rate as in

[3] Cole, *Wholesale Commodity Prices*, p. 258.
[4] Conference on Income and Wealth, *Trends*, p. 49.
[5] In the computations that follow, data on animals stocks, production of corn and population are taken from the Census Reports for 1840 and 1860; the ratio of slaughter weight to dressed weight is taken from G. K. Holmes, *Meat Supply and Surplus*, USDA, Bureau of Statistics, *Bulletin No. 55* (Washington, 1907). A barrel of beef or pork is assumed to have weighed 200 pounds. As previously noted, only four states are included under the designation "South Atlantic States."

TABLE 3

AVERAGE EXPORT PRICES AT ATLANTIC AND GULF PORTS FOR THE YEAR
ENDING JUNE 30, 1857
(Dollars per Barrel)

	Flour	Pork
Baltimore, Maryland	6.72	18.53
Alexandria, Virginia	7.00	
Norfolk, Virginia	7.87	20.00
Richmond, Virginia	8.10	22.76
Wilmington, N.C.	7.26	
Charleston, S.C.	7.85	21.30
Savannah, Georgia	7.71	23.00
Key West, Florida	9.14	
Mobile, Alabama	6.72	
New Orleans, Louisiana	6.67	19.72

SOURCE: U.S. Treasury Department, *Annual Report on Commerce and Navigation, 1857* (Washington, 1857), Table 7.

the nation as a whole, then the maintenance of regional self-sufficiency required a production of 783,000 head in 1860. However, production appears to have been only 561,000 head, indicating a deficit of 222,000 head or 558,000 barrels.[6] This amounts to about 64 percent of the beef and cattle that Fishlow estimates were shipped from the West to the North.

Applying the same method to pork, it appears that for the nation as a whole, per capita consumption declined by 33 percent over the twenty years between 1840 and 1860. This odd conclusion is the result of the fact that the number of swine in stock grew more slowly than the population and the assumption of a constant average slaughter weight on swine.[7] If one goes on to assume that the South Atlantic States were self-sufficient in 1840 and that per capita consumption in the region declined at the same rate as in the nation as a whole, then maintenance of self-sufficiency would have required a production of 289,000 tons of pork. However, the estimated 1860 production in the region appears to have been 351,000 tons. Consequently, the assumptions of this computation lead to a second startling conclusion: in 1860 the South Atlantic States were a surplus area in pork production.

The unacceptability of these conclusions is revealed by an examination

---

[6] Following Towne and Rasmussen, the average slaughter weight of cattle is assumed to be 950 pounds. Conference of Income and Wealth, *Trends,* p. 283.

[7] Following Fishlow, the average slaughter weight of hogs used in the computation was 200 pounds.

of trends in corn production and consumption. Corn production increased at an extremely rapid rate between 1840 and 1860, rising by 453,000,000 bushels or 120 percent. Since corn was primarily a feed grain — human consumption did not amount to more than 10 percent of the total crop — trends in per capita production figures are relatively meaningless. One can, however, construct an index of "consuming units," establishing a swine as one consuming unit, and counting each other type of animal as some multiple of the "swine unit."[8] On this basis, after making due allowance for exports and seed requirements, corn consumption per consuming unit rises from a national average of 8.7 bushels in 1840 to 13.6 bushels in 1860 — an increase of 56 percent.

Since no plausible increase in human corn requirements could have accounted for more than a very small portion of the indicated rise in per unit consumption, these figures imply a major change in animal husbandry over the twenty-year period. There was obviously a major movement away from grazing (in the case of horses and cattle) and mast feeding (in the case of swine) to corn feeding. Such a turn suggests a rise in the slaughter weight of hogs and cattle.

Did this change from mast feeding and grazing to corn feeding and the consequent rise in animal weights extend to the South? A recent study by Professor Eugene D. Genovese indicates that it did not. Referring to the period of the 1850's, Genovese states that "the quality of southern hogs was far inferior to the better fed, better bred, better housed hogs of the Middle West" and that southern hogs were "allowed to run wild in the woods and feed themselves throughout the winter as best they could, often receiving no grain at all during the year." According to a sample of plantation records drawn by Genovese, the average slaughter weight of 4,000 hogs on plantations in eight states in the year 1860 was 140 pounds, as contrasted to an average 1860 weight of 228 pounds in Chicago, and about 200 pounds in both Cincinnati and St. Louis.[9]

The data on corn support Genovese's finding. In order for corn consumption in the South Atlantic States to have risen at the same rate as the rest of the nation, the four states in the region would have had to have imported 43,400,000 bushels of corn in 1860. But this figure is 130 percent larger than Kohlmeier's estimate of the amount of western corn shipped to the North in 1860. Indeed, it exceeds his estimate of total western corn shipments to all points outside of the region by 90 percent.

---

[8] The weights used in the construction of this index are based on data in USDA, Agricultural Research Service, *Production Research Report,* No. 21 (Washington, 1958); and Fogel, *Railroads,* Chaps. II and III.

[9] "Livestock in the Slave Economy of the South — A Revised View," *Agric. Hist.,* July, 1962, pp. 147-48.

The data on corn consumption and Genovese's findings on average weights imply that the apparent decline in per capita pork consumption in the nation between 1840 and 1860 may be an illusion produced by the failure to take account of the rise in the average weights. Since the national corn consumption per consuming unit in 1840 was somewhat below the corresponding figure in the South Atlantic States in 1860,[10] we may take Genovese's estimate of the average weight of hogs in the South in 1860 as indicative of the national average in 1840. This suggests a rise of 43 percent in the national average slaughter weight of hogs between the two dates (from 140 to 200 pounds) a rise that just offsets the decrease in the stock of swine per capita. It also suggests that the per capita consumption of pork remained stable during the period in question.

If the previous computation of the pork import requirements of the South Atlantic States is altered to reflect a constancy in per capita consumption, one finds that pork production in the region fell short of consumption requirements by 787,000 barrels or about 62 per cent of the Kohlmeier-Fishlow estimate of western pork shipments to the north Atlantic area in 1860.

Using Fishlow's prices, it thus appears that if one limits oneself only to beef and pork, western meats and animals amounting to about $21,000,-000 which Fishlow assigns to northern consumption may actually have been destined for the South. But such a shift would significantly alter one's appraisal of the South as a market for western goods. Its share in the internal consumption of western exports would rise from 25 percent to 40 percent.

The preceding estimates are too crude to be more than an illustration of the scope of the issue posed by Professor Fishlow's specification of a one-route model in West-South trade. The resolution of the issue requires research on trends in the average weight of animals, on the shifts in the proportion and amounts of the various grains fed to particular categories of animals, and on the human consumption of particular foods in the major regions of the nation prior to the Civil War — research of a magnitude that could not be undertaken in the limited time available for the preparation of this paper.

Professor Fishlow raises a second issue of model specification when he writes:

> On the other side, the southern states were far from dependent upon the agricultural largess of the West for their needs. The greater than average per capita production of corn, peas, and beans in the South supports this observation, so too do the larger cattle and swine inventories. The southern social structure, with its large number of landowners with few slaves

---

[10] The respective figures are 8.7 and 10.6 bushels.

or none at all, also lends support. It is suggestive of an economic organization with both widespread self-sufficiency and local sale of foodstuffs
to nearby plantations.

This position is not only a consequence of Professor Fishlow's single-
route model of West-South trade, and an assumption of constancy in the
average weights of livestock in the various regions, but also of the high
level of aggregations in Fishlow's overall model of interregional trade.
The statement that on a per capita basis cattle inventories in the South
exceeded that of the rest of the nation is true in 1860 only if one lumps
Texas and Arkansas together with the South Atlantic and Eastern Gulf
States. Without the two trans-Mississippi states, the rest of the South had
a per capita cattle inventory equal to only 94 percent of the national figure.

Texas, which alone had cattle stock exceeding that of all the South
Atlantic States, had only one-seventh of the combined population of these
states. It is of interest therefore to ask, "What happened to this enormous cattle surplus?" Fragmentary data suggest that large numbers of
Texas cattle were sold in Louisiana and the Gulf States to the east of it
during the 1850's. Between 2,900 to 6,000 head per year were reportedly
sent by boat to New Orleans from Galveston alone during 1850-56. In
the first ten months of 1856 an additional 32,412 "beeves from western
Texas crossed the Sabine River into Louisiana." The Galveston *News*
reported that most of these animals were being driven to New Orleans.[11]

A different structuring of regions and the elimination of the one-route
hypothesis thus appears to reveal a steady decline in self-sufficiency in the
South Atlantic and Eastern Gulf States. The relative decline which
Fishlow observed in receipts at New Orleans appears to be explained
partly by the rise of a new western region between 1840 and 1860 — the
Southwest — which replaced the Northwest as a supplier of the deficits of
the Eastern Gulf States, and partly by the cost advantage that enabled
the northern route to the Southeast to usurp the hegemony of the
Mississippi.[12]

Professor Fishlow's paper thus illustrates two of the main issues of model
specification that confront the new economic historians. The first issue
pertains to the empirical validity of the assumptions that underlie their

---

[11] Wayne Gard, *The Chisholm Trail* (Univ. of Oklahoma Press, 1954), pp. 24-25.

[12] Further consideration must also be given to the possibility that large numbers
of cattle and swine were trailed into various parts of the South from the Northwest
and thus have been omitted from Fishlow's figures (cf. Genovese, "Livestock,"
passim). To the extent that the southern deficit noted above was supplied in this
manner, Fishlow's estimates will be off not only with respect to the division of
western exports between the North and the South, but also on the overall magnitude of the exports.

models; it involves the determination of the extent to which errors in specification will lead to a distortion of the reality that historians wish to reconstruct. In the present case, this problem is illustrated by scope of the error that might be introduced by the assumption that there was only one nontrivial commercial route from the West to the South in the antebellum era. The second issue pertains to the power of a model to yield information of the type required to successfully evaluate a given set of circumstances. In the present case, this problem appears in connection with the extremely high level of aggregation on which Professor Fishlow chose to cast his analysis, a level of aggregation that may be too high to permit one to determine either the direction, or the magnitude or the developmental significance of changes in the degree of local self-sufficiency in the South.

Postscript

ALBERT FISHLOW

Professor Fogel has admirably performed the function of attorney for defense of the traditional hypothesis that western flows to the South indeed were large before 1860. By skillfully introducing the specter of an extensive western-southern trade via the North Atlantic ports, he has injected a "reasonable doubt" that may incline the reader to acquittal of the defendant. It seems appropriate therefore to take advantage of this opportunity briefly to re-inforce the case presented in my original article.

Fogel's espousal of such an indirect West-South trade derives from three separate considerations. First, there are the actual measured flows of 1881–82 presented in the *Report on the Internal Commerce of the United States for 1886*. These, he concludes, show that "the overwhelming proportion of southern bound western goods reached the major South Atlantic cities by way of New York and Baltimore rather than by direct rail connection with the West." Second, there are the data on relative prices between New Orleans and New York that seem to indicate a trend decline in the initial advantage of New Orleans over the Atlantic port. By 1859 Fogel actually finds a disadvantage, suggesting that shipments logically might be expected to originate in New York rather than the Crescent City by that date. Third, there are the estimates of 1860 pork and beef consumption requirements for the South Atlantic states. They testify to substantial deficits and as a consequence of meeting them, Fogel feels the share of the South in domestictic western exports could have been as great as 40 per cent instead of the 25 per cent originally estimated. These points will be considered in turn.

The post-Civil War experience, while relevant to many ante-bellum issues, is a particularly inappropriate citation in this context. The increased integration of southern and western railroads, through the formation of the Green Line in 1868, naturally increased direct rail shipments beyond what they had been formerly. As Sindell writes, "the Green Line worked a great revolution in the traffic business from the West and Northwest to the South and Southeast." [1] Accordingly, the 1881-82 proportions are of academic interest. This may seem only to strengthen Fogel's objections inasmuch as he finds water shipments predominating at the later date *despite* more forceful rail competition. In fact, however, Fogel, by his selection of shipments originating in Chicago alone and terminating only at South Atlantic ports has shown the West-South trade in a peculiar perspective. Considered totally, 506,000 tons were shipped by rail from the West to the South in 1881-82, 45,000 by water.[2] Moreover, if the purpose of the later comparison is to contend that under pre-Civil War conditions it was cheaper to ship from Chicago to Charleston via Baltimore than directly by rail, again the illustration is inept; the relevant comparison is shipments from the Ohio Valley to Charleston via New Orleans or via Baltimore. The essential ingredients to this determination, ante-bellum Mississippi River, plus Gulf coastal rates, on the one hand, and rail rates plus Atlantic Ocean coastal rates on the other, cannot be inferred from Fogel's evidence.

As regards relative prices, again I am dubious as to what Table I really proves. For example, had 1858 or 1860 been selected to compare New York and New Orleans prices of corn rather than 1859, New Orleans would have been the cheaper market — in 1858 by almost 25 per cent and in 1860 by 3 per cent.[3] A similar change of year to 1858 makes New Orleans pork the better buy. Or had a comparable grade of flour, superfine, valued at Philadelphia been compared with New Orleans superfine, the latter would have come out the less expensive by some 4 per cent. In the instance of the commodity with the largest differential, mess beef, the gap is due to this inexplicably low price quotations at New York beginning in mid-1859 which are less than half those prevailing in Philadelphia. This last inconsistency argues forcefully that early price quotations are not to be relied upon as precise measures, or imprecise for that matter, of the most profitable shipping point. Needless to say, such a large difference between New York and Philadelphia should not have persisted over many months. Yet there are other instances too, where items entering trade, like lard, exhibit a bigger gap between Philadelphia and New York than New Orleans and Charleston. In addition, intra-year variations frequently were large to

---

[1] U. S. Bureau of the Treasury, Report on Internal Commerce for 1886, p. 681.
[2] *Ibid.*, Table 4 and Table 6.
[3] All price data are taken from Arthur Cole, *Wholesale Commodity Prices in the United States, 1700-1861* (Cambridge, 1938).

the point of exceeding inter-city differentials. For all these reasons, there must be serious reservations concerning the implications drawn from the price data.

What, then, of the consumption requirements showing substantial pork and beef deficits in the South Atlantic states? Without seeking to comment in detail upon the results, there are certain internal contradictions that are relevant here as well. In the first place, note that the calculations invoke different assumptions concerning the temporal pattern of beef and pork consumption per capita as they suit convenience. Declining per capita consumption of beef is satisfactory, but constancy must be rationalized for pork. If pork consumption per capita is permitted to decline only at the same 7 per cent rate — not at the observed 33 per cent national pace — and still conceding a slaughter weight in the South some 70 per cent that in the west, the deficit is reduced almost by 20 per cent. The point, simply, is that the deficit is very sensitive to alternative assumptions — a slightly larger southern slaughter weight would have the same effect — and is not to be relied upon unduly. Furthermore, to reckon the effect of the deficit by diverting shipments entirely from the East to the South is to exaggerate its role unduly. From New Orleans to southern coastwise ports in the year 1859-1860 some 187,000 barrels of pork and bacon were in fact shipped.[4] If they went to the South Atlantic states, this is a fourth of the deficit calculated by Fogel and would not have to be subtracted from eastern shipments as he does. Likewise, why not direct satisfaction of these deficits from the surplus border states of Tennessee and Kentucky, both of which were important suppliers to the South?

In sum, Fogel's attempts to create a substantial flow from the West to the South via the East seem less persuasive after closer analysis. My reluctance to accede to his suggestion is fortified by additional evidence relating to that Atlantic coastal trade itself. Whereas Fogel has not offered any direct indication of a great trade in breadstuffs and provisions from North to South, there are pertinent data that straightforwardly deny such a possibility. In the first instance, the trade data from New Orleans confirm an increasing coastwise trade to other southern ports rather than the reverse. Secondly, as far as wheat, corn, and flour are concerned, there were actual exports to the North of the latter two commodities from Norfolk and Charlestown during the 1850's, a circumstance suggesting both limited flow northward, and partial cancellation in any event.[5] The evidence of coast-

---

[4] *New Orleans Price Current*, Aug. 31, 1861.

[5] See the Boston Board of Trade reports at the end of the 1850's for evidence of receipts of corn and flour from southern ports. Also note the exports from Charleston and Norfolk in *DeBow's Review*, XXIX (1860), 526 and *Hunt's Merchant Magazine*, XLII (1860), 480.

wise exports from Baltimore in 1860 tightens the case. In that year, the prime source of supply to the South Atlantic cities shipped 1,358,033 bushels of corn, 120,000 barrels of flour, and 562,339 bushels of wheat.[6] Even if all went South — which we know from Boston receipts a goodly part did not — total imports would have supplemented output by less than one and a half per cent, and reliance upon external supplies of wheat would have remained short of 15 per cent.

Unfortunately, the Baltimore reports do not explicitly give coastwise provisions exports. Yet that fact itself is of significance. A trade whose value would greatly exceed that of breadstuff shipments — if Fogel were correct — hardly figures to go unrecorded. Nonetheless it is possible to calculate what its maximum extent might have been. Total receipts of livestock and provision by the Baltimore and Ohio railroad approximate the total supply of beef and pork available to the city.[7] Subtraction of consumption requirements and foreign exports leaves a surplus of pork, but none of beef.[8] Potential exports are then less than 175,000 barrels of pork at a valuation of $3 million, which raises the share of the South in consumption of western products only from 23 to 24 per cent. The assumptions that the city population alone consumed the available supply, and that all shipments went southward assure that this is an upper limit. Since, by all accounts, Baltimore dominated in what Atlantic coastal trade there was, exclusion of other ports is not a major factor.

Some additional commerce there undoubtedly was — and I confess to error in not pointing it out — but not so large as to affect significantly the conclusions or the underlying interregional trade estimates. The same applies to the implications of the possible, but minor, cattle trade from Texas to the eastern Gulf states.

---

[6] *Eleventh Annual Report of the Baltimore Board of Trade for 1860* (Baltimore, 1861), pp. 21-56. From the Boston reports it appears that perhaps half of the Baltimore flour and a quarter of the corn found their way to that city.

[7] *Thirty-Fourth Annual Report of the Baltimore and Ohio Railroad for 1860* (Baltimore, 1860), pp. 64, 105 and 106. 140,274 hogs, 32,131 cattle, and 25,212 tons of provisions — apparently entirely pork and bacon — were received at Baltimore.

[8] Per capita consumption requirements of 1278 pounds of pork and 79.3 pounds of beef were employed. If the lower 1860 per capita consumption of pork products were used instead, exports of another 25,000 barrels would then be possible. The assumption therefore is not of great significance. Foreign exports were taken from *Annual Report on Commerce and Navigation for 1860.*

AMERICAN INTERREGIONAL TRADE
IN THE NINETEENTH CENTURY*

ROBERT W. FOGEL*

The purpose of this paper is two-fold. First, it represents my reply to Professor Fishlow's "Postscript." Second, it elaborates certain points in my original comments[1] which may transcend the immediate dispute over the magnitude and pattern of interregional trade in the ante-bellum era.

In pursuing the second objective I suggest the existence of a revolution in animal husbandry that probably extended at least from 1840 to 1860. A discernible change in feeding practice appears to have produced both an increase in the average slaughter weight of animals and an increase in the importance of corn relative to other crops. If correct, the finding suggests that recent computations of gross farm income during the ante-bellum period, may be in error.

I also estimate coastwise shipments of cargo to the South from New York in 1872. The indicated volume is over a million tons, with perhaps as much as 60 per cent originating in the West. The connection of this finding with Fishlow's estimate of trade flows in 1860 follows from a point to which Fishlow alludes in his Postscript. Namely, the cost of direct rail shipments from the West to the South Atlantic states (relative to the cost of reaching the South Atlantic via New York, Boston and Baltimore) dropped after the Civil War when the South established "through-line" rail links with the West. Hence one would expect that the indirect route to the South Atlantic states was relatively more important in 1860 than in 1872. Beyond this, however, the large volume of cargo shipped from New York to the South after the Civil War suggests that coastal shipping probably played a major role in internal trade well after the advent of the railroad — a role that may have escaped attention because of the paucity of data on coastal shipping and a preoccupation with newer forms of transportation.

*   *   *

In "Antebellum Interregional Trade Reconsidered," Professor Fishlow sought to determine the magnitude and pattern of trade flows during the

---

* Robert Fogel is Professor of Economics at the University of Chicago.

period from 1839 to 1860.[2] Professor Fishlow's results and his defense of them involve the following assumptions: (a) Virtually all goods shipped from the West to the South were sent down the Mississippi River to New Orleans and then shipped by coastal vessels to other Southern cities. (b) The ratio of annual meat production to the June 1 stock of animals was constant (over time and among regions).[3]

In my original comments on Professor Fishlow's paper I attempted to test these assumptions and the conclusions derived from them by exploring their implications. Specifically, I showed that assumption (b) implied that between 1840 and 1860 the national average consumption of beef declined by 7 per cent and the national average consumption of pork declined by 33 per cent.

The magnitude of the implied decline in pork consumption is particularly suspicious. The Department of Agriculture has published estimates of per capita consumption of pork for the 59 years from 1899 through 1958.[4] It is possible to combine these estimates in 1,711 pairs. Only one of these combinations shows a percentage difference in pork consumption between years as large as that implied by Fishlow's assumption. In 1935, one of the worst years of the depression, average pork consumption fell to a six-decade low. In 1944, the peak year of the World War II boom, average consumption rose to a six-decade high.

In Fishlow's case, income moves in the wrong direction. While 1840 belongs to the contraction phase of a business cycle. 1860 marked the peak of a boom. Moreover, between 1840 and 1860 the prices of cattle and swine fell relative to the prices of grains.[5] Hence both income and price movements militate against the likelihood of a decline in meat consumption — especially a decline of the magnitude implied for pork.

If one brings assumption (a) into play, Fishlow's difficulties become compounded. Assumptions (a) and (b) together imply a regional breakdown in national meat consumption. For on the basis of assumption (a) Fishlow computes net imports into the South; and assumption (b) applied to census data on the stock of animals in the Southern states yields an estimate of meat production in that region. Computations based on these two assumptions produce the following dubious results:[6]

1.　In 1840 average Southern consumption of beef exceeded that of the North by 36 per cent while average Southern consumption of pork exceeded the Northern average by 118 per cent. Thus total meat consumption per person in the South was nearly twice as great as in the North.

2.　In 1860 average Southern consumption of beef exceeded that of the North by 66 per cent while average Southern consumption of pork exceeded the Northern average by 186 per cent. Thus total meat consumption per person in the South was more than twice as great as in the North.

3. Between 1840 and 1860 average beef consumption rose by 6 per cent in the South while it declined by 13 per cent in the North.

4. Between 1840 and 1860 pork consumption fell in both the South and the North by 21 and 40 per cent respectively.

The implausible implications of Fishlow's assumptions with respect to levels and trends in the average consumption of meats throws his assumptions, and hence arguments based on them, into doubt. Nor does Fishlow extricate himself from the dilemma with his Postscript. Quite the contrary; he worsens his position by insisting that the cattle trade between Texas and the Southern states east of the Mississippi was small enough to be ignored. This statement (together with his previous assumptions) implies that the average consumption of beef in the Southwest rose by over 100 per cent between 1840 and 1860, reaching an incredible level of 246 pounds per person in the latter year.[7] It simultaneously implies that average beef consumption in Southern states east of the Mississippi declined by 29 per cent. One could of course argue that while shipments to the other Southern states were small, substantial quantities of Texas cattle were trailed to the North. But this requires an increase in Fishlow's estimate of Southern import capacity. It also requires either an increase in the volume of shipments into the South along the routes Fishlow designated or the identification of additional routes of trade between the North and the South.

Fishlow falls into a similar contradiction during the attempt to refute my conjecture that the Southern deficit in pork production may have been as large as 787,000 barrels. That deficit was computed on the basis of Fishlow's assumption (b) and the further assumption that the average consumption of pork remained constant between 1840 and 1860. In his postscript Fishlow argues that it is reasonable to assume that the average Southern consumption of pork dropped by 7 per cent between the two years. He suggests that this would reduce the figure I put forward for the deficit to 483,000 barrels. In appraising Fishlow's argument on this point it must be remembered that my computation was aimed at testing the sensitivity of a particular argument to the assumptions on which it was based. It was not an attempt to replace Fishlow's original estimates with a set of alternative figures. Hence for my purposes it was sufficient to focus on just the four South Atlantic states. The pork deficit that I computed of 787,000 barrels then was the deficit in only these states. However, Fishlow's assumptions imply a deficit throughout the South. Thus if average consumption remained constant between 1840 and 1860,

Fishlow's assumptions imply that the Southwide production deficit of pork was not 787,000 barrels but 2,722,000 barrels. And if one accepts Fishlow's suggestion that average pork consumption declined by 7 per cent, the Southwide deficit (calculated on the basis of this assumption) is still 1,815,000 barrels. Indeed, to reduce the Southwide deficit to 483,000 barrels one must assume that average consumption fell not by 7 but by 17 per cent. Finally, Fishlow in fact contradicts himself when he argues that a 7 per cent fall in average pork consumption in the South is reasonable. For as I have already pointed out, his computations imply a 21 per cent decline.

The implausible implications of Fishlow's assumptions led me to search for evidence that might shed light on the manner in which the assumptions should be altered. In my original comment I suggested that available evidence contradicted the most basic proposition underlying assumption (b): the proposition that the slaughter weight of animals remained constant between 1840 and 1860. The growth of corn production indicates a veritable revolution in animal husbandry between 1840 and 1860 — a movement that has previously escaped attention because of the practice of computing indexes of corn consumption per person. However, since corn was primarily an animal feed, a proper index must show the movement in corn production relative to growth not only of population but also of the stock of corn consuming animals.

Such an index[8] reveals that corn consumption per consuming unit increased by close to 60 per cent for the nation as a whole between the dates in question. But there is a marked disparity between the North and the South. Corn production per consuming unit rose by 120 per cent in the North but only by 15 per cent in the South. Moreover, in the North the rise in corn consumption was accompanied by a rise in the production of oats. In the South, however oats production fell by 32 per cent between 1840 and 1860, suggesting that a substantial part of the rise of the Southern index represents not an increase in the total amount of grain fed to animals but a substitution of one grain (corn) for another (oats). The implications of these findings are that: (1) the slaughter weight of animals in the North and the Northern ratio of meat production to stocks of cattle and swine rose between 1840 and 1860; (2) the slaughter weight of animals in the South and the Southern ratio of meat production to stocks of cattle and swine rose much less, if at all; (3) by 1860 there was a substantial regional differential in the slaughter weight of animals and in the ratio of meat production to stocks.

I also questioned assumption (a), suggesting that Fishlow had overlooked the possibility of substantial trade between the West and the South over routes other than the Mississippi River. In particular, I suggested the possibility that substantial numbers of cattle and swine might have been trailed overland from the Northwest into the South; that large numbers of cattle may have been trailed from Texas into the Southeast; and that Northwestern products bound for the South Atlantic states may have been shipped increasingly via New York, Philadelphia and Baltimore rather than via New Orleans.[9] Because the last of these three possibilities is most novel, I focused my main attention on it. I argued that changes in prices of comparable products in New Orleans and in New York indicate that by the 1850's, if not sooner, it may have cost less to ship from the Northwest to the coastal cities of the South Atlantic states via New York, Philadelphia and Baltimore rather than via New Orleans. I also suggested that post-Civil War data supported this possibility.

In his Postscript Fishlow argues that monthly and annual price movements were too variable to lend support to my conjecture. In the case of pork, for example, he points out that while in 1859 the average New York price of mess pork was below that of New Orleans, the reverse situation prevailed in 1858. Yet despite monthly and annual variability in price differentials, the shift of prices in favor of New York is unmistakable. Over the decade 1831-1840 the New Orleans price of pork was below the New York price in 89 out of 120 months (74 per cent of the time) and the average differential in favor of New Orleans was 94 cents per barrel. During the next decade (1841-50) New Orleans' edge dropped to an average of 28 cents. During the five years from 1851 to 1855, New Orleans' edge again dropped, this time to an average of only 15 cents. And in the final quiquennium (1856-60) the advantage shifted to New York which had lower prices than New Orleans in 37 of 60 months (62 per cent of the time), the average differential in its favor being 9 cents per barrel.[10] Hence it seems quite clear, that despite daily, monthly and annual variability in price differentials, New Orleans progressively lost its *average* price advantage to New York. This shift in favor of New York must have affected relative sales in the two cities and by 1856-1860, if not sooner, probably made New York a better market for the deficit areas of the South Atlantic states than New Orleans.

Fishlow attempts to prove that Northwestern shipments to the South via the cities of New York, Philadelphia and Baltimore must have been small by roughly estimating pork shipments from Baltimore to the South and then arguing that it is unnecessary to perform similar computations for the other cities because "Baltimore dominated what Atlantic coastal trade there was." The difficulty with this position is not only that it assumes what has to be proved but also that the assumption is probably wrong. Post-Civil War data indicate that New York rather than Baltimore dominated the coastal trade. The earliest time for which we have comprehensive data on coastal shipments from the Middle Atlantic ports is 1890. In that year shipments from New York to all Atlantic and Gulf points exceeded those of Baltimore by 160 per cent. Shipments from Philadelphia exceeded the Baltimore's total by 17 per cent. If consideration is limited to shipments to the South, the totals (in tons) are: New York, 1,206,342; Baltimore, 842,458; and Philadelphia, 502,160.[11]

Available data further suggest that shipments to the South represented a bigger share of New York's coastal trade in the early 1870's than it did in 1890. It also appears likely that the absolute volume of coastal shipments from New York to the South was nearly as large in 1872 as it was 18 years later.

It is possible to estimate the volume of freight shipped from New York to Southern ports on steamships during 1872 by combining the data on the tonnage of the steamships engaged in the Southern trade with information on average load factors, average rates of speed, and distances from New York to specified ports. This is done in Table 1 which shows that total shipments from New York to the South via steamship were 825,000 tons in 1872. Since a total of 1,243,000 tons were shipped from New York on coastal steamships bound for all ports,[12] it appears that two-thirds of the total was bound for the South. By contrast, the South received only 23 per cent of New York's coastal shipments in 1890.[13]

It should be noted that the figure of 825,000 tons given for 1872 represents shipments to the South only by steamboat. However, in 1872 sailing vessels were still an important factor in the coastal trade. If the shipments to the South from New York are estimated on the assumption that the sailing trade was divided between the South and the other coastal regions in the same proportion as the trade of steam vessels, then coastwise shipments from New York to the South must be increased by 230,000 tons.[14] This puts New York's total coastal shipments to the South in 1872 at 1,055,000 tons.

Fishlow is also mistaken in his interpretation of Sindall's data.[15] The figure of 45,000 tons cited by Fishlow represents neither the total shipments from the West to the South by water nor the total shipments from the West to the South via New York and Baltimore. The first interpretation is unwarranted, among other reasons, because the stated figure completely omits Western shipments to the South via the Mississippi River — shipments which Sindall does not discuss and which are not included in his tables. The error in the second interpretation becomes obvious when one recognizes that 45,000 tons which Sindall classified as shipments from Chicago, St. Louis, Indianapolis, Cincinnati and other Western points to the South via New York and Baltimore must have been sent on through bills of lading. For otherwise, Sindall would not have been able to identify the origin of these commodities. However shipments received by New York and Baltimore from the West on through bills of lading were but a small fraction of their total receipts from the West.

To put it another way, Fishlow's second interpretation of the 45,000 ton figure is in effect a statement that no Southerners purchased Western grain, provisions and goods from supplies available in the markets of New York and Baltimore; i.e., that no Western commodities sold to the

TABLE 1

ESTIMATED SHIPMENTS BY STEAMSHIP FROM NEW YORK TO THE SOUTH IN 1872 COMPARED WITH TOTAL COASTWISE SHIPMENTS FROM NEW YORK TO THE SOUTH IN 1890

1	2	3	4	5	6
District Receiving Shipments from New York	Number of ships	Estimated average cargo per ship per trip (tons)	Estimated number of trips per year per ship	Estimated annual shipments by steamship in 1872 (tons)	Annual shipments in 1890 by all types of ships (tons)
1. Norfolk	14	692	46.40	450,000	422,329
2. Savannah	15	829	19.35	241,000	567,141
3. Mobile	—	—	—	—	17,553
4. New Orleans	12	711	8.01	68,000	12,653
5. Galveston	11	827	7.22	66,000	186,666
Totals					

SOURCES AND NOTES:

COLUMN 1. The districts and the ports included in them are given *Census of Transportation, 1890,* Part II, p. 4. The Norfolk District includes Alexandria in 1872 but not in 1890.

COLUMN 2. The New York Produce Exchange, *Annual Report, 1872-73,* pp. 315-20, lists 52 steamships as being regularly engaged in trade between New York and designated Southern ports. The enrolled tonnage of these ships was 57,000 tons.

COLUMN 3. The average weight of New York steamships engaged in the coastal trade in 1890 was 754.70 tons. The average freight per trip by a steamboat leaving New York was 518.54 tons. The indicated load factor of 0.6871 was multiplied by the average tonnage of the ships given in Column 2. The resulting figure is the estimated average cargo per ship per trip. *Census of Transportation, 1890,* Part II, Table 15; New York Produce Exchange, *Annual Report, 1872-73,* pp. 315-20.

COLUMN 4. New York's steamships averaged 90.007 trips per year in 1890, indicating that the average number of days per trip (including time in port) was 4.056. The average distance per trip was 303.1 miles. Hence the number of days (including time in port) required to go one mile was 0.01338. The last figure multiplied by the round trip distance from New York to the ports indicated in Column 1 yields the average number of days per trip. The average number of days per trip was divided into 365 to obtain the estimated number of trips per year per boat. *Census of Transportation, 1890,* Part II, Table 15; U. S. Coast and Geodetic Survey, *Distance Between United States Ports,* Serial No. 444 (Washington: GPO, 1938).

COLUMN 5. Col. 2 x Col. 3 x Col. 4. Line 1 includes 38,000 tons estimated to have been sent from New York to Alexandria, Va. Since shipments to Alexandria are not included in the Norfolk district in 1890, the entry in Line 1 should be reduced by 38,000 to make it directly comparable with the entry in Column 6, Line 1. A similar reduction should be made for Line 6 to make it directly comparable with the entry in Column 6, Line 6.

COLUMN 6. *Census of Transportation, 1890,* Part II, Table 10. This column excludes shipments to Southern cities included in the Baltimore district.

South became part of the New York and Baltimore supplies because they were all shipped on through bills of lading. But this is clearly false. For at least in the case of grains and provisions we know that most of New York's supply originated in the West. We also know that New York shipped such commodities not only to New England but also to the South. The 1876 *Report on the Internal Commerce of the United States* records the following question and the reply to that question given by the General Agent of the New York Cheap Transportation Association:

> "Question 22. Will you please to describe approximately the area in the Atlantic States within which the New York grain-market competes with other markets for the distribution of western grain and flour?
>
> "Answer. This is a very difficult question to answer with any degree of definiteness. I have conferred with such men as Mr. Blanchard, of the Erie Road, and all concur in the statement that a line can be drawn nowhere in the Atlantic States limiting the market for grain and flour distribution from New York. There is a constant trade with every Atlantic port — both a regular and incidental trade.
>
> "The incidental trade is where a return freight is desired, and is enjoyed in a greater or less degree by all of the chief seaports . . . but in addition to this, New York has a regular trade with all the coast states."[16]

Unfortunately there are no data which reveal how large a share of the commodities sent by the West through New York and other port cities was shipped on through bills of lading. However, we do have such information for goods destined for foreign ports. According to reports by their respective boards of trade less than 3 per cent of grain exported from New York and less than 10 per cent of grain exported from Baltimore were on through bills in 1876.[17] Moreover, the primary advantage of through bills of lading to shippers was the savings on intermediate costs (weighing, transfer and commission charges). In the case of grains these usually amounted to 1.25 to 1.50 cents per bushel in the late seventies and early eighties.[18] However according to the U. S. Bureau of Statistics it took intermediate charges of 2.5 cents per bushel on grain to deflect sales away from the markets of the Eastern port cities to the markets of the West.[19] Thus only a small proportion of the foreign sales were on through bills originating in the West because intermediate charges were usually such for most shippers that it was more efficient to purchase Western grain in Eastern markets.

Essentially the same considerations must have entered into the determination of the importance of through bills in shipments from the West to the South via the Eastern port cities. Consequently it does not seem unreasonable to compute a first — and very rough — approximation of South-bound shipments on the assumption that the ratio of total to through-bill shipments for the South was the same as that observed in the foreign trade. If ones uses Sindall's data for 1881-82, total shipments from the West to the South are 630,000 tons via New York and 260,000 tons via Baltimore.[20]

While the crude and uncertain nature of these estimates is too obvious to need emphasis, the results are by no means implausible. The computation suggests that about 60 per cent of New York's coastwise shipments to the South and about 30 per cent of Baltimore's originated in the West. This would put Western shipments to the South via New York in 1881-82 at about 15 per cent of New York's recorded receipts of domestic produce and livestock in that year or about 25 per cent of her foreign exports of such commodities.[21] Moreover, if Fishlow is right in his assumption that Sindall's fourth table gives the total direct[22] rail shipments from the West to the South (the total given by that table for 1881-82 is 506.211 tons), then it may well be that as late as the 1880's more than half of the West's shipments to the South reached the latter region by way of New York, Baltimore and Philadelphia.[23]

*   *   *

Where then does this debate leave us? Professor Fishlow has clearly shown that one cannot use aggregate receipts at New Orleans to establish the proposition that during 1840-1860 the South purchased a consistently large share of Western exports. As he perceptively points out, this fallacious interpretation of the New Orleans data arises from a failure to consider the composition of New Orleans' receipts and a neglect of New Orleans' role as an exporter.

The validity of Fishlow's reconstruction of the magnitude of trade among the three regions he designates is less clear cut. The assumptions on which his reconstruction is based imply highly dubious levels and trends in the per capita consumption of leading commodities. His contention that the Mississippi River was the only substantial link between the Northwest and the South is also open to doubt.

I do not mean to imply that either my critique of Professor Fishlow's argument or the alternative assumptions I have proposed are definitive. They are not. I cannot, and did not try to, verify a substitute set of assumptions. I am not in possession of the evidence needed for so formidable a task. I sought instead to show that alternative assumptions were consistent with readily available scraps of data and hence are at least plausible.

I do not believe that the wide range of issues posed by Professor Fishlow's searching re-examination of ante-bellum trade can be resolved with the skimpy evidence currently in hand. We will not have a reasonably reliable set of figures in interregional trade flows during the antebellum era until we explore more fully than we have so far such current mysteries as the extent of the coastal trade, the nature and dimensions of the revolution in animal husbandry, and the extent to which non-railroad forms of overland transportation persisted down to the Civil War. I would particularly stress the need to investigate the role of coastal shipping. Preoccupation with the railroad may have led us to overlook the continuing importance of this form of transportation through much of the nineteenth century. Professor Fishlow's essay emphasizes the need for these studies. It also suggests fruitful lines along which such research may be pursued.

FOOTNOTES

* I am indebted to Peter Mieszkowski, Albert Rees, Eugene Smolensky and Harold Vatter for their comments on a draft of this paper. Michael R. Lav assisted in the computations.

[1] Robert William Fogel, "A Provisional View of the 'New Economic History'," *American Economic Review,* LIV (May, 1964).

[2] Albert Fishlow, "Antebellum Interregional Trade Reconsidered," *American Economic Review,* LIV (May, 1964), 352-64.

[3] Fishlow implicitly invokes assumption (b) when he infers Southern self-sufficiency from the size of Southern stocks of cattle and swine relative to the stocks of other regions. Assumption (b) also follows directly from two assumptions that he uses in his unpublished technical appendix to correct Kohlmeier's estimates of cattle and swine shipments. These are: (1) the slaughter weight of cattle and hogs was constant; (2) the annual number of cattle and swine slaughtered was a constant percentage of the respective stocks.

It should be noted that assumption (a) is probably more basic to the magnitude of Fishlow's trade flows than assumption (b). The latter affects the magnitude of the flows only through the correction of Kohlmeier's figures on cattle and swine shipments. Fishlow leans most heavily on assumption (b) when he uses regional differentials in animal stocks to support his low estimate of Western shipments to the South and in his computation of potential beef and pork exports from Baltimore.

4 U. S. Bureau of the Census, *Historical Statistic of the United States, Colonial Times to 1957* (Washington, D. C.; 1960), p. 186.

5 Marvin W. Towne and Wayne D. Rasmussen, "Farm Gross Product and Gross Investment in the Nineteenth Century," Conference on Income and Wealth, *Trends in the American Economy in the Nineteenth Century*, Vol. 24 of *Studies in Income and Wealth* (Princeton: Princeton University Press, 1960), pp. 283, 284, 294, 297.

6 The method of computation and the sources of data are given in Fogel, "A Provisional View," p. 385. As defined in this paper, the states comprised in "the South" are Virginia, North Carolina, South Carolina, Georgia, Florida, Kentucky, Tennessee, Alabama, Mississippi, Louisiana, Arkansas and Texas.

7 The annual per capita consumption of beef during the 59 years from 1899 through 1957 varied between a low of 53 and a high of 95 pounds. *Historical Statistics*, p. 186.

8 The index is defined in Fogel, "A Provisional View," p. 385.

9 *Ibid.*, pp. 382, 387 and 388n25.

10 Computed from data in Arthur Harrison Cole, *Wholesale Commodity Prices in the United States 1700–1861, Statistical Supplement* (Cambridge, Mass.: Harvard University Press, 1938).

11 U. S. Bureau of the Census, *Eleventh Census of the United States: 1890, Report on Transportation Business in the United States*, Part II, Table 10; thereafter referred to as *Census of Transportation, 1890*.

12 Estimated by multiplying the total tonnage in the coastal trade cleared from New York during the year ending June 30, 1872 by the average load factor for 1890. U. S. Treasury Department, *Annual Report on Commerce and Navigation, 1872*, p. 718; note to Col. 3 of Table 1, above.

13 *Census of Transportation, 1890*, Part II, Table 10.

14 About 66.37 per cent of the goods carried from New York by steamship were bound for the South. The average load factor for sailing vessels cleared from New York in 1890 was 0.6637. The total tonnage of sailing ships in the coastal trade cleared from New York in 1872 was 521,559. See the sources cited in note 12.

15 Charles A. Sindall, "Development of the Traffic Between the Southern States and the Northern and Northwestern States," U. S. Treasury Department, *Report on the Internal Commerce of the United States, 1886* (Washington: GPO, 1886), pp. 679-738.

In this connection, it is worth noting the lake ports became the dominant centers for the collection, and shipping of the agricultural products of the Old Northwest before the Civil War, rather than after it. Their hegemony over the Ohio River ports in 1860 is striking. In that year flour and grain shipments from Chicago exceeded those of Cincinnati by 483 per cent. For Toledo and Milwaukee the corresponding figures are 128 and 74 per cent. Chicago also eclipsed Cincinnati in shipments of beef and cattle. It lagged behind only in shipments of pork. Lewis Bernard Schmidt. "The Internal Grain Trade of the United States 1860–1890," *Iowa Journal of History and Politics*, XIX (1921), 449; U. S. Bureau of Statistics, *Monthly Summary of Commerce and Finance* (February, 1900), p. 2287; Chicago Board of Trade, *Annual Report, 1859*, p. 56.

16 U. S. Treasury Department, *Report on the Internal Commerce of the United States, 1876*, (Washington: GPO, 1876), Appendix, pp. 74-75.

17 *Ibid.*, p. 132.

18 U. S. Treasury Department, *Report on the Internal Commerce of the United States, 1879* (Washington: GPO, 1879), Appendix, p. 31.

19 *Report on Internal Commerce, 1876*, p. 129.

20 The computation is as follows: $\dfrac{18,996}{0.03} = 633,200$; and $\dfrac{26,200}{0.10} = 262,000$.

Sindall, "Development," p. 725.

21 New York Produce Exchange, *Annual Report, 1882,* pp. 433-35, 711.

22 In contradistinction to shipments via New York, Baltimore, Philadelphia and Boston.

23 However, it is unlikely that Sindall's figure does represent total direct rail shipments. Sindall's fourth table gives the tonnage of rail shipments from the West to 12 Southern cities and to a scattering of points in Florida and on the S. & N. A. Railroad. It does not give receipts at such important centers as Knoxville, Tenn.; Raleigh, N. C.; Columbia, S. C.; Nashville, Tenn.; Memphis, Tenn.; Jackson, Miss.; and New Orleans. Hence Sindall's table would give total direct shipments only if all Western commodities shipped directly to the South were unloaded at the points listed by Sindall before being sent to the points that he does not report on.

RAILROADS AND THE AXIOM OF INDISPENSABILITY †

ROBERT W. FOGEL*

The prevailing interpretation of the influence of railroads on American economic growth during the nineteenth century is still dominated by ideas spawned during that era. This long but questionable rule has been facilitated by two features of recent historiography: first, the acceptance of certain propositions propounded during the Gilded Age as truths so obvious that they did not require critical examinaton; second, a tendency to analyze issues connected with the construction and operation of railroads within the conceptual framework established by the antagonists of yore. Escape from the confines of the past is never an easy task; it has been particularly difficult in this case. The evidence which must be re-examined is vast and the economic significance of railroads is intricately intertwined with a host of social and political issues. Under these circumstances the re-evaluation of the nineteenth century conception of the place of railroads in American economic development must be a proccess rather than a single act. Such a process has in fact been underway for some time. However, the required revisions are much more extensive than has been generally recognized. The discussion that follows focuses on the most important of the "self-evident truths" of the Gilded Age: the axiom of indispensability.

The Evolution of the Axiom

The railroad was not born with the distinction attributed to it by later

* Robert W. Fogel is Professor of Economics at the Univ. of Chicago.
† This paper was first presented to the annual meeting of the Mississippi Valley Historical Association held in Omaha, Nebraska in May of 1963. Professor Fogel's paper was in the nature of a preliminary progress report of a much larger and detailed study which has subsequently been published as, *Railroads and American Economic Growth: Essays in Econometric History* (Baltimore: Johns Hopkins Univ. Press, 1964). The present version of Professor Fogel's earlier paper is reprinted here with three changes: social savings estimates are updated as are the indexes of canal construction and iron consumption. Though this paper serves as a most brilliant introduction to Professor Fogel's work — and a topic which has become controversial — it is no substitute for the more comprehensive and far-ranging material contained in Professor Fogel's book noted above. Students and professors, therefore, are urged to use the present paper as a starting point in assaying the role of railroads in our national economic growth.

generations. Far from being viewed as essential to economic development, the first railroads were widely regarded as having only limited commercial application. Extreme skeptics argued that railroads were too crude to insure regular service, that the sparks thrown off by belching engines would set fire to buildings and fields, and that speeds of twenty or thirty miles an hour could be "fatal to wagons, road and loading, as well as to human life." More sober critics questioned the ability of railroads to provide low cost transportation, especially for heavy freight. Benjamin Wright, a superintendent of construction on the Erie Canal and adviser to the New York Legislature on the Erie railroad, placed "a railroad between a good turnpike and a canal" in transportation efficiency. Even railroad executives appear to have had, at least initially, a limited conception of the role of railroads. Most of the first enterprises expected to make their profit largely in the carriage of passengers, by serving small localities and by serving as feeders to waterways. The prevailing opinion of the thirties appears to have been expressed in a report presented to the New York Legislature by three engineers. "We are . . . led to the conclusion," they wrote, "that in regard to the cost of construction and maintenance and also in reference to the expense of conveyance at moderate velocities, canals are clearly the most advantageous means of communication. On the other hand, where high velocities are required, as for the conveyance of passengers, and under some circumstances of competition, for light goods of great value, in proportion to their weight, the preference would be given to a railroad." [1]

By the mid-forties, most of the early doubts about railroads were squelched. Some four thousand miles of track had ben built in the East and South and iron rails were pushing past the Appalachian barrier into the states of the Old Northwest. Considerable advances had been made in railroad technology. Engines were larger, more powerful and less prone to breakdowns. These and other developments made it possible for trains to pass through mountainous regions as well as over level terrain. Railroad advocates no longer argued the feasibility of railroads. Although waterways still carried the great bulk of the nation's freight, far-sighted innovators now declared that the "iron horse" had superceded the waterway in inland transportation and proposed vast projects for the railroadization of the nation. J. W. Scott, editor of the *Toledo Blade* was typical of these prophets. "The railroad," he proclaimed, "has become the great instrument of land commerce and trade." But railroads were not being built rapidly enough. "No nation," he asserted, "can maintain its position among the foremost in civilization" without fully exploiting this new means of transportation. He, therefore, called on Congress to finance the construction of

---

[1]Thurman William Van Metre, *Early Opposition to Steam Railroads* (New York, 1924). The three quotations are from pages 10, 37 and 42 respectively.

six great trunk lines: two running North and South — along the Atlantic
seaboard and from the Great Lakes to New Orleans; four leading from the
Atlantic seaboard to the West — along routes which today roughly parallel the New York Central, the Pennsylvania, the Chesapeake and Ohio,
and the Southern railroads. Such a system of trunk lines, said Scott, would
transform the nation:[2]

> To commercial exchanges through the interior, it would give an activity
> beyond anything witnessed heretofore in inland trade. A face of gladness
> would animate every department of toil, and new motives be held out to
> activity in enterprise. Social as well as commercial intercourse of the
> people of distant States, would break down local prejudices and annihilate
> sectional misunderstandings. The wages of labor would be improved, and
> the profits of capital increased beyond the whole cost of these works . . .
> As long as the hills stand, or the valleys disclose their beauty, so long
> will these works bear evidence to prosperity of the energy and spirit of
> those who erected them.

Congress did not adopt the specific program called for by Scott. But it
did turn in the direction suggested by such prophets. Between 1850 and
1872 the Federal government gave an empire of land to promoters who
promised to build railroads across the sparsely settled territory of the
West. While Congress dispensed over 100,000,000 acres of the public
domain, state and local governments provided an additional $280,000,000
in cash or credit (about 30 percent of the total capitalization of railroads)
in the decades preceding the Civil War.[3] Spurred by such inducements the
railroad network expanded swiftly. The legacy left to the Gilded Age included a system of track over 35,000 miles long — almost half the world's
total.[4]

In 1867 the *North American Review* surveyed the effects wrought by
railroads and found that they were stupendous. "With perhaps two exceptions," it said, the railroad was "the most tremendous and far-reaching
engine of social revolution which has ever either blessed or cursed the
earth." It was this innovation which "made our century different from all
others, — a century of greater growth, of more rapid development." The
railroad, the distinguished journal held, had peopled the "wilds of America"
and turned "the very Arabs of civilization" into "substantial communities."
It cosmopolitanized the nation; removed the old distinctions between
classes, changing both dress and manners; "abolished" the Mississippi

[2] J. W. Scott, "A National System of Railways," *Merchants' Magazine and Commercial Review*, XVII (December, 1847), 564-71.
[3] Carter Goodrich, *Government Promotion of American Canals and Railroads,
1800-1890* (New York, Columbia University Press, 1959), 268-270.
[4] U. S. Bureau of the Census, *Historical Statistics of the United States, Colonial
Times to 1957* (Washington, D. C., 1960), 427.

River; crushed the southern rebellion; made "the grass grow in the once busy streets of small commercial centres like Nantucket, Salem, and Charleston"; robbed "New Orleans of that monopoly of wealth which the Mississippi River once promised to pour into her lap" and simultaneously turned New York into "an overgrown monster." The "iron arms" of the railroad, the *Review* concluded, "have been stretched out in every direction; nothing has escaped their reach, and the most firmly established institutions of man have proved under their touch as plastic as clay." [5]

Thus by the opening of the Gilded Age the railroad had already won a strong claim to the title of indispensability. During the next three decades the view of the railroad as the chief agent of economic and social transformation became an integral part of popular thought. The further extension of the railroad network — to 181,000 miles in 1895 — made what was an imposing industry at the close of the Civil War even more monumental.[6] Companies engaged in competing forms of transportation were vanquished one after the other as the railroad technology advanced. The size, speed and pulling power of locomotives increased, the substitution of steel for iron rails permitted larger and heavier loads. At the same time the rail network which had been a discontinuous conglomeration of segments with track gauges varying from three to six feet was rationalized into an integrated system with a uniform gauge of 4'8½". As a result of these and other changes the average cost of commodity transportation by railroad dropped over fifty percent during the Gilded Age — from 1.925 cents per ton-mile in 1867 to 0.839 cents in 1895.[7] By 1890 railroads had achieved almost complete domination of inter-city freight shipments. The magnitude of the railroad victory over its chief competitor — waterways — is summarized by two sets of figures: in 1851-52 boats carried six times as much freight as railroads; in 1889-90 railroads carried five times as much freight as boats.[8]

To the men of the Gilded Age the primacy of the railroad in the promotion of American economic growth became an indisputable fact. Among the most obvious of the many obvious effects assigned to the railroad was the rapid growth of the internal market. Available statistical data, particularly

---

[5] "The Railroad System," *North American Review*, CIV (1867), 476-511.

[6] U. S. Bureau of the Census, *Historical Statistics*, 429.

[7] H. T. Newcomb, *Changes in the Rates of Charge for Railway and Other Transportation Services*, U. S. Dept. of Ag., Division of Statistics, Bull. No. 15, revised, 1901, 14.

[8] There was double counting in the data on which these ratios are based. U. S. Congress, Senate, *Andrews Report*, Executive Document No. 112, 32nd Cong., 1st Sess., 903-906; U. S. Bureau of the Census, *Eleventh Census of the United States: 1890, Report on the Transportation Business*, part I, 452, 548, 640. Part II, 9, 10, 163, 308, 384, 436, 479.

those bearing on the development of states West of the Alleghanies, appeared to give unambiguous support to this attribution. States such as Indiana, Illinois, Michigan, and Ohio experienced a marked increase in population, construction and manufacturing following the completion of rail lines across their territories. And these states together with Minnesota, Nebraska, Iowa, Wisconsin and Kansas replaced New York and Pennsylvania as the granary of the nation. Common sense also supported the attribution. "If produce cannot be carried," said an observer in 1866, "it can only find local markets. If it only finds local markets, prices must abate. If prices abate the stimulus to cultivation is lost. . . . The prosperity of the West, the value of its produce, the value of its land, and the extent of land cultivated — all depend, therefore, upon increased facilities for the conveyance of produce; and these facilities railroads must afford."[9] Economic theory also appeared to support the attribution. Richard T. Ely, a distinguished economist of the era, deduced "a universal dependency on the railway" from the proposition that productivity depended on the division of labor. For a "primary condition" for the "widespread, far-reaching, division of labor" that characterized their epoch, said Ely, was "the improved means of communication and transportation which the inventions and discoveries of our century have place at our disposal."[10] Sidney Dillon gave vivid expression to the dominant opinion at the close of the Gilded Age when he wrote:[11]

> The growth of the United States west of the Alleghenies during the past fifty years is due not so much to free institutions or climate, or the fertility of the soil, as to railways. If . . . railways had not been invented, the freedom and natural advantages of our Western states would have beckoned to human immigration and industry in vain. Civilization would have crept slowly on, in a toilsome march over the immense spaces that lie between the Appalachian ranges and the Pacific Ocean; and what we now style the Great West would be, except in the valley of the Mississippi, an unknown and unproductive wilderness.

The ability of railroads to determine the course of economic growth also appeared to be inherent in the great power that railroads exercised over the commercial destinies of individual firms and groups of firms. The investigations of railroad rate practices by a special committee of the Assembly of the State of New York (the Hepburn Committee) in 1879 did much to develop public consciousness of the rate-making power. The

---

[9] Sir S. Morton Peto, *Resources and Prospects of America* (New York and Philadelphia, 1866), 281.

[10] Richard T. Ely, "Social Studies; I. The Nature of the Railway Problem," *Harper's Magazine,* 73 (1886), 252.

[11] Sidney Dillon, "The West and the Railroads," *North American Review,* CLII (1891), 443.

proceedings revealed a pattern of special contracts with favored shippers at rates below those rates generally charged. The most publicized example of the practice was the Standard Oil case. The Pennsylvania Railroad entered into a contract with the Rockefeller organization under which it agreed to maintain the business of Standard Oil "against injury or loss by competition" by raising the rates charged to other refiners "as far as it legally may, for such times and to such extent as may be necessary to overcome such competition." [12] The Standard Oil Company, said Ely, received "$10,000,000 in eighteen months in rebates. If it had done business at what would have been cost for others, it would still have had that enormous sum as profit . . . It is a matter of course that its competitors were ruined." [13]

Few rebates were as large as those granted to Standard Oil. But few had to be. In the shipment of such commodities "as wheat, coal and flour," noted William Larrabee, Governor of Iowa, "a small advantage in rates is sufficient to enable the favored shipper to 'freeze out' all competitors." [14] According to the Hepburn Committee, a concession on railroad rates equal to less than 4 percent of the market price of wheat enabled two firms to control the grain trade of the largest secondary market in the nation — New York City — during the Winter of 1877.[15] "The railway charge is so important an element in the price of every commodity carried for a distance in the United States . . ." declared Simon Sterne, counsel for the New York Board of Trade, "that it is within the power of our railway magnates to become partners in every special line of occupation, and it is this power to destroy and to build up which no community can allow to roam and exercise itself unchecked, which must be restrained, curbed and rendered subservient to the general public weal through the instrumentality of wise legislation rigidly enforced." [16]

During the course of the bitter battles over government control, the indispensability of railroads to American economic growth was elevated to the status of an axiomatic truth. Critics and defenders of railroad management argued about the appropriate basis for setting rates, the size of a fair profit, the necessity of various types of discrimination, the effectiveness of competition, and the wisdom of private pools, but they rarely debated the indispensability of railroads. Quite the contrary, the

---

[12] State of New York, Legislature, Assembly, *Proceedings of the Special Committee on Railroads* (8 vols., Albany, 1879); 6:41. Hereafter referred to as Hepburn Committee.

[13] Richard T. Ely, "Social Studies; II. The Economic Evils in American Railway Methods," *Harper's Magazine*, 73 (1886), 455.

[14] William Larrabee, *The Railroad Question* (Chicago, 1893), 141.

[15] Hepburn Committee, Proceedings, 6:57.

[16] *Ibid*, 4:3971.

invocation of the "axiom of indispensability" was usually the first step in the argument of every disputant. "By the aid of railroads," said an advocate of strong government action, "the wilderness has been made productive, countless farms brought within the reach of the great markets, mines opened, mills, factories, and forges built, villages, towns and cities brought into existence, and populous States carried to a higher level of development than would have been possible in centuries without such aid." This great power, he argued, made railroads "public trusts." However managers of railroads had violated the trust placed in their care by using "watery fiction, to extort from railway users the enormous sum of $1,592,280,471" in 15 years. It was therefore the duty of legislatures "to formulate such statutes as will protect user and investor, both of whom are at the mercy of a small body of men who can and do make and mar the fortunes of individuals, cities and States, without let or hinderance." [17] Opponents of government control found the axiom equally useful in opposing government action. "Let us imagine for a moment," the president of one of the nation's leading railroad complexes suggested, "that all railways in the United States were at once annihilated. Such a catastrophe in not, in itself, inconceivable; the imagination *can* grasp it; but no imagination can picture the infinite sufferings that would at once result to every man, woman, and child in the entire country. Now, every step taken to impede or cripple the business and progress of our railways," he concluded, "is a step towards just such a catastrophe, and therefore of a destructive tendency." [18]

The Logical and Empirical Foundation of the Axiom

While many eminent volumes have been written on railroad history and related topics in recent decades, it is no slight to the importance of these works to point out that their central focus has not usually been the analysis of the effects of railroads on economic growth. Most studies of railroad history tend to subordinate the interaction between the railroads and the growth process to more limited issues — to tracing the origin of the railroad "idea," to the early difficulties in winning popular support, to descriptions of the spread and integration of the network, to the study of railroad entrepreneurship, to the anatomy of railroad finance and organization, to the examination of railroad land policies, and to narratives of such technological questions as the increase in the capacity of locomotives and cars, the standardization of track and the introduction of the air brake.

---

[17] C. Wood Davis, "The Farmer, the Inventor, and the Railway," *The Arena,* 3 (1891), 291-313.
[18] Dillon, "The West", 450.

The effect of these events on the growth of the economy as a whole usually enters only tangentially. A chapter or section may attempt to show how the particular subject matter of the study related to the emergence of the railroad as an indispensible agent of social and economic transformation. But the proposition of indispensability as such has not been subjected to critical investigation. Like all axiomatic truths it has been too obvious to require analysis.

As a consequence the echoes of the Gilded Age still reverberate in contemporary historiography. Virtually all the leading text books on economic history repeat, in one way or another, the themes formulated almost a century ago. In his compenduous *Economic History of the United States* Chester Wright declared that "few things did more to change the economic organization" of the nation than the railroad. "Its revolutionizing effects," he continued, "can scarcely be exaggerated." [19] In a more recent text Gilbert C. Fite and Jim E. Reese state that railroads, at the close of the nineteenth century, had "the power of life and death over the economy. Access to railroads or even differences in freight rates determined the growth and decline of whole cities." [20] Herman E. Krooss refers to railroads as "the principal single determinant of the levels of investment, national income, and employment in the nineteenth century." [21] And August C. Bolino writes: "Besides stimulating investment and creating a demand for goods and factors, the railroad also provided a transportation service which was essential to the development of capitalism in America." [22]

The Fallacy of Composition

The firm faith our generation continues to have in the axiom formulated by the men of the Gilded Age is unwarranted. For if the axiom is considered skeptically, the apparently powerful body of evidence on which it is based appears much less sturdy. Indeed it quickly becomes obvious that the "axiom of indispensability" is founded on a series of logical errors, questionable inferences and unverified assumptions. Consider, for example, the argument that because the railroad could crush a particular firm by denying it access to railroad service, the absence of the railroad system would have represented a crushing blow to the economy as a whole. To reason in this way is to fall victim to the fallacy of composition. The

---

[19] Chester W. Wright, *Economic History of the United States* (1st ed.: New York, 1941), 343.

[20] Gilbert C. Fite and Jim E. Reese, *An Economic History of the United States* (Cambridge, 1959), 325.

[21] Herman E. Krooss, *American Economic Development* (Englewood Cliffs, N. J., 1959), 439.

[22] August C. Bolino, *The Development of the American Economy* (Columbus, Ohio, 1961), 173.

presence of the fallacy is demonstrated by the following example. In 1890 Kansas City merchants sold large quantities of wheat in New York City. If success in this operation required a profit of six percent on the sale price, the average profit of the merchants would have been $1.98 per ton.[23] Suppose now that railroads denied their facilities to one of the merchants and that the next most favorable form of transportation involved a fifty percent increase in shipping charges. Such an occurrence would have been a catastrophe for the merchant involved. A rise in shipping costs of the stipulated magnitude would have transformed the merchant's normal profit into a seven percent loss.[24] However, the total freight revenue of all railroads in 1890 was $714,000,000.[25] Consequently, if in the absence of railroads there were a fifty percent increase in the cost of shipping all those goods that were actually carried by railroads in 1890, the reduction in the production potential of the economy would have been only $357,000,000 or about three percent of gross national product.

While the absence of railroads would in this illustrative case have left the economy worse off than it actually was, the reduction in transportation efficiency is hardly enough to justify the characterization of "indispensable." Given the historical stability of the aggregate saving and capital-output ratios, the hypothetical example implies that an increase in transportation costs sufficient, when *discriminatorily applied,* to ruin individual firms, would have retarded the development of the economy by just one year — that is, reduced the economy's production potential to the level that prevailed in 1889. The great power of railroads over the destiny of individual firms or groups of firms does not necessarily imply a similar influence over the economy as a whole. The former existed because of the sensitivity of profits to relatively small changes in cost conditions; the latter depends on the ratio of the aggregate of such changes in costs to total national product.

The preceding argument is based on a hypothetical case and is not intended to prove that railroads were inessential to economic growth. But it does point to the weakness of one of the main bodies of evidence on which the "axiom of indispensability" has been based — the various governmental investigations of the effects of railroad rate discrimination during the Gilded Age. While these investigations provided convincing demonstration of the power of railroads to redistribute wealth and income among

---

[23] The average New York price of spring wheat was $33.03 per ton in July, 1890. U. S. Congress, Senate, *Wholesale Prices, Wages and Transportation,* Report of the Committee on Finance, Rept. No. 1394, Part 2, 52nd Cong. 2nd Sess., 63.

[24] The rail rate on the shipment of wheat from Kansas City to New York was $8.72 per ton in the summer of 1890. Fifty percent of this figure is $4.36 or 2.2 times the hypothetical profit. *Ibid.,* Part I, 516, 517, 551.

[25] U. S. Bureau of the Census, *Historical Statistics,* 431.

both individuals and regions, large equity effects do not necessarily imply large changes in the productive efficiency of the economy. Of course the Rochester miller whose business was ruined by the low through rates granted to Milwaukee millers found it expedient to pose his personal loss in income as a loss to society. However, the loss in national income, if it existed, was the amount by which the gain to Westerners fell short of the loss to Easterners. Whether this difference was positive, zero or negative can only be settled empirically. There is no basis for making such a determination on *a priori* grounds even in situations where one of the consequences of rate discrimination was the establishment of industrial monopolies. For it is entirely feasible that, as Joseph Schumpeter argued, the reductions in cost due to large scale operations more than compensated for any misallocations of resources due to monopolistic practices. Thus to accept the arguments of merchants and farmers that railroad practices which annihilated their particular businesses necessarily reduced national income is to accept a nonsequitur. The establishment of the efficiency effects of railroad rate discrimination requires methods of analysis and sets of data much different from those on which historians have traditionally relied.

The Assumption on Costs

It is also erroneous to leap from data that demonstrate the victory of railroads over waterways in the competition for freight to the conclusion that the development of the railroad network (particularly the trunk lines) was a prerequisite for the rapid continuous growth of the internal market. The only inference that can safely be drawn from such data is that railways were providing transportation services at a cheaper cost to the buyer than other conveyances. For if rail transportation was a perfect or nearly perfect substitute for waterways, all that was required for a large shift from waterways to railroads was a small price differential in favor of the latter. Whether the shift produced a significant increase in the width of the internal market depends, not on the volume of goods transferrred from one medium to the other, but on the magnitude of the associated reduction in transportation costs. If the reduction in costs achieved by railroads was small, and if waterways could have supplied all or most of the service that railroads were providing without increasing unit charges, then the presence of railroads did not substantially widen the market and their absence would not have kept it substantially narrower. The conclusion that the railroad was a necessary condition for the widening of the market thus flows not from a body of observed data but from the unverified assumption that the cost per unit of transportation service was significantly less by rail than by water.

The most celebrated instance of the substitution of rail for water haulage took place in the interregional movement of the agricultural surpluses of the North Central states. The distributional process began with the concentration of farm surpluses in the great primary markets of the Midwest — Chicago, Minneapolis, Duluth, Milwaukee, Peoria, Kansas City, Omaha, St. Louis, Cincinnati, Toledo and Detroit. Over 80 percent of the agricultural products that entered into interregional trade were shipped from the farms to these cities. These commodities were then transshipped from the primary markets to some 90 secondary markets in the East and South. Among the most important secondary markets were New York City, Baltimore, Boston, Philadelphia, New Orleans, Albany (N. Y.), Portland (Me.), Pittsburgh, Atlanta, and Savannah. After arriving in the secondary markets, the commodities were distributed to retailers in the immediately surrounding territory or exported.

The difference between the actual cost of distributing agricultural products and what it would cost to distribute them without railroads may be called the "social saving" attributable to railroads in the shipment of agricultural products. An estimate of this social saving for the year 1890 has recently been computed. While the results are still preliminary, they appear to be sufficiently reliable to justify their presentation. In the summary that follows the term "interregional" will be used to refer to movements from primary to secondary markets. Movements from farms to primary markets will be called "intraregional."

One of the surprising results of the preliminary calculation is the finding that the direct cost of the interregional transportation of agricultural commodities was less by water than by railroad; that is, when only the payments to rail and water carriers are considered, the social saving in interregional transportation is negative by $38,000,000. The odd result is not difficult to explain. While direct payments to railroads included virtually all of the cost of interregional transportation, direct payments to water carriers did not. In calculating the cost of shipping without the railroad, one must account for six additional items of cost not included in the payments to water carriers. These items are: cargo losses in transit, transshipment costs, wagon haulage from water points to secondary markets not on water routes, the cost resulting from time lost when using a slow medium of transportation, the cost of being unable to use water routes for five months out of the year, and finally, capital costs not reflected in water rates.

When account is taken of these six neglected costs, the loss attributable to railroads is transformed into a positive saving of $70,000,000 (see Table 1). Since the actual 1890 cost of shipping

TABLE 1

THE SOCIAL SAVING IN THE INTERREGIONAL
TRANSPORTATION OF AGRICULTURAL COMMODITIES

Social saving on direct payments	$-38,000,000
Neglected cargo losses	6,000,000
Transshipping costs	16,000,000
The cost of slow transportation	8,000,000
The cost of the unavailability of water routes during certain times of the year	40,000,000
Supplementary wagon haulage	20,000,000
Neglected capital costs	18,000,000
Total	70,000,000

the specified commodities was approximately $88,000,000, the absence of railroads would have almost doubled interregional shipping costs on agricultural commodities. It is quite easy to see why the great bulk of agricultural commodities (75 percent) were sent East by rail, water transportation being used only over a few favorable routes. The disadvantage of water transportation to firms that faced keen competition was even greater than the figures in Table 1 imply. For in a situation in which rapid transportation was available to some firms, slow delivery might have led to the loss of sales and other consequences that would not have existed in the absence of railroads. Here then is a specific case in which denial of access to rail facilities was capable of destroying competitive firms. However, in the absence of railroads, the social loss would have been less than one percent of gross national product. [26]

The analysis can be extended to the intraregional movement of farm products. As one might suspect, estimation of the intraregional social saving is more difficult than in the case of long-haul shipments. Interregional transportation represented a movement between a relatively small number of points — eleven great collection centers in the Midwest and 90 secondary markets in the East and South. Moreover many of the secondary markets fell on the same route. Five of the most important out along the Atlantic Coast. On the other hand, intraregional transportation required the connection of an enormous number of locations. Con-

[26] For a more rigorous discussion of the analytical problems involved in the estimation of the inter-regional social saving as well as for the sources of data, see Robert William Fogel, "A Quantitative Approach to the Study of Railroads in American Economic Growth: A Report of Some Preliminary Findings," *Journal of Economic History*, XXII (June, 1962), 163-197. [Ed. The estimate of Table 1 was revised to $73,000,000 in Fogel's book, p. 47.]

sidering each farm as a shipping point, there were not eleven but 4,565,000 interior shipping locations in 1890; the number of primary markets receiving farm commodities was well over a hundred.[27] Clearly, not all of these points could have been connected by 26,000 miles of navigable streams, 4,000 miles of canals, the Great Lakes and the coastal routes. These points were not even connected by the 167,000 miles of railroad track that laced the nation in 1890. The movement of commodities from farms to primary markets was never accomplished exclusively by water or by rail. Rather it involved a mix of either wagon and water or wagon and train services. The size of the social saving attributable to interior railroads depends not only on the relative efficiency of the trains and boats but also on the amount of wagon transportation that had to be combined with each of these services.

Preliminary calculations indicate that the social saving in the intraregional distribution of agricultural commodities in 1890 was about $238,000,000 or 2 percent of gross national product. This can be broken down into two parts: the social saving due to the superiority of rail over water transportation and the social saving due to the reduction in the required amount of supplementary wagon haulage. Only the latter is positive. Thus the great incentive for the use of railroads in short-haul movements of agricultural commodities was not the inherent superiority of rail service as such but the fact that railroads required a much smaller amount of supplementary wagon services than did waterways.[28]

It is important to note that the 2 percent social saving attributed to railroads in the overall movement of agricultural products is an upper limit. The procedures followed in the preliminary calculations introduced a series of upward biases. The most important of these arose from the assumption that only waterways in actual existence in 1890 would have been used in the absence of the railroad. As a result 24 percent of all agricultural land (by value) fell beyond a range in which commercial agriculture would have been feasible without railroads. However, it is quite clear that in the absence of railways, canals would have been extended. The construction of just 5,000 miles of additional waterways would

---

[27] In the intraregional case the term "primary markets" refer not merely to the 11 midwestern collection centers listed above but to all cities that received products directly from farms. Thus New York City is classified as a primary market with respect to intraregional trade since it was the first market for dairy products, fruits and other commodities produced by local farmers.

[28] The procedures employed in the preliminary estimate of the intraregional social saving and the sources of data are discussed in Robert William Fogel, *Railroads and American Economic Growth: Essays in Econometric History* (Baltimore, 1964), Chapter 3.

have reduced agricultural land lying beyond the feasible region to less than 10 percent of the national total.[29] It seems likely that when this and other adjustments are made, the social saving in agricultural distribution in 1890 will be cut in half.*

It is also important to note that the advantage of railroads was greater in 1890 than in earlier years. It can be shown, for example, that the relative social saving of 1870 was one-half of the figure for 1890.[30]

The Assumptions on the Demand for Manufactured Goods

The proposition that the quantity of manufactured goods used in the construction and maintenance of railroads was of decisive importance in the growth of manufacturing industry during the nineteenth century is a third foundation of the "axiom of indispensability." This theme, while enunciated by writers of the Gilded Age, has been put forth even more vigorously by modern scholars. W. W. Rostow, for example, argues that railroads triggered the American "take-off" into "self-sustained growth," and that the quantity of manufactured goods consumed by railroads "led on to the development of modern coal, iron and engineering industries." [31] However, the belief that railroads dominated the market for various manufactured products involves at least three unverified assumptions. It not only assumes the volume of goods purchased by the railroad was very large relative to the total output of the supplying industries, but also that purchases were directed toward the domestic rather than foreign markets. It assumes further that if there had been no railroad, the demand for manufactured goods by other forms of transportation, such as boats, would have been significantly smaller and its impact strategically different from the demand associated with railroads.

The iron industry is frequently cited as the classic example of the effect of railroads on manufacturing. However, the analysis of the position of railroads in the market for iron has been distorted by use of an erroneous measure. Since the iron industry did not produce one homogeneous product and since railroads consumed various types of iron, the usual problem of how to aggregate these products arise. The most desirable procedure would be to aggregate by prices and to use

---

29 Construction estimates were calculated on some of this mileage by the Army engineers and other organizations.

30 Fogel, *Railroads,* chapter 3.

* [Ed: cf. Fogel, *Railroads,* p. 110, where the social saving as a per cent of GAP, after accounting for a Reduction in wagon rates and the extension of internal navigation, is reduced to between 1.0% and 1.2% .]

31 W. W. Rostow, *The Stages of Economic Growth* (Cambridge, 1960), 55.

$$I_1 = \frac{\text{value of domestically produced railroad iron}}{\text{value of all final products of the iron industry}}$$

as an index of the proportion of the output of the American iron industry consumed by railroads. The numerator of I_1 is defined to exclude railroad iron purchased from abroad. The denominator is defined to exclude double counting. Unfortunately the available data are not complete enough to permit the construction of this index. Even for the years following the Civil War, the breakdown of production by type of product is not detailed enough and prices of many individual products are not available.

As a consequence, writers dealing with the impact of railroads on the iron industry have resorted to indices based on the tonnage of iron production and consumption. The most frequently used measure is

$$I_2 = \frac{\text{tons of iron used in the construction \& maintenance of railroads}}{\text{tons of pig iron produced}}$$

The implicit assumption made in using I_2 is that $I_1 = I_2$. This assumption would be true if (1) all railroad iron was purchased from domestic producers; (2) the amount of pig iron required to produce a ton of more highly manufactured iron was the same for all products; (3) only pig iron was used to produce more highly manufactured iron; and (4) the values of the final products of the iron industry were proportionate to the amounts of pig iron used in their production.

In actual fact all of these conditions were violated in such a way that I_2 is greater than I_1 by a substantial amount in most of the relevant years. A large part of railroad iron consumed through the seventies was purchased from abroad. During the 1850's foreign rails represented nearly two-thirds of all rail purchases; in 1871 they still accounted for 37 percent of purchases. The pig iron requirement of a ton of rolled iron differed from that of cast iron and hammered iron. Pig iron was not the only form of crude iron used in the production of final products; scrap iron became an increasingly important part of total crude iron consumption in years following 1850. Finally, the value of all final products was not directly proportional to the amount of pig iron required to produce them; the ratios of the price of a ton of steel and the price of a ton of hammered bar to the amount of pig used in their production exceeded the ratio of the price of a ton of rolled bar to its pig iron content. Consequently the use of I_2 as a measure of the share of output of the domestic iron industry consumed by railroads contains a considerable upward bias.

It is possible, even within the limitations imposed by aggregation based on tonnages rather than prices, to define two indexes that reduce the upward bias of I_2. These are

$$I_3 = \frac{\text{tons of domestic crude iron consumed in the iron industry}}{\text{tons of domestic crude iron used in domestically produced rails}}$$

and

$$I_4 = \frac{\text{tons of all crude iron consumed in the iron industry}}{\text{tons of all crude iron used in domestically produced rails}}$$

If imported crude iron were distributed between the production of railroad iron and other items in proportion to the amount of domestic crude iron each consumed, I_3 would equal I_4. While I_4 is less than I_2, it is still greater than I_1 because the ratio of price per ton of finished product to crude iron per ton of finished product was greater in the production of hammered iron, cast iron, rolled bar other than rails, and in steel than in the production of railroad iron. However, it is closer to I_1 than previously used indexes based on tonnage and it represents a significant improvement over I_2.

The extent of the improvement can be demonstrated by comparing the pattern of development implied by I_2 and I_4 during the two decades preceding the Civil War. According to Hofstadter, Miller and Aaron, the railroad was "by far the biggest user of iron in the 1850's." They estimate that "as early as 1860 more than half the iron produced annually in the United States went into rails" and associated items.[32] I_2 certainly supports this conclusion. It shows that the average share of the output of the iron industry going into rails during the decade of the fifties was 46 percent — three times the average proportion of the preceding decade. I_2 reaches a peak in 1851; rail consumption in that year is pegged at 67 percent of domestic iron production. The pattern suggested by I_4 is much different. It indicates that the average share of domestic iron output going into rails was only 15 percent during the fifties. The peak share, attained in 1856, was just 20 percent; the proportion then declined to 15 percent in 1860. Moreover the rise between the forties and fifties was under 10 percentage pig iron used for rails was only 7 percent of the total output of pig iron during the fifties. It can also be shown that erroneous procedures have led to a similar exaggeration of the importance of railroads in the market for such other products as coal, lumber, machinery and transportation equipment.[33]

* * *

This essay has argued for the rejection of the "axiom of indispensability." The preceding discussion should not, however, be interpreted as a state-

---

[32] Richard Hofstadter, William Miller and Daniel Aaron, *The American Republic* (2 vols.; Englewood Cliffs, N. J., 1959), I:557.

[33] See Fogel, *Railroads,* Chapters 4 and 5 for a more complete discussion of the position of the railroads in the market for various manufactured goods and for the sources of the data.

ment of the unimportance of railroads in American economic growth. "Indispensable" and "important" are not equivalent terms. The long reign of the "axiom of indispensability" has inhibited rather than promoted our understanding of the contribution of railroads to American economic progress. Rejection of the axiom will therefore facilitate the process of acquiring a body of tested knowledge on the developmental impact of the most celebrated innovation of the nineteenth century.

PART FOUR

The Civil War to 1914

Contents

I.

EDITOR'S INTRODUCTION

It was stated in the Preface to this collection that it was aimed at teachers and students of American history. The topics covered in the following introductory material and in the articles and notes collected in this Part of the book are ideal subjects for seminars or lecture halls.

First we pose some alternative views to a question raised by Thomas Cochran concerning the impact of the Civil War on the pace of American industrialization.[1] Next we sketch some broad dynamic factors affecting the overall development of the American economy from the Civil War to the first decade of the 20th Century. Finally, certain factors affecting the changing structure of the American economy in the industrial sector are discussed. In each instance, the topics are bursting with controversy and with conflicting and alternative interpretations of the same data. Finally, the papers collected, though overlapping in time with other periods already examined, cover the main domestic issues of American industrialization in the last quarter of the 19th Century: the contribution of the entrepreneur, the dynamic factors affecting the massive changes in industrial organization, and an examination of one of the key industries where the network of forces influencing changes in industrial structure reached their fullest development.

II.

What effect did the Civil War have on the long-term growth rate of the American economy? The variety of possible answers to this question will astound even the most gifted teacher and student of American history. The question has been raised in a quite narrow context by Cochran and others, and has turned on a comparison of rates of changes in commodity production during the decades preceding and following the war. Cochran concluded that the war did not accelerate the pace of American industrialization but may well have retarded it. He also suggests that most of the advances in national output were achieved in the two decades before the war, and that it was not until 1880 that the economy fully

---

[1] Cochran's article, as well as several others relevant to this topic, have been collected in Ralph Andreano, ed., *The Economic Impact of the American Civil War,* Schenkman Publishing Co., Cambridge, Mass. 1963.

regained its prewar momentum. Cochran's critics have made some points against his hypothesis on the following grounds: the choice of base years for comparison of the time series distorts the influence of the war; the inability to quantify certain institutional changes that occurred during the war but which were of fundamental importance to our long term economic performance; the importance and weight to be assigned to the variability in rates of output for key industries and commodities; inability to assess the war's impact on trend rates of growth because of pre and postwar business contractions; the inapplicability of quantitative data to test broad, essentially verbal, historical generalization.[2]

Clearly the debate has gotten out of hand. There are three possibilities: the war had no effect on the overall growth rate, it had a retarding effect, it had an accelerating one. Or, one could suggest that the war could well have accelerated some sectors of the economy, retarded others, and had no effect on still others; thus, on net the impact would cancel out and keep the effect of the war neutral. Certain suggestions may be offered which may help clarify the premises upon which answers to any of the set of questions implied by Cochran's original article may be approached.

The Civil War, in terms of human and economic experience, lasted only four years. It was both preceded and followed by rather sharp contractions in the general economy. Physical destruction was largely limited to the South, though human destruction was large for both regions. Technological developments in manufacturing, which ultimately proved of importance to our long term economic possibilities for growth, were known and occurred both before and after the war. A shift in the locus of national political power, already underway before the war, became clearly evident after it. To this observer, the information most relevant to the issue of whether or not the Civil War retarded, accelerated, or had neutral effects on our long term growth rate is only partially related to the data cited by Cochran and criticized by his attackers.

Did the structure of the economy differ fundamentally after the war from what it was before it, and can one trace the structural changes to events that occurred because the war happened at that time in our history? This question is probably unanswerable. The term structure is used here to mean the change in the percentage distribution of output among the various industries constituting the total economy. If the war accelerated our growth, one should expect to find statistically significant changes in the percentage distribution of outputs. Gallman's data are for commodity

---

[2] Most of the points noted above are mentioned by Pershing Vartanian, "The Cochran Theses: A Critique in Statistical Analysis," *Journal of American History*, LI; June 1964; pp. 77-89.

producing industries and are measured by value added — not by income originating within each sector; it is the latter which one really needs to have in order to document structural changes. The fact that data availability is only for quinquennia or decades further complicates any attempted answer, even if one uses the Gallman series on commodity output as a first approximation to total output and income originating by sector. We must also assign causative weights to any structural changes observed; this is probably impossible in the absence of detailed industry-wide and region-wide studies. Finally, no theory about structure alone can suffice to illuminate the importance of changes in our basic political and social institutions resulting from the war; these qualitative changes in the character of American economic life may well have been the most important results of the war, and it is not likely that their impact on the structure of the economy would be noticed until long after the event.

Rostow has labeled the period 1843-1860 as our take-off, which may be taken to mean that our secular growth path, despite short term deviations, was a sustained and upward one. Goldsmith, in a piece collected in this volume, has calculated our long-term trend growth rate in real income per head from 1839 to 1959 at 1 5/8% per annum. To prove whether the war nudged this rate downward, or upward, (which compounded over a century would be quite significant) seems an impossibility. Apparently before, during, and after the war, the American economy was not in danger of slipping back into a period where increases in our national output and income would be episodic rather than automatic. The issue of the impact of the war ought to turn on matters relating to personal economic welfare, rather than on long-term growth rates or the build-up or destruction of output capacity. But personal economic welfare is just as elusive a thing to document as is the set of factors affecting determinatively our pace and pattern of long term economic development.

With all these *caveats* aside, it still may be profitable to inspect rates of change in value added by manufacturing and agricultural sectors of the economy from 1840-1880, and in the major time series used by Cochran, pig iron production, 1850-1880. Both items are shown in Tables IV-I IV-II. The data are arranged by quinquennia.[3] In any case, the ten year increases show that the rate of change for manufacturing was at about one half its 1840 level during the 1850's. Five year increases indicate this decline was not only due to the 1857 depression, as Cochran suggests, but fell in the quinquennia, 1849-54, when the percentage rate of change was thirty points below the previous five year period. Meanwhile, the

---

[3] I am grateful to a former student of mine, Michael Locker, for the computational work in Tables IV-I and IV-II.

value added by agriculture rose at twice the 1840's rate during the 1850's, and was reflected in a rise of the total value added. Not until 1884 did the value added for manufacturing exceed agriculture.

There is little doubt that the statistical performance of the economy during the 1860's was relatively poor. But without more refined statistical data, it is hard to be sure which half of the decade was responsible for this. Indications, particularly in manufacturing, point to a low rate during the war and a higher one after it, though it is extremely difficult to make any kind of definitive judgment. In any case, it *is* clear that during the 1870's the rate of increase for manufacturing was *higher* than for the 1850's, while for agriculture and the total value added it remained at about the same level.

TABLE IV-I

Per Cent Increase in Value Added by Selected Industries in 1879 Prices: 1839 to 1889 in Five* and Ten Year Intervals

	Total		Agriculture		Manufacturing	
	Five Year Interval	Ten Year Interval	Five Year Interval	Ten Year Interval	Five Year Interval	Ten Year Interval
1839						
	27		19		53	
1844		52		25		157
	21		5		69	
1849	—	—	—	—	—	—
	39		33		39	
1854		62		51		76
	16		13		26	
1859	—	—	—	—	—	—
1864		23		15		25
1869	—	—	—	—	—	—
	31		15		56	
1874		62		51		82
	23		31		16	
1879	—	—	—	—	—	—
	38		15		59	
1884		63		25		112
	19		8		29	
1889	—	—	—	—	—	—

*1864 figures are missing so only ten year interval for the 1860's.

Source: Computed from figures in *Historical Statistics of the United States* (1960), p 139, as cited in R. Andreano (ed.), *The Economic Impact of the American Civil War* (Cambridge, 1962), p. 172. (after Gallman).

In the 1870's the rate of growth for manufacturing during the first half of the decade, or that half closer to the war years, was 40 percentage points higher than during the second half. The same is true for the 1880's The increase for the ten year period is 112% while from 1879-84 it is 59%, or only a fraction greater than the first half of the 1870's (56%. From 1884-89 the increase was 29%, a figure comparable to the rate achieved during the latter half of the 1850's (26%). Similar up and down movements took place in agriculture and for total value added. Finally, if we take the average of the four quinquennia percentage increases in value added for manufacturing before (1839-59) and after the war (1869-89), we find that it was 47% in the former and 40% for the latter. For total value added the figures are 26% and 28% respectively. These data may suggest a "no growth" conclusion, but a more judicious suggestion is that when value added figures are viewed in terms of five year intervals, the pattern is one of constant *fluctuation* before and after the war.

In writing about pig iron production Cochran noted that "The period from 1840 to 1850 shows a 97% increase in shipments, while for the period 1870 to 1880 the increase was 130%." [4] First, this hardly shows

TABLE IV-II

Per Cent Changes:
Pig Iron Production: 1850 to 1880*

(A)		(B)		(C)		(D)	
Five Year Interval	Per Cent Increase	Five Year Interval	Per Cent Increase	Five Year Interval	Per Cent Increase	Ten Year Interval	Per Cent Increase
1850-54‡	17			1850-55	24		
1855-59	7	1856-60	4	1855-60	17	1850-60	46
1860-64	23	1861-65	27	1860-65	1		
1865-69	106	1866-70	38	1865-70	100	1860-70	103
1870-74	44	1871-75	19	1870-75	21		
1875-79	35	1876-80	105	1875-80	89	1870-80	130

Average: (39)+   Average: (39)   Average: (42)

*Each five year series (A, B, C) is computed from the same absolute yearly figures for pig iron production; the intervals have been rearranged in each.

‡The figure for 1851 is missing.

+(Average of percentage increases in that series.)

SOURCE: Computed from *Historical Statistics of the United States, Colonial Times to 1857*, pp. 365-366.

---

[4] Ralph Andreano, ed., *The Economic Impact of the Civil War*, Schenkman Publishing Co., Cambridge, Mass. 1963, page 158.

that the war retarded the rate of growth for this important material. A more careful look at pig iron production figures reveals the following per cent increases by decades from 1850 to 1880; a 46% increase from 1850 to 1860, a 103% increase from 1860 to 1870, and a 130% increase from 1870 to 1880. The increases over five year intervals are set forth in Table IV-II. Neither series A, B, or C of this table, nor any of the other figures cited above, prove that the war retarded the long-run growth curve of pig iron production.

I leave to the students and teachers who read these pages the further questioning of the logical foundations upon which an examination of the long term impact of the war on our national development should rest. The topic may be an insoluble one, but the pedagogic value of examining the war in the context of the movement of the national economy is surely an improvement over the traditional treatment it receives in the literature of American history.

III.

The period immediately following the Civil War until the first decade of the 20th Century was one of the greatest change in the structure and performance of the American economy. It is a period which gives us much contradictory data, characterized by a generally falling price level, by severe and frequent business contractions, by high rates of increase in productivity on an economy-wide basis, by huge waves of immigration, by a levelling in the natural rate of population increase, and by truly substantial increases in national product and per capita income. The period was also the most creative one in our history as regards the conditions affecting the structure of leading manufacturing industries. The pace of consolidations and mergers, the colorful and creative (and destructive) activities of entrepreneurs in nearly every phase of our economic life, and the first rumblings of an organized labor movement, were equally important parts of this dynamic period in our national development. One cannot hope to resolve these developments here into a systematic appraisal of the economic history of this period, but certain relevant data are offered to enable students and teachers to premise their discussions on grounds that are not solely emotive.

Further, the selections printed below all relate to the mainstream of economic history of this period. Hughes offers an interpretative framework for judging entrepreneurial behavior which could well be applied to men of the last quarter of the 19th Century different from those he has chosen for case analysis. Similarly, the brilliant article by Chandler gets behind the external dynamic forces that affected the structure of firms and industries, and presents conclusive evidence of the action and reaction of the strategy of business decisions upon the nation's industrial structure. The piece by Williamson and Andreano casts considerable doubt on the completeness of Rockefeller's control over the domestic petroleum industry. The exhortation to historians to read Alfred Marshall's *Industry and and Trade* is included, not without justification, as relevant to a basic understanding of the dynamic ingredients of economic change at work in this impressive period of our national history.

Finally, it should be noted that though the focus of the following introductory material and the readings collected below is on the domestic aspects of the 1865-1910 period, the international repercussions as well as independent developments in international trade and finance were equally momentous as regards national economic development: the dramatic inflow of foreign long-term and short-term capital into the United States, the neomercantilist rivalries in international trade and markets, and the "American Commercial Invasion of Europe," as two writers have recently put it, conjure up a period of intense activity in international economic affairs and policy.[5] It is only because of considerations of space that these international developments are not illuminated here. But certain data are discussed below on the following topics; price movements, business cycles, income and product growth, productivity. The last section of the Introduction is reserved for comments on the data relating to industrial organization and structure.

IV.

As will be noted below, by almost any measure of economic development the rate of overall advance in the American economy in the period 1867 to 1913 was unprecedented in our economic history. What is of particular interest is that this development was accompanied by a rapid secular decline in the general price level between 1867 and 1897, and the slower growth rate in the following decade was accompanied by a rapid rise in the general price level between 1897-1913. The point we stress is that for almost three decades the trend of commodity prices was downward — the general level of prices in 1897 was less than half of that in 1867. With 1913 as a base year, the index of wholesale prices for all commodities declined from 162 in 1867 to 82 in 1890. Taking 1926 as the base year, the index of wholesale prices fell from 56.2 in 1890 to 46.6 in 1897. As shown in Chart IV-I, however, the distinguishing feature of price movements during this period was the fairly broad range of

---

[5] See Matthew Simon and David Novack, "Some Dimensions of the American Commercial Invasion of Europe, 1871-1914: An Introductory Essay" in *Journal of Economic History*, XXIV; Dec. 1964; pp. 591-605.

Chart IV-I.

PERCENT CHANGE IN GENERAL INDEX OF PRICES, 1872-1911

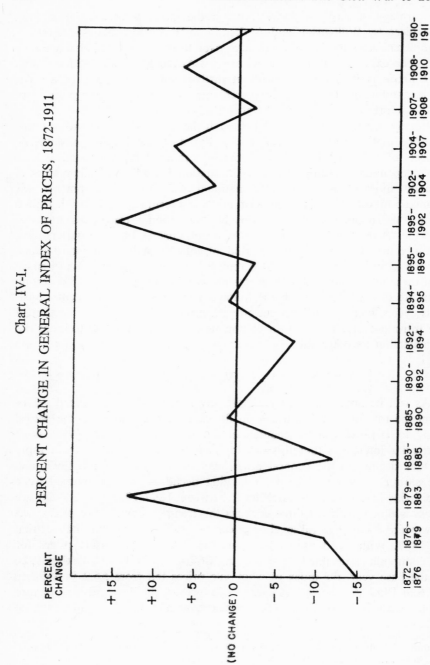

Source: Computed from *Historical Statistics of U.S.*, pp. 115-117.

amplitude in year to year fluctuations. The years in Chart IV-I are at one, two, three or five year intervals; the years of greatest change are indicated without attempting to present an annual account of price movements.

Rising relative prices are generally associated with rapid advances in national income and product, but from 1867 to 1897 the reverse was the case in the United States. In Table IV-III it can be seen that Gross National Product in constant 1929 dollars increased nearly fourfold between the periods 1869-73 and 1897-1901, and rose in per capita terms about 2 1/2 times. Kuznets' recent data on capital formation show decennial rates of increase in net capital formation, 1869 to 1888, of nearly 52% and from 1889 to 1908 of about 24%.[6] National wealth or physical reproducible assets increased 2 1/2 times in real terms during the last two decades of the 19th Century. All of these data conjure up a picture of an economy which has undergone massive increases in its national income and product. One could further document the structural changes these increases entailed by viewing rates of growth in population, changes in the industrial distribution of the labor force and its growth rate, and other demographic and economic magnitudes.

No one seriously challenges the fact that the rate of growth of the American economy in the last quarter of the 19th Century was an impressive one. But certain important questions do remain. Was this growth consistent with a secular decline in the price level? Was personal economic welfare raised significantly because of the high growth rate? There are a subset of questions that also relate to these two broader ones: What caused the decline in prices and in turn the sensitivity of the economy to business contractions? Were gains in personal economic welfare evenly spread among the population, or was the rate of growth accomplished by squeezing resources from one income group and allocating it to others? It is only possible to make suggestive statements here, it being doubtful that a definitive answer actually exists.

In the first instance, a secularly falling price level ought to have had some effect on the expectations of investors as to whether or not investment decisions should be made at any given point in time. We certainly know that the rate of investment is very much influenced by the state of expectations prevailing in an economy. What is clearly the case for the American economy during this period, however, is that, as Kuznets' data show, there was an acceleration in the level of productive investments made in the economy. This would seem to indicate that business investment decisions were not materially influenced by appraisals of long term price behavior. What is more likely the case is that only on a short term

---

[6] Simon Kuznets; *Capital in the American Economy;* Princeton University Press; Princeton, New Jersey 1961; p. 56.

TABLE IV-III

| | GNP (constant 1929 dollars) annual or average annual | |
Years	Total (in billions)	Per Capita
1869-73	$9.11	$223
1872-76	11.2	254
1877-81	16.1	327
1882-86	20.7	374
1887-91	24.7	388
1889-93	27.3	424
1892-96	29.6	434
1897-1901	37.1	496
1902-06	46.8	569
1907-14	55.0	608

SOURCE: *Historical Statistics of the United States,* p. 139.

basis, when the price level underwent drastic annual changes, would the level of expectations be likely to affect the rate of productive investment. This, of course, raises another question regarding the relationship of changes in investment spending and the periodicity of business contractions in the last quarter of the 19th Century, as well as the role of price expectations on general economic conditions. For the moment it is sufficient to note that the relationship between the price level and the rate of economic development is a complicated one, and one which is yet to be even partially explored for the American experience of these years.

The most probable explanation for the secular decline in prices from the end of the Civil War to the turn of the Century is to be found in the competitive structure of industry and in the rate and incidence of productivity advances in the economy. Productivity gains can be noted for the two major sources of income and employment — the raw materials resources industries (including agriculture), and manufacturing. It has generally been supposed that the agricultural sector of the economy did not participate in the overall national growth of the economy to the extent that other sectors did, specifically manufacturing. Agricultural growth has been noted, but its path was taken as somewhat autonomous, as releasing resources for the higher growth possibilities in the greater productivity-type manufacturing and mining industries. Both Schumpeter and Alfred Conrad have commented on the somewhat passive role of agriculture in national growth, and it is worth quoting a passage from Conrad on this.

Agriculture, in most respects the losing sector, maintained or supported the pace of industrial development by a series of technological improvements and geographical relocations that released a growing labor force for industry and made possible the feeding of the growing urban work force at steadily declining prices.[7]

Nonetheless, it is true that even if the agricultural sector was being squashed by industry growth, it still achieved a fairly high growth rate, and its own productivity advances account for a large fraction of the decline in the secular price level.[8]

A somewhat more interesting set of statistics are those shown in Table IV-IV, where agricultural output is treated as part of the natural resources base along with that of timber and mineral output. One gets a fairly good picture of the resource base of the American economy in the 1870-1910 period and the growing relative efficiency of their use (viz, lines 4 and 6) as well as the larger GNP supported by a given relative level of resource consumption by the economy (lines 1, and 3).

Only two indicators of the growth of manufacturing production during this period need be indicated here — the index of total manufacturing output as shown in Chart IV-II, and the sectoral origin of national income. As may be noted from this chart, the trend rate of growth of manufacturing production was exceptionally high with an overall increase of nearly 170 percentage points in the 4½ decades and about 75 percentage points for the 1869-1899 period. Further evidence of the structural changes implied by the high growth rate of manufacturing output can be found in the changes that occurred in the industrial distribution of the labor force. In 1870 nearly 52% of the gainful workers were in the agriculture and related industries and 16.2% in manufacturing; by 1900 the respective figures were 37.4% and 22%, and by 1910, 31% and 23%. Moreover the total labor force, heavily augmented by immigration, increased threefold from 1870 to 1900, and fourfold by 1910. Most of the increases in manufacturing production can be accounted for by the growth in domestic demand, augmented, to be sure, by the growing resource base of the economy and the impressive technological advances made on a broad front in the major income and employment sectors of the economy. (For certain industries, export markets were also crucially important for their growth.)

---

[7] Alfred H. Conrad; "Income Growth and Structural Change," in Seymour Harris ed., *American Economic History;* McGraw-Hill Co.; New York 1961; p. 52. Also note Schumpeter's remarks on the same subject in *Business Cycles,* Vol. I; New York 1939; pp. 316, 321-22.

[8] Alvin Tostlebe, *Capital in American Agriculture;* Princeton University Press; Princeton, New Jersey 1955, has the most authoritative data on productivity and output gains in agriculture from 1870 onwards.

TABLE IV-IV

Resource Trends in the United States, 1870-1910

		1870	1880	1890	1900	1910
(1)	Consumption of Resources[a] (1947-49 equal 100)	17	23	30	41	53
(2)	Per Capita Resource Consumption (1954 dollars)	$174	$191	$195	$221	$237
(3)	Output of Resources as % of GNP in 1954 prices	36%	32%	29%	27%	22%
(4)	Prices of Resources (deflated by BLS WPindex, 1947-49 equal 100)	78	66	66	68	76
(5)	Net Resource imports (1947-49=100)	(—)31	(—)75	(—)77	(—)107	(—)69
(6)	Employment in resource industries as % of total employment	51.9%	51.9%	45.4%	40.5%	33.9%

[a]Agriculture, Timber products, Minerals.

SOURCE: Adapted from Joseph L. Fisher and Edward Boorstein, *The Adequacy of Resources for Economic Growth in the United States,* Study Paper No. 13, Joint Economic Committee (December 1959), 43.

Against this general background of overall and sectoral growth, one needs to place the extent to which individuals participated. At first glance, and assuming such data are reasonably accurate measures of personal welfare, the two and one-half fold increase in per capita Gross National Product (in 1929 prices) shown by the Kuznets data would seem to indicate a fairly broad and general increase in personal welfare. Various measures of real wage trends in manufacturing and in agriculture also indicate secular advances that were statistically significant. One study has shown an increase at annual compounded rates for real wages in manufacturing from 1860 to 1890 of slightly in excess of 1.3%. From 1890 to 1914 the increase was somewhat smaller.[9] On the other hand, for the period during which the secular decline in prices was greatest — the last

---

[9] Clarence Long, *Wages and Earnings in the United States, 1860-1890;* Princeton University Press; Princeton, New Jersey 1960, and Albert Rees, *Real Wages in Manufacturing, 1890-1914;* Princeton 1961, esp. Chapter I.

Chart IV-II.

INDEX OF MANUFACTURING PRODUCTION, 1869-1914
(after Frickey, 1899 = 100)

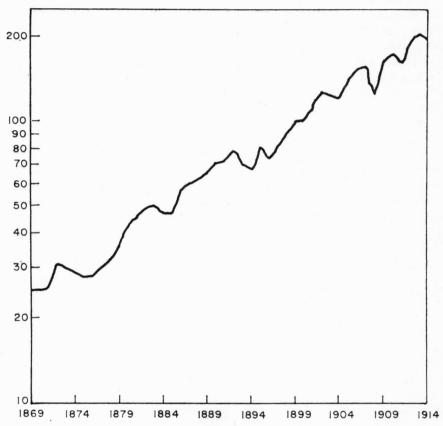

Source: *Historical Statistics of U.S.,* p. 409.

paper reprinted in Part V of this book, the frequency and duration of three decades of the 19th Century — there are indications that the personal distribution of income worsened for the first part of the period and probably did not improve until the beginning of the 20th Century, certainly not markedly so until the 1930's.[10] Moreover, as Lebergott shows in his

---

[10] See Simon Kuznets, "Economic Growth and Income Inequality" in *American Economic Review;* March 1953; pp. 1-28.

paper reprinted in Part V of this book, the frequency and duration of unemployment in the last quarter of the 19th Century was a phenomenon new to American life; this must, of course, be balanced off against the overall gains in per capita real income. There seems little to question concerning the gains in personal welfare over the course of four decades despite previous disclaimers; all contemporary observers noted the "high living standard" of the American. But what is being stressed here is that long term improvement is of little comfort to those suffering the costs of this advance in the short run. American cities and slums, urban and rural, had their start during this heyday of our economic expansion, and though relative improvements in the level of living surely did occur, the extent of poverty, ignorance, and disease was high, and the difficult and painful social costs of adjusting to life in an industrialized society must be considered as important results of this period in our national history.

The social discomforts that accompanied the rapid growth of the period were exacerbated, as indeed the growth of the economy may well have been affected, by the periodic and severe business contractions that occurred between 1865 and 1900. The turning points of the major cyles for this period and the duration from bottom point (trough) to bottom point as calculated by the National Bureau of Economic Research is shown in Table IV-V. Many scholars have studied these cycles and as yet there is no generally accepted single version of the reasons causing them as to timing and length. The two major positions on the cause of the cycles can be best termed "monetary" and "real." In the former it is alleged that the insufficiencies in the financial structure and institutions, and the unrespon-

TABLE IV - V

Business Cycle Turning Points, 1864 - 1900

Peak Year	Trough Year	Years Duration Trough to Trough
1869	1870	3
1873	1878	8
1882	1885	7
1887	1888	3
1890	1891	3
1892	1894	3
1895	1896	2
1899	1900	4

SOURCE: W. C. Mitchell and A. F. Burns, *Measuring Business Cycles* (New York: 1947), p. 78.

siveness of the money supply to changing economic conditions resulted in periodic contractions in investment demand. Proponents of the view that the cycles were caused by "real" forces allege that a shortage of investment opportunities initiated each of the downward phases of the cycles, and technological changes the upward phases.[11] The arguments of both points of view can become quite technical and it is not necessary to discuss them here. The point to be noted is that the business contractions did occur with greater regularity than ever before in our history, and that by their very nature they affected the whole fabric and structure of American social, economic, and political life. One needs to keep this seemingly simple observation in mind when appraising the quality of social and economic change which the massive industrial effort of the last quarter of the Century produced.

V.

One other feature of the period after the Civil War, concurrent with those already mentioned above, was the fundamental structural change which occurred in the size of firms and size of industries. As is well known, the entrepreneurial talent which sparked much of the visible industrial changes of these decades included some of the giants of American economic biography. In this connection the article by Hughes, as well as that by Chandler, offers suggestive interpretations of the roles played by the late 19th Century industrial entrepreneurs in shaping the modern structure of American industry.

Three questions ought to be raised as background discussion for the reading of the pieces reprinted in this part of the book and for the remarks of the Editor in Part One of the work done on the First Merger Wave: What forces affected the high rate of mergers that took place, at first slowly in the 1870's and 1880's, and then reaching a peak in the 1895-1904 period? What forces were most contributory to the size of firms in key manufacturing and mining industries as achieved by 1900? Would the changes in industry structure and industrial concentration have occurred in the absence of the dynamic entrepreneurs commonly associated with each industry (viz. Rockefeller in petroleum, Harriman in railroads, Morgan in finance, etc.)? As is true throughout this book, such questions are raised, not necessarily to be finally answered, but to serve as the springboard for discussions about dynamic elements of change.

The most reasonable explanation of the growing pattern and increase in industrial concentration is that all those factors were important: the desire

---

[11] The best summary and analysis of all the views can be found in Rendigs Fels, *American Business Cycles;* North Carolina University Press; Chapel Hill, N. C. 1959. The most exhaustive treatment of the monetary issues involved is in Milton Friedman and Anna J. Schwartz, *A Monetary History of the United States, 1867-1960;* Princeton 1963; esp. Chapter III.

for market control, the creative aspirations of the leading industrial entrepreneurs to build firms and industries of long-term significance to the growth of the economy, and the inexorable set of economic forces that worked independently of human decision because of conditions of technology and aggregate demand. There is little doubt that the modern structure of American industry was formed during the last two decades of the 19th Century, but as yet the mix of conditions that enabled this to happen has not been properly balanced by traditional scholarship. The papers in this section do not pretend to accomplish this most needed result, but do suggest certain standards that are necessary for it.

Three of the papers — Hughes, Chandler, and Williamson and Andreano — are attempts to bring some analytical order out of a morass of empirical observation. Hughes attempts to provide a framework of analysis for appraising the historical role of the entrepreneur. Chandler examines the impact of exogenous economic forces on the decision-making structure of firms and industries. Williamson and Andreano, working with an implicit model of the conditions of entry as the fundamental area for analysis of industry structure, suggest that for one industry, petroleum, economic forces indigenous to that industry permitted a size distribution of firms quite different from what traditional scholarship has assumed was the case.

Finally, a word or two about the Alfred Marshall selection. It is purely an idiosyncratic twitch on the part of the Editor: Alfred Marshall had much to say about American industrial development and historians should read his work, especially *Industry and Trade*.

EIGHT TYCOONS: THE ENTREPRENEUR AND AMERICAN HISTORY*

J. R. T. Hughes‡

It is customary in certain circles to preface a methodological essay with apologies. Mine are offered, even though I will put some factual flesh on my methodological bones as we go along and thus hope to lighten the offense to good taste. But it seems to me that now is an opportune time to look into certain basic methodological problems of Entrepreneurial History. The journal, *Explorations in Entrepreneurial History*, has been resurrected, and new interest seems to be building up in the use of the entrepreneur as a vehicle for the study and comprehension of American economic history and of economic development generally. It is to this view of the uses of Entrepreneurial History that I shall address my remarks.

I

Doubtless, the main difficulty in the study and writing of Entrepreneurial History is the choice of an appropriate frame of reference within which study is to be conducted. The social geography of the entrepreneurial domain, as it stands at any moment, is primarily a map of social artifacts, a map of the results of past actions. And there are, and have been, an enormous number of entrepreneurs involved in the creation of those artifacts. How does one decide who is worth studying? Some of the most successful business and industrial leaders led uninspiring careers, and some of the most dramatic and original leaders in entrepreneurial activity have been relatively unsuccessful. The situation is reminiscent of the statement of the Victorian scholar, Arnold Toynbee, who argued that the roll of English landholding was scarcely susceptible to pure economic analysis.[1] It was the singular product of centuries of intrigue, violence, political favoritism, accidents of birth and economic upheaval held tightly within the grip of primogeniture and entail. It was a history of individual cases, the landscape at any moment being inhabited by survivors of a

---

* This paper was presented to the 11th annual conference of the Business History Association held March 28-29 at Indiana University. The author is indebted to the discussant, Professor Ralph Hidy, and to others present at this gathering for criticisms and suggestions.

‡ J. R. T. Hughes is Professor of Econ. at Purdue Univ.

[1] *The Industrial Revolution* (Boston, 1956), pp. 2-3 and Chapter V.

process that was anarchistic from the point of view of rigorous economic analysis.

Can Entrepreneurial History do better than this? On what general grounds do certain entrepreneurial achievements emerge from the whole universe of them and come into the historian's focus? Surely we can do better than merely measure entrepreneurial achievement by the index of lifetime net dollar earnings. In the long pull of the nation's life many financial failures had important effects. I would argue, in fact, given the record of successes, the failures are important information; William Penn's colony (a loss to him) and Edison's electric light company (he claimed to have lost money on it) are cases in point.

If failures are important, then one indicator of appropriate subjects of study in the whole entrepreneurial galaxy is not too useful, and that, of course, is price theory. It does not inform the scholar much in a general way if profits are negative and the index of efficiency is successful, non-negative, profit maximization. And, moreover, *all* failures were not important; failure, no more than financial success, illuminates the contributions of the entrepreneur to the nation's economic development. There must be some more meaningful frame of reference. Aggregative economic theory also is not too useful initially, as it tends to blot out the achievements of individuals. Even if the individual contributions could be measured on a current basis, the larger contributions at any moment of time are not necessarily the most fruitful in the long run; sailing ships were making greater contributions than the steamships in the "transportation sector" in the early 1850's, but the smallness of the steam sector is misleading as an indicator of the growth path. Steam, after all, was the wave of the future, however diminutive and unprofitable were the activities of the entrepreneurs launching that innovation.

The standard gauges of the importance of the industry in question are of course useful, except that the focus is again upon success alone, and, as I said before, failures can be important information about the direction of the nation's growth. Here I am thinking, for example, of the canals in the ante-bellum period, or perhaps railroads today. In such cases it can be argued that the record of failures in entrepreneurial activity can be as informative of the nation's economic growth pattern over time as is the customary catalogue of entrepreneurial triumph. For example, I think that Henry Villard's failures with the Northern Pacific tell us a great deal about which of James J. Hill's methods were crucial in the success of the Great Northern.

The problem of the appropriate "unit of history" in entrepreneurial studies is so inordinately complex and difficult primarily because it encompasses two sets of historical information: (1) economic criteria, such as markets and technology, and (2) personalities. Each set of information has members in common with the other, and each would be difficult to comprehend in isolation. The two kinds of information taken together condemn the student of entrepreneurial activity to the life of the proverbial "lion-taming snake charmer." The fine old notion that one need merely find and study "forces of history" is muddled by the undoubted influence of personality; and the *simpliste* grandeur of the Carlylian hero is subverted by the need of each hero to deal with a complex economic world in order to come into the historian's focus at all. Each entrepreneur in history faced the others, and none acted except in response to the others, all of whom employed skills and techniques determined by the "market" and by the "state of the arts." I think this is a sufficient statement of the problem to underscore the unhappy fact that realistic entrepreneurial history cannot be a simple enterprise.

I do not mean to present a cry of despair, or a blueprint for historiographical anarchy in which each man is a "thing in himself." But I do not think that some careful methodological thinking is not warranted by the difficulties of the problem.

II

If "economic theory" is not a sufficient guide, and if I consider financial success by itself to be an excessively facile and superficial approach, what alternatives are open? I think there are many alternatives, and they constitute a problem of simple taxonomy — a problem, initially, of basic classification.

The efforts of men in economic life can be classified according to the nature of their historical achievements in their economic environments. The environment needs to be defined, and this can be done by sub-dividing the whole entrepreneurial domain on a functional basis. We ask ourselves not "how much money did they make," but rather, "how, and in what circumstances, did they make, or lose, their money?" Each student of entrepreneurial activity is not only considering men, but the whole ecological world of the men in question. Whether it be on a micro or macro level, both the selection of men and the "interesting" actions of these men are determined by our notions of what facts were important ones in the relevant historical segment we are considering. The facts, as always in historical studies, are illumined by bias, preference, theory or what have you. Enough ink has been spilled on this last issue to render nugatory any fresh remarks I might have to make. But a rigorous application of this method to the economic history which is the ecology of any entrepreneur provides some bench marks for study. After that, theory and ingenuity inform the student in his analyses of individual entrepreneurial actions.

III

I would like to illustrate the usefulness of this taxonomic approach by outlining a somewhat grandiose but simple scheme wherein the biographies of eight entrepreneurial figures were used to illuminate some broad channels of American economic development.[2] Here I am using the entrepreneur as my vehicle to study American economic development, which is my main interest. I could have chosen any number of historical figures for this purpose, but I selected eight well-known figures for purposes of simplicity. It is my contention that an explicit ordering of these men on the basis of their functional contributions throws a bright and different light upon our history. The initial question I asked was simple "What goes on in economic life, at any time, in the broadest sense?" Out of the infinity of possible answers I constructed an inclusive five part "stage system" in which the stages are functional. Events flow through the stages, but the stages are the framework of analysis, and they do the job of selection of "facts." Time is passive, to be used as suits the analysis. This arbitrary stage system is thus a functional, and not a chronological one.[3] Nations do not pass through these stages in sequence; economic life is enmeshed in these functional stages constantly, simultaneously.[4]

---

[2] *The Vital Few — American Economic Progress and Its Protagonists,* a manuscript of a book recently completed by the present author.

[3] Two decades ago Arthur Cole urged the use of functional, timeless categories as the framework for utilizing entrepreneurial studies in economic history in opposition to chronological stage systems. "An Approach to the Study of Entrepreneurship," reprinted in F. C. Lane and J. C. Riemersma, *Enterprise and Secular Change* (Homewood, Ill., 1953), p. 189. I have not used Professor Cole's scheme, but my neglect of it was due to my own ignorance of its existence until the work under discussion was completed. Cole's suggestions seem to me to have great merit. As I will argue below, any number of such schemes would be appropriate, depending upon the ends the scholar has in view.

[4] In fact it ought to be clear enough that any serious attempt to weight the economic life of a community in terms of any of the better-known chronological stage systems would be a Herculean task. Reliance upon a single indicator such as net investment as a percentage of net national product as a growth indicator is most useful in studying the transition from rural unemployment stagnation into industrial growth in a market economy. One might be interested in something else; in the case of American economic development, something else altogether. For example, suppose that the historian is examining a fully-employed frontier society, output equals income, and output (in lieu of any market exchanges) is measured as the total application of human and animal energy in felling trees, clearing land, making buildings, growing, processing and consuming domestic commodities and services. We measure output as a kind of "embodied labor" reminiscent of Marx. In such a case investment is a very large part of output, and might easily be *greater* than consumption in the crucial early years, consumption only rising later on as the community becomes more developed and markets develop. A *falling* investment-output ratio in this instance is a concomitant of economic progress. How does this fit into Professor Rostow's stages of economic

My justification for this approach is a simple one. *Men,* after all, make "history," not changes in rates of capital formation, or other quantitative or qualitative measures of change. One needs a method of analyzing men themselves;[5] *their* contributions to some general aspect of development form the important set of questions.

The American economy is the deliberate product of the sum of individual human actions. I think it is vital for the entrepreneurial historian to be most explicit about this. Otherwise, why bother with individual entrepreneurs at all?

The five simultaneous "stages of history," or, if you prefer, "conceptual categories," are: (1) idealism, (2) invention, (3) innovation, (4) organization, and (5) stagnation and decline. Allow me to explain these categories for a moment.

1. It is clear that every identifiable economic product or sustained activity represents some vested interest, weak or powerful, that will likely oppose change, since change implies that other products or activities will be produced. Competition will thus exist to confront virtually any new idea, even ideas of a wholly abstruse nature. To overcome resistance to change, then, is almost by necessity to fly in the face of some "convention." To press ideas against existing reality in the face of argument, and perhaps threat, is to be idealistic or fanatical (I'm not sure there is really any difference). A vast and largely unplumbed region of American economic life and history is the role of systematic idealism about such non-economic matters as religion and social organization in provoking change. The wholly recondite can be, and has been, burning reality to men who built empires, but whose metaphysics could not be comprehended by mere reason.

2. Invention must supply the wares of economic change. Viable growth in a nation usually depends upon some self-generating inventive activity, even if there is a great deal of borrowing from others. Inventors are mainly creatures of the "state of the arts." [6] But invention also advances the arts,

---

growth? It doesn't. Yet the frontier is an important "unit of history" in the study of the American economy. Professor Rostow's frame of reference is inappropriate, except to study *his economy,* a market economy with underemployment in agriculture generating an industrial sector, moving on to his "promised land," high mass consumption.

[5] A problem recognized explicitly early in the life of the Research Center in Entrepreneurial History. See generally, *Change and the Entrepreneur* (Cambridge, Mass., 1949), especially L. H. Jenks, "The Role Structure of Entrepreneurial Personality," and T. C. Cochran, "Role and Sanction in American Entrepreneurial History." Suggestive as these two essays are, I chose to attack the problem in another way, treating personality characteristics of the men I studied as part of the determinants of their reactions to the external world.

[6] A singular little essay on the general question of inventiveness (in this case,

and economic change crucially depends at any time upon the flow of choice to the seller or user of economic products.

3. As Schumpeter emphasized, the man who changes the stream of the allocation of resources over time by introducing new departures into the flow of economic life is not necessarily an inventor of anything. He is an innovator, and plays a vital role in the economy. Andrew Carnegie, for example, invented nothing in the technology of the steel industry, and is credited with the remark "Pioneering don't pay." What he meant by "pioneering" was activity in which the probability of failure seemed to him to be high. Yet he was a real pioneer in the steel industry and his pioneering paid off in astronomical figures. He was an innovator *par excellence,* and American history has many like him.

4. A significant feature, in many ways a singular feature in American economic life, is the presence of great size of enterprises at crucial junctures in manufacturing, communications and transportation. In many cases access to internal economies of scale meant that the nation's pool of wealth and the flow of current savings had to be tapped through capital markets. To organize and tap capital and money markets some men had to develop the means of reconciling the demand for resources and available supplies of those resources on a massive scale. In any nation there is a pool of wealth and a flow of savings. But it may take organizational genius to effect even the simplest markets for securities and transfer buying power from savers to users of resources, especially where the individual sources of wealth and savings are widely dispersed.

5. Finally, as Simon Kuznets and A. F. Burns [7] demonstrated more than three decades ago, the history of separate firms and industries shows that their rate of growth tends to slow down, and, moreover, that they tend to stagnate and decline once the retardation has advanced. Because of the power of ideas and technology in individual cases these stagnating tendencies do not necessarily find expression in aggregative measures of growth; youth replaces age in economic life. Bureaucracy presides over retardation and decline. But bureaucracy performs useful and necessary functions. After all, someone needs to replace the burnt-out light bulbs at the River Rouge, but the job hardly requires a Henry Ford. In fact, one wonders how an entrepreneurial historian would approach the problem of the role of bureaucracy. I haven't tried, but someone should. I'm certain that many tired economic activities have had their Robert McNamaras. The post-

---

architecture), its technical antecedents, and the influence of contemporary environment, is: Aldous Huxley, "Faith, Taste, and History," *Encounter,* Feb., 1954.

[7] Simon Kuznets, "The Retardation of Industrial Growth," reprinted in *Economic Change* (London, 1954); A. F. Burns, *Production Trends in the United States* (New York, 1934).

1945 history of the Ford Motor Company shows clearly enough that the arts of management contain certain powers of corporate rejuvenation.

IV

I would now like to put some flesh on this framework. It follows that if I really think that these arbitrary categories can be sufficiently bent and twisted to cover, roughly, all facets of economic activity, the whole history of the American economy could be squeezed within this framework. Moreover, because I am using actual entrepreneurial action as the basis for constructing the history, and those entrepreneurial actions are chosen by my framework, I ought to be able to provide a new and more meaningful interpretation of both sides of my problem, the history itself and the contributions of the men in question. If these categories form an operational taxonomy of the main species, who are the fishes that reflect the wealth of individuals in the entrepreneurial ocean? Remember that I have defined "species" arbitrarily to include only a minimal number. Instead of selecting a large number of historical figures suggested by this framework, I have kept the number of individuals to a minimum, deliberately choosing men in these categories whose functional contributions cover the main part of the historical canvas, the economic growth of the United States. To gain the advantages of contrast and comparison, I have chosen my men in pairs. As I said earlier, the "stage" of stagnation and decline was not treated in this way since it is growth that presently concerns me.

The way our individuals operated within their environments illustrates the importance of personality in the shaping of action. The framework within which the men operated explains, given the personalities, why each contribution came in the form it did. It is important to recall that the men acted upon each other, and the whole environment at any time contained men acting in all categories. One of my men, John Pierpont Morgan, acted partly as a lover of order (mathematics) with the rules of an ancient art (finance) to change a world of vigorous activity created by men of elemental and sometimes undisciplined force. His achievements reflected largely the power of technique systematically applied to a hostile world. Another of my men, Andrew Carnegie, had Morgan in his environment. After he went into steel, Carnegie gave up his activities as a seller of securities, and even became highly and socially contemptuous of bankers and "finance." Morgan I count as an organizer, and Carnegie as innovator. They lived in the same waters and made common cause just as the whale and the shark both contribute to ecological balance in the ocean. To simply lump the two together as "entrepreneurs" is to miss the crucial parts of the mosaic; all "big business" is not the same, and entrepreneurial activity is not a set with a single member.

My choice of men in my problem are as follows:[8]

1. Idealists: William Penn and Brigham Young
2. Inventors: Eli Whitney and Thomas Edison
3. Innovators: Andrew Carnegie and Henry Ford
4. Organizers: Edward Harriman and Pierpont Morgan

1. In the first category the choice of men was easy enough. Given the supply of manpower, America required two things initially, a viable and developable institutional system and the land itself. Our institutions are largely descendants of the upheavals of seventeenth-century England, and in fact, largely the outgrowth of the Charter of Liberties and Frame of Government of Penn's colony.[9] The selection of basically democratic in-

---

[8] The minimal number of secondary works I would recommend concerning these eight men are: Augustus C. Buell, *William Penn* (New York, 1904); Catherine Owens Peare, *William Penn* (Philadelphia, 1957); Leonard J. Arrington, *Great Basin Kingdom* (Cambridge, Mass., 1958); M. R. Werner, *Brigham Young,* (New York, 1925); Constance Green, *Eli Whitney and the Birth of American Technology* (Boston, 1956); Jeanette Mirsky and Allan Nevins, *The World of Eli Whitney* (New York, 1952); Frank L. Dyer, Thomas C. Martin, and W. H. Meadowcroft, *Edison, His Life and Inventions* (2 vols., New York, 1929); Matthew Josephson, *Edison, A Biography* (New York, 1959); Andrew Carnegie, *Autobiography* (Boston, 1924); Burton J. Hendrick, *The Life of Andrew Carnegie* (2 vols., New York, 1932); Allan Nevins and F. E. Hill, *Ford* (3 vols., New York, 1954-1963); Keith Sward, *The Legend of Henry Ford* (New York, 1948); Charles Sorenson, *My Forty Years with Ford* (New York, 1956) (I recommend Sward as an antidote to Nevins and Hill, and Sorenson as an antidote to Sward); George Kennan, *E. H. Harriman* (2 vols., Boston, 1922); Robert A. Lovett, *Forty Years After* (New York, 1949); F. L. Allen, *The Great Pierpont Morgan* (New York, 1949); Herbert L. Satterlee, *J. Pierpont Morgan* (New York, 1939).

[9] With due apologies to Roger Williams, the House of Burgesses and so forth. Such a judgment cannot be anything but controversial since it is impossible to measure the proportional ancestry of such things as our present liberties in the many historical strands that make up the present fabric. It seems to be the *balance* of liberties, lawfulness, longevity and pervasiveness of statutory democratic power vested in the franchised voters, the egalitarian tradition, the purity of conception and lucidity of writing in the basic Pennsylvania documents, together with the success of the colony, that have combined to place William Penn in such a high place among specialists in American Constitutional History. Indeed, the historian Edward Channing was willing to call William Penn *the* founding father of the United States, if any one person were to receive that appellation. Edward Channing, "William Penn," *Annual Report of the American Historical Association,* Vol. I., 1906. Before his financial losses in Pennsylvania became settled Penn was immensely proud of his entrepreneurial success in America: "I have led the greatest colony into America that ever any man did upon a private credit. . . ." S. E. Morison and H. S. Commager, *The Growth of the American Republic* (New York, 1962) vol. I., pp. 77-78. Discussing, in a wartime edition of their classic, the resistance of the United States to the fascist powers, Morison and Commager handed Penn their highest laurels: "And if the American experiment has so far withstood the assaults made upon it by the totalitarian powers, William Penn and his "Holy Experiment" are more directly responsible than any other colonial founder, or any other colonial commonwealth." *Ibid.,* p. 79. Penn failed to collect the modest

stitutions from the chaos of seventeenth-century English autarchy was the gift of history, and was due in large part to Penn's single-minded, perhaps even simple-minded, devotion to a set of religious beliefs which brought death, maiming, imprisonment and banishment to thousands. Much of the Leveller doctrine had permeated the Quakers, and Penn's thinking. It was Penn's largely egalitarian democracy (allowed to operate within a private fief), and not the bigotry of the New England theocracy that found expression in the basic American documents, and finds a home today in typical American organizational structures, economic as well as political. Penn's decisions were a product of a fanatical adherence to a system of theology. This country scarcely knows a more profound entrepreneurial contribution to its development. As a business venture Pennsylvania was a disaster to Penn, but it was a great legacy to future generations.

From the time of the first settlement the taking of the Continent engaged all sorts of people. But from Plymouth onwards, systematic idealization of thought — national, religious, racial, economic and political — and mixtures of all played critical roles. At the end of the trail, in the mountain deserts of the West were Brigham Young and the Mormons. They were not only acting out the closing of the American geographical frontier, but were themselves a kind of distillation of several main strains of American utopianism. The New England village, the Puritan millenialism, the social experimentation of Oneida, Brook Farm, New Harmony and a hundred other frontier settlements, and the movement of the physical frontier across the middle west into the acquisitions of the Mexican War. Young's radical pragmatism, mixed with self-effacing devotion to his singular religious principles were a reflection of a main stream of American life of the ante-bellum period, which was permanently deflected after the 1840's.[10] Young's successes as well as his failures were partly the results of his personality, partly the outcome of the movement he represented, and partly were compromises with an alien environment. He represented a multitude of individuals whose lives were fulfilled on the American frontier. In the cases of both Penn and Young the contribution of the individual to the historical outcome was striking, yet their environment was "given" by the actions of others. Adherents to systematic idealism today make the same sorts of impacts on the flow of events, even though, in our time, the idealism is not so likely to be a religious one.

---

quit rents he had imposed upon his feudal *seigniorie* and hence lost a fortune. At the time of his death he was still negotiating for the sale of his rights in the colony. Of the vast literature on Penn's contribution to the United States, a particularly incisive and well-balanced view is one of the oldest, George Bancroft, *History of the United States of America* (Boston, 1879) Vol. II, ch. XX and XXIV.

[10] The first chapter in Arrington's *Great Basin Kingdom, op. cit.,* is a particularly brilliant exegesis developing this point.

2.   Through the life of Eli Whitney (and others like him in his time) ran two fundamental threads of American development: the rise of the ante-bellum South with its slave economy, and the nascent industrial and commercial power of the North. Whitney contributed to both developments, as did scores of other men who converted the "state of the arts" to American needs. Whitney's early career, from the cotton gin, financed by expropriated British crown property, through his weary negotiations and battles over his government musket contracts, was deeply concerned with the growth of governmental power and methods in the new nation. The proliferation of invention from his hands and those of his colleagues in the armament field, into a broader spectrum of industrial uses mirrored a remarkable chapter of American industrial history.[11]

Edison's career, on the other hand, was not importantly connected to government, but straddled a more complex technological world developed primarily in the private sector after the Civil War. The vast new world of electricity and chemistry went from crude beginnings to a powerful adolescence in the lifetime of Edison, and he participated in the new technology at its beginnings. Edison dealt with most of the great inventors of this crucial time in American history on terms that ranged from open patent infringements (the telephone) to the more subtle oligopolistic jostling of the old motion picture cartel.

The study of Edison's role as an inventor raises an interesting line of inquiry for entrepreneurial historians. His dictum, "A patent is an invitation to a lawsuit" would have found a welcome "Amen" from Whitney, and from other inventors all the way down to our own times. I think that the history of patent infringement is by itself an illuminating view of the permeation of new technology into the nation's economic life over time. The entrepreneurs involved might sometimes seem to be slightly disreputable but ours is the study of facts, and not the judging of ethics.

Both Edison and Whitney made their contributions in a certain way because of properties of their own personalities and private circumstances, and subtly influenced the course of economic history in the process. But they also were reacting to a changing world created not only by men like themselves, but by men in our other "stages" of development, entrepreneurs like Westinghouse and Morgan, men whose visions were part of circumstances which only touched the inventor tangentially.

---

[11] "Who did what with which first?" in the early American machine tool industry is a lively area for the revisionist. So far as I am aware, Eli Whitney is still accorded *some* role in the story. For our purposes Whitney can be partly considered as a symbol of the whole set of machine-tool makers associated with the arms industry in the ante-bellum period. On the genesis of the Machine Tool Industry see Nathan Rosenberg, "Technological Change in the Machine Tool Industry, 1840-1910," *Journal of Economic History*, 23" 4;4-43 (Dec., 1963).

3.   Schumpeterian innovators have, of course, held the center of the stage from the very beginning of entrepreneurial studies. These were men who invented nothing, but adapted and forced new technology and products into economic life. Carnegie and Ford were two such men. Their careers not only determined important departures in the course of economic change, their personalities powerfully determined their contributions — and, I hasten to add, the nature of the reaction, especially the violence and single-mindedness of labor-union action in America from Homestead to the River Rouge and after.

Carnegie's great contribution, from the establishment of the Edgar Thomson works at Braddock Field in 1873 until Pierpont Morgan loosened the aged Spencerian's grip in 1900, was to make the American steel industry one of the wonders of industrial history. His methods were those of ruthless and unremitting competition. Carnegie Steel was the cutting edge of progress in the basic industry during the great industrial transformatic of 1873-1900, an epoch in which the United States outstripped all others in industrial development. Carnegie himself was a product of two deeper and older economic phenomena. His father, Thomas, was actually a hand-loom weaver, a master weaver of linen in Dunfermline, displaced by the power-loom. The classic Industrial Revolution was thus one progenitor of Carnegie Steel. The other was the Atlantic migration of the nineteenth century, to which was added, in 1848, the little Scottish family of Thomas Carnegie. Andrew Carnegie's contributions to his new country were many-sided, ranging from steel to philanthropy, and remain with us. But the entire story is most clearly framed by the single fact that, in the growth of the American economy in the late nineteenth century, the poor lad from Dunfermline became the Schumpeterian entrepreneur *par excellence*. Carnegie's own development was a microcosm of much of American experience in economic affairs in the last half of the nineteenth century.

Perhaps the greatest change in American economic history thus far in the twentieth century has been due to the transformation of a European "invention" into an American innovation — the automobile. And the automobile industry was almost spelled Ford in its vital formative years, when a rich man's plaything became the basic mode of American transport. The automobile set off a vast change in the demographic and social structure of the country that still shows few signs of stabilizing. To really understand this phenomenon, and its main instrument, the Model T, one must begin by looking closely into the character of the tyrant of Dearborn, the Napoleon of the River Rouge, and oppressor of the worker, who probably brought more freedom to more people than all the liberators of history. Ford was a corn-fed Bolivar to the twentieth century. His greatest contribution to American life was to free the common man from his geography. After

Ford, no man needed to stay in any locale if he had the few dollars it cost to buy some sort of an automobile. And here I do not mean to include only inter-regional mobility in the national economy, but also, and perhaps mainly, the local freedom of movement which has diminished the farmtown and made the new shopping-center world of suburbia a threat to the conventional city itself. Model T was Ford's religion and the mass-produced world of the automobile his monument. His own life and work take American history from the horse-drawn plough to the mechanical farm, from the wagon road to the superhighway. Oddly enough, both of these men, Carnegie and Ford, are now associated in the public mind with vast philanthropies. It was not always so. The details of these careers in industrial revolution comprise a key which unlock a rich understanding of this country's past and its present.

4. I chose Harriman and Morgan as my men of organization to illustrate a singular and continuous thread in economic history, the essentially conservative power of the financial art. Finance imposes a logic of its own upon both the borrower and the lender. Even financial frauds and chicaneries follow identifiable, almost predictable patterns. There is great continuity in techniques in arts and crafts over time, and the mind follows the action of the hand. Pierpont Morgan was like the Medicis in more ways than his personal tastes; over the gulf of centuries, they were essentially in the same trade. If the users of savings, the tycoons of a new technology, wanted contact with accumulated wealth and with current flows of savings, that contact had to come from an intermediary whose rules were fixed by customs far older than the Newtonian science from which that new technology had developed.[12] Financiers set terms for repayment of debt. To meet those terms, borrowers had to regulate their own activity according to schedules of repayment and even, commonly, to accept bankers into direct management in order to guarantee the necessary safeguards. The decisions of industry were thus powerfully influenced by the needs of the manipulators of engraved paper. Hence, men like Carnegie and Ford, who did not use the capital markets, had a freedom of action quite different from those like Gary and Durant who did need to come to terms with the world of high finance.

In the late nineteenth century, as certain American transportation and industrial ventures generated ambitions which outstripped their own current earning capacities, the builders of these systems sought contractual partnerships with those who wanted earning assets in place of cash hoards.

---

[12] The financial historian might well contemplate the degree of sophistication implied in Babylonia by Article 112 of Hammurabi's Code, which laid down penalties for default on maturing bills of exchange. Paul Einzig, *The History of Foreign Exchange* (New York, 1962), p. 15.

The resulting unions were arranged for and sanctified by the financial organizers. The result has been called such names as the "age of finance capitalism," the "age of trusts," and the like. These phrases described a reality, and a vital one, in American economic history. Without the union of finance and industry the massive size of many of our great companies might well not have developed. There is no evidence that most of these are not based upon efficiency. The charge of "monopoly power" sounded good, but it has not held up as the origin of economic strength among the industrial giants. Internal economies made access to the capital markets desirable. In industry after industry in the late nineteenth century, the union of technology and the capital market provided an opening for growth, where reliance upon current earnings for expansion seemed to constrain management.

I chose Harriman as one of my financial organizers to illustrate the contribution of the specialist. He is the paragon of the railroad financier. From his reorganization of the Ontario and Southern through the Northern Pacific Trust (in which Morgan had a hand) and on to the posthumous liquidation of the Southern Pacific empire under the Sherman Act, Harriman's activities showed a consistent pattern of rationalization, conservative reorganization, and expansion. Men like Villard built the railroads, but they didn't run them. Time after time it seemed that the empire-builders had to "hand over" to the financial organizers. Harriman, like Carnegie, was both thoughtful and ruthless. He also represented Thomas Mun's ideal, the man whose private ambitions embraced the public interest, or at least advanced the public interest. Harriman was apparently not an attractive person in business, and historians have gleefully followed the unsubstantiated and bitter charges of Harriman's defeated enemies. Yet a careful study of Harriman's career as an organizer provides a vivid lesson in the mechanics of transportation finance at the turn of the century. Harriman was no hero to the historians, but he was a whale of a financial organizer, and his volcanic and controversial career creates a bright light on the American past when that career is viewed as an example of a particular kind of contribution; viewed merely as a "Robber Baron," as he traditionally has been treated, Harriman has almost been lost to the history books.

My final entrepreneur is John Pierpont Morgan himself. Sometimes it seems that all roads led to the Morgan library until Morgan died in 1913. Personally he was an enigma, but as a financial organizer he knew no peer. We have not seen his like since, nor, in my opinion, are we likely to. Almost every facet of his life was a side of American economic history. One part of Morgan's personality, the hard-eyed Yankee moralist studying the imperfections of his fellow tycoons, is an essay in Americana. One imagines the astonished forefather of our race, in his threadbare suit and mud-covered boots looking upon his affluent progeny with both dismay and disapproval — yet recognizing his own. On the other hand, Morgan's tastes in matters of personal consumption, and his esthetic senses, were extravagant in his time, and perhaps foreshadowed a future when affluence came within the reach of millions. Morgan had a passion to impose discipline and order upon everything he touched. When men came to him for help they took away orders. In fact, when Wall Street's elite came voluntarily to the old man for help, as they did that Sunday half a century ago in the panic of 1907, they knew that orders would come which would be painful but effective. The portly old gentleman with the blazing eyes, long cigar, whose words were few, who reorganized a vast portion of the nation's industry during his endless games of solitaire, was a one-man segment of American financial history. His banking house grew out of the older tradition of merchant banking, and he presided over the growth of American investment banking practice virtually from its beginning. His actions in national emergencies from 1877 to 1907 were examples for those who yearned for the restoration of central banking to the United States. His promotion of the arts was a great beginning of the infusion of high quality into everyday American life — the Metropolitan Museum of Art is as much his monument as is United States Steel, but few remember that today.

In my scheme of organization of American economic development the Morgans are as essential as the Penns, and if neither kind is identifiable today on such a heroic scale, it is the scale of the national framework that has changed, not the basic economic functions of idealism, invention, innovation and organization. We sometimes overlook the extent to which our society automatically systematizes useful art. Entrepreneurship of the Morgan or Harriman variety was most rare in their time. The *talent* is still rare enough, but business schools now teach the skills those men had.

V

I have outlined this view of American economic development in order to underscore two points: (1) the entrepreneur can quite properly be used as a focal point in the interpretation of American economic history generally, but (2) the entrepreneurial role can be made coherent *only* within some sort of explicit analytical framework. Because I chose to try this scheme on the grandest scale, my analytical framework is one of desperate simplicity. One presumes that more specific problems would yield more complex analytical systems. As any experienced economist is aware, it is in disaggregation that complications develop. But I want to insist upon the view that the entrepreneurial historian should be as much concerned with *what* he is talking about as with *whom* he is dealing. Sub-division of the entrepreneurial function into conceptual categories is a useful device for clarification. If his work is to be a coherently integrated part of the whole fabric of American history, the entrepreneurial historian owes it to his reader to commit himself as much to identifying and analyzing his problem as to getting his biographical facts straight. This is so, even if for no other reason than this simple one: *it is the underlying problem that determines which facts shall be chosen.* My conceptual framework determined how I was to pick my men, and why. The "facts" themselves are silent, unless ordered by ideas. Brigham Young was a religious enthusiast, and Pierpont Morgan was a financier. But, given my frame of reference, I argue that Young's great contribution, including even his banking, came primarily from his religious commitment, and Pierpont Morgan's from his financial acumen (perhaps soothed by appropriate scripture).

Let me add two points. First, I doubt that there will ever be any single, generally accepted way to write Entrepreneurial History, because there will be as many analytical frames of reference as there are ideas about what is important in economic life. That will always be a large number indeed. Second, there is more, much more, than economic motivation in the lives of men. For example, let me make a "far out" but entirely serious suggestion about these men in particular, and Entrepreneurial History in general. It seems to me that my men could have been studied most profitably indeed from a type of Freudian analysis. What were the effects upon Penn, Brigham Young and Morgan of their all-powerful fathers? Whitney was a "solitary," a bachelor into his fifties. Were these facts, together with his inventiveness, and with the secretiveness of his actions, all related in an important way? Did they have important effects? Did Harriman, the "Little Giant," act out the part in a defensive reaction to his small stature? What was the impact of strong mothers and weak fathers upon Carnegie, Harriman, Ford and Edison? I am almost asking what was the effect of family life on American history *through* these men. Yet, if we are seriously interested in understanding the individual entrepreneur's impact, I don't really see how we can avoid the problems of the determination of personality.

It also seems to me that the "lessons" of history aren't really very easily found by entrepreneurial historians. For the Victorian period especially, there were powerful motivations which might not seem reasonable to our age, but these must be learned and taken into account if the historian is to make any sense of some Victorian entrepreneurs. I'm not saying that unvarnished greed — or profit maximization — was not important. But

I am saying that profit maximization isn't a sufficient identification of motivation. For example, there was millenialism in both Penn and Young, there was a powerful belief in inexorable *moral* progress in both Carnegie and Morgan. In Edison and Ford there was a rich strain of what might be called cracker-barrel chauvinism — disdain for formal science and for expertise. The chauvinism was sincere, and partly armed those two classic "country boys" to triumph over a world in which science and expertise were both largely hostile. Of the men I've studied here, possibly only Whitney and Harriman were sufficiently examples of *homo oeconomicus* to satisfy the most mundane model of human motivation. But even in these two it can be shown that the "public interest" intruded at times.

Our hideous age of wars and atrocities, the impact of income taxes upon the aggregation and control of great wealth by individuals, remorseless inflation adding to the persistent social disorganization of our times, may make the Victorian world more obsolete as a model of basic motivation and behavior than the passage of time alone might indicate. The student of entrepreneurship, no less than any other variety of historian, needs to acclimate himself in the culture of the period he is studying, and this is an added burden.

All such considerations lead me back to one of my earliest statements: informed Entrepreneurial History is difficult and complex, and must necessarily be so. The biographer-historian-economist-social psychologist-philosopher who scales all these heights in a really professional way will indeed be worthy of our admiration. But what is most difficult of all, is that this lion-taming snake charmer needs the broad as well as the narrow view. And this is an unkind fate.[13]

---

[13] The approach I suggest may be thought to be a departure from the view held by Arthur Cole: " . . . limitation of the term 'entrepreneurship' to the purveyance of economic goods and services on certain terms seems necessary for purposes of clear analysis, especially relative to motivations and to sources of power." *Business Enterprise in its Social Setting* (Cambridge, Mass., 1959), p. 10. Yet I don't think the approach I suggest is really a departure from "purveyance of economic goods" at all. Even in the cases of Penn and Young, the successful application of men and resources to religion resulted in new economic horizons, empires, and these were "economic goods," if one wants to interpret Cole broadly — and I do. I think the entrepreneurial role ought to be conceived by the historian in the broadest sense. The full impact of Henry Ford was not just the Ford car, but a whole world of change set in motion. It is not necessarily at the expense of "clear analysis" that the entrepreneurial historian attempts to paint the broad picture. A river flows to the sea, but a river, painted as mere water, is uninteresting, and is a distortion, especially if one is interested in the full economic, social and aesthetic impact of it. Viewed in his full ecology, the entrepreneur in American history ought to open a new window on the past.

The Beginnings of "Big Business" in American Industry*

ALFRED D. CHANDLER, JR. ‡

CRITERIA FOR SELECTION AND ANALYSIS

The historian, by the very nature of his task, must be concerned with change. What made for change? Why did it come when it did, and in the way it did? These are characteristically historians' questions. For the student of American business history, these basic questions can be put a little more precisely. What in the American past has given businessmen the opportunity or created the need for them to change what they were doing or the way they were doing it? In other words, what stimulated them to develop new products, new markets, new sources of raw materials, new ways of procuring, processing, or marketing the goods they handled? What encouraged them to find new methods of financing, new ways of managing or organizing their businesses? What turned them to altering their relations with their working force, their customers and competitors, and with the larger American public?

The question of what constitutes the dynamic factors in American business history, dynamic in the sense of stimulating change and innovation, can be more clearly defined if the country's land, natural resources, and cultural patterns are taken as given. Land and resources were the raw materials with which the businessmen had to work, and the cultural attitudes and values helped set the legal and ethical rules of the game they had to play. Within this cultural and geographic environment a number of historical developments appear to have stimulated change. These provide a framework around which historical data can be compiled and analyzed.

The following major dynamic forces are visible in the American business economy since 1815: the western expansion of population; the construction and initial operation of the national railroad network; the development of a national and increasingly urban market; the application of two new sources of power: the internal combustion engine and electricity, to industry and transportation; and the systematic application of the natural and physical sciences, particularly chemistry and

* This study was supported by the Sloan Research Fund of The School of Industrial Management and the Center for International Studies, Massachusetts Institute of Technology.

‡ Alfred D. Chandler is Professor of History at the Johns Hopkins University.

physics, to industry through the institutionalizing of research and development activities.

The first, the westward expansion, appears to have provided the primary impetus, except possibly in New England, to business innovation in the years from 1815 to about 1850; the building of the railroads appears to have been the major factor from the 1850's to the late 1870's; the growth of the national and urban market from the 1880's until a little after 1900; the coming of electricity and the internal combustion engine from the early 1900's to the 1920's: and, finally, the growth of systematic and institutionalized research and development since the 1920's.

These five factors are essentially aspects of fundamental population changes and technological advances. There were, of course, other factors that encouraged business innovation and change. The coming of the new machines and mechanical devices may have been a more important stimulant to innovation in New England than the growth of her markets and sources of supply in the expanding South and West. Wars usually precipitated change. The business cycle, flow of capital, government policy and legislation all played a significant part in business innovation. But such political and financial developments appear to have intensified or delayed the more basic changes encouraged initially by fundamental population shifts and technological achievements.

The purpose of making such a list is, however, not to argue that one development was more dynamic than the other. Nor are these five factors to be considered as "causes" for change; nor are they "theses" to be argued as representing reality, nor "theories" to provide an over-all explanation of change or possibly of predicting change. They are, rather, a framework on which historical information can be tied and inter-related. They provide a consistent basis upon which meaningful questions can be asked of the data.

This framework and these questions are, it should be emphasized, concerned only with fundamental changes and innovation in the business economy. They do not deal with the day-to-day activities to which businessmen must devote nearly all of their time. They are not concerned with the continuous adaptation to the constant variations of the market, sources of supply, availability of capital, and technological developments. Nor do they consider why some businesses and businessmen responded quickly and creatively to the basic population and technological changes and others did not. But an understanding of the continuous response and adjustment would seem to require first an awareness of the meaning of the more fundamental or "discontinuous" changes.

Since historical compilation and analysis must be selective, it is impossible to undertake any historical study without some criteria either implicit or explicit for selection. Further study and analysis, by indicating the defects of this approach and framework, will suggest more satisfactory ones. In the process, an analysis and interpretation of change in the American business past should come a little nearer to reality.

The purpose of this article then is, by using the framework of basic, dynamic forces, to look a little more closely at the years that witnessed the beginnings of big business in American industry. What types of changes came during these years in the ways of marketing, purchasing, processing, and in the forms of business organization? Why did these changes come when they did in the way they did? Was the growth of the national market a major prerequisite for such innovation and change? If not, what then was? How did these innovations relate to the growth of the railroad network or the coming of electricity and the internal combustion engine?

In addition to secondary works on this period, the data used in seeking answers to these questions have been annual and other corporation reports, government documents, articles in periodicals, histories, and biographies concerning the 50 largest industrial companies in the country in 1909. Nearly all these companies, listed in Table I, had their beginnings in the last years of the nineteenth century.

MAJOR CHANGES IN AMERICAN INDUSTRY AT THE END OF THE NINETEENTH CENTURY

Between the depression of the 1870's and the beginning of the twentieth century, American industry underwent a significant transformation. In the 1870's, the major industries serviced an agrarian economy. Except for a few companies equipping the rapidly expanding railroad network, the leading industrial firms processed agricultural products and provided farmers with food and clothing. These firms tended to be small, and bought their raw materials and sold their finished goods locally. Where they manufactured for a market more than a few miles away from the factory, they bought and sold through commissioned agents who handled the business of several other similar firms.

By the beginning of the twentieth century, many more companies were making producers' goods, to be used in industry rather than on the farm or by the ultimate consumer. Most of the major industries had become dominated by a few large enterprises. These great industrial corporations no longer purchased and sold through agents, but had their own nationwide buying and marketing organizations. Many, primarily those in the extractive industries had come to control their own raw materials. In other words, the business economy had become industrial. Major industries were dominated by a few firms that had become great, vertically integrated, centralized enterprises.

In the terms of the economist and sociologist a significant sector of American industry had become bureaucratic, in the sense that business decisions were made within large hierarchical structures. Externally, oligopoly was prevalent, the decision-makers being as much concerned with the actions of the few other large firms in the industry as with over-all changes in markets, sources of supplies, and technological improvements.

These basic changes came only after the railroads had created a national market. The railroad network, in turn, had grown swiftly primarily because of the near-desperate requirements for efficient transportation created by the movement of population westward after 1815.[1] Except for the Atlantic seaboard between Boston and Washington, the construction of the American railroads was stimulated almost wholly by the demand for better transportation to move crops, to bring farmers supplies, and to open up new territories to commercial agriculture.

By greatly expanding the scope of the agrarian economy, the railroads quickened the growth of the older commercial centers, such as New York, Philadelphia, Cincinnati, Cleveland, and St. Louis, and helped create new cities like Chicago, Indianapolis, Atlanta, Kansas City, Dallas, and the Twin Cities. This rapid urban expansion intensified the demand for the products of the older consumer goods industries — particularly those which processed the crops of the farmer and planter into food, stimulants, and clothing.

At the same time, railroad construction developed the first large market in this country for producers' goods. Except for the making of relatively few textile machines, steamboat engines, and ordnance, the iron and non-ferrous manufacturers had before 1850 concentrated on providing metals and simple tools for merchants and farmers. Even textile machinery was usually made by the cloth manufacturers themselves. However, by 1860, only a decade after beginning America's first major railroad construction boom, railroad companies had already replaced the blacksmiths as the primary market for iron products, and had become far away the most important market for the heavy engineering industries. By then, too, the locomotive was competing with the Connecticut brass industry as a major

---

[1] The factors stimulating the growth of the American railroad network and the impact of the earlier construction and operation of this network on the American business economy and business institutions is suggested in Chandler, *Henry Varnum Poor — Business Editor, Analyst, and Reformer* (Cambridge, 1956), especially chaps. 4, 6-9.

consumer of copper. More than this, the railroads, with their huge capital outlay, their fixed operating costs, the large size of their labor and management force, and the technical complexity of their operations, pioneered in the new ways of oligopolistic competition and large-scale, professionalized, bureaucratized management.

The new nation-wide market created by the construction of the railroad became an increasingly urban one. From 1850 on, if not before, urban areas were growing more rapidly than rural ones. In the four decades from 1840 to 1880 the proportion of urban population rose from 11 per cent to 28 per cent of the total population, or about 4 per cent a decade. In the two decades from 1880 to 1900 it grew from 28 per cent to 40 per cent or an increase of 6 per cent a decade. Was this new urban and national market, then, the primary stimulant for business innovation and change, and for the coming of big business to American industry?

Changes in the Consumers' Goods Industries

The industries first to become dominated by great business enterprises were those making consumer goods, the majority of which were processed from products grown on the farm and sold in the urban markets. Consolidation and centralization in the consumers' goods industries were well under way by 1893. The unit that appeared was one which integrated within a single business organization the major economic processes: production or purchasing of raw materials, manufacturing, distribution, and finance.

Such vertically integrated organizations came in two quite different ways. Where the product tended to be somewhat new in kind and especially fitted for the urban market, its makers created their businesses by first building large marketing and then purchasing organizations. This technique appears to have been true of the manufacturers or distributors of fresh meat, cigarettes, high-grade flour, bananas, harvesters, sewing machines, and typewriters. Where the products were established staple items, horizontal combination tended to precede vertical integration. In the sugar, salt, leather, whiskey, glucose, starch, biscuit, kerosene, fertilizer, and rubber industries a large number of small manufacturers first combined into large business units and then created their marketing and buying organizations. For a number of reasons the makers of the newer types of products found the older outlets less satisfactory and felt more of a need for direct marketing than did the manufacturers of the long-established goods.

Integration via the Creation of Marketing Organization

The story of the changes and the possible reasons behind them can be more clearly understood by examining briefly the experience of a few innovating firms. First, consider the experience of companies that grew large through the creation of a nation-wide marketing and distributing organization. Here the story of Gustavus F. Swift and his brother Edwin is a significant one. Gustavus F. Swift, an Easterner, came relatively late to the Chicago meat-packing business. Possibly because he was from Massachusetts, he appreciated the potential market for fresh western meat in the eastern cities.[2] For after the Civil War, Boston, New York, Philadelphia, and other cities were rapidly outrunning their local meat supply. At the same time, great herds of cattle were gathering on the western plains. Swift saw the possibilities of connecting the new market with the new source of supply by the use of the refrigerated railroad car. In 1878, shortly after his first experimental shipment of refrigerated meat, he formed a partnership with his younger brother, Edwin, to market fresh western meat in the eastern cities.

For the next decade, Swift struggled hard to carry out his plans, the essence of which was the creation, during the 1880's, of the nation-wide distributing and marketing organization built around a network of branch houses. Each "house" had its storage plant and its own marketing organization. The latter included outlets in major towns and cities, often managed by Swift's own salaried representatives. In marketing the products, Swift had to break down, through advertising and other means, the prejudices against eating meat killed more than a thousand miles away and many weeks earlier. At the same time he had to combat boycotts of local butchers and the concerted efforts of the National Butchers' Protective Association to prevent the sale of his meat in the urban markets.

To make effective use of the branch house network, the company soon began to market products other than beef. The "full line" soon came to include lamb, mutton, pork, and, some time later, poultry, eggs, and dairy products. The growing distributing organization soon demanded an increase in supply. So between 1888 and 1892, the Swifts set up meat-packing establishments in Kansas City, Omaha, and St. Louis, and, after

---

[2] Swift's story as outlined in Louis F. Swift in collaboration with Arthur Van Vlissingen, *The Yankee of the Yards — the Biography of Gustavus Franklin Swift* (New York, 1928). The United States Bureau of Corporations, *Report of the Commissioner of Corporations on the Beef Industry, March 3, 1905* (Washington, 1905), is excellent on the internal operations and external activities of the large meat-packing firms. There is additional information in the later three-volume *Report of the Federal Trade Commission on the Meat Packing Industry* (Washington, 1918-1919). R. A. Clemen, *The American Livestock and Meat Industry* (New York, 1923) has some useful background data.

the depression of the 1890's, three more in St. Joseph, St. Paul, and Ft. Worth. At the same time, the company systematized the buying of its cattle and other products at the stockyards. In the 1890's, too, Swift began a concerted effort to make more profitable use of by-products.

Before the end of the 1890's, then, Swift had effectively fashioned a great, vertically integrated organization. The major departments — marketing, processing, purchasing, and accounting — were all tightly controlled from the central office in Chicago. A report of the Commissioner of Corporations published in 1905 makes clear the reason for such control: [3]

> Differences in quality of animals and of their products are so great that the closest supervision of the Central Office is necessary to enforce the exercise of skill and sound judgment on the part of the agents who buy the stock, and the agents who sell the meat. With this object, the branches of the Selling and Accounting Department of those packing companies which have charge of the purchasing, killing, and dressing and selling of fresh meat, are organized in the most extensive and thorough manner. The Central office is in constant telegraphic correspondence with the distributing houses, with a view to adjusting the supply of meat and the price as nearly as possible to the demand.

As this statement suggests, the other meat packers followed Swift's example. To compete effectively, Armour, Morris, Cudahy, and Schwarzschild & Sulzberger had to build up similar integrated organizations. Those that did not follow the Swift model were destined to remain small local companies. Thus by the middle of the 1890's, the meat-packing industry, with the rapid growth of these great vertically integrated firms had become oligopolistic (the "Big Five" had the major share of the market) and bureaucratic; each of the five had its many departments and several levels of management.

This story has parallels in other industries processing agricultural products. In tobacco, James B. Duke was the first to appreciate the growing market for the cigarette, a new product which was sold almost wholly in the cities.[4] However, after he had applied machinery to the manufacture of cigarettes, production soon outran supply. Duke then concentrated on expanding the market through extensive advertising and the creation of a national and then world-wide selling organization. In 1884, he left Durham, North Carolina, for New York City, where he set

---

[3] *Report of Commissioner of Corporations on the Beef Industry*, p. 21.

[4] Some information on James B. Duke and the American Tobacco Company can be found in John W. Jenkins, *James B. Duke, Master Builder* (New York, 1827), chaps. 5-7, 10. More useful was the United States Bureau of Corporations, *Report of the Commissioner of Corporations on the Tobacco Industry* (Washington, 1909).

up factories, sales, and administrative offices. New York was closer to his major urban markets, and was the more logical place to manage an international advertising campaign than Durham. While he was building his marketing department, Duke was also creating the network of warehouses and buyers in the tobacco-growing areas of the country.

In 1890, he merged his company with five smaller competitors in the cigarette business to form the American Tobacco Company. By 1895 the activities of these firms had been consolidated into the manufacturing, marketing, purchasing, and finance departments of the single operating structure Duke had earlier fashioned. Duke next undertook development of a full line by handling all types of smoking and chewing tobacco. By the end of the century, his company completely dominated the tobacco business. Only two other firms, R. J. Reynolds & Company and P. Lorillard & Company had been able to build up comparable vertically integrated organizations. When they merged with American Tobacco they continued to retain their separate operating organizations. When the 1911 antitrust decree split these and other units off from the American company, the tobacco industry had become, like the meat-packing business, oligopolistic, and its dominant firms bureaucratic.

What Duke and Swift did for their industries, James S. Bell of the Washburn-Crosby Company did during these same years in the making and selling of high-grade flour to the urban bakeries and housewives, and Andrew J. Preston achieved in growing, transporting, and selling another new product for the urban market, the banana.[5] Like Swift and Duke, both these men made their major innovations in marketing, and then went on to create large-scale, departmentalized, vertically integrated structures.

The innovators in new consumer durables followed much the same pattern. Both Cyrus McCormick, pioneer harvester manufacturer, and William Clark, the business brains of the Singer Sewing Machine Company, first sold through commissioned agents. Clark soon discovered that salaried men, working out of branch offices, could more effectively and at less cost display, demonstrate, and service sewing machines than could the agents.[6] Just as important, the branch offices were able to provide the customer with essential credit. McCormick, while retaining the dealer to handle the final sales, came to appreciate the need for a strong selling and distributing organization, with warehouses, servicing facilities, and a large

---

[5] The story of Bell is outlined in James Gray, *Business Without Boundary, the Story of General Mills* (Minneapolis, 1954), and of Preston in Charles M. Wilson, *Empire in Green and Gold* (New York, 1947).

[6] The early Singer Sewing Machine experience is well analyzed in Andrew B. Jack, "The Channels of Distribution for an Innovation: the Sewing Machine Industry in America, 1860-1865," *Explorations in Entrepreneurial History*, Vol. IX (Feb., 1957), pp. 113-141.

salaried force, to stand behind the dealer.[7] So in the years following the Civil War, both McCormick and Singer Sewing Machine Company concentrated on building up national and then world-wide marketing departments. As they purchased their raw materials from a few industrial companies rather than from a mass of farmers, their purchasing departments were smaller, and required less attention than those in the firms processing farmers' products. But the net result was the creation of a very similar type of organization.

Intergration via Horizontal Combination

In those industries making more standard goods, the creation of marketing organizations usually followed large-scale combinations of a number of small manufacturing firms. For these small firms, the coming of the railroad had in many cases enlarged their markets but simultaneously brought them for the first time into competition with many other companies. Most of these firms appear to have expanded production in order to take advantage of the new markets. As a result, their industries became plagued with overproduction and excess capacity; that is, continued production at full capacity threatened to drop prices below the cost of production. So in the 1880's and early 1890's, many small manufacturers in the leather, sugar, salt, distilling and other corn products, linseed and cotton oil, biscuit, petroleum, fertilizer and rubber boot and glove industries, joined in large horizontal combinations.

In most of these industries, combination was followed by consolidation and vertical integration, and the pattern was comparatively consistent. First, the new combinations concentrated their manufacturing activities in locations more advantageously situated to meet the new growing urban demands. Next they systematized and standardized their manufacturing processes. Then, except in the case of sugar and corn products (glucose and starch), the combinations began to build large distributing and smaller purchasing departments. In so doing, many dropped their initial efforts to buy out competitors or to drive them out of business by price-cutting. Instead they concentrated on the creation of a more efficient flow from the producers of their raw materials to the ultimate consumer, and of the development and maintenance of markets through brand names and advertising. Since the large majority of these combinations began as regional groupings, most industries came to have more than one great firm. Only oil, sugar, and corn products remained long dominated by a single company. By World War I, partly because of the dissolutions under

---

[7] William T. Hutchinson, *Cyrus Hall McCormick* (New York, 1935), Vol. II, pp. 704-712.

the Sherman Act, these industries had also become oligopolistic, and their leading firms vertically integrated.

Specific illustrations help to make these generalizations more precise. The best-known is the story of the oil industry, but equally illustrative is the experience of the leading distilling, baking, and rubber companies.

The first permanent combination in the whiskey industry came in 1887 when a large number of Midwestern distillers, operating more than 80 small plants, formed the Distillers' and Cattle Feeders' Trust.[8] Like other trusts, it adopted the more satisfactory legal form of a holding company shortly after New Jersey in 1889 passed the general incorporation law for holding companies. The major efforts of the Distillers Company were, first, to concentrate production in a relatively few plants. By 1895 only 21 were operating. The managers maintained that the large volume per plant permitted by such concentration would mean lower costs, and also that the location of few plants more advantageously in relation to supply and marketing would still reduce expenses further. However, the company kept the price of whiskey up, and since the cost of setting up a distillery was small, it soon had competition from small local plants. The company's answer was to purchase the new competitors and to cut prices. This strategy proved so expensive that the enterprise was unable to survive the depression of the 1890's.

Shortly before going into receivership in 1896, the Distillers Company had begun to think more about marketing. In 1895, it had planned to spend a million dollars to build up a distributing and selling organization in the urban East — the company's largest market. In 1898, through the purchase of the Standard Distilling & Distributing Company and the Spirits Distributing Company, it did acquire a marketing organization based in New York City. In 1903, the marketing and manufacturing units were combined into a single operating organization under the direction of the Distillers Securities Company. At the same time, the company's president announced plans to concentrate on the development of brand names and specialties, particularly through advertising and packaging.[9] By the early years of the twentieth century, then, the Distillers Company had

---

[8] The major sources of information on combination and consolidation in the distilling industry are Jeremiah W. Jenks, "The Development of the Whiskey Trust," *Political Science Quarterly,* Vol. IV (June, 1889), pp. 296-319; J. W. Jenks and W. E. Clark, *The Trust Problem* (rev. ed.; New York, 1917), pp. 141-149. The annual reports of the Distilling and Cattle Feeding Company and its various successors provide some useful additional data, as does the Industrial Commission, *Preliminary Report on Trusts and Industrial Combinations* (Washington, 1900), Vol. I, pp. 74-89, 167-259, 813-848, and Victor S. Clark, *History of Manufacturers in the United States* (New York, 1929), Vol. II, pp. 505-506. Changes in taxes on liquors also affected the company's policies in the early 1890's.

[9] *Annual Report of the President of the Distillers Securities Company* for 1903.

become a vertically integrated, departmentalized, centralized operating organization, competing in the modern manner, more through advertising and product differentiation than price.

The experience of the biscuit industry is even more explicit. The National Biscuit Company came into being in 1898 as a merger of three regional combinations: the New York Biscuit Company formed in 1890, the American Biscuit and Manufacturing Company, and the United States Biscuit Company founded a little later.[10] Its initial objective was to control price and production, but as in the case of the Distillers Company, this stategy proved too expensive. The Annual Report for 1901 suggests why National Biscuit shifted its basic policies:[11]

> This Company is four years old and it may be of interest to shortly review its history. . . . When the Company started, it was an aggregation of plants. It is now an organized business. When we look back over the four years, we find that a radical change has been wrought in our methods of business. In the past, the managers of large merchandising corporations have found it necessary, for success, to control or limit competition. So when this company started, it was thought that we must control competition, and that to do this we must either fight competition or buy it. The first meant a ruinous war of prices, and a great loss of profit; the second, a constantly increasing capitalization. Experience soon proved to us that, instead of bringing success, either of those courses, if persevered in, must bring disaster. This led us to reflect whether it was necessary to control competition. . . . we soon satisfied ourselves that within the Company itself we must look for success.
>
> We turned our attention and bent our energies to improving the internal management of our business, to getting full benefit from purchasing our raw materials in large quantities, to economizing the expenses of manufacture, to systematizing and rendering more effective our selling department; and above all things and before all things to improve the quality of our goods and the condition in which they should reach the customer.
>
> It became the settled policy of this Company to buy out no competition. . . .

In concentrating on distribution, the company first changed its policy from selling in bulk to wholesalers to marketing small packages to retailers. It developed the various "Uneeda Biscuit" brands, which immediately became popular. "The next point," the same Annual Report continued,

---

[10] The information on National Biscuit comes largely from its annual reports.

[11] *Annual Report of the National Biscuit Company for the Year Ending December, 1901,* January 3, 1902. References to centralizing of manufacturing facilities appear in several early annual reports. As this was written before Theodore Roosevelt had started to make the Sherman Act an effective antitrust instrument and Ida Tarbell and other journalists had begun to make "muck raking" of big business popular and profitable, the Biscuit Company's shift in policy could hardly have been the result of the pressure of public opinion or the threat of government action.

"was to reach the customer. Thinking we had something that the customer wanted, we had to advise the customer of its existence. We did this by extensive advertising." This new packaging and advertising not only quickly created a profitable business, but also required the building of a sizable marketing organization. Since flour could be quickly and easily purchased in quantity from large milling firms, the purchasing requirements were less complex, and so the company needed a smaller purchasing organization. On the other hand, it spent much energy after 1901 in improving plant layout and manufacturing processes in order to cut production costs and to improve and standardize quality. Throughout the first decade of its history, National Biscuit continued the policy of "centralizing" manufacturing operations, particularly in its great New York and Chicago plants.

In the rubber boot, shoe, and glove industries, the story is much the same. Expansion of manufacturing facilities and increasing competition as early as 1874, led to the formation, by several leading firms, of the Associated Rubber Shoe Companies — an organization for setting price and production schedules through its board of directors.[12] This company continued until 1886. Its successor, the Rubber Boot and Shoe Company, which lasted only a year, attempted, besides controlling prices and production, to handle marketing, which had always been done by commissioned agents. After five years of uncontrolled competition, four of the five firms that had organized the selling company again combined, this time with the assistance of a large rubber importer, Charles A. Flint. The resulting United States Rubber Company came, by 1898, to control 75 per cent of the nation's rubber boot, shoe, and glove output.

At first the new company remained a decentralized holding company. Each constituent company retained its corporate identity with much freedom of action, including the purchasing of raw materials and the selling of finished products, which was done, as before, through jobbers. The central office's concern was primarily with controlling price and production schedules. Very soon, however, the company began, in the words of the 1896 Annual Report, a policy of "perfecting consolidation of purchasing, selling, and manufacturing."[13] This was to be accomplished in four ways. First, as the 1895 Annual Report had pointed out, the managers

---

[12] The background for the creation of the United States Rubber Company can be found in Nancy P. Norton, "Industrial Pioneer: the Goodyear Metallic Rubber Shoe Company" (Ph.D. thesis, Radcliffe College, 1950), Constance McL. Green, *History of Naugatuck, Connecticut* (New Haven, 1948), pp. 126-131, 193-194, and Clark, *History of Manufactures,* Vol. II, pp. 479-481, Vol. III, pp. 235-237. The company's annual reports provide most of the information on its activities.

[13] *The Fifth Annual Report of the United States Rubber Company, March 31, 1897,* pp. 6-7.

agreed "so far as practicable, to consolidate the purchasing of all supplies of raw materials for the various manufactures into one single buying agency, believing that the purchase of large quantities of goods can be made at more advantageous figures than the buying of small isolated lots."[14] The second new "general policy" was "to undertake to reduce the number of brands of goods manufactured, and to consolidate the manufacturing of the remaining brands in those factories which have demonstrated superior facilities for production or advantageous labor conditions. This course was for the purpose of utilizing the most efficient instruments of production and closing those that were inefficient and unprofitable." The third policy was to consolidate sales through the formation of a "Selling Department," which was to handle all goods made by the constituent companies in order to achieve "economy in the distribution expense." Selling was now to be handled by a central office in the New York City headquarters, with branch offices throughout the United States and Europe. Of the three great new departments, actually manufacturing was the slowest to be fully consolidated and centralized. Finally, the treasurer's office at headquarters began to obtain accurate data on profit and loss through the institution of uniform, centralized cost accounting.

Thus United States Rubber, National Biscuit, and the Distillers Securities Company soon came to have organizational structures paralleling those of Swift and American Tobacco. By the first decade of the twentieth century, the leading firms in many consumers' goods industries had become departmentalized and centralized. This was the organizational concomitant to vertical integration. Each major function, manufacturing, sales purchasing, and finance, became managed by a single and separate department head, usually a vice president, who, assisted by a director or a manager, had full authority and responsibility for the activities of his unit. These departmental chiefs, with the president, coordinated and evaluated the work of the different functional units, and made policy for the company as a whole. In coordinating, appraising, and policy-making, the president and the vice presidents in charge of departments came to rely more and more on the accounting and statistical information, usually provided by the finance department, on costs, output, purchases, and sales.

CHANGES IN THE PRODUCERS' GOODS INDUSTRIES

Bureaucracy and oligopoly came to the producers' goods industries somewhat later than to those making products for the mass market. Un-

---

[14] This and the following quotations are from the *Fourth Annual Report of the United States Rubber Company, May 25, 1896,* pp. 4-5, 7-8.

til the depression of the 1890's, most of the combinations and consolidations had been in the consumers' goods industries. After that, the major changes came in those industries selling to other businesses and industrialists. The reason for the time difference seems to be that the city took a little longer to become a major market for producers' goods. Throughout the 1880's, railroad construction and operation continued to take the larger share of the output of steel, copper, power machinery, explosives, and other heavy industries. Then in the 1890's, as railroad construction declined, the rapidly growing American cities became the primary market. The insatiable demand for urban lighting, communication, heat, power, transportation, water, sewerage, and other services directly and indirectly took ever growing quantities of electric lighting apparatus, telephones, copper wire, newsprint, streetcars, coal and iron, steel, copper, and lead piping, structures and fixtures; while the constantly expanding urban construction created new calls on the power machinery and explosives as well as the metals industries. Carnegie's decision in 1887 to shift the Homestead Works, the nation's largest and most modern steel plant, from rails to structures, symbolized the coming change in the market.[15]

Also the new combinations and consolidations in the consumers' goods industries increased the demand for producers' products in the urban areas. Standard Oil, American Tobacco, Swift and other meat packers, McCormick's Harvesting Machinery and other farm implement firms, American Sugar, Singer Sewing Machine, and many other great consumer goods companies concentrated their production in or near major cities, particularly New York and Chicago.

The changes after 1897 differed from the earlier ones not only in types of industries in which they occurred but also in the way they were promoted and financed. Combinations and vertical integration in the consumer goods industries before 1897 had been almost all engineered and financed by the manufacturers themselves, so the stock control remained in the hands of the industrialists. After 1897, however, outside funds and often outside promoters, who were usually Wall Street financiers, played an increasingly significant role in industrial combination and consolidation. The change reflected a new attitude of investor and financier who controlled capital toward the value of industrial securities.[16] Before the

---

[15] Clark, *History of Manufactures,* Vol. II, chap. 19.

[16] The story of the shift from rails to industrials as acceptable investments is told in Thomas R. Navin and Marian V. Sears, "The Rise of the Market for Industrial Securities, 1887-1902," *Business History Review,* Vol. XIX (June, 1955), pp. 105-138. Government securities were, of course, important in the years before 1850 and during and after the Civil War, but in the late 1870's and 1880's, as in the 1850's, railroads dominated the American security exchanges. As Navin and Sears point out, some coal and mining firms were traded on the New York

depression of the 1890's investment and speculation had been overwhelmingly in railroad stocks and bonds. The institutionalizing of the American security market in Wall Street had come, in fact, as a response to the needs for financing the first great railroad boom in the 1850's.

The railroads, however, had made a poor showing financially in the middle years of the 1890's when one-third of the nation's trackage went through receivership and financial reorganization. The dividend records of some of the new large industrial corporations, on the other hand, proved unexpectedly satisfactory. Moreover, railroad construction was slowing, and the major financial and administrative reorganizations of the 1890's had pretty well stabilized the industry. So there was less demand for investment bankers and brokers to market new issues of railroad securities.

Industrials were obviously the coming field, and by 1898 there was a rush in Wall Street to get in on this new business. The sudden availability of funds stimulated, and undoubtedly overstimulated, industrial combination. Many of the mergers in the years after 1897 came more from the desire of financiers for promotional profits, and because combination had become the thing to do, and less from the special needs and opportunities in the several industries. Moreover, as the financiers and promoters began to provide funds for mergers and expansion, they began to acquire, for the first time, the same type of control over industrial corporations that they had enjoyed in railroads since the 1850's.

The changes in the producers' goods industries were essentially like those in the consumer goods firms before the depression. Only after 1897 the changes came more rapidly, partly because of Wall Street pressures; and the differences that did develop between the two types of industries reflected the basic differences in the nature of their businesses. Like the companies making consumer goods, those manufacturing items for producers set up nation-wide and often world-wide marketing and distributing organizations, consolidated production into a relatively few large plants and fashioned purchasing departments. Because they had fewer customers, their sales departments tended to be smaller than those in firms selling to the mass market. On the other hand, they were more concerned with obtaining control over the sources of their supply than were most of the consumer goods companies.

Here a distinction can be made between the manufacturers who made semi-finished products from raw materials taken from the ground, and those who made finished goods from semi-finished products. The former,

---

Exchange, but the only manufacturing securities, outside of those of the Pullman Company, were some textile stocks traded on the local Boston Exchange. The connections between the railroad expansion and the beginnings of modern Wall Street are described in detail in Chandler, *Poor,* chap. 4.

producing a uniform product for a few large industrial customers, developed only small sales departments and concentrated on obtaining control of raw materials, and often of the means of transporting such materials from mine to market. The latter, selling a larger variety of products and ones that often required servicing and financing, had much larger marketing and distributing organizations. These makers of finished goods, except for a brief period around 1900, rarely attempted to control their raw materials or their semi-finished steel and other metal supplies. They did, however, in the years after 1900, begin to buy or set up plants making parts and components that went into the construction of their finished products.

Except in steel, integration usually followed combination in the producers' goods industries. And for both makers of semi-finished and finished goods, integration became more of a defensive strategy than it was in the consumers' goods industries processing agricultural products. In the latter the manufacturers had an assured supply of raw materials from the output of the nation's millions of farms. In the former, on the other hand, they had to consider the threatening possibility of an outsider obtaining complete control of raw materials or supplies.

Integration and Combination in the Extractive Industries

By the early twentieth century nearly all the companies making semi-finished product goods controlled the mining of their own raw materials. The industries in which they operated can, therefore, be considered as extractive. This was also true of two consumers' goods industries: oil and fertilizer. The experience of these two provides a good introduction to the motives for integration and the role it played in the coming of "big business" in steel, copper, paper, explosives and other businesses producing semi-finished goods.

In both the oil and fertilizer industries, control over raw materials came well after combination and consolidation of groups of small manufacturing firms. The Standard Oil Trust, after its formation in 1882, consolidated its manufacturing activities and then created a domestic marketing organization. Only in the late 1880's, when the new Indiana field began to be developed and the older Pennsylvania ones began to decline, did the Trust consider going into the production of crude oil. Both Allan Nevins in his biography of John D. Rockefeller and the Hidys in their history of Standard Oil agree that the need to be assured of a steady supply of crude oil was the major reason for the move into production.[17] Other

---

[17] Ralph W. Hidy and Muriel E. Hidy, *Pioneering in Big Business, 1882-1911* (New York, 1955), pp. 176-188. Allan Nevins, *Study in Power, John D. Rockefeller, Industrialist and Philanthropist* (New York, 1953), Vol. II, pp. 1-3.

reasons, the Hidys indicate, were a fear that the producers might combine and so control supplies, and the desire of the pipeline subsidiaries to keep their facilities operating at full capacity. Although neither Nevins nor the Hidys suggest that the desire to obtain a more efficient flow of oil from the well to the distributor was a motive for this integration, both describe the committees and staff units that were formed at the central office at 26 Broadway to assure more effective coordination between production, refining, and marketing.

What little evidence there is suggests somewhat the same story in the fertilizer industry. Shortly after its organization in the mid 1890's, the Virginia-Carolina Chemical Company, a merger of many small southern fertilizer firms, began, apparently for the same defensive reasons, to purchase phosphate mines. Quickly its major competitor, the American Agricultural Chemical Company, a similar combination of small northeastern companies formed in 1893, responded by making its own purchases of mines. As the latter company explained in a later annual report: "The growth of the business, as well as the fact that available phosphate properties were being fast taken up, indicated that it was the part of wisdom to make additional provision for the future, and accordingly . . . available phosphate properties were purchased, and the necessary plants were erected and equipped, so the company now has in hand a supply of phosphate rock which will satisfy its growing demand for 60 years and upwards."[18] However, neither of these companies appeared to have set up organizational devices to guide the flow of materials from mine to plant to market; nor did the managers of a third large integrated fertilizer company, the International Agricultural Corporation, formed in 1909.

Defensive motives were certainly significant in the changes in the steel industry. Here the story can be most briefly described by focusing on the history of the industry's leader, the Carnegie Steel Company.[19] That company's chairman, Henry C. Frick, had in the early 1890's consolidated and rationalized the several Carnegie manufacturing properties in and

---

Nevins adds that another reason for the move into production was "partly to limit the number of active wells and reduce the overproduction of crude oil," Vol. II, p. 2, but he gives no documentation for this statement.

[18] *Annual Report of the American Agricultural Chemical Company, August 14, 1907;* also the same company's *Annual Report* dated August 25, 1902. In addition to the annual reports of the two companies, Clark, *History of Manufactures*, Vol. III, pp. 289-291, provides information. There is a brief summary of the story of the International Agricultural Corporation in William Haynes, *American Chemical Industry — A History* (New York, 1945), Vol. III, p. 173.

[19] The information on the Carnegie Steel Company is taken from Burton J. Hendrick, *The Life of Andrew Carnegie*, 2 vols. (New York, 1932), George Harvey, *Henry Clay Frick, the Man* (New York, 1928), James H. Bridge, *The Inside Story of the Carnegie Steel Company* (New York, 1903.)

about Pittsburgh into an integrated whole. At the same time, he systematized and departmentalized its purchasing, engineering, and marketing activities. The fashioning of a sales department became more necessary since the shift from rails to structures had enlarged the number of the company's customers.

Then in 1896 the Carnegie company made a massive purchase of ore lands when it joined with Henry W. Oliver to buy out the Rockefeller holdings in the Mesabi Range. As Allan Nevins points out, the depression of the 1890's had worked a rapid transformation in the recently discovered Mesabi region.[20] By 1896, the ore fields had become dominated by three great interests: the Oliver Mining Company, the Minnesota Mining Company, and Rockefeller's Consolidated Iron Mines. A fourth, James J. Hill's Great Northern Railroad, was just entering the field. Frick's purchases, therefore, gave the Carnegie company an assured supply of cheap ore, as well as providing it with a fleet of ore ships. Next, Frick and Carnegie bought and rebuilt a railroad from Lake Erie to Pittsburgh to carry the new supplies to the mills.

Yet the steel company's managers did little to coordinate systematically the mining, shipping, and manufacturing units in their industrial empire. These activities did not become departments controlled from one central office but remained completely separate companies under independent managements, whose contact with one another was through negotiated contracts. This was the same sort of relation that existed between the Frick Coke Company and Carnegie Steel from the time Frick had joined Carnegie in 1889. If the Carnegie company's strategy had been to provide a more effective flow of materials as well as to assure itself of not being caught without a supply of ore and the means to transport it, then Frick and Carnegie would have created some sort of central coordinating office.

The steel industry responded quickly to the Carnegie purchases.[21] In

---

[20] Nevins, *Rockefeller,* Vol. II, p. 252.

[21] The experience of the other steel firms comes primarily from their annual reports and from prospectuses and other reports in the Corporation Records Division of Baker Library. A company publication, *J & L — The Growth of an Amreican Business* (Pittsburgh, 1953) has some additional information on that company. Also, books listed in footnote 26 on the United States Steel Corporation have something on these companies. Two other steel companies listed in Table I made major changes somewhat before and after the period immediately following 1898. One, the Colorado Fuel & Iron Co., established in 1892, quickly became an integrated steel company in the Colorado area. The Bethlehem Steel Corporation was formed in 1904 when Charles F. Schwab, formerly of the Carnegie company and the United States Steel Corporation, reorganized the finances, corporate structure, and administrative organization of the bankrupt United States Shipbuilding Company.

1898, Chicago's Illinois Steel Company, with capital supplied by J. P. Morgan & Company, joined the Lorain Steel Company (with plants on Lake Erie and in Johnstown, Pennsylvania) to purchase the Minnesota Mining Company, a fleet of ore boats, and railroads in the Mesabi and Chicago areas. Again, little attempt was made to coordinate mining and shipping with manufacturing and marketing. In the same year, many iron and steel firms in Ohio and Pennsylvania merged to form the Republic and National Steel Companies. Shortly thereafter, a similar combination in the Sault Sainte Marie area became the Consolidated Lake Superior Company. These three new mergers began at once to set up their marketing organizations and to obtain control by lease and purchase of raw materials and transportation facilities. In 1900, several small firms making high-grade steel did much the same thing by the formation of the Crucible Steel Company of America. In these same years, the larger, established steel companies, like Lackawanna, Cambria, and Jones & Laughlin obtained control of more supplies of ore, coke, and limestone and simultaneously reorganized their manufacturing and marketing organizations. Like Carnegie and Federal, they at first made little effort to bring their mining and coke operations under the direct control of the central office.

In copper, defensive motives for integration appear to have been somewhat less significant. In the 1890's, mining, smelting and refining were combined on a large scale. During the 'eighties the railroad had opened up many western mining areas, particularly in Montana and Arizona; a little later the new electrical and telephone businesses greatly increased the demand for copper. Mining firms like Anaconda, Calumet & Hecla, and Phelps, Dodge moved into smelting and refining, while the Guggenheims' Philadelphia Smelting & Refining Company began to buy mining properties.[22] In the copper industry, the high cost of ore shipment meant that smelting and — after the introduction of the electrolytic process in the early 1890's — even refining could be done more cheaply close to the mines. Of the large copper firms, only Calumet & Hecla and the Guggenheims set up refineries in the East before 1898, and both made use of direct water transportation.

After 1898, several mergers occurred in the nonferrous metals industries. Nearly all were initially promoted by eastern financiers. Of these, the most important were Amalgamated Copper, engineered by H. H. Rogers of Standard Oil and Marcus Daly of Anaconda, the American Smelting and Refining Company which the Guggenheims came to control,

---

[22] Information on the mining companies came from their annual reports and from Isaac P. Marcosson's two books, *Magic Metal — the Story of the American Smelting and Refining Company* (New York, 1949), and *Anaconda* (New York, 1957), also Clark, *History of Manufactures,* Vol. II, pp. 368-369.

and United Copper promoted by F. Augustus Heinze. United Copper remained little more than a holding company. Amalgamated set up a subsidiary to operate a large refinery at Perth Amboy and another, the United Metals Selling Company, with headquarters in New York City, to market the products of its mining and processing subsidiaries. The holding company's central offices in New York remained small and apparently did comparatively little to coordinate the activities of its several operating companies. The Guggenheims formed a much tighter organization with direct headquarters control of the company's mining, shipping, smelting and marketing departments. On the whole, there appears to have been somewhat closer coordination between mining and processing in the large copper than in the major steel companies.

Lowering of costs through more effective coordination appears to have been a major motive for consolidation and combination in three other businesses whose raw materials came from the ground: explosives, paper, and coal.[23] The mergers that created the Pittsburgh Coal Company in 1899 and greatly enlarged the Consolidation Coal Company in 1903 were followed by a reorganization and consolidation of mining properties and then by the creation of large marketing departments which operated throughout most of the country. The merger of close to 30 paper companies, forming the International Paper Company in 1899, was followed first by consolidation and reorganization of the manufacturing plants, next by the formation of a national marketing organization with headquarters in New York City, and then by the purchase of large tracts of timber in Maine and Canada. These three activities were departmentalized under vice presidents and controlled from the New York office. In all these cases, the central office was responsible for the flow of materials from mine or forest to the customer or retailer.

The explosive industries underwent a comparable sweeping change in 1902 and 1903. Since the 1870's, price and production schedules had been decided by the industry's Gunpowder Trade Association, and almost from its beginning, that Association had been controlled by one

---

[23] The story of the leading explosives, paper, salt and coal companies comes from annual reports and also from Charles E. Beachley, *History of the Consolidation Coal Company 1864-1934* (New York, 1934), George H. Love, *An Exciting Century in Coal* (New York, 1955), the company-written, *The International Paper Company, 1898-1948* (n.p., 1948), William S. Dutton, *DuPont — One Hundred and Forty Years* (New York, 1940), and *U. S. v. E. I. DuPont de Nemours & Company et al.* in Circuit Court of the United States for the District of Delaware, #280 *in Equity* (1909), *Defendants' Record Testimony*, Vol. I, and for the paper industry, Clark, *History of Manufactures*, Vol. III, pp. 245-252. The American Writing Paper Company, though less successful, had many parallels to International Paper.

firm, the E. I. DuPont de Nemours & Company. However, the member concerns had retained their own corporate identities and managements. In 1902, the DuPonts bought out a large number of these independent companies through exchanges of stock, and then consolidated them into a single centralized organization. In the process, plants were shut down, others enlarged, and new ones built. A nation-wide selling organization was created, and centralized accounting, purchasing, engineering and traffic departments formed. Once the new organization was completed, then the company's executives obtained control of their raw materials through the purchase of nitrate mines and deposits in Chile.

Except possibly in paper, the control of price and production does not appear to have been a major motive for the initial combinations in the extractive industries making producers' goods. In steel before 1901, and in nonferrous metals and coal, there were several combinations, but none acquired as much as 20 per cent of the market. Nor is there any evidence that the creators of the different mergers, while they were forming their organizations, were arranging with one another to set over-all price and production schedules. In explosives, control of competition could not have been a significant reason for the 1902 changes since the DuPont company had enjoyed such control since the 1870's. In coal and explosives, and possibly in copper, the major motive for combination, consolidation, and the integration of supply with the manufacturing and marketing processes seems to have been an expectation of lowered costs through the creation of a national distributing organization, the consolidation of manufacturing activities, and the effective coordination of the different industrial processes by one central office. In steel and possibly copper, the desire for an assured supply of raw materials appears to have been more significant in encouraging combination and integration.

Changes and Integration in the Finished Producers' Goods Industries

Control of price and production was, on the other hand, much more of an obvious motive for combination and resulting consolidation in the industries manufacturing finished products or machinery from the semi-finished materials produced by the extractive firms. Concern over supply, however, was also a cause for change, for after 1898 the users of steel, copper, coal, and other semi-finished materials felt threatened by the growing number of combinations among their suppliers. In any case, between 1898 and 1900 there was a wave of mergers in these industries, largely Wall Street financed, which led to the formation of American Tin Plate, American Wire & Steel, American Steel Hoop, National Tube, American Bridge, American Sheet Metal, Shelby Steel Tube, American

Can, National Enameling & Stamping Company and a number of other combinations among steel-fabricating firms.[24] At the same time, there were many amalgamations in the power machinery and implement businesses, such as American Car & Foundry, American Locomotive, Allis-Chalmers, International Steam Pump, and International Harvester. The largest combination among the copper users, the American Brass Company, came a little later, in 1903, after the Guggenheims, Rogers, and Heinze had completed the major copper mergers.

Nearly all these combinations quickly consolidated their constituent companies into a single operating organization. Manufacturing facilities were unified and systematized, over-all accounting procedures instituted, and national and often world-wide distributing organizations formed. Many set up central traffic and purchasing departments; some even began to assure themselves control over supply by building up their own rolling mills and blast furnaces. As American Wire & Steel and National Tube began to make their own steel, they cancelled contracts with Carnegie and other semi-finished steel producers. This development, in turn, led Carnegie to develop plans for fabricating his own finished products.[25]

The resulting threat of overcapacity and price-cutting led to the formation of the United States Steel Corporation.[26] This giant merger, which included Carnegie, Federal and National Steel, and the first six of the fabricating companies listed above, continued on as a combination. Although the activities of the various subsidiaries were re-formed and redefined, there was no consolidation. United States Steel remained a holding company only, and the central office at 72 Broadway did comparatively little to coordinate the operations of its many subsidiary companies.

After 1901, the fabricators and the machinery manufacturers made little attempt to produce their own steel or copper. Nor did the makers of semi-finished products try, for some years to come, to do their own fabricating. Possibly the metal users realized that even with the formation of United States Steel they were fairly certain of alternative sources of supply. Also they may have found that once they had combined they had

---

[24] The best brief summary of these mergers and the formation of the United States Steel Corporation is in Eliot Jones, *The Trust Problem in the United States* (New York, 1924), pp. 189-200. The companies' annual reports and prospectuses provide additional material.

[25] Hendrick, *Carnegie,* Vol. II, pp. 116-119.

[26] The beginnings and the operation of the United States Steel Corporation are outlined in Abraham Berglund, *The United States Steel Corporation: A Study of Growth and Combination in the Iron and Steel Industry* (New York, 1907), Arundel Cotter, *The Authentic History of the United States Steel Corporation* (New York, 1916), Ida M. Tarbell, *The Life of Elbert H. Gary, the Story of Steel* (New York, 1925).

enough bargaining power to assure themselves of a supply of steel and other materials more cheaply than they could make it themselves.

While such firms no longer sought to control their basic materials, many, particularly the machinery makers like General Electric, Westinghouse, American Car & Foundry, International Harvester and, a little later, General Motors, began to purchase or set up subsidiaries or departments to make parts and components.[27] Here again the motive was essentially defensive. Since much of their manufacturing had now become mainly assembling, they wanted to be sure to have a supply of parts available at all times. The lack of a vital part could temporarily shut down a plant. However, they expected to take only a portion of the output; a major share was sold to outsiders. One outstanding exception to this pattern was Henry Ford. He came to control his raw materials as well as his parts and components, and rarely sold such parts to outside companies. But Ford's insistence on having a completely integrated organization from mine to market, concentrated largely in one huge plant, proved to be one of the most costly mistakes in American business history.

Control of parts and accessory units led to a diversification of the types of products these manufacturing companies made and sold. Such diversification brought, over time, important changes in business organization. Even more significant for stimulating product diversification was the new "full line" strategy adopted by a number of these recently consolidated concerns. Such a policy, initiated largely to help assure the maximum use of the new departments, encouraged technological as well as organizational change.

Pioneers in developing "full lines" in the producers' goods industries were the two great electrical companies: General Electric and Westinghouse. Unlike almost any other of the leading American industrial companies in 1900, these two had begun as research and development rather than manufacturing organizations. Because of their origins, they had the skilled personnel and the necessary equipment to move, in the mid-1890's, from making lighting equipment alone to manufacturing many lines of electric traction and power machinery products.[28] Allis-Chalmers, International Steam Pump, and American Locomotive began, shortly after their formation and subsequent consolidations, to develop new lines using electric and gasoline engines.[29] International Harvester, building up a

---

[27] This generalization is based on the annual reports of the several companies.

[28] As is well described in Harold C. Passer, *The Electrical Manufacturers* (Cambridge, 1953).

[29] The development of new lines by Allis-Chalmers, International Steam Pump, and American Locomotive is mentioned in their annual reports in the first decade

number of farm implement lines, also started to experiment with the use of the gasoline engine for machinery on the farm. In this same first decade of the twentieth century, rubber, explosive, and chemical companies began to turn to industrial chemistry in their search to develop broader lines of products.

Continuing diversification came, however, largely in industries where science, particularly chemistry and physics, could be most easily applied. And it was in these industries, and in those which were directly affected by the coming of two new sources of power, electricity and the internal combustion engine, that the major innovations in American industry came after 1900. The chemical, automotive, power machinery, rubber, and petroleum industries led the way to the development of new processes and products, new ways of internal organization and new techniques of external competition as the new century unfolded. The metals industries and those processing agricultural goods have, on the other hand, changed relatively little since the beginning of the century. In these industries, the same firms make much the same products, use much the same processes, and compete in much the same manner in the 1950's as they did in the 1900's. For them the greatest period of change came in the last decade of the nineteenth century.

CONCLUSION: THE BASIC INNOVATIONS

The middle of the first decade of the new century might be said to mark the end of an era. By 1903, the great merger movement was almost over, and by then the metals industries and those processing agricultural products had developed patterns of internal organization and external competition which were to remain. In those years, too, leading chemical, electrical, rubber, power machinery and implement companies had initiated their "full line" policy, and had instituted the earliest formal research and development departments created in this country. In this decade also, electricity was becoming for the first time a significant source of industrial power, and the automobile was just beginning to revolutionize American transportation. From 1903 on, the new generators of power and the new technologies appear to have become the dominant stimuli to innovation in American industry, and such innovations were primarily those which created new products and processes. Changes in organizational

---

of the twentieth century. International Harvester's similar "full line" policies are described in Cyrus McCormick, *The Century of the Reaper* (New York, 1931), chaps. 6-9, and United States Bureau of Corporations, *The International Harvester Co., March 3, 1913* (Washington, 1913), especially pp. 156-158.

methods and marketing techniques were largely responses to technological advances.

This seems much less true of the changes during the 20 to 25 years before 1903. In that period, the basic innovations were more in the creation of new forms of organization and new ways of marketing. The great modern corporation, carrying on the major industrial processes, namely, purchasing and often production of materials and parts, manufacturing, marketing, and finance — all within the same organizational structure — had its beginnings in that period. Such organizations hardly existed, outside of the railroads, before the 1880's. By 1900 they had become the basic business unit in American industry.

Each of these major processes became managed by a corporate department, and all were coordinated and supervised from a central office. Of the departments, marketing was the most significant. The creation of nation-wide distributing and selling organizations was the initial step in the growth of many large consumer goods companies. Mergers in both the consumer and producer goods industries were almost always followed by the formation of a centralized sales departent.

The consolidation of plants under a single manufacturing department usually accompanied or followed the formation of a national marketing organization. The creation of such a manufacturing department normally meant the concentration of production in fewer and larger plants, and such consolidation probably lowered unit costs and increased output per worker. The creation of such a department in turn led to the setting up of central traffic, purchasing, and often engineering organizations. Large-scale buying, more rational routing of raw materials and finished products, more systematic plant lay-out, and plant location in relation to materials and markets probably lowered costs still further. Certainly the creators of these organizations believed that it did. In the extractive and machinery industries integration went one step further. Here the motives for controlling raw materials or parts and components were defensive as well as designed to cut costs through providing a more efficient flow of materials from mine to market.

These great national industrial organizations required a large market to provide the volume necessary to support the increased overhead costs. Also, to be profitable, they needed careful coordination between the different functional departments. This coordination required a steady flow of accurate data on costs, sales, and on all purchasing, manufacturing, and marketing activities. As a result, the comptroller's office became an increasingly important department. In fact, one of the first moves after a combination by merger or purchase was to institute more effective and detailed accounting procedures. Also, the leading entrepreneurs of the period, men like Rockefeller, Carnegie, Swift, Duke, Preston, Clark, and the DuPonts, had to become, as had the railroad executives of an earlier generation, experts in reading and interpreting business statistics.

Consolidation and departmentalization meant that the leading industrial corporations became operating rather than holding companies, in the sense that the officers and managers of the companies were directly concerned with operating activities. In fact, of the 50 companies with the largest assets in 1909, only United States Steel, Amalgamated Copper, and one or two other copper companies remained purely holding companies. In most others, the central office included the heads of the major functional departments, usually the president, vice presidents, and sometimes a chairman of the board and one or two representatives of financial interests. These men made major policy and administrative decisions and evaluated the performance of the departments and the corporation as a whole. In the extractive industries a few companies, like Standard Oil (N.J.) and some of the metals companies, were partly holding and partly operating companies. At Standard Oil nearly all important decisions were made in the central headquarters, at 26 Broadway, which housed not only the presidents of the subsidiaries but the powerful policy formulating and coordinating committees.[30] But in some of the metals companies, the subsidiaries producing and transporting raw materials retained a large degree of autonomy.

The coming of the large vertically integrated, centralized, functionally departmentalized industrial organization altered the internal and external situations in which and about which business decisions were made. Information about markets, supplies, and operating performance as well as suggestions for action often had to come up through the several levels of the departmental hierarchies, while decisions and suggestions based on this data had to be transmitted down the same ladder for implementation. Executives on each level became increasingly specialists in one function — in sales, production, purchasing, or finance — and most remained in one department and so handled one function only for the major part of their business careers. Only he who climbed to the very top of the departmental ladder had a chance to see his own company as a single operating unit. Where a company's markets, sources of raw materials, and manufacturing processes remained relatively stable, as was true in the metals industries and in those processing agricultural goods, the nature of the business executive's work became increasingly routine and administrative.

When the internal situation had become bureaucratic, the external one tended to be oligopolistic. Vertical integration by one manufacturer forced others to follow. Thus, in a very short time, many American industries

---

[30] Hidys, *Pioneering in Big Business,* chap. 3 and pp. 323-388.

became dominated by a few large firms, with the smaller ones handling local and more specialized aspects of the business. Occasionally industries like oil, tobacco, and sugar, came to be controlled by one company, but in most cases legal action by the federal government in the years after 1900 turned monopolistic industries into oligopolistic ones.

Costs, rather than interfirm competition, began to determine prices. With better information on costs, supplies, and market conditions, the companies were able to determine price quite accurately on the basis of the desired return on investment. The managers of the different major companies had little to gain by cutting prices below an acceptable profit margin. On the other hand, if one firm set its prices excessively high, the other firms could increase their share of the market by selling at a lower price and still maintain a profit. They would, however, rarely cut to the point where this margin was eliminated. As a result, after 1900, price leadership, price umbrellas, and other evidences of oligopolistic competition became common in many American industries. To increase their share of the market and to improve their profit position, the large corporations therefore concerned themselves less with price and concentrated more on obtaining new customers by advertising, brand names, and product differentiations; on cutting costs through further improvement and integration of the manufacturing, marketing, and buying processes; and on developing more diversified lines of products.

The coming of the large vertically integrated corporation changed more than just the practices of American industrialists and their industries. The effect on the merchant, particularly the wholesaler, and on the financier, especially the investment banker, has been suggested here. The relation between the growth of these great industrial units and the rise of labor unions has often been pointed out. Certainly the regulation of the large corporation became one of the major political issues of these years, and the devices created to carry out such a regulation were significant innovations in American constitutional, legal, and political institutions. But an examination of such effects is beyond the scope of this paper.

Reasons for the Basic Innovations

One question remains to be reviewed. Why did the vertically integrated corporation come when it did, and in the way it did? The creation by nearly all the large firms of nation-wide selling and distributing organizations indicates the importance of the national market. It was necessary that the market be an increasingly urban one. The city took the largest share of the goods manufactured by the processors of agricultural products. The city, too, with its demands for construction materials, lighting, heating and many other facilities, provided the major market for the metals and other producers' goods industries after railroad construction slowed. Without the rapidly growing urban market there would have been little need and little opportunity for the coming of big business in American industry. And such a market could hardly have existed before the completion of a nation-wide railroad network.

What other reasons might there have been for the swift growth of the great industrial corporation? What about foreign markets? In some industries, particularly oil, the overseas trade may have been an important factor. However, in most businesses the domestic customers took the lion's share of the output, and in nearly all of them the move abroad appears to have come after the creation of the large corporation, and after such corporations had fashioned their domestic marketing organization.

What about the investor looking for profitable investments, and the promoter seeking new promotions? Financiers and promoters certainly had an impact on the changes after 1897, but again they seem primarily to have taken advantage of what had already proved successful. The industrialists themselves, rather than the financiers, initiated most of the major changes in business organization. Availability of capital and cooperation with the financier figured much less prominently in these industrial combinations and consolidations than had been the case with the earlier construction of the railroads and with the financing of the Civil War.

What about technological changes? Actually, except for electricity, the major innovations in the metals industries seem to have come before or after the years under study here. Most of the technological improvements in the agricultural processing industries appear to have been made to meet the demands of the new urban market. The great technological innovations that accompanied the development of electricity, the internal combustion engine, and industrial chemistry did have their beginning in these years, and were, indeed, to have a fundamental impact on the American business economy. Yet this impact was not to be really felt until after 1900.

What about entrepreneurial talent? Certainly the best-known entrepreneurs of this period were those who helped to create the large industrial corporation. If, as Joseph A. Schumpeter suggests, "The defining characteristic [of the entrepreneur and his funtion] is simply the doing of new things, and doing things that are already done, in a new way (innovation)," Rockefeller, Carnegie, Frick, Swift, Duke, McCormick, the DuPonts, the Guggenheims, Coffin of General Electric, Preston of United Fruit, and Clark of Singer Sewing Machine were all major innovators of their time.[31] And their innovations were not in technology, but rather in organization

---

[31] Joseph A. Schumpeter, "The Creative Response in Economic History," *Journal of Economic History,* Vol. VII (May, 1947), p. 151, and also his *Theory of Economic Development,* trans. Redvers Opie (Cambridge, 1934), pp. 74-94.

TABLE I

THE FIFTY LARGEST INDUSTRIALS
(Numbers indicate relative size according to 1909 assets)

Consumers' Goods Companies

Agricultural Processing	*Extractive*	*Manufacturing*
3. Am. Tobacco	2. Standard Oil	4. Int'l. Harvester
8. Armour & Co.	26. Va.-Carolina Chem.	10. U.S. Rubber
9. American Sugar	35. American Agri.	12. Singer Mfg. Co.
13. Swift & Co.	Chem.	
30. Nat'l. Biscuit		
32. Distillers' Securities		
50. United Fruit		

Producers' Goods Companies

Agricultural Processing	*Extractive*	*Manufacturing*
6. Central Leather	1. U.S. Steel	7. Pullman
18. Corn Products Co.	5. Amalgamated	15. Gen. Elec.
21. Am. Woolens	(Anaconda) Copper	16. Am. Car & Foundry
	11. Am. Smelting & Refining	19. Am. Can
	14. Pittsburgh Coal	22. Westinghouse
	17. Colo. Fuel & Iron	24. DuPont
	20. Lackawanna	29. Am. Locomotive
	23. Consolidation Coal	36. Allis-Chalmers
	25. Republic Steel	44. Int. Steam Pump
	27. Int'l. Paper	46. Western Electric
	28. Bethlehem Steel	
	31. Cambria Steel	
	33. Associated Oil	
	34. Calumet & Hecla	
	37. Crucible Steel	
	38. Lake Superior Corp.	
	39. U.S. Smelting & Ref.	
	40. United Copper	
	41. National Lead	
	42. Phelps Dodge	
	43. Lehigh Coal	
	45. Jones & Laughlin	
	48. Am. Writing Paper	
	49. Copper Range	

and in marketing. "Doing a new thing," is, to Schumpeter, a "creative response" to a new situation, and the situation to which these innovators responded appears to have been the rise of the national urban market.

There must be an emphasis here on the words "seem" and "appear." The framework used is a preliminary one and the data itself, based on readily available printed material rather than on business records are hardly as detailed or accurate as could be desired. More data, more precise and explicit questions, and other types and ranges of questions will modify the generalizations suggested here. For the moment, however, I would like to suggest, if only to encourage the raising of questions and the further compilation and analysis of data, that *the* major innovation in the American economy between the 1880's and the turn of the century was the creation of the great corporations in American industry. This innovation, as I have tried to show, was a response to the growth of a national and increasingly urban market that was created by the building of a national railroad network — the dynamic force in the economy in the quarter century before 1880. After 1900 the newly modified methods of interfirm and intrafirm administration remained relatively unchanged (as did the location of major markets and sources of raw materials) except in those industries directly affected by new sources of power and the systematic application of science to industry. In the twentieth century electricity, the internal combustion engine, and systematic, institutionalized research and development took the place of the national urban market as the dynamic factor in the American industrial economy.[32]

---

[32] This point has only been considered briefly here, but has been developed at some length in my "Development, Diversification and Decentralization," to be published in a book of essays tentatively titled *The Postwar American Economy* under the sponsorship of the Department of Economics, Massachusetts Institute of Technology.

[Ed. note: The book referred to is Ralph Freeman, ed.; *The Postwar American Economy;* Harper's, New York 1960.]

Competitive Structure of the American Petroleum Industry
A Reappraisal

HAROLD F. WILLIAMSON * AND RALPH L. ANDREANO

It is quite commonly assumed, even among certain scholars, that for some 30 years prior to 1911 Standard Oil's dominant position in the American Petroleum Industry was virtually unchallenged.[1] A close examination of the data covering the history of the industry during this period, however, strongly suggests that changes in the structure of the industry through the entry of new firms after 1911 were essentially a projection of a trend already well advanced at the time of the formal dissolution of the Standard Oil Company.[2]

Quite aside from any deterioration in Standard's market position attributable to general economic growth, the circumstances leading to new entrants into the industry may be grouped under three main headings:[3]

1. A growth in the number and location of new flush fields that, because of minimal barriers to entry posed by absolute capital requirements and economies of scale, enabled established firms to expand and new firms to obtain crude supplies necessary to begin operations.
2. The quality and quantity of crude oil discoveries, which played an important role in types of products produced and sold and, in turn, facilitated the process of entry via effects on market segmentation.
3. Incorrect, or insufficiently rapid, market response on the part of the dominant firm (Standard Oil) which left market opportunities, or market space, not only for the exploitation of crude deposits but also for the distribution of "old" and "new" products.

---

* Harold F. Williamson is Professor of Economics at Northwestern Univ.

[1] Joel Dirlam, for example, author of the chapter, "The Petroleum Industry," in *The Structure of American Industry,* Walter B. Adams, ed. (New York, 1954), pp. 236-237, says: "From 1883, when the Standard Oil Company acquired the last independent pipeline of importance, to 1911 when it was dissolved under the anti-trust laws, Standard bought, transported, refined, and marketed some 90% of U. S. petroleum."

[2] Source materials for this article were: Harold F. Williamson and Arnold R. Daum, *A History of the American Petroleum Industry 1859-1900: The Age of Illumination* (Evanston, Ill., 1959); Ralph and Muriel Hidy, *Pioneering in Big Business: History of Standard Oil Company (New Jersey),* vol. I (New York, 1955); Ralph L. Andreano, "The Emergence of New Competition in the American Petroleum Industry Before 1911" (unpublished doctoral thesis, Northwestern University, Evanston, Ill., 1960).

[3] Some indication of the magnitude and relative importance of crude production by major fields is given in Table I.

TABLE I

U. S. CRUDE OIL PRODUCTION, BY MAJOR FIELDS: 1874–1911
(In millions of 42-gallon barrels)

	Appalachian	Lima-Indiana	Gulf Coast	California	Mid-Continent	Illinois	All Other	Total
1874								
No. of barrels	10.9	....	....	....	....	....	....	10.9
Percentage of total production	100	....	....	....	....	....	....	100
1879								
No. of barrels	19.8	....	....	....	....	....	.1	19.9
Percentage of total production	100	....	....	....	....	....	a	100
1884								
No. of barrels	23.9	....	....	....	....	....	.3	24.2
Percentage of total production	99	....	....	....	....	....	1	100
1889								
No. of barrels	22.3	12.2	....	....	....	....	.7	35.2
Percentage of total production	63	35	....	....	....	....	2	100
1894								
No. of barrels	30.8	17.3	....	....	....	....	1.2	49.3
Percentage of total production	63	35	....	....	....	....	2	100
1899								
No. of barrels	33.0	20.2	....	2.6	....	....	1.3	57.1
Percentage of total production	58	35	....	5	....	....	2	100
1901								
No. of barrels	33.6	21.9	3.6	8.8	1.0	....	.6	69.5
Percentage of total production	48	32	5	13	1	....	1	100
1903								
No. of barrels	31.5	24.0	18.4	24.4	1.6	....	.6	100.5
Percentage of total production	31	24	18	24	2	....	1	100
1905								
No. of barrels	29.4	22.3	36.5	33.4	12.5	.2	.4	134.7
Percentage of total production	22	16	27	25	9	a	a	100
1907								
No. of barrels	25.3	10.0	15.8	44.9	46.9	24.3	....	167.2
Percentage of total production	15	6	9	27	28	15	....	100
1909								
No. of barrels	26.5	8.2	9.7	55.5	50.8	30.9	1.6	183.2
Percentage of total production	14	4	5	30	28	17	2	100
1911								
No. of barrels	23.7	6.2	11.0	81.1	66.6	31.3	.5	220.4
Percentage of total production	11	3	5	37	30	14	a	100

a Less than 1 per cent.
SOURCE: Basic data from Ralph Arnold and William Kemnitzer, *Petroleum in the U. S. and Possessions* (New York, 1931), p. 33.

TABLE II

SUMMARY OF STANDARD OIL'S POSITION
IN THE AMERICAN PETROLEUM INDUSTRY
1880–1911

PERCENTAGE CONTROL OVER CRUDE OIL SUPPLIES

Fields	1880	1899	1906	1911
Appalachian[a]	92	88	72	78
Lima-Indiana	..	85	95	90
Gulf Coast[b]	..	..	10	10
Mid-Continent[c]	..	..	45	44
Illinois[d]	..	..	100	83
California[e]	..	..	29	29

PERCENTAGE CONTROL OVER REFINERY CAPACITY

	1880	1899	1906	1911
Share of Rated Daily Crude Capacity	90-95	82	70	64

PERCENTAGE OF MAJOR PRODUCTS SOLD[f]

	1880	1899	1906 — 1911[g]	
Kerosene	90-95	85	75	
Lubes	..	40	55	
Waxes	..	50	67	
Fuel Oil[h]	..	85	31	
Gasoline	..	85	66	

[a] Share of pipeline runs. Does not include sales of crude by Standard to independents. If these are included, Standard's share of Appalachian crude should read: 1899, 80%; 1906, 40%; 1911, 50%. Approximately 2% of Standard's Lima-Indiana runs were sold to independents.

[b] Standard had no pipeline connection in the original Gulf fields; it was a relatively passive buyer of crude. In 1909 Standard had a trunk line connection from Mid-Continent through Louisiana; but this was to tap Mid-Continent crude rather than Gulf-Louisiana crude. Above figures are Standard Oil consumption of Gulf crude.

[c] Figures refer to Prairie Oil & Gas Company share of Mid-Continent crude available for shipment to consumption points.

[d] Ohio Oil Company pipeline runs as per cent of total field production.

[e] Standard did not formally enter California in an integrated way until 1900 when it acquired Pacific Coast Oil Company.

[f] These are all rough estimates.

[g] Figures available only for 1906 and 1910 from Standard; 1908 for other firms. Because of this, both the lube and wax estimates may be overstated. In general, however, for somewhere in the middle of the 1906-1911 period the above figures are a close approximation of relative market shares in the respective products.

[h] Includes residual fuel oil and unrefined crude sold as fuel.

Changes in Standard Oil's relative position in the industry between 1880 and 1911 are summarized in Table II. In respect to crude oil, for example, Standard maintained its predominant control over production in the Appalachian, Lima-Indiana, and Illinois fields between 1880 and 1911. But the proportion of crude from California, Mid-Continent, and Gulf Coast fields going to independents had by 1911 reduced Standard's share of total domestic production during this period from over 90 per cent to approximately 60–65 per cent. This decline in the company's relative share of domestic crude production was closely matched by a decrease in the proportion of total refining capacity under Standard's control from approximately 90–95 per cent in 1880 to 60–65 percent in 1911. The impact of these shifts on Standard's general marketing position was varied. By 1911, however, the independents were supplying nearly 70 per cent of the fuel oil; some 45 per cent of the lubricants; a third of the gasoline and waxes; and about one quarter of the kerosene distributed by the American Petroleum Industry.

These changes, coupled with the emergence of a dozen or more integrated concerns plus a large number of smaller companies specializing in one or more phases of the oil business, suggest a competitive structure in 1911 that was a far cry from the late 1870's, when Standard Oil and the American Petroleum Industry were practically synonymous.

The circumstances and processes by which new companies entered the industry during the period before 1911 may be illustrated by reference to developments associated with the emergence of the major new crude producing areas.

APPALACHIAN

Standard Oil's position in the American industry late in the 1870's was based essentially on ownership (or lease) of some 90 per cent of domestic refining capacity, plus virtually a monopoly control of facilities for gathering and transporting crude oil. But even Standard found it impossible between 1876 and 1882 to expand its gathering lines, storage, and transport facilities rapidly enough to accommodate an approximate trebling of output of crude — largely from Bradford, the first modern flush field, in the Appalachian oil regions.

The result was a sufficient supply of crude outside Standard's control to provide the basis for the emergence of two types of firms: (1) fully integrated companies producing a complete line of refinery products, such as the Tidewater Oil Company and a group that was subsequently merged to form the Pure Oil Company, and (2) companies (partially or fully integrated), including the Union Petroleum Company, Crew-Levick, and the Pennzoil Company, that specialized in the production of lubricating oils and wax.

The immediate impact of Bradford on Standard's position in the industry is reflected in the Trust's share of total refining capacity, which fell from about 90 per cent in the late 1870's to approximately 75 per cent by 1884. Some of this loss was subsequently regained and for the entire 1880-1899 period Standard's share of total refining capacity declined about 10 percentage points; its share of Appalachian crude production over the same period dropped from 92 to 88 per cent. The most important effect of Bradford (supplemented by the growth of production in Lima-Indiana), however, was in the reduction of Standard's share of the production of lubricants and waxes from 75 per cent or more in 1880 to approximately 40 per cent of lubricants and 50 per cent of waxes by 1899.

LIMA-INDIANA

Production that began to expand in the Lima-Indiana fields in the mid-1880's, and reached a peak in 1896, prompted Standard Oil to move quickly into the area with an extensive system of gathering lines, storage facilities, and crude trunk lines. Even so, Standard's control over output that, measured by pipeline runs, was approximately 93 per cent in 1894, declined to about 85 per cent by 1899.

Chiefly because of the quality of the crude (sold largely as fuel oil until the development by Standard of the Frasch process) and the costs of entry, Standard Oil was the only established company to move into the Lima-Indiana fields.

The Lima-Indiana fields did, however, provide an opportunity for new entrants, including the Sun Oil Company, the National Refining Company, and the Paragon Oil Company. Moreover, these companies were fully integrated, with their own production, pipelines, and refining and marketing facilities. While fuel oil was their major product, by adopting refining techniques similar to the Frasch process, all were producing a full product line by 1899.

While the independents' share of the market was relatively modest — probably no more than 15 per cent in respect to fuel oil and much less in other products — the experience gained in exploiting the industrial demand for petroleum fuel oil was an important factor in subsequent decisions to move into the Gulf area after the turn of the century.[4]

---

[4] Production of crude in Ohio and Indiana also had repercussions on the organization of the eastern segment of the industry that may be labeled the "Lima-effect."

GULF COAST

In contrast to Lima-Indiana, Standard Oil did not formally enter the Gulf Coast region, where crude production reached its peak about 1905. Three reasons have generally been cited in explaining this response on the part of Standard: (1) the legal climate in Texas — where an antitrust action had been instituted against the Waters-Pierce Company, Standard's major marketing affiliate in the state; (2) the refining quality of the Texas crude, which yielded relatively small amounts of kerosene, the product that Standard was primarily interested in refining; and (3) the feeling on the part of Standard officials that Mid-Continent and California offered better investment opportunities than Gulf, both in respect to the quantity and quality of crudes needed for their operations. Standard's role in the Gulf Coast development was thus limited to the purchase of an estimated 10 per cent of the output from the region.

With some 90 per cent of Gulf Coast crude output available for "outsiders," the impact on the structure of the industry — and on Standard's position — was quite significant. Of the already established firms in the Appalachian and Lima-Indiana regions, Sun Oil Company moved most rapidly to use Gulf crude as a springboard for a highly successful program of expansion that made the company one of the leading factors in the industry, particularly in the production and distribution of fuel oil and lubricants. Pure Oil was also able to acquire a modest interest in the Gulf fields.

The most significant structural changes stimulated by Gulf Coast developments, however, were attributable to *de novo* entrants into the industry. These were of two types. First, there were fully integrated companies such as Gulf Oil Company and the Texas Company that attempted to produce a full product line but were more successful for several years as distributors of fuel oil. Second, there were the fuel oil companies, about 20 in all, that did not operate refineries (because the crude oil could be sold as fuel after exposure to the sun had evaporated the light ends), but were integrated from production to marketing facilities.

As a result of these developments in the Gulf region, Standard Oil, for the first time since the mid-1880's, did not "establish" crude prices in the United States. Moreover, with the expansion of the established firms

---

In brief, the process may be described as follows: (1) crude from the Lima fields could only be refined to produce fuel oil and kerosene; (2) firms making lubricants and wax from Appalachian crude — which yielded more desirable (in terms of market acceptance) qualities of lubricants and wax, changed their product mix to maximize outputs of these products, rather than kerosene; (3) the effect was to increase the proportion of these products supplied by eastern firms relative to Standard Oil which was committed to processing Lima crude.

and the addition of the new entrants drawing their crude from the Gulf fields, oligopoly behavior — a characteristic commonly associated with the present-day petroleum industry — became distinctly recognizable. This was particularly true in respect to the fuel oil market, where less than a dozen firms accounted for the great bulk of sales. The increasing importance of independents in the expanding fuel market was further reflected by a decline in Standard's relative market share from about 85 per cent in 1899 to 31 per cent in 1906–1911.

MID-CONTINENT

Mid-Continent provided the basis for an even more significant expansion of established independents and the entry of new firms in the industry. Not only did the strike at Glenn Pool in 1905 establish the region as a major producing area in the United States, but the crude was an Appalachian type that yielded relatively large proportions of gasoline and kerosene as well as high quality lube stocks.

Standard Oil understandably was quick to acquire leases and to build gathering lines, storage facilities, and trunk pipelines in Mid-Continent. But other companies were also quick to move into Mid-Continent. Among the leaders were the firms already operating in the Gulf region, notably Gulf Oil and the Texas Company; National Petroleum and Sun Oil, that had started in Lima-Indiana; the Associated Oil Company, a California concern; the Union Petroleum Company; Crew-Levick; and Pure Oil and Tidewater, pioneer processors of Appalachian crudes. In addition, the Mid-Continent provided the basis for the emergence of almost a score of partially or fully integrated firms, listed in Table III.

With Standard's control over Mid-Continent crude production limited to about 45 per cent during 1905–1911, the effect of the growth of independents was to extend competition beyond the fuel oil market into the sale and distribution of kerosene, gasoline, and lubricants. The results of this expansion were most noticeable in the reduction between 1899 and 1906–1911 of Standard's share of kerosene distribution from about 85 per cent to 75 per cent, and of gasoline from about 85 per cent to approximately 66 per cent.

ILLINOIS

Standard's relative position in the industry would no doubt have deteriorated even more by 1906–1911 if the organization had not succeeded

TABLE III

Size Characteristics of Oklahoma-Kansas Independents, 1906-1911

Name of Firm	Crude Production	Daily Crude Oil Capacity of Refineries (in 42-gallon barrels)	Pipeline Mileage (miles)	No. of R.R. Tankers	No. of Distribution Stations
American Refining Co.[a b]	c	1500	c	c	c
Chanute Refining Co.[d]	Yes	1750	60	290	33
Cudahy Refining Co.[a d]	Yes	6000	128	335	610
Great Western Refining Co.[a]	Yes	2000	24	40	1
Indiahoma Refining Co.	Yes	1200	43	83	3
Kansas City Refining Co.[a]	No	1000	c	42	e
Kansas Oil Refining Co.	c	1800	60	52	c
Kansas Co-operative Refining Co.[a]	Yes	500	6	30	20
Kanotex Refining Co.[f]	Yes	1000	33	41	31
Milliken Refining Co.[a d]	c	4000	65	370	c
Muskogee Refining Co.[a b]	Yes	1440	18	49	8
National Refining Co.[a g]	Yes	3000	110	315	50[h]
Oklahoma Refining Co.[b]	c	600	7	40	50
Petroleum Producing Co.[a]	Yes	3500	170	182	c
Paola Refining Co.[i b]	Yes	(150)[i]	40	c	c
Sapulpa Refining Co.	No	3000	35	69	c
Uncle Sam Oil Co.	Yes	1400	c	88	7

a Also had separate lube oil plants.
b Merged into Cities Service Corp.
c Not available.
d Became part of Sinclair Oil Co.
e Used Mid-Continent crude by tank cars; sold all its refined output, including considerable fuel oil, to jobbers in Kansas City, Missouri, area.
f Now property of Anderson-Prichard Oil Co.
g Absorbed by Ashland Oil & Refining Co.
h Does not include operations in East.
i Taken over in 1907 by Standard Asphalt and Rubber Co. Standard continued to operate the petroleum refinery, and by end of 1911 had expanded daily crude capacity to about 2000 barrels. The asphalt plant had another 1000 barrels per day crude capacity. Standard was an extremely successful manufacturer of roofing and paving material, marketing its products under the brand name "Sarco." In 1917, J. Ogden Armour, who then owned Standard Asphalt, sold all his holdings to Cities Service.

Source: Andreano, "The Emergence of New Competition in the American Petroleum Industry Before 1911."

in controlling some 85 per cent of the Appalachian type crude produced in the Illinois fields, which reached their peak during 1907-1911. Yet the remaining 15 per cent of the Illinois output was sufficient to make it worthwhile for Tidewater to acquire production in the area and extend its trunk pipeline from Pennsylvania to southeastern Illinois, as well as to enable the Indiana Refining Company (later absorbed by The Texas Company) to emerge by 1911 as a fully integrated concern.

CALIFORNIA

In many respects the structure of the petroleum industry in California to 1911 followed a pattern of development that was radically different from the evolution of the industry east of the Rockies. It is true that by extending its marketing organization into California during the 1880's, Standard Oil remained the dominant distributor of kerosene on the West Coast until 1911. But the asphaltic based California crude, ill-suited for the production of kerosene or lube stocks, had little attraction for Standard, which did not acquire any producing properties, pipelines, or refineries in California until 1900. By that date, however, production in California (which by 1906 was as important quantitatively as output from Mid-Continent) was already split more or less equally among some seven integrated companies engaged primarily in the production and distribution of fuel oil.[5] Thus for a decade or more prior to 1911, the California industry had virtually all the characteristics of an oligopoly.[6]

CONCLUSION

If, as suggested by the foregoing material, the American Petroleum Industry was significantly influenced by the characteristics associated with new flush fields, it would seem that some revision is necessary in appraising the emergence of the modern structure of the industry. In other words, it appears that the basic forces generally recognized as stimulating the entry and expansion of vertically integrated firms during the 1920's were also operating in the 30-year period prior to 1911.

Similarly, it may be instructive to reinterpret the conservation and prorationing movement in terms of what historically was the most common route for new firms to enter the industry. There are, of course, other important barriers to entry besides access to crude oil, notably product differentiation, economies of scale in refining, and aggregate capital re-

---

[5] In addition to Standard of California, these included the Union Oil Company, Associated Oil Company, Kern Trading & Oil Company, General Petroleum Company, Independent Oil Producers' Agency, and the Santa Fe Railroad.

[6] Mention should be made of the participation by the major California oil companies along with a dozen or more smaller concerns in the production and distribution of asphalt.

quirements. Yet it can be argued that the effect of prorationing, introduced early in the 1930's, was a major factor in freezing the competitive structure of the petroleum industry; that the driving competitive forces formerly unleashed by flush field developments became a thing of the past.

If it is desirable to have more firms of more nearly equal size competing under reasonably similar structural conditions, a policy favoring free access to crude supplies via the flush field mechanism would appear to have considerable merit from the national standpoint. It may well be that the social-welfare gains through conservation and prorationing more than offset any advantages that might be realized through a policy that would allow flush field developments. The prorationing and conservation movement should, however, be re-examined in strictly economic, as well as social and political terms, and it is clear that flush fields played a more positive contributory role than hitherto assumed in the historical development of the industry's structure.

Alfred Marshall's *Industry and Trade:* A Neglected Classic in Economic History

Ralph L. Andreano *

The purpose of this note is to reactivate interest in Marshall's *Industry and Trade* as a classic work in economic history and economic development. It seems ludicrous at this late date to treat any of Marshall's writings as "neglected." So much of modern economic analysis is in the Marshallian tradition that it is difficult to separate Marshall's specific contributions from the general stream of economic thought. Nevertheless, Marshall's *Industry and Trade* is rarely read by economic historians. The writings of the classical economists, no less than those of Marshall and his immediate successors, are grist for the mill of economic history. Unfortunately, the classical and neoclassical writers have rarely been sprung from the box labelled "history of economic thought." The current vogue for formal systems of economic development has considerably broken down this particularism, but still, the enormous insights of Smith, Ricardo, Malthus, and most notably Marshall for the economic history of the western world, have yet to infiltrate into general usage in anywhere near the same degree that one discusses their correct or incorrect theorems of economic analysis.

Marshall as an Economic Historian

All who have been raised on Marshall's writings are well aware of the extensive historical materials included in the *Principles.*[1] In the first edition there were two historical chapters, relegated in later editions to an Appendix. Soon after the publication of the *Principles*, William Cunningham, the noted British economic historian, accused Marshall of trying to squeeze economic history into the fundamental "laws" of then contemporary economic analysis.[2] Marshall, breaking his usual silence, accepted Cunningham's challenge, and the reply provides the clearest statement of his

---

* The author is in the debt of Professor Eric Lampard of University of Wisconsin who not only read this note critically, but generously offered to me his own valuable insights on Marshall.

[1] Alfred Marshall; *Principles of Economics;* 8th edition; MacMillan and Co., Ltd.; London 1952. See Appendix A. All references to 8th edition.

[2] The controversy which developed from Cunningham's criticism is reminiscent of the Clapham-Robertson "empty-box" discussion of many years later.

principal suggestions for the scope and method of historical economic inquiry.[3]

The nub of Cunningham's attack on Marshall (his article was entitled "The Perversion of Economic History") was twofold: (1) he criticized Marshall's interpretation of certain historical data, and (2) objected strenuously to Marshall's use of economic analysis to illuminate the past. "From the point of view of economic theory neglect of patient study of actual fact seems excusable; from my point of view," Cunningham argued, "it is disastrous, because it prevents the economist from finding out the narrow limits within which his generalizations are even approximately true."[4]

"Dr. Cunningham," Marshall wrote, "is mistaken in supposing that my book proceeds on the 'underlying assumption . . . that the same motives have been at work in all ages,' " and that all one need do is discover fundamental economic laws for the historical past to become fully understood. As for the use of economic analysis by economic historians, Marshall uses an analogy with geologists and the study of subsurface structures: "Now my only suggestion was that the economic historian should in like manner explore contemporary customs on the spot; and that, aided in like manner by modern analysis, he should use his knowledge to guide him . . . for subterannean channels of change; we can examine and cross-examine the living, but not the dead."[5]

Keynes concluded that Marshall came out the better in the controversy, and this judgement seems even more persuasive some thirty years later. Marshall, as is well known from his own statements and those in the *Keynes Memoir*, had great respect for economic history as a fruitful area of investigation for even the theoretical economist, and decided at one time to "write a treatise on economic history, and for many years collected materials for it."[6]

Talcott Parsons, in several highly original articles written during the 1930's, finds in Marshall a much more specific conception of economic

---

[3] Cunningham's criticism and Marshall's reply are in *Economic Journal,* II (1892), pp. 491-519.

[4] *Ibid.,* 495.

[5] All quotations above from *Ibid.,* 507, 511.

[6] *Ibid.,* 507. Buried in a footnote of the *Keynes Memoir* is a letter to Keynes from J. H. Clapham which credits Marshall at the time of the controversy as understanding the "seventh to the nineteenth centuries better than Cunningham, and he had — naturally — a feeling for their quantitative treatment to which Cunningham never attained." J. M. Keynes; "Alfred Marshall, 1842-1924," in A. C. Pigou (ed.), *Memorials of Alfred Marshall;* MacMillan and Co.; London 1925; 46 n 2. Cited hereafter as *Keynes Memoir.* Clapham and Court, *A Concise Economic History of Britain* (Cambridge: 1955) and Clapham's other work make frequent references to the chapter in *Industry and Trade* dealing with Western Economic Development.

history. According to Parsons, he describes and analyzes the modern economic order for a purpose, and thus "economic history becomes for Marshall essentially the history of the development of free enterprise."[7]

> With all the set-backs the process [the development of free enterprise] is conceived as in principle continuous, and the things which really need explanation are not the specific forms of behavior and organization but the removal of barriers and the development of certain arrangements facilitating exchange, communications, etc., such as money and credit, which are generally themselves included in the developing rationality. This is on the whole the orthodox Anglo-Saxon view of economic history: the barriers must be removed, but once they are removed, modern capitalism — or free enterprise — becomes established of itself. It needs no specific propelling force — and if it consists merely in rational conduct, why should it?[8]

Whether or not one accepts the Parsonian stricture, it is clear that Marshall had a particular methodological approach to economic history: use the tools of modern economic analysis, quantify, and then examine the rationality of past economic behavior.[9] To be sure, Parsons' interpretation of Marshall offers invaluable insights for interpreting *Industry and Trade* as a study in comparative economic development and not as a series of isolated fragments with historical materials as an afterthought. Nevertheless, for whatever objective Marshall had in mind, the process by which economic history becomes important for his argument is the interesting thing. The methodology which he brought to historical materials in a sense predetermined the objectives he hoped to achieve; namely, to discover how the past is related to the economic and social institutions

---

[7] Talcott Parsons, "Wants and Activities in Marshall," *Quarterly Journal of Economics,* XLVI; November 1931; p. 123, p. 150. Also see, Bruce Glassburner, "Alfred Marshall on Economic History and Historical Development," *Quarterly Journal of Economics,* LXIX (Nov. 1955), pp. 577-595. This is an excellent and detailed examination of all of Marshall's historical writings.

[8] *Ibid.,* 129-130.

[9] One of Marshall's observations in the reply to Cunningham is worth repeating. In Marshall's view the mobility of labor in the Middle Ages was much greater than economic historians had suspected: custom and tradition were plastic not inflexible and market forces, however below the surface they might have been, were still operative. It is inappropriate to report on the extent to which Marshall's hunch was justified; rather, the point is that Marshall with the theorist's keen sense for an illogical proposition demonstrated what significant use could be made of the tools of economic analysis in studying the economic past. Several writers have suggested that there is evidence of vertical mobility of the labor force judging from the diminishing gap (particularly in England) in the wage levels of unskilled and skilled workers. A number of hypotheses have been advanced. See William Beveridge, "Wages in Winchester Manors," *Economic History Review,* November 1936; pp. 22-43; M. Postan, "Some Evidence of Declining Population in the Later Middle Ages," *Economic History Review* (1950), pp. 221-246; J. Schreiner, "Wages and Prices in England in the Later Middle Ages," *Scandinavian Economic History Review,* II (1954), pp. 61-73.

of the present, and whether or not one can discern guide lines for the future. His conception of economic history is not, as the criticism of Cunningham seemed to suggest, static; but is on the contrary quite dynamic, for it traces the adjustment path of individuals and institutions to a myriad set of economic, social, and political forces. He had a theory of social evolution far more complicated and sophisticated than that of Mill, Malthus, or Ricardo.

Industry and Trade as a Treatise in Economic History

Keynes tells us that Clapham, perhaps the leading economic historian at that time, thought highly of the historical materials in *Industry and Trade,* and Keynes himself called the work valuable as economic history.[10] Keynes and even Marshall thought of Book One as the "historical" part. From a present perspective, however, all three books and the 16 appendices should be considered as economic history. Keynes thought that the book lacked structural unity. The suggestion of the following paragraphs is just the contrary: *Industry and Trade* is indeed a unified study of the comparative economic history of Western European nations and the United States during the nineteenth century. It may be, as Parsons insists, a study of the development of "free trade and industry" but that is precisely why it is a book unified in scheme, outlook, and perception.

Marshall gave the book the motto "The many in the one and the one in the many" not without reason. It is, as it were, a study of all the external forces in history which led to the development of an industrialized society and the inner structure (institutions and individuals) of an economy. In the preface of the First Edition, Marshall stated his perspective for the entire work:

> Many tendencies have gone to the making of each industry, and each economic institution; therefore a thorough realistic study of any part of the economic field, calls for some reference to the interaction of many diverse tendencies, and gives occasion for some care in analysis. And, conversely, almost every important tendency is so far modified by the conditions under which it operates, that an exhaustive study of it may need to range over many fields of work.[11]

Marshall came closer to achieving his goal than is generally regarded, and again, the interpretation of Marshall by Parsons is suggestive of the structural unity of *Industry and Trade*. Social evolution for Marshall "consists in the progressive approximation to action according to the prin-

---

[10] *Keynes Memoir,* 46 n 2, 62.

[11] Alfred Marshall, *Industry and Trade;* Fourth Edition; MacMillan and Co.; London 1923; V. All succeeding references are to the Fourth Edition.

ciple of substitution, i.e., to economically rational action." [12] The burden of all Marshall's writings, Parsons argues, is to study the influence of economic conditions on human character — for Marshall the development of character is the main issue of human life.[13] Marshall placed great emphasis on the "human condition" in economic history, and had a clear awareness of man's social as well as economic dimensions.

In Book One — Some Origins of Present Problems of Industry and Trade — Marshall attempts what few economic historians have dared to do: a comparative analysis of the growth of industrialization in the United Kingdom, France, Germany, and the United States.[14] In each case, his approach is to first determine what forces accounted for the particular form of economic development which emerged in each country. Second, Marshall identifies distinguishing features of the character of economic change in each country and the prospects of future growth. In each case he seeks to pick out determinants of growth (social and economic in Parsons' view) which might be successfully reformulated for the United Kingdom. Book Three — Monopolistic Tendencies: Their Relation to Public Well-Being — is closely related to Book One, for it provides the mechanism, as Marshall saw it, of the processes of economic change. Indeed, one way to view Book Three is as a study of the inter-relationship of industrial structure, scale economies, and the comparative rate of economic growth in the major industrialized countries of the western world. Book Two — Dominant Tendencies of Business Organizations — might well be considered as Marshall's attempt to link economic history with the then actual behavior of the large-scale corporation. It is more a study of Industrial Organization, but in the overall perspective of *Industry and Trade* it is the pivotal point — "the one in the many" of Marshall's motto — which links the process of economic change with the operations of the business institutions that are the engines of that change. The sixteen appendices — that range from a discussion of the Zollverein to American industrial statistics — are in the nature of separate monographs that support in greater depth the stream of economic change described in the text.

---

[12] Parsons, *op. cit.,* 129-130.

[13] *Ibid.,* 107, 110.

[14] The only work close to that found in *Industry and Trade* is the remarkable book by Lillian C. A. Knowles, *Economic Development in the Nineteenth Century: France, Germany, Russia and the United States,* George Routledge & Sons, Ltd.; London 1932. There are no specific references to *Industry and Trade* in the Knowles study, yet the similarity of the two books is quite impressive. Schumpeter recognized Marshall's contributions to economic history in *Ten Great Economists,* p. 94, 101. Also see G. F. Shove, "The Place of Marshall's *Principles*" in Spengler and Allen, *Essays in Economic Thought,* esp. 207-22.

Industry and Trade and Economic Development

In a recent article in the *Scottish Journal of Political Economy*, Professor A. J. Youngson attempted to construct a theory of economic growth from Marshall's writings, mainly *Industry and Trade*. "Marshall never produced a theory of economic growth," Youngson writes, "and there is no such thing as a 'Marshallian system.' " [15] Youngson isolates, however, what he believed to be Marshall's "fundamental determinants," and "major and minor" influences that condition economic growth. The unstated conclusion of Youngson's article, nevertheless, is that Marshall indeed had very much to say about the process of economic development and the necessary and sufficient economic conditions for rapid industrialization. What Youngson meant is that one could not find in any single source a comprehensive and rigorous statement by Marshall of a "theory" of economic growth. Neo-classical growth theories, best represented by the work of W. Arthur Lewis, are related generically to Marshallian economic analysis.[16] Neo-classical growth theorists have been criticized as sterile and void of concern for the non-economic dimensions of development, but one finds no such narrow conception of the process in Marshall. To be sure, Marshall's orientation is "Western," and for some critics this severely restricts the usefulness of Marshall's observations for contemporary problems of economic underdevelopment.[17] As already indicated, Parsons treated all of Marshall's work in the framework of a theory of social evolution with strong economic underpinnings.[18] At the end of Book Three of *Industry and Trade* is a section titled "Possibilities of the Future." One can not only see the guidelines of strict neo-classical growth theory, but also the specific human and social characteristics Marshall felt were essential to economic growth and development.[19]

In these pages Marshall discusses seven conditions that are pre-

[15] "Marshall on Economic Growth," in *Scottish Journal of Political Economy* (February 1956), 1-18.

[16] See, W. Arthur Lewis, "Economic Development With Unlimited Supplies of Labor," *Manchester School of Economic and Social Studies*, XXIII, May 1955, 153-160.

[17] See the discussion of Boeke's writings on the inapplicability of "Western" economic theory to economic development in Benjamin Higgins, *Economic Development: Problems, Principles, and Policies*, W. W. Norton & Co., Inc.; New York 1959; pp. 274-293, esp. 288-290.

[18] See Talcott Parsons, "Economics and Sociology: Marshall in Relation to the Thought of His Time," *Quarterly Journal of Economics*, XLVI (February 1932), 316-347. Marshall wrote soon after the publication of *Money, Credit and Commerce* (1923) that he hoped to now complete a volume on "Progress: Its Economic Condition." See *Keynes Memoir*, 65. Perhaps this reference has thrown historians of economic thought off base in their assessment of Marshall's contribution to the theory of development.

[19] *Industry and Trade*, 663-665.

requisites of economic development in the past and economic growth in the future.

1. An increasing supply of "mechanical inventions."

2. Increasing investment in human capital; education, particularly the education for businessmen and "trades."[20]

3. Social class mobility — Marshall, much impressed by the character of United States economic development in the last quarter of the nineteenth century, placed great stress on this condition. There were two dimensions to it: the free movement of factors necessary for a smooth production process, and class mobility which would encourage segmented, but flexible, specialized markets.[21]

4. Economic institutions — Marshall stressed the necessity for "risk taking" to be a way of life, and that tax laws, for example, should allow sufficient incentives for capital accumulation.

5. The supply of labor and entrepreneurs should not be "artificially restricted."

6. The burden of investment should be in the private sector.

7. The role of government and the size of the public sector should be kept to a minimum but could be used with discretion for leverage effects: encouraging and promoting fundamental scientific research, making grants or subsidies to "key" or "pivotal" industries (not by protective tariffs, however), etc.

Marshall stressed other conditions such as climate, natural resource endowments, human character, and human freedom. In the more illuminating passages of *Industry and Trade,* he also examined income distribution, the population's propensity to save, financial institutions, and external economies, specifically as they affect and condition the possibilities for economic growth. But the strictly "economic" aspects of growth receive equal weight with social conditions.

It is inappropriate here to dwell further on Marshall's comments on economic growth. What is suggested, however, is that *Industry and Trade* is not only a work in comparative economic history, but also contains a broad-gauged theoretical framework for appraising the process of industri-

---

[20] Marshall earlier stressed that the only way for the United Kingdom to maintain productivity in the industrial race with Germany and the United States in the last quarter of the nineteenth century was by reforming its educational system. Marshall felt in particular that labor productivity could be increased through education and on this he placed great confidence for the economic future of United Kingdom. *Industry and Trade*, 663-665, 97, 75 n 1.

[21] The importance of class mobility in Marshall's scheme can be inferred from Parsons' insistence on the linearity of "activities" and "wants" in the development process: "Each new step upwards is to be regarded as the development of new activities giving rise to new wants." Parsons, *op. cit.*, 113; *Principles*, 89.

alization. To this extent, Marshall's *Industry and Trade* is as much a study of the theory and practice of economic development as Smith's *Wealth of Nations* and Marx's *Das Kapital*. The intellectual achievement represented by *Industry and Trade* is all the more remarkable than hitherto believed, for we know that most of the material was originally written during the last twenty-five years of the nineteenth century, a period in which the outlines of the economic development of the western world were just beginning to be solidified. In its view of the process of economic development, *Industry and Trade* was prophetic. The simple causistic models of growth built around technological change, population growth, and capital formation, have been known to be inadequate when placed in the realistic framework of underdeveloped economies of the present. Rigorous growth theories leave little room for public policy. Marshall's overall conception of the fundamentals of economic change for growing or less developed economies is closer to the point of view now adopted by practicing development theorists in the non-Marxian world: growth is a process dependent not only on purely economic factors, but also on institutions and individual reaction, and on the accidents of nature.[22]

Observations on American Economic Development in the Nineteenth Century

Marshall's observations on the characteristics of early and later nineteenth century American economic history are still refreshing some 40 years after the publication of *Industry and Trade* and possibly some 60 years since he first formulated his ideas on this subject. The range of his observations is quite broad and it would be impossible to examine all aspects within the limits of a note. Only three particular sets of Marshall's observations will be noted: (1) an explanation of American industrialization, (2) commentaries on the "trust" movement, and (3) tariff policies and economic development.

Explanation of American Economic Growth

The intention here is not to insist that Marshall had a closely formed theory of "what made America great." Rather, the point is that Marshall saw in American experience, a combination of unique characteristics that

---

[22] A. O. Hirschmann's, *The Strategy of Economic Development;* Yale University Press; New Haven, Connecticut, 1958 is a most sober and balanced account of processes of economic development. It contains in more rigorous format the range of speculation about economic change one reads in *Industry and Trade*. And as a guide for public policy it is much closer to the mark than the more popular and heuristically pleasing growth models of Harrod, Domar, and others.

both explained and predicted the course of United States economic development.[23] He called the mainspring of American industrial development "Multi-form Standardization," a corollary of his concept of "massive production." [24] He was persuaded that despite differences in native background, Americans had a homogeneous demand for manufactured goods; commodities that were stylized, yet could be standardized. There was both an apparently high propensity to consume, and a very strong consumption demonstration-effect working on new immigrants. Homogeneity of demand plus the external economies of the city enabled Americans to take full advantage of the economies of massive production and, most important, economies of mass distribution.[25] Secondly, the interaction of consumer demand with the supply of labor and entrepreneurs produced a unique combination of the faculties and aptitudes needed for inventing the machinery suitable for standardized production. To go with the special endowments of the labor force (i.e., little skill, willingness to work hard at menial tasks, and for low wages relative to the economy), entrepreneurs provided the "right" kind of technological change. Finally, social class mobility, the proper investment in humans, and the timing of economic change relative to the United Kingdom, all propelled the American economy during the nineteenth century into a position of industrial leadership at the beginning of the twentieth century. In Marshall's view, there was little indication that the American position would deteriorate in the near future; rather he predicted that if all the parameters remained the same, American economic growth would in the twentieth century be more impressive than in the nineteenth century.

Marshall's explanation is today not entirely original, yet few writers since his time have taken quite as comprehensive a view of American economic development. Marshall's explanation does suggest that a combination of stimuli, both economic and non-economic, can be fitted together

---

[23] The following paragraphs are drawn from *Industry and Trade*, 146-159, 303-305, although the point of view expressed above recurs constantly throughout the entire book.

[24] Massive production for Marshall was not synonomous with heavy or factory industry. Basically, he meant by the concept production far more than a local market on a scale requiring co-ordinated distribution. See *Industry and Trade*, 59-63.

[25] Marshall's contribution to the economics of urbanization was summarized by Eric Lampard in his excellent paper, "The History of Cities in the Economically Advanced Areas," *Economic Development and Cultural Change*, III (January 1955), 96-98. Lampard wrote; "Marshall did not, of course, formulate a theory of urban-industrial growth. The gleanings of his wisdom gathered here are scattered through two major books [*Principles*, and *Industry and Trade*] and three decades or more of careful observation and reflection. Yet his remains the boldest, most imaginative, account of urban influences to appear in the literature." (p. 98)

to explain and appraise American industrialization.[26] To a certain extent parts of the explanation have been investigated in great detail by scholars, but the synthesis has yet to come. Marshall attempted it nearly a half-century ago and whether or not we approve of his construction, it is surely economic history on a grand scale.

Commentaries on the Trust Movement

Marshall had an appreciation and understanding of the underlying drives to horizontal industrial concentration and vertical integration that were characteristic of the United States in the last quarter of the nineteenth century, which surpassed most, if not all, writers of his time. Historians specializing in the period 1870-1914 will find a reading of Chapters VII and VIII of Book Three most rewarding. For purposes of this note, however, only two of Marshall's observations are mentioned. First, he offers a challenging generalization concerning the importance of scale economies in the Trust Movement:

> The large majority of industrial trusts are of course to be found in those manufacturing industries, in which an increased scale of production brings with it increased economies. But in fact they do not owe very much of their power to that advantage: for, with some exception for the steel industries, a capital very much less than that required to dominate the market, will suffice to obtain every important advantage that belongs to production on a large scale. Nearly all the chief trusts . . . owe more to the economies of marketing on a vast scale than to those of production on a vast scale.[27]

A second observation is one which most American historians of the Trust Movement consider to be quite valid:

> One rule alone is almost universal. It is that each great industrial trust has owed its origin to the exceptional business genius of its founder. In some cases the genius was mainly constructive: in others it was largely strategic and incidentally destructive; sometimes even dishonest.[28]

Both of Marshall's observations appear to be quite instructive, and one must remember that they were virtually recorded at the time the event described was taking form. Recent researchers of the American petroleum

---

[26] Professor Harold F. Williamson in a recent paper has forged these Marshallian ingredients into a very interesting explanation of the United States economy during the nineteenth and early twentieth century. See H. F. Williamson, "Mass Production, Mass Consumption, and American Industrial Development," in M. M. Poston (ed.), *First International Conference of Economic History,* Mouton and Co., 1960, pp. 137-148.

[27] *Industry and Trade,* 515.

[28] *Ibid.*

industry, for example, support Marshall's contention of the minimal importance of plant scale economies and the greater importance of distribution economies as a concentration-inducing force.[28a] Some new information on these points as they related to the merger movement has been provided by a recent National Bureau of Economic Research Study.[29] Nevertheless, there still is need of testing the Marshallian observation on scale economies for the trusts on a comparative, industry-wide basis.

Marshall's second observation — the "great man" theory of the Trust Movement — is a fitting hypothesis for business historians to examine critically.[30] One obvious view to juxtapose next to the "great man" theory is that external forces — the forces of demand, the nature of technology, etc. — exerted as much influence on the character of industrial organization, i.e. the Trusts, as did individual entrepreneurs. Much business historiography in recent years, has greatly circumscribed the "great man" approach. The work of the Hidys on Standard Oil and Allan Nevins on John D. Rockefeller has helped to add more varied dimensions to the drives of the industrial leaders in the Trust Movement. Yet the issue is hardly settled. Reference to an important textbook in American economic history reveals that the work of the revisionist business historians has yet to infiltrate these pages.[31] In Marshall's broader conception of economic change, human character occupied a central role, and perhaps his original judgment concerning the men behind the American Trust Movement is very much closer to the truth. In any case the Marshallian generalization is testable and offers a direct challenge to business and economic historians.

[28a] Ralph and Muriel Hidy, *Pioneering in Big Business, 1882-1911, History of Standard Oil Company (New Jersey)*; Harper and Bros.; New York 1955; Harold F. Williamson and Arnold Daum, *The American Petroleum Industry: The Age of Illumination, 1859-1900*: (Northwestern University Press; Evanston, Illinois 1959); R. L. Andreano "The Emergence of New Competition in the American Petroleum Industry Before 1911," (unpublished Doctoral Dissertation, Department of Economics, Northwestern University, Evanston, Illinois, 1960). Marshall further explored the problem of scale in relation to concentration in Appendix II, *Industry and Trade*, pp. 785-792.

[29] Ralph Nelson, *Merger Movements in American Industry, 1895-1956*; Princeton University Press; Princeton, New Jersey; esp. pp. 71-104.

[30] We have seen earlier that in the Parsonian version of Marshall the "character" of the business leader formed a key element in the development process: America had businessmen, by this interpretation, of "superior character," i.e. they developed faster.

[31] See Lance Davis, J. R. T. Hughes, D. M. McDougall, *American Economic History* (Homewood; 1961), p. 371: "How was it possible to gain almost complete control of an entire growth industry in such an incredibly short period of time? The principal reason was undoubtedly the business acumen of Rockefeller and his group of advisers. The organizational ability of these men plus the technical ability of Andrews made them an unbeatable group."

American Tariff Policies and Economic Development

Marshall devoted an entire appendix of *Industry and Trade* to a discussion of American tariff policy and its effect on industrialization.[32] He visited the United States in 1875 and at that time made extensive inquiries concerning "protection." Marshall made a number of quite interesting observations but only two will be offered in this note (again a careful reading of Appendix G would reward the reader with a number of "researchable" ideas).

Three things impressed Marshall concerning American tariff policy: (1) the importance of tariff levels to industrial development up to about 1833, (2) the diminishing importance of "Protection" as a spur to economic development after that date, and (3) the inability to measure precisely the effects of tariffs on industrialization when their "educative" value had diminished. Only one suggestive paragraph and one of Marshall's buried footnotes can be reported here.

> Looking away from details to broad considerations, we can see that Protective tariffs increased the manufacturing population relatively to the agricultural; and thus developed centres of complex and various social life and high culture, and provided an ever-widening choice of occupations for people of varying temperaments and capacities; but at the same time they hindered the development of the agricultural resources of the country. This involved some retardation of the growth of commercial centres; which are nearly, though not quite, as important from the social point of view as the industrial centres.[33]

On measuring the economic effects of tariffs in America, Marshall wrote:

> It may be noted that Carey's *Social Science* and Grosvenor's *Does Protection Protect?*, basing themselves on almost identical statements of fact, applied them the one to prove that nothing but good had ever resulted from a high tariff and nothing but evil from a low tariff, and the other to prove the exact opposites. I endeavored on my return from America in 1875 to form an independent opinion by tracing in a book (each page of which contained a hundred horizontal lines, one for each year of the nineteenth century) curves showing all the available and relevant statistics for the United States and other countries; grouping each class on a separate page, and writing across the page brief statements of relevant events which were not in statistical form. That plan led me to the conclusion that each party to the controversy unconsciously stretched or compressed, so as to suit his case, the length of time which he supposed to elapse between a particular tariff charge and its chief results. But in this matter, as well as in the neglect of important causes relevant to the issues under discussion, the laxity seemed greater on the Protectionist than on the Free-trade side.[34]

---

[32] Appendix G, 773-784.
[33] *Industry and Trade*, 779.
[34] *Ibid.*, 784 n 1.

Economic historians assessing American tariff policy in the last quarter of the nineteenth century would do well to undertake a quantitative analysis of the type suggested by Marshall.[35]

Concluding Remarks

This note does not pretend to exhaust the historical insights of Alfred Marshall. Its purpose is to direct the interest of economic historians to the writings of a scholar and thinker who is customarily neglected by economic historians. As Keynes wrote some thirty years ago about *Industry and Trades:*

> The book is a mine rather than a railway — like the *Principles,* a thing to quarry in and search for buried treasure. . . . It contains the suggestions, the starting points for many investigations. . . . For the ignorant the broad generalizations of the book are too quiet, smooth, urban, undogmatic, to catch him.[36]

Industry and Trade is a classic work in comparative economic history and this author, for one, urgently hopes this much neglected work will attract an enterprising publisher to reissue it so that it may receive the wide distribution and readership it demands.

---

[35] Davis, Hughes, and McDougall, *op. cit.,* 321-327 reflect precisely the type of analysis Marshall attempted in respect to American tariff policy. Unfortunately, however, this particular textbook is an exception in this regard. Moreover. their analysis of tariff policy is largely theoretical.

[36] *Keynes Memoir,* 63.

PART FIVE

The Long View of American Economic Development

Contents

EDITOR'S INTRODUCTION

In the late 1950's and early 1960's there was great concern among government officials and economists about the present rate of growth of the American economy and prospects for the coming years. The Joint Economic Committee, charged with overseeing the efforts of the Executive to meet the objectives of maximum employment outlined in the Full Employment Act of 1946, commissioned a number of studies on this problem. The three papers reprinted here were part of this broader inquiry made by the Joint Economic Committee. The papers by Goldsmith and Lebergott require little editorial introduction. They assess in aggregate detail the long term growth record of the economy in output and personal economic welfare, and the performance of one of the most important of the economy's resources and indicators of the growth and its relative performance over the course of a century and one-half of American history. Given the purposes for which these papers were commissioned, it is appropriate to raise a larger question concerning the usefulness of economic history for contemporary problems of economic policy.

If there are any lessons from economic history for contemporary policy, one is hard pressed to state these in a concrete fashion. It is certain, however, that the basic conditions of American economic progress does have importance for our future growth. As Abramovitz has shown in his paper before the Joint Economic Committee, economic history can at least isolate the elements from which the determinants of secular growth can be separated. By this essentially statistical procedure, one can point to the American record as having taken place through a close interaction of build-up in our capacity to produce both by and in the intensity of use of this capacity. What this portends for contemporary economic policy is clear: it must be directed toward measures which enlarge our production resources and their productivity and intensity of use.

When these three papers were presented to the Joint Economic Committee there was concern at the highest professional levels for the ability of the economy to generate a sustained full employment and maximum productive capacity growth rate. Through the decade of the 1950's, the United States growth rate of national product per capita was at an average annual rate of 1.6%; this was about half the combined average rate for the major non-Communist industrialized nations of the West and Japan. What is more, the unemployment rate appeared to be creeping upward on a secular basis, giving rise to an argument over whether or not unemployment had now become a structural problem rather than one solely due to the low growth rate of national income and product. On this issue, the perspective of a century or more of experience in American economic history enables Lebergott to assuage the fears of policy makers concerning the probable upward drift of the secular level of unemployment. Though one cannot say the effort fully succeeded, centainly the insights provided by economic history on this important issue of public policy may well have been a factor in the decision to attack the current (1964) high level of unemployment by the more traditional method of stepping up the economy's aggregate demand for goods and services. Similarly, Professor Goldsmith's emphasis on the relative constancy of the trend rate of growth in real national product per person also provided a perspective for public policy which was desperately needed. Whether or not these can be called "lessons" of economic history, I leave for others more skilled to say; but there is little doubt that without the perspective of our past record of growth and its fundamental components, the task of today's public policy makers in economic matters would be appreciably more difficult.

The matter of long swings in American economic growth is an issue related to the relevance of economic history for public policy of today. The full testimony of Abramovitz is reprinted here because the matter of long swings in our growth is so important that it was felt that a better understanding of this phenomenon could be achieved by following the laymen type queries of members of the Joint Economic Committee.

The phenomena of long swing was first discovered by Simon Kuznets, and they are therefore sometimes called Kuznets Cycles.[1] The Kuznets Cycle, or long swing, describes a condition in the behavior of economic magnitudes which is distinguished from both the trend occurring during ordinary business cycles and the primary secular trend. The former are characterized by month to month or year to year changes in total output — first predominantly upward and then succeded by periods of downward movements. The primary secular trend can be found in the behavior of the major economic magnitudes for periods longer than a normal business cycle movement. One can see in data between business cycles that the average level of output tends to be higher in the latter than in the former period. This persistence of output growth is an underlying characteristic of industrialized nations.

The Kuznets Cycle is something different from either a business cycle

---

[1] The best exposition of the history and meaning of Kuznets Cycles is to be found in Moses Abramovitz; "The Nature and Significance of Kuznets Cycles"; *Economic Development and Cultural Change,* IX; April 1961; pp. 225-248.

or a primary secular trend. It is possible statistically to remove the influence of these two occurrences from basic economic data for an economy, and still find a wave-like movement in total output and its components of a 15-25 years' duration. What this procedure has shown for the growth record of the American economy is that our development during the 19th and 20th Century occurred in an upward surge in the series of output, capital, and labor resources, followed by periods during which the growth for the same series was retarded. In all, these wave-like movements in output and economic resources were of 15-20 years' duration. Abramovitz's article reprinted here collects the most comprehensive information available for the American economy on the Kuznets Cycle and its relationship to other pulses of economic life in the 19th and 20th Centuries.

What does this all mean? Abramovitz has written that the **Kuznets** Cycles have a two-sided character:

"They involve first, an ebb and flow in the pace of economic growth in the basic sense that the development of our capacity to produce, of our supplies of labor and capital and, perhaps, of their productivity at optimum rates of utilization, has alternately proceeded faster and slower in waves that, in the past, have been longer than ordinary business cycles. Secondly, they involve swings in the intensity of resource use in which periods of relatively high unemployment, or low intensity of use, alternate with periods in which the labor market is tighter and capital is used more intensively. The two sides of the phenomenon interact and each stands in relation to the other both as cause and effect."[2]

Certain questions may be raised concerning this new characteristic of economic development. Do Kuznets Cycles contribute to a theoretical underpinning for economic growth and development? Do they have relevance for current issues in economic policy? Do they have relevance in the American case beyond the necessarily restrictive limits of economic history? An answer to the first question is probably too extended to be discussed here; but it is certain that the occurrence of the Kuznets Cycles in virtually every economic magnitude to which the technique has been applied, suggests that conventional theories of economic growth must now be expanded to include not only the interactions between capital, output, and income, but also "repercussions via growth of population and labor force, the composition of capital formation, the terms of finance, the balance of international payments, and the supply of, and demand for, money." [3] Similarly, one needs also to integrate into such a theory of growth explanations of the very occurrence and duration of the long-swings. Are they self-generating and systematic, or are they caused by episodic and exogenous

[2] *Ibid.,* p. 241.
[3] *Ibid.,* p. 247.

forces independent of the interaction of the main variables of economic development? The evidence to date, for America at least, suggests that the former is correct, but the questions still are not resolved conclusively.

The relevance of the long swings to current issues of economic policy comes out very effectively in Abramovitz's paper. But the relationship of the Kuznets Cycle to the sweep of general American history — social, cultural, political and economic — is a serious matter deserving of further examination by students and scholars. Shown in Table V-1 are the peak and trough years for long swings in American Gross National Product in the past two centuries. Surges in American and political life were no less common a feature of our national development than were the wave-like Kuznets Cycles in our economic history. It may be impossible to quantify non-economic variables such as social customs, political philosophy, and the like, but if one views the peak and trough years shown in Table V-1 as reference points for turning phases in our national life, perhaps it may be the beginning of a useful synthesis of economic and general history. The temptation to list national events of lasting significance which correspond

TABLE V-1

LONG SWING PEAKS AND TROUGHS IN AMERICAN ECONOMIC ACTIVITY ON GROSS NATIONAL PRODUCT

Peaks	Troughs
1814	1819
1834	1840
1846	1858
1864.25	1874.25
1881	1886.5
1889.75	1892.25
1899	1911
1914.5	1920.25
1923	1930.25
1938.5	———

SOURCE: Abramovitz, *Economic Development and Cultural Change*, IX (April 1961), p. 231.

quite closely to the dating of Kuznets Cycles is strong, but must be resisted. On the other hand, it may be simplifying our national history far too much to suggest that social, political, and economic development take place in such a rhythmic fashion. Nonetheless, the proposition still persists: what is the degree of correspondence between facets of our national economic development as exemplified by the Kuznets Cycles and the main drift of American history in politics, national character, and social customs and values?

Long Period Growth in Income and Product, 1839-1960

RAYMOND W. GOLDSMITH *

I. CONCLUSIONS

The growth of this country's national product per head — the best simple measure of economic growth that we have — has averaged about 1¾ percent a year over the last 120 years after adjustment for price changes, and has shown remarkable steadiness if periods of at least 40 years' duration are considered. This trend under which real income per head doubles every 40 years and increases almost sixfold every century, is far above the growth rate experienced by the United States in its earlier history; has hardly if ever been equaled for as long a stretch of time in any other country or period; and has been the vehicle which has propelled the United States to its present eminence in the world as the country with the largest aggregate output, the most advanced technology and the highest standard of living; and as the main source of foreign capital for less developed areas.

The fact that the secular trend in real output and income per head of the population has been fairly steady at 1¾ percent per year since the middle of the 19th century must not be used as the basis for either of two conclusions, one refering to the past and the other to the future. It must not be interpreted as denying the possibility or asserting the easy achievement of a higher rate of growth during the past century if our economy had been able to operate at a higher average rate of utilization of its labor, capital, and natural resources. Nor must it be regarded as forecasting the future rate of growth, even if peace prevails and even if the average rates of utilization of resources follow their customary trends. An economist may be permitted to point out, however, that if the future trend of real output and income per head is to average considerably above its level of the last 120 years, either technological progress in the narrow sense must become much more rapid than it has been in the past; or far-reaching changes — whose nature and chance of success cannot as yet be specified with confidence — must take place in the economic and financial organization of the United States.

---

* Raymond W. Goldsmith is Professor of Economics at Yale University.

The rest of this statement will be limited to explaining, qualifying, and occasionally interpreting some of these assertions.

II. THE MEANING OF NATIONAL PRODUCT AND TREND

Let me begin by explaining what is meant by gross national product, how the current estimates are reduced to a constant price basis, why per head instead of aggregate figures are used, and what economically significant facts are measured by real gross national product per head.

Gross national product can be defined very simply and quite accurately, as the heap of finished goods and services produced each year. To use more learned language, gross national product is the total final unduplicated output of an economy. Unduplicated in this connection means that, for instance, the sale of bread by the grocery store to the housewife is counted as part of the value of gross national product, while the sale of the bread by the bakery to the grocery store, the sale of flour by the mill to the bakery, the sale of wheat by the farmer to the elevator, are all excluded from gross national product.

Since we are primarily interested in changes in the quantities of goods and services produced rather than in the fluctuations of their current monetary values, particularly when we are studying long-term growth, we must deflate the current values with the help of appropriate price indexes. The result of the division of the current values of output by these price indexes is the value that a given year's production of goods and services would have had at the prices prevailing during the base period — in our case during the year 1929.

The estimation of gross national product does not allow for the fact that some of the stock of capital, in the sense of durable reproducible assets, is used up during the year and is, so to speak, transformed into a part of final output. If capital consumption allowances are deducted from gross national product we obtain net national product, the amount of goods and services produced during a given period that could be used up while keeping capital intact.

Chart VII illustrates these and other main relations among the chief national accounting aggregates and their principal components. I shall not specifically discuss these relationships, but have added this chart to facilitate orientation in the sometimes a little complicated national accounting terminology.

An economy may grow in two ways which must be carefully distinguished. It may grow, first, by adding to the number of producers and consumers while average output or consumption per unit remains unchanged. This we may call extensive, or, more graphically, amebic growth. An economy may, secondly, increase output and consumption per head with or without concurrent expansion of the number of producing and consuming units. This may be called intensive growth. Most observed increases in total national product or income are the result of both extensive and intensive growth. The two components may be separated by dividing aggregate output or income by the appropriate number of units.

From some points of view interest may center on aggregate growth, for instance when a comparison of the actual or potential economic strength of different countries is wanted as a part of the evaluation of the political or military situation. In studying the trend in either productive efficiency or economic welfare we are, however, primarily interested in intensive growth. Since tomorrow's session will be devoted to the subject of productivity I shall not discuss what denominator ought to be applied to total output to measure productive efficiency. If we want to measure the trend in the standard or level of living as an indicator of economic welfare, consideration should be given only to that part of output that reaches consumers, and allowances should be made for the fact that consumption requirements vary among consumers of different age and sex. Hence, in measuring the trend in the level of living we should use consumer expenditures reduced to a constant price basis as the numerator and the number of equivalent full consumers as the denominator. This is what we shall actually do a little later. For the broader picture of the trend in intensive growth of the American economy, we shall however use total real gross national product divided by the number of inhabitants. This, it should be noted, is not an ideal concept theoretically as it measures neither productivity — in the sense of output per unit of input — nor economic welfare. Real national product per head is, however, the broadest simple measure of intensive economic growth that we have and is therefore used as the basis of our discussion.

By "trend"— also called secular trend or basic movement — economists understand a movement in one direction of reasonable regularity, i.e., without very wide or irregular deviations, continuing for a period at least as extensive as the longest authenticated wave-like movement in the series, and preferably several times as long as it. As you will hear at a later session, economic statisticians now feel that a wave-like movement of about 20 years' duration has been fairly well established in many basic American economic series for a period back to the early 19th century. Hence, the minimum period for which a trend in national product or income should be calculated is about two decades. Periods covering an integral multiple of these so-called long swings, i.e., periods of 40, 60, 80, or more years are, however, much to be preferred as a basis of trend analysis.

It is not as yet possible in studying the long-term trend of national product and income in the United States to go back to the founding of the

Republic, let alone to the beginning of white settlement. We are, however, in a position to study the long-term trend for a period of approximately 120 years. I want to stress immediately, so as not to have to repeat it, that the available data are considerably more reliable beginning with the late 1870's on than for the preceding 40 years for most of which estimates can be derived only at 5-year intervals. This presentation, therefore, will have to be limited to the period from 1839 to 1959. Fortunately this period as well as the two 60-year and the three 40-year subperiods into which it can be divided have considerable internal unity as distinctive phases in our economic history. This justifies studying the trends in national product and income during the subperiods as well as the trend observable over the entire 120-year period.

By starting our series in 1839 we are able to reach back virtually to the time when industrialization started in earnest and thus to cover the entire period of what may be regarded as the modern economic history of the United States. It is well to remember that in 1839 the area of continuous settlement ended at approximately the 95th meridian; railroads were but 10 years old; steamships were far outnumbered by clipper ships; petroleum, gas, and electricity were as yet unheard of; and the thought of moving men, goods, or messages through the air was regarded as chimerical.

If we divide the entire period for which we have statistics into two 60-year subperiods, the first of these, running from 1839 to 1899, encompasses the interval between the time "the Nation took shape" and the "watershed of the nineties," to use the characterization of two eminent historians. The second subperiod extending from 1899 to the present may have less unity, but it represents economically speaking all that we have witnessed of contemporary America.

Fortunately, a division into three 40-year subperiods also seems to make historical sense. The first of them, from 1839 to 1879, can be regarded as the formative period of modern America, politically and economically. The second subperiod, stretching from 1879 to 1919, witnessed the creation of the country's industrial and financial system as we still know it, notwithstanding all the extensive and intensive changes that have since taken place. The last subperiod, extending from 1919 to the present, circumscribes fairly accurately the period of economic preeminence of the United States, a position characterized by a share in total world production of not less than one-fourth; the highest standard of technology and of consumer welfare anywhere in the world; and the role as the chief supplier of capital and technical assistance to less developed countries.

III. THE TREND OF NATIONAL PRODUCT AND INCOME

We are now ready to look at the figures. We shall deal first with gross national product and then with consumption, and shall progress from aggregates in current prices to aggregates in constant (1929) prices, to per head values in constant prices, so that you may see the extent to which observed growth in total national product or consumption is due to (1) changes in the price level, primarily a monetary phenomenon; (2) increases in population, reflecting extensive growth; and (3) increases in average real output or consumption, the basic measure of intensive growth.

The estimates of gross national product and personal consumption shown in the chart are a combination of two or three sets of data. For the last 50 years use is made of the estimates of the National Income Division of the Department of Commerce. The figures for 1879 to 1908 (for consumption for 1879 to 1929) are taken from an unpublished study by Professor Kuznets,[1] but they are very similar to estimates contained in some of his earlier work.[2] For estimates of gross national product during the four decades before 1879, I have used estimates of the value of the commodity product, i.e., the output of agriculture, manufacturing, mining, and construction, which have been prepared recently by Professor Gallman for every fifth year between 1839 and 1899.[3] Since commodity product, which excludes transportation and services, increases less rapidly than gross national product, these estimates have been adjusted for the difference as reflected in the percentage of the labor force engaged in commodity production.[4]

To bring out differences in the rate of growth and in changes in it, all charts depicting time series are plotted on a ratio (logarithmic) scale under which a steady rate of growth is reflected by a straight line sloping upwards, and the rapidity of growth is proportional to the steepness (slope) of the line.

---

[1] "Capital Formation and Its Financing" (unpublished, National Bureau of Economic Research, mimeograph, 1958). [Published as *Capital in the American Economy,* NBER, Princeton Univ. Press, 1961.]

[2] See, e.g., "Long-Term Changes in the National Income of the United States of America Since 1870" in "Income and Wealth," series II (1952), ch. I.

[3] "Commodity Output in the United States, 1839-99" [published in National Bureau of Economic Research, "Studies in Income and Wealth," vol. 24, *Trends in the Am. Econ. During the 19th Century,* NBER, Princeton U. Press, 1960.]

[4] Professor Kuznets' estimates are available back to 1869, and Professor Gallman's series could have been linked in 1869 (or 1874) rather than in 1879. The decision to effect the link in 1879 was influenced by the unusually sharp upward movement shown in Professor Kuznets' estimates between 1869 and 1879. Use has not been made here of the older estimates by Martin ("National Income in the United States, 1799-1938") that are available for decennial census years back to 1799 since the criticism by Professor Kuznets ("Income and Wealth," op. cit., p. 306) casts very grave doubt on the reliability of Martin's series for the first half of the 19th century. If Martin's estimates had been used the growth of gross national product between 1839 and 1879 would have been considerably smaller than shown in the charts, viz, 1.2 percent against 1.6 percent for real national product per head.

Chart I shows the course of aggregate gross national product over the last 120 years, cyclical variations, long swings and extraneous disturbances all being reflected in the unadjusted annual data plotted from 1869 on. The light line follows the current value of gross national product while the heavy line represents the result of an attempt to reduce these current values to the measuring rod of the price level of 1929. Since the trend of prices has been upward during much of the past century, the light line rises more rapidly than the heavy line — deflated aggregate gross national product.

Chart II permits us to segregate intensive from extensive growth. The lower (thin) line is aggregate deflated gross national product, the heavy line of Chart I. The heavy (upper) line shows real gross national product per head, our key measure of intensive growth.

Chart III presents comparable information for consumer expenditures, the upper (light) line again showing aggregate real consumption while the lower (heavy) line represents real consumption per full consumer (i.e., in terms of adult males), the closest simple approach to a welfare measure of national product that we have.

In Chart IV we reach the heart of our subject, the long-term trend in intensive economic growth as reflected in real (deflated) gross national product per head. To minimize the effects of cyclical fluctuations, the light line shows 5-year moving averages of real gross national product per head for the period from 1869 on when annual estimates are available. The heavy straight line is the trend of 1⅝ percent a year determined by mathematical fitting for the period 1879 to 1929, and extended forward to 1959 and backward to 1839.

Because the two main disturbers of the secular trend — the great depression and the Civil War — lie just beyond and slightly before the core period of 1879 to 1929, it has seemed preferable to calculate the trend for the entire 120-year period from the core period rather than to determine the secular trend by means of an algebraic fit to all annual values between 1839 and 1959 (apart from the difficulty that before 1869 figures are available only at 5-year intervals). This is justified only if the extensions from the trend, forward and backward for three or four decades, produce values close to the actual observations for 1959 and 1839. The trend based on the core period meets this test. The extrapolated value for 1959 is only 2 percent away from the observed value; similarly, the difference between the extrapolated and the observed values for 1839 is only 1 percent. This close coincidence should permit regarding a growth rate of 1⅝ percent a year as the trend not only for the core period 1879–1929, but also for the more extended period from 1839 to 1959. The probably more familiar rate of growth of aggregate real gross national product averages a little over 3½ percent a year for the entire period, but shows a declining trend reflecting the slowing down of population growth, and thus comes to 3 percent for the final 40-year period of 1919–59.

A second test of the appropriateness of a 1⅝ percent trend as an expression of the growth in real national product per head throughout the entire 120-year period, is to observe the closeness of the annual values, or their 5-year moving averages, to the trend. This comparison is helped by plotting a trend line 10 percent above and another 10 percent below the trend line as is done in Chart IV. It will then be seen that only in three instances do the observed values fall outside the band of 10 percent above or below the trend. The first of these is the period of the Civil War and its aftermath; the second, the great depression; and the third, the years of World War II. The third of these exceptions is subject to doubt. If a deflation had been applied to the current national product estimates for these years that eliminated the effect of the relatively high cost of armaments more completely, real gross national product per head for the war years might fall within the 10-percent band, or exceed it only to a negligible extent. The existence of these two or three exceptions, of course, is hardly astonishing as they occur exactly at those periods in our economic history where they would be expected.

The conclusion thus seems justified that an average growth rate of real national product per head of 1⅝ percent is a satisfactory description of the basic movement of national product and income throughout the last 120 years.

The story is a very similar one for real consumption per full consumer. The trend here is about 1½ percent per year for the period 1879 to 1959, only slightly below the trend for real gross national product per head. The small difference between these two measures of intensive growth reflects the near-constancy of the ratio of consumption to gross national product and the slight upward trend in the ratio of full consumers to total population, which in turn is due to slow aging of the population.

Chart V based on the figures of Table I illustrates how increases in population, changes in the prices level, and increases in output per head have combined to produce the observed rates of growth of aggregate gross national product in current prices during the last 120 years and during the two and three sub-periods of 60 and 40 years' duration respectively. These rates have been calculated on the basis of the values at the beginning and the end of the period, not as in Chart IV by determining mathematically the average rate of growth that fits all annual figures within the period as closely as possible. The differences between the rates of growth determined in the elementary and the more sophisticated way, however, are usually quite small.

TABLE 1. — *Trend of gross national product and personal consumption,*
1839–1959

[Percent increase per year[1]]

	Entire period 1839-1959	60-year subperiods		40-year subperiods		
		1839-1899	1899-1959	1839-1879	1879-1919	1919-1959
	(1)	(2)	(3)	(4)	(5)	(6)
A. Gross national product:						
1. Aggregate, current prices	4.85	4.13	5.59	4.48	5.69	4.40
2. Price level	1.15	—0.10	2.42	0.16	1.91	1.40
3. Aggregate, constant prices	3.66	4.23	3.09	4.31	3.72	2.97
4. Population	1.97	2.50	1.45	2.71	1.91	1.30
5. Per head, constant prices	1.64	1.67	1.62	1.55	1.76	1.64
B. Personal consumption:						
6. Aggregate, current prices	......	......	5.48	......	5.27	4.49
7. Prices	......	......	2.18	......	1.53	1.28
8. Aggregate, constant prices	......	......	3.22	......	3.68	3.17
9. Consumers (equivalent adult males)	......	......	1.46	......	2.01	1.30
10. Per full consumer, constant prices	......	......	1.74	......	1.64	1.85

Let us start with the simplest series, current aggregate gross national
product. Its average rate of growth over the entire period is 4.8 percent.
In other words, over the last 120 years on the average, this year's gross
national product in current prices has been almost 5 percent above last
year's. I do not need to expand on the buoying effects of such a tendency
on many economically relevant factors, not the least businessmen's expectations of a noticeable increase in volume of sales as the normal course
of events.

The differences in the rate of growth of aggregate current gross national
product between subperiods are not negligible, but they are not radical
either. Even if we take subperiods of 40 years' length — probably the
shortest period for which one ought to calculate trends — the average
rate of growth of aggregate current gross national product varies only

---

[1] Calculated from values in first and last year of period.

between 4.4 and 5.7 percent per year. More interesting, there does not appear to be a trend toward acceleration in the rates of growth of the monetary value of aggregate national product. If 40-year periods are used, the rate of growth is highest in the period from 1879 to 1919, not in that from 1919 to 1959 or that from 1839 to 1879.

Population is the only one of the three factors to show a definite change in trend over the full period, declining from an annual average rate of growth of 2.7 percent in 1839–79 to one of only 1.3 percent in 1919–59. This trend, as you know, appears to have been reversed or at least halted recently, the average rate of growth of the population for the postwar decade reaching 1¾ percent, not far below the level which prevailed early in this century.

The largest variations in the average rate of change are shown by the price level, more specifically by the gross national product deflator which is a weighted average of the prices of all final goods and services produced. For the 120 years as a whole, prices have increased on the average at the rate of 1⅛ percent per year, a rate which probably now would be regarded as within the range of price rise characterizing a "creeping inflation." Price trends in the first half of the period, when the average rate of change was virtually zero, differed considerably from those observed during the second half starting in 1899, during which the rise in prices averaged 2½ percent per year, probably near the upper boundary of what is thought to be compatible with a creeping inflation. However, if subperiods of 40 years' duration are taken, prices advanced most rapidly from 1879 to 1919 when the rise averaged 1.9 percent per year rather than in the last 40 years, during which the average rise amounted to only 1.4 percent.

The result of these variations in rates of increase of total gross national product in current prices, in the price level, and in population is that the residual, the rate of growth in real national product per head, shows more stability within the range of 1½ to 1¾ percent than any of the other three series. The contribution of the three factors — real output per head, population, and prices — to the average rate of growth of aggregate current output thus has differed greatly in the different periods.

For the entire 120 years population growth has accounted for two-fifths of the total increase in the monetary value of aggregate output; the rise in the price level for one-fourth; and intensive growth, the rise in real output per head, for one-third. In some of the subperiods the change in the price level has contributed nothing to the increase in aggregate gross national product at current prices, as for instance from 1839 to 1899, or has even offset part of the increase in population and intensive growth, e.g., from 1869 to 1899. There is no period during which the rise in the price level accounted for as much as one-half of the rate of growth in total current aggregate output. During the last 40 years the rise in the price level has been responsible for fully one-third of the rate of growth of current aggregate output, while population growth has contributed three-tenths and intensive growth almost two-fifths.

No clear relation seems to exist between the rate of intensive growth — to repeat, the magnitude in which we are primarily interested — and either price level movements or the rapidity of population growth. Intensive growth proceeded at approximately the same rate during the first and the second half of the 120-year period although the price level showed no trend during the first half but advanced at an average rate of 2½ percent per year during the second half. The only instance in which a relationship between the movement of the price level and the rate of intensive growth can be observed — without detailed analysis no such relationship can be regarded as reflecting cause and effect — is the period from 1869 to 1899 during which the rate of intensive growth at 2.2 percent per year was the highest one observed during any period of 30 years' or more duration while the price level declined at the rate of 1.7 percent per year, the only case of a downward trend in prices for any period of such length. All that possibly needs to be added to avoid misunderstanding is that substantial sustained intensive growth and an upward trend in prices, at a moderate rate, are obviously not incompatible.

The movements in the rate of growth of aggregate consumption in current prices and the contributions to it made by increases in real consumption per full consumer, growth in the number of consumers, and changes in the price level are so similar to those observed in the case of gross national product, that a separate discussion is unnecessary. The relevant figues, however, are given in table 1.

IV. THE GROWTH OF THE PRINCIPAL COMPONENTS OF NATIONAL PRODUCT AND INCOME

Stability in the rate of growth of gross national product per head (or, for that matter, stability in the rate of growth of real income per full consumer) does not mean stability of the rate of growth of the components of gross national product or income. Specifically, it does not mean stability of the rate of growth of the different industrial sectors of the economy (such as agriculture, manufacturing, trade and services); of the private and the Government sector; of the different regions of the country; of the different types of commodities and services produced; of the different forms of income, particularly labor and property income; and of incomes of different size. As a matter of fact, we know that the rates of growth over the past century have been quite different for different industrial sectors, for the Government as against the private sector, for different types of commodities, and for different regions; and it is at least possible that considerable differences have existed also in the rates of growth of different types of income and of different income size classes.

These differences in the rate of growth of the different constituents of national product or income are the essence of the process of economic development. The national rate of growth is nothing but an average of the rates of growth in different sectors, regions, etc. The national rate of growth, therefore, is influenced by two sets of factors. The first is the rate of growth prevailing in the different sectors of the economy; the second, the share of the different sectors in aggregate national product or income. The national rate of growth can remain the same even if sectoral growth rates change, increasing rates in some sectors being offset in their effect on the national average by decreasing rates of growth in other sectors. Similarly, the national rate of growth can and will change although there is no change in the rates of growth of any sector. If the share of one sector in national product or income increases over a given period, this shows that the sector has been growing more rapidly than the national aggregate. Similarly, a decline in the share of a sector indicates that the sector has been growing less rapidly than the Nation as a whole.

It would go far beyond my assignment and ability — and at times would exceed the reliable statistical material now available — to trace in detail the differences that have existed during the last century in the rates of growth of the constituents of national product and income. I shall have to limit myself to summarizing in a few sentences the main features of these differences in growth rates insofar as they are known.

1. Capital formation versus consumption

While rates of growth have differed greatly for the different specific commodities and services that make up the national product, with the consequence that the distribution of total national product among groups of commodities and services has changed substantially, one relation — and possibly the most important single relation in this field — has shown a remarkable degree of constancy over the last 100 years.

When the total national product is divided into two parts, one consisting of durable goods (including changes in business inventories and in net foreign investment) and the other made up of all nondurable goods and services, it is found that the two parts have grown over the long run at approximately the same rate. Hence, the share of durable goods in total gross national product, a relation often referred to as the gross capital formation ratio, has been fairly constant since the Civil War. If consumer durables are included in capital formation its share in gross national product has deviated but little from 30 percent from decade to decade with the sole exception of the decade including the Great Depression. Eliminating consumer durables, but still including residential housing and Government construction, the gross capital formation ratio has in most decades been slightly above one-fifth without showing a definite upward or downward trend. The decade of the Great Depression is again the main exception.

The equality of the long-term rate of growth of the production of durable goods on the one hand and of nondurable goods and services on the other, and the consequent stability in the gross capital formation ratio, however, do not mean that the same relationships persist when account is taken of capital consumption allowances. Capital consumption allowances have been increasing in proportion to gross capital formation, partly because of the shortening of the average life of durable goods which reflects the increasing share of producer and consumer durables and the decline of the share of construction expenditures in total gross capital formation. The long-term rate of growth of net capital formation, has, therefore, been somewhat smaller than that of the output of nondurable goods and services or of total gross national product. As a necessary consequence the share of net capital formation in net national product has declined somewhat, the exact extent of the decline depending on assumptions made regarding the length of life of the different components of capital formation, the method of depreciation applied and the price indexes used to deflate the original data.

Considerable changes have taken place in the structure of capital formation. The output of producer and consumer durables has risen more rapidly than that of residential or nonresidential construction. From 1879 to 1959 average rates of growth have been fully 4 percent for producer durables: 2½ for residential construction and for other private construction; and over 4½ for public construction. (All rates calculated from values at beginning and end of period; they are aggregate deflated, not per-head, values.) The share of gross capital formation represented by increases in inventories has shown a slight decline reflecting a somewhat slower growth of additions to inventories than of total gross capital formation.

2. Sectoral differences in growth

No economist is needed to tell you that rates of growth of the main sectors of the economy have differed considerably, since changes in the distribution of gross national product among sectors, which reflect these differences in rates of growth, are obvious even to the casual student of American economic history. The outstanding features of these changes in industrial structure, of course, have been the declining shares of agriculture; and the increase in the shares of manufacturing and mining and of government. Between 1839 and 1959 the share of agriculture in national product has declined from about one-third to about 5 percent. On the other hand, that of manufacturing and mining has risen sharply from about one-tenth to one third, while that of Government has shot up even more rapidly from only 2 percent to approximately one-eighth of total national product.

Obviously, very pronounced changes in average rates of growth underlie these changes in the sectoral structure of gross national product. The average rate of growth (aggregate — not per head, calculated from deflated values at beginning and end of period only) for the entire period is thus about 1¾ percent for agriculture; 2¾ percent for transportation and public utilities; 3¼ percent for services and construction; 4 percent for trade; 4½ percent for manufacturing and mining; and 5 percent for Government — all compared to the 3½ percent rate for the entire economy. It would take us too far afield to explore the trends in the rate of growth of each of these sectors, the more so as some of them do not by any means move along the regular straight path which we have observed in the case of total national product.

3. Regional differences in growth

Substantial differences also exist in the rates of growth of real income per head among different regions of the United States. The outstanding feature here has been the tendency toward a reduction of the differences existing between the level of real income per head in the different parts of the country. This, of course, means that the average rate of growth of real income per head has been more rapid in those regions in which income was relatively low in the mid-19th century than in those in which it was then high compared to the national average. Thus, to take the extremes, the southeastern and southwestern states have shown an average rate of growth of real income per head between 1929 and 1957 of almost 3 percent per year, while the rate of growth has been as low as 1¼ percent for the mideastern states and 1½ percent for New England.[5]

4. Differences among types of income

In contrast to the pronounced differences in the rates of growth observed among different industrial sectors, different regions and different types of commodities and services, the differences in the rates of growth of the main functional types of income seem to have been rather moderate. Great caution, however, is necessary in making statements in this field as the figures are subject to considerably more disagreement among experts than is the case for the divisions of national product with which we have dealt so far.

If total national income is divided only into the part going to labor and that accruing to property, entrepreneurial income being allocated throughout the period in the ratio of 2 to 1 between labor and property, then there appears to have been a slight increase in the share of labor, possibly from seven-tenths in the 1860's to nearly four-fifths in the last decade, if recent, not uncontested, estimates by Professor Kravis are used. Within property income the share of interest and rent has declined sharply while entrepreneurial property income has held its own, corporate profits, of course, gaining rapidly at the expense of property income from unincorporated business enterprises. These changes, of course, reflect differences in rates of growth.

5. *Changes in income size distribution*

Finally, there have also been changes in the rate at which the average real income of people of different affluence has increased, differences which are reflected in changes in the shape of the size distribution of personal income. In this case, unfortunately, reliable figures do not go beyond 1929.

In the last 30 years the per head real, before-tax income of the lowest two-fifths of the population, arrayed by size of income, has tended to increase at a more rapid rate (2.6 percent per year) than average personal income (1.7 percent), while the rate of growth has been below the national average for the top fifth of income recipients (1.0 percent). The result, of course, has been some reduction in the degree of inequality of incomes. Most of the net change occurred during the few years of World War II.

In interpreting these figures it is well to remember that 1929 was a year of a particularly high degree of relative income inequality. If comparable figures were available for a longer period of time, preferably back to the middle of the 19th century, differences in the rates of growth of the different strata of the population might therefore be smaller, on an annual basis, than they now appear to be when we can follow them for only a 30-year period. Notwithstanding all the qualifications that must be made, it appears likely that even for the entire last century the rate of growth has been higher for the lower than for the higher income groups, and that in consequence the degree of inequality in income distribution has diminished somewhat.

V. STATISTICAL QUALIFICATIONS

I now reach a section of my presentation which, I am afraid, may tax your patience. After having presented briefly the statistical record on the rate of growth of national product during the last 120 years I now must discuss, be it ever so incompletely, the qualifications to which these figures are subject. This I shall do, as far as possible, in nontechnical terms.

To spare you any discussion of the statistical limitations of the figures I have used in this presentation would, I feel, be a disservice to this committee. Before you can judge the significance of the average rate of growth of national product and income for the last century or parts of it you should be aware of some of the statistical limitations to which the figures are subject and to some of the qualifications which must be made in their interpretation.

I have told you that the gross national product per head, reduced to the constant price level of 1929, has increased over the past 120 years, and through the three 40-year subperiods into which it can be divided, at an average annual rate of 1⅝ percent. How accurate is this figure as a measure of the trend in the physical output of the U.S. economy?

Of the many factors which make the observed average rate of growth of real gross national output per head differ from a perfect measure of the growth of physical output, if such exists, I shall discuss only half a dozen; three factors which make the observed rate of growth appear higher than a perfect measure would show it to be, and three others that have the opposite effect of reducing the observed rate below the perfect one. This restriction is, of course, dictated partly by limitations of time and the desire to avoid overly technical points, but it seems justified by the likelihood that the six factors to be mentioned cause the most important discrepancies between the observed and the perfectly measured rate of growth.

To begin with factors which tend to make the observed rate of growth appear higher than it should be, the first is the increase in the share of those economic activities that can be brought within the measuring rod of money, and, hence, are covered by our measures of national product. To put it in a different and possibly more easily understandable way, the part of economic activities that takes place within the household, including cooking, baking, dressmaking, home repairs, vegetable gardening, and so forth, and is not included in our measures of national product, has been de-sumption of capital. In the long run only that part of gross national product means that the rate of growth in measured national product is somewhat higher than it would be if these intrahousehold economic activities had been included. There are no reliable or close estimates of the relative size of these activities — this is one of the reasons why they are not covered by the usual measures of national product — but it is unlikely that their inclusion would reduce the average annual rate of growth of real national product per-head by as much as one-eighth of 1 percent.

A second factor tending to make the measured rate of growth too high is the increasing share of output that is required to make good the consumption of capital. In the long run only that part of gross national product can be regarded as available either for consumption or addition to the stock of capital that exceeds the current using-up of part of the stock of capital. In this case we are fortunately in a position to make a reasonably close estimate of the magnitudes involved. If our calculations had been based on net national product, that is, gross national product less capital consumption allowances, the average annual rates of growth for the entire period from 1839 to 1959 would have been one-tenth of 1 percent lower than the figures presented.

The third of the factors that tend to overstate the observed rate of growth of national product is more difficult to define and almost impossible to measure. It concerns certain increases in the economic cost of producing the national output, expenditures which are not treated in our statistics as cost because they are borne by consumers rather than by producers. The most important item in this category probably is the increased cost of transportation borne by consumers as the distance between home and place of work has increased. Others are various expenses necessitated by the increasing strain of participation in the modern production process. These items, which are now included in gross national product, but according to many national income experts should not be, are difficult to measure exactly even if agreement could be obtained as to their scope. It is unlikely, however, that their elimination from gross national product would significantly reduce its long-term rate of growth.

Let us now turn to the factors which tend to make the calculated rate of growth of national product smaller than it ought to be if appropriate definitions were used and all necessary information were available.

The first, and probably the most important of these factors, is the improvement in the quality of goods and services which has not been taken into account in the price indexes which are used to reduce the estimates of national product in current prices to the constant prices figures you have seen. In principle, of course, price indexes should be based on items of identical quality so that the difficulty we are now discussing would not arise. Actually, however, it has proved impossible to take account fully of the process of quality improvement that goes on continuously though not at constant speed nor in all sectors of the economy. (I am doubtful, for instance, whether the quality of bread or haircuts is superior now to what it was a century ago.) As a result, the price indexes we use as deflators have a tendency to overstate the rise in prices (or to understate the decline in prices) that has actually occurred. Exactly how important this failure to take full account of quality improvement may be, it is impossible to say. While it is undoubtedly substantial for certain types of commodities, particularly producer and consumer durables, that are mass produced, it would seem to be slight or nonexistent or negative for a considerable proportion of national product particularly many custom made products and services. While failure to take account of quality improvement leads on balance to some understatement of the measured rate of growth of national product, the understatement would seem not to have been very large in proportion to the level of the observed rate.

The second of the factors, inclusion of which would increase the rate of growth above its observed level, is the omission in all available estimates of the services rendered by the stock of consumer durables, of durable assets of nonprofit institutions, and of Government structures, civilian as well as military. Since these categories have increased in importance over the last century the omissions of the services they provide to the population imparts a slight downward bias to the observed rate of growth of national product. Even at the present time, however, inclusion of these services would add only a few percent to measured gross national product. Hence, their omission can influence the rate of growth of national product over the past century to only a minor extent.

The third factor that tends to make the observed rate of growth appear smaller than it should be is unfortunately both important and highly technical. The price indexes that have been used, directly or by a process of linking, to reduce gross national product in current prices to a constant price level are based on the relative importance of the different commodities and services near the end of the period of observation. Specifically, they are based on the relative prices of 1879 for the period from 1839 to 1879; on the prices of 1929 for the period of 1879 to 1909; and on the relative prices of 1954 for the period from 1909 to 1959. Statisticians have found that price indexes using weights at or near the end of the period tend to overstate the rise in prices. Hence, estimates of current national product deflated by means of these indexes tend to show too low a rate of growth, too low that is in comparison to the figures that would be obtained by using relatives for the middle or the average of the period as weights. The reason for this phenomenon is a fact of which every housewife is aware even if but hazily, the tendency for commodities and services that increase in price less than the average to grow in volume more than the average. This negative correlation between relative price and relative quantity movements, to use the technical expression, necessarily leads to an understatement of the rate of growth of national product when a weight system based on the situation at or near the end of the period of observation is used. While an exact measure of the effect of the use of late period weights on our estimates of gross national product in constant prices is not available for most of the period, scattered observations indicate that while far from negligible this factor is unlikely to have led to an overstatement of the rate of growth of national product by an amount that is substantial in proportion to that rate.

It is not easy to evaluate to what extent the three factors which tend to make the observed rate of growth of gross national product larger than it should be, offset the three factors operating in the other direction; nor to assess the net effect of other factors working in both directions which have not been discussed specifically. It is, therefore, not more than a personal judgment to say that on balance the economically relevant factors that are not, or not adequately, reflected in the figures on which we base the calculation of the observed rate of growth would result in a slight increase of the observed annual average rate of growth for the entire period from 1839 beyond the level of 1⅝ percent. The adjusted rate is likely to be least as high as 1¾ percent. It may even have been a little higher than that. It is very unlikely, however, that adjustment for all the factors discussed would raise the adjusted rate of growth to 2 percent a year or even very close to it. This conclusion, however, I repeat, is to a good extent a matter of personal judgment.

VI. A LOOK BACKWARD AND ABROAD

Although our usable statistical record does not go back beyond 1839 — and the data have already been stretched to the utmost for the 40 years before 1879 — I cannot well evade the question whether the trend in national product and income that has been observed over the last 120 years and has shown considerable long run stability at the rate of about 1⅝ percent per year for real national product per head is likely to, or could have extended into the period before 1839, possibly as far back as the coming of the white man.

There are two ways of obtaining if not a reliable answer to this question at least an idea about it. The first approach is provided by the very rough estimates by students who have worked on the quantitative aspects of the earlier periods of American economic history. They feel that average real income per head in 1760 is very unlikely to have been below one-half of the level of 1860. This judgment — and it is not more than that — implies an average rate of growth in real income per head between 1760 and 1839 of not more than 0.6 percent per year. Granting all possible errors in the evaluation of the figure for 1760, these are rates of growth radically lower than those observed for any substantial period over the next 120 years.

The second approach is along the lines of the logician's indirect proof.

Let us start from the level of real income per head in 1839, and see where we shall arrive on the assumption that the measured rate of growth actually had averaged 1⅝ percent before 1839 as it has since. This is very easy to do, since an annual growth of 1⅝ percent implies a halving of national income every 43 years as we go back. Average real income per head in 1839 may be estimated at about $400 in present prices. If the trend observed since 1839 had been in force before that date, average income per head in today's prices would have been about $145 in 1776, $80 in 1739, and less than $30 in 1676. It takes only a little consideration of the minimum requirements for keeping body and soul together, even in the simpler conditions prevailing in colonial America, to conclude that at present prices for individual commodities an average level of income below $200 is fairly well ruled out for 1776 or even the early 18th century. Indeed, we do not have to rely entirely on speculations of this type, but may recall that the average real income per head, in current American prices, is in the order of $200 in countries such as Mexico, Turkey, and Portugal, whose present standard of living for the mass of the population is hardly higher than that prevailing in colonial America.

There seems little doubt, then, that the average rate of growth of real income per head was much lower than 1⅝ percent before 1829. If we consider periods of at least 50 years' length, it is questionable that we would find an average rate of growth as high as 1 percent for any of them. There thus must have occurred a fairly sharp break in the trend of real national product per head sometime before 1839. Exactly when this break occurred we cannot yet say, on the basis of the statistical data available. I would hazard a guess, however, which may shock scrupulous economic historians, that the break occurred not very long before 1839 and that it reflects both the transition of the United States from a predominantly agricultural to a more and more industrial country and the advent of the railroads.

In the case of the United States we can study the trend of national product and income for a period of only 120 years unless we want to lose ourselves in the realm of speculation — at least in the present state of the statistics. There exists, however, fortunately, a country, not incomparable in its industrial structure and its economic development to the United States, in which we are able to measure the trend in national income for a period of almost 300 years — Great Britain. It may therefore be worthwhile to review very briefly the British record illustrated in Chart VI, if only to bring out one salient fact, viz, that the rate of growth in real product per head was much slower before the 19th century than over the last 150 years.

British real product per head has increased at an average rate of about

1.2 percent between 1870 and 1957. The average rate of growth for the entire period from 1839 to 1959 is likely to have been close to 1⅛ percent. This rate, while substantially lower than that observed in the United States for the same period, is of the same order of magnitude. The average rate of growth for the 150 years before 1840 — specifically, from 1688, the year for which we have the remarkable estimate of Gregory King — appears to have been below 0.5 percent, according to the studies of P. Deane. While we cannot use this sharp break in the trend of national product and income in England, which seems to have occurred a few decades before 1840, to infer a similar movement in the United States, it may at least be not without value as collateral evidence.

It is also interesting to see how the seemingly small difference of one-half of 1 percent between the trend of intensive growth of national product in the United States and in Britain — 1⅝ percent against 1⅛ percent — has sufficed to produce within one century the present very substantial difference in the level of average real output per head in the two countries. If we assume that at the present time output per head in the United States is 60 to 100 percent above that in Britain, as specialized inquiries indicate (Gilbert and Associates, Comparative National Products and Price Levels) then it would have taken not more than 100 and 140 years respectively, for a difference of one-half of 1 percent per year in the rate of intensive growth to result in the present large difference in level of average income. In other words we should expect average real income per head to have been the same in the United States and Britain as late as 1860 or 1820. This conclusion is quite compatible with the fragmentary direct evidence of relative output per head we have for those dates — another example of the power of even small differences in compound interest rates, if operating over long periods of time.

Chart I

AGGREGATE GROSS NATIONAL PRODUCT
CURRENT AND CONSTANT (1929) PRICES

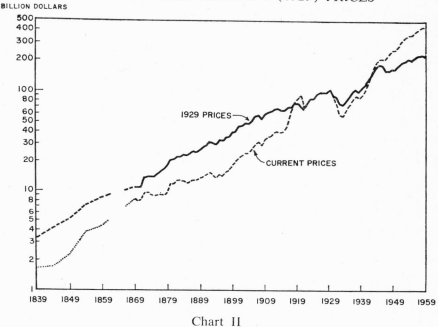

Chart II

REAL GROSS NATIONAL PRODUCT (1929 PRICES)
AGGREGATE AND PER HEAD

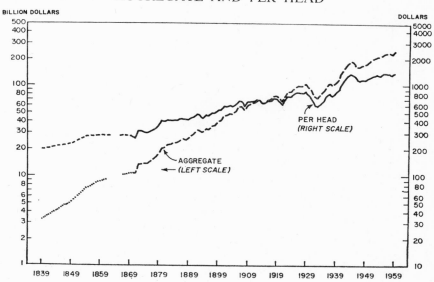

Chart III

PERSONAL CONSUMPTION EXPENDITURES (1929 PRICES)
AGGREGATE AND PER FULL CONSUMER

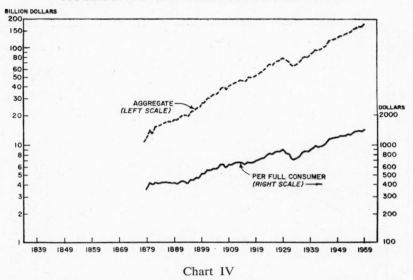

Chart IV

THE TREND IN REAL GROSS NATIONAL PRODUCT PER HEAD
1839-1959

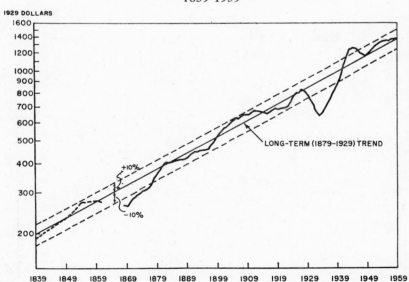

Chart V

CONTRIBUTION OF GROWTH OF PRICES, POPULATION AND REAL GNP PER HEAD TO GROWTH OF AGGREGATE CURRENT GNP

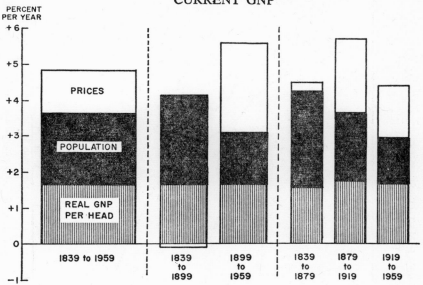

Chart VI

SECULAR GROWTH OF REAL NATIONAL INCOME PER HEAD
IN U.S.A AND GREAT BRITAIN (1929 PRICES)

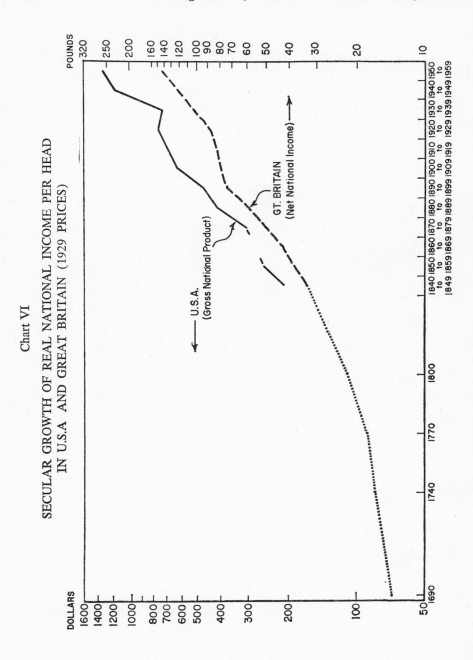

Chart VII

THE MAIN NATIONAL ACCOUNTING AGGREGATES
AND THEIR COMPONENTS, 1957

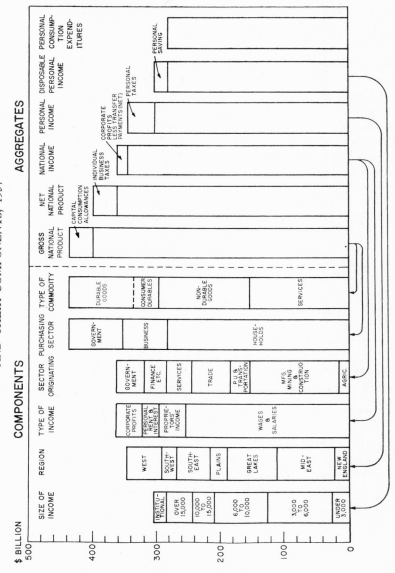

Labor Force Mobility and Unemployment, 1800-1960

STANLEY LEBERGOTT *‡

A few years ago a book on English history appeared in which the writers rambled through the decades, labeling the events that were "a good thing" and those that were not. It is clear that current discussions generally treat labor mobility as "a good thing" — not to be confused with labor turn-over, which is "a bad thing." Without attempting to draw the delicate boundary lines that separates those two, I shall simply define labor mobility as the movement of persons into and out of jobs. Such changes commonly involve a shift from one employer to another, but they may only take the form of entrances into the labor force or exits from it.[1]

What can we say about the American historical record? Essentially this — that the main currents of American life have tended, with some vital exceptions, to reduce labor mobility over the past century. Of course, we may single out one of these forces and make a plausible case, say, for seniority systems, or pension plans, or social security being "the" major cause. But if we look to the broad pattern of our national growth we will find, I think, a great many causes powerfully working to reduce labor mobility. Let us review some of the main ones, not as opponents or sup-porters of any of them, including even the first, which is:

1. The American home: At the beginning of this century about 36 percent of our nonfarm families owned their homes.[2] Today the ratio is half again as great.[3] Higher real incomes and improved construction tech-

---

* The opinions expressed are purely personal and have no connection with the work of any organization.

‡ Stanley Lebergott is Professor of Economics and Chairman of the Dept. at Wesleyan Univ. in Conn.

[1] In recent years basic research has been done, almost for the first time, in labor mobility. Among the ablest studies have been Gladys L. Palmer, "Labor Mobility in Six Cities" (1954); Wight Bakke et al., "Labor Mobility and Economic Opportunity" (1954); Charles Myers and George Shultz, "Dynamics of a Labor Market" (1951); Lloyd Reynolds and Joseph Shister, "Job Horizons" (1949). Two perceptive shorter works are an essay by Myers in John Dunlop, "The Theory of Wage Determination" (1957), and Arthur M. Ross, "Do We Have a New Industrial Feudalism?" American Economic Review (December 1958). The latter looks to long-run factors in quit rates. The penumbra of union rules have been covered in two outstanding studies, Sumner Slichter's "Union Policies and Industrial Management" (1941), and John Dunlop's "Wage Determination Under Trade Unions" (1944).

[2] "Historical Statistics of the United States, 1789-1945." p. 174.

[3] "The 1957 Statistical Abstract," p. 771, gives a rate of 53.4 for 1960, which we extrapolate by the the trend for dwelling units inside standard metropolitan areas *ibid.,* p. 769).

niques have played a part. And a significant factor was agreement by the Congress and the Executive in that long line of actions from the mortgage moratorium of the early 1930's, the FHA insurance program of the late 1930's, to the VA loan program of the late 1940's.

However, converting a tenant into a homeowner inevitably reduces his mobility. A man who has sown his crop of crabgrass wants to be around next year to see how it made out. Men who become homeowners develop neighborhood ties, other commitments, that keep them from picking up as readily as a renter and heading for areas where alternative opportunities may beckon.

2. A second factor is motherhood. Women in the child-bearing years today have borne 37 percent more children than women of the same age group in 1941.[4] From data in the 1950 census we may make a crude estimate of migration rates among families with children, an estimate which indicates that the rate of this group is less than half that for families in comparable age groups without children.[5] A moment's reflection indicates how the links that children and family develop with their school, neighbors, and even the PTA tend to reduce geographic mobility. In turn this reduces the willingness of the head of the family to seek work in new areas when the pattern of labor opportunities changes.

3. A third force is that of education. The proportion of our children (aged 5-14) attending public school a century ago was 55 percent.[6] Today it is nearer 85 percent.[7] No less important has been the rise in school guidance work — local school systems providing counselors, and Department of Labor materials helping to tell the counselors how the outlook for different occupations shapes up. What do these factors imply for

---

[4] Bureau of the Census, Current Population Reports, Series P–20, No. 84, "Fertility of the Population: March 1957," table A.

[5] From the 1950 census report, "Population Mobility, Characteristics of Migrants," we can estimate migration rates of 7 percent for the youngest children, and lower rates, down to 4 percent for those aged 14 to 19. If we compute the percentage for married males aged 20-24 it runs to 13 percent with 10 percent for those aged 25-29, 7 percent for those 30-34, and 5 percent for age 35-44. From the census, Current Population Reports, Series P–20, No. 83, "Social and Economic Characteristics of Households and Families, March 1957," table 4, we can estimate 2.5 children per family in the 20-44 age interval. Assuming 2.5 children under 18 to families with children, and subtracting them from the figures for all married males, we derive figures for married males without children. The resultant migration rate is enormously greater than that implied above for families with children. Because of the lack of direct measures, however, the only conclusion drawn here is that the rate for those without children must be at least double that for those with children. It must be realized that the above data are in no way standardized out for color, rural, urban, etc., differences, and doing so would presumably affect the influence on mobility of children per se.

[6] "The Seventh Census of the United States: 1850" (1954), p. lx, xlii-xliv.

[7] 1950 census, vol. 11, "Characteristics of the Population," pt. 1, tables 38, 111.

mobility? Well, they suggest that young men and women enter today's labor market better trained, with a better idea of both their own abilities and the prospects in different occupations than did their grandparents. If so, does it not follow that these youngsters are less likely to wander from unskilled job to unskilled job before they find their way? And more likely to begin closer to their occupational limit without as many preliminary jobs? As a result mobility has decreased among the very group that traditionally has shown the highest mobility.

4. Ending of large scale immigration: In Jefferson's day about half our labor force was composed of immigrants.[8] By President Harding's time the ratio had fallen to 20 percent and today it stands at about 8 percent.[9] Now the very name we use for this group — immigrant — emphasizes its high mobility. When the typical immigrant landed he would first find temporary work where the ship docked — Philadelphia, New York, New Orleans. He would then move across the land from job to job. Whether it was building the Chesapeake & Ohio Canal here along the Potomac, cutting timber in the Wisconsin woods, or breaking stone for the national road to the West, his jobs tended to be short-lived. Each move, and each advance up the occupational ladder, added to mobility. Hence the declining share of our labor force in this category in turn brought a reduction in labor mobility.

5. Personnel work: Personnel men early discovered the high cost to industry of hiring and training new workers, only to have them quit, or prove unsatisfactory. What was more natural than for them to try to reduce labor turnover (and thereby mobility) by entrance and exit interviews, by changes in working conditions?

A now widespread personnel practice when employment has to be cut is to spread the work. During the great depression a survey of many thousand manufacturing firms found that 64 percent of their employees were on part-time work.[10] And anyone who watched the monthly census figures during the recessions of 1949 and 1953 could discern how industry sought first to reduce hours, to spread the work, rather than initially adjusting by outright firings. The common sense of holding on to a trained labor force, and the growing feeling for human values, have tended to reduce the outright firings that in an earlier day would have meant high mobility.

---

[8] The derivation of these estimates is described in the writer's chapter, "The Pattern of Employment Since 1800," S. E. Harris, ed., *American Economic History,* New York 1962.]

[9] Idem.

[10] William J. Barrett, "Extent and Methods of Spreading Work," Monthly Labor Review, September 1932, p. 490.

6. The family farm program: The Government's farm program in the 19th century took the form of land sales at low prices. Differences of opinion turned on whether land should be given away or should merely be sold at low prices. Its entire purpose led to the encouragement of labor mobility. Representative Allison of Pennsylvania called one homestead bill "a seductive lure which is well calculated to induce many laborers and mechanics, who are now doing well at their home in the old States, to leave them and engage in agriculture." [11]

The Federal farm program in the 20th century has been designed to achieve quite other purposes than getting men to move westward and acquire farms. It seeks to assure prices, and thereby incomes, to farmers. By doing so it makes it possible for farmers to remain on the farms on which they are already located. So far as it affects mobility, therefore, it tends to reduce it — just as our 19th century policies tended to encourage it.

7. The defense program: Although the Congressional Record in the days of President Adams and Jackson was filled with bitter debate on the amount of Government spending, the total amount spent could hardly have had a sizable impact on the economy. Even as late as 1940 the Federal Government's spending in the hard goods industries only ran to $1 for every $27 spent by consumers and businessmen.[12] By 1953, however, Federal spending matched private spending in this area dollar for dollar, the ratio declining mildly since then. We are not looking here to total Federal spending — but to the rise of Federal spending from less than $2 billion to more than $44 billion in one sector of the economy. A rise of this magnitude, timing, and local concentration could hardly fail to bid up prices of land, labor, and capital in that sector. In a free market economy this in turn meant pressures transmitted to the other sectors of the economy, which likewise require the use of these factors.

Now the basic cause of labor quits, an important component of total labor

---

[11] Quoted in Helen S. Zahler, "Eastern Workingmen and National Land Policy, 1829-1962" 1941, p. 149.

[12] Office of Business Economics, "U.S. Income and Output, 1958 Supplement to the Survey of Current Business," table I–1. The private expenditure figure used here is the sum of the figures for personal consumption expenditures on durable goods plus producers' durable equipment. The Federal national defense purchases figure shown in this table includes pay of the Armed Forces, excludes unilateral transfers under the aid programs. For 1940 the $2.223 billion figure was reduced to $2 billion as an approximate method of excluding military pay. For 1957 the reported figure was used on the assumption that the military pay inclusion would roughly offset the exclusion of durables bought by aid transfers.

More important, a substantial volume of producers' durables purchased for the production of defense goods with Government funds are included under the private heading whereas for present purposes they should be shifted to the Government category.

mobility, is the desire for higher wages.[13] But with the tremendous impact of the spending noted above it was to be expected that those who sell their labor just as those who sell raw materials, components, or entrepreneurial ability, could get higher rates in this sector without moving to other markets.

Economic theory has not yet, I believe, described the phenomenon of the weak monopsonist. But both the Congress and the executive have long since recognized that neither the Government, nor the enterprises who operate as its relay men in the defense race, drive the tightest of possible bargains in the swift procurement of immense quantities of goods, particularly where these are new and undeveloped. Such recognition has led to setting up procedures for defense contract renegotiation. Should it surprise us, therefore, that in the purchase of factory inputs, whether raw materials, finished components, or labor that a similar flexibility should develop? And if it has, how should it not diminish the mobility of all factors, by diminishing one of the key forces that make men and capital move on in search of higher rewards?

8.   The last factor I shall mention is an encompassing one, probably best termed "The Search for Security." Roller coaster changes in economic activity have been the traditional source of profits, bankruptcies, ulcers — and heavy labor mobility. Like flash floods the panics of the 19th century threw hundreds of thousands of men onto the labor market, and firings in the 20th century's major depression threw millions out of work. Mobility was also high when prosperity returned, turnover among new employees normally being high in the process of shaking down to a mutually suited employer-employee relationship.

Today, most groups in the economy are more insistent upon security than were their predecessors in the 19th century. We have noted above the interest that the personnel man has in a stabler work force. But the comptroller has found no endearing qualities in irregular demands for cash, in unpredictable ups and downs in requirements for financing inventories or new plants. And the company president has discovered that evening out the seasonal pattern of production, spreading out product lines to stabilize long-run production is an endeavor worthy of his best talents. Every step taken toward such goals reduces hirings, firings — and mobility. It is unnecessary to labor the major point that seniority systems, pension plans and other measures that preceded the massive growth of union membership in recent decades have, in general, been firmly supported and pressed for by the labor unions.

Towering above all this has been the endeavor of many groups to have the Federal Government help to create greater economic stability. In the 19th century the tariff program was the only one of consequence (and then not great by today's standards) that tended to immobilize capital and labor. In our day we have seen an enormous battery of programs that work to that end, whatever their primary purposes — I refer to the programs for farm parity, resale price maintenance, minimum wages, unemployment insurance, deposit insurance on through to the broad principle of stability adopted in the Employment Act of 1946. We need pass judgment on the merits of none of these widely supported programs to note that one by one they have tended to slow down the mobility of labor, whether self-employed or employee.

9. Summary: Let me summarize the above in two sentences. First, big numbers are not better than small ones, even those measuring labor mobility. Second, the main currents of American economic development in the past century, powerfully aided by an impressive number of Federal programs, have worked to reduce labor mobility because other goals, such as economic stability, an educated labor force, more homeowners, etc., were felt to be worthy of national support.

Two observations might be added. (1) We have been dealing with the long-term trends. It may be useful to consider the absolute amount of labor mobility today, adding up all the shifts from job to job, all the entrances into and exits from the labor force. Making such an estimate for 1955 we arrive at the crudely accurate, if fairly sensational figure of 70 million job changes in that year.[14] The ratio of this figure to our 69 million labor force may well indicate that despite a long-term decline, U. S. mobility rates are the highest of any nation, free or otherwise. A recent report by the leading Swedish economist, Bertil Ohlin, and experts from five other European countries states flatly that "the extent to which the objective of full employment is interpreted (in Europe) as implying security of employment in the same job and in the same place has sometimes amazed outside observers."[15]

---

[14] The derivation of this estimate, based on BLS data for manufacturing turnover, and census data for nonmanufacturing shifts and for entrances into and exits from the labor force is outlined in the writer's "On the shape of the Income Distribution," to appear in the May 1959, American Economic Review. [Published, vol. XLIX (No. 3), pp. 328-347.]

[15] The entire paragraph reads as follows: "Most Western European workers appear to be reluctant to change their occupation or place of employment. They consequently view with some apprehension the possibility that schemes for higher productivity or freer trade may lead to changes in the overall pattern of employment and may thus make it necessary for some workers to change their jobs. The extent to which the objective of full employment is interpreted as implying security of employment in the same job and in the same place has sometimes amazed outside observers. For example, an American author was struck by the fact that it is not unheard of for European employers to refuse lucrative new business on the ground that it would require adding to the work force new workers for whose continued employment the employer would then be legally or morally responsible. Conversely, unemployment tends to mean patient waiting for a new job in the same occupation and area without consideration of the possibility of moving to an occupation or area of more active demand." Inter-

(2) In specific instances where workers and industries have been left behind by the retreating economic tide, community organizations and government will presumably still continue to take action to assist mobility. One may refer to such programs as that proposed by the administration in 1956 to assist in the training of farm families in new skills; to the proposals made by the Steel Workers to the Randall Committee; to suggestions of various economists in the fine symposium on foreign trade policy issued by the Boggs subcommittee.

Let us turn now to the long-term forces affecting unemployment. I. Seasonal unemployment gets relatively little attention in our day but in the last century it was a major factor, the nation's dependence on nature then being so much greater. The declining role of farming alone, occupying 83 percent of the gainful workers in 1800, but only a little more than 10 percent today, would tend to a marked moderation in seasonal employment.[16] When iron was becoming a major industry in the 1830's, it was common for ironworks to shut down for 2 months of frost and snow. It is difficult to imagine blast furnaces today shutting down for winter however unforeseen the weather on the Great Lakes may be. II. Technological unemployment is, of course, no novelty in human history. The engineers and master mechanics of the 19th century had their own brilliant accomplishments. When the reaper came into prominence in President Buchanan's day, it did the work of 4 to 5 men cutting grain with hand cradles.[17]

This is much better for example, than the 2½-fold advantage offered by the mechanical cornpicker in our own time.[18] And pallet loading of ships raises smaller problems than those brought by the invention of the steamboat. For while broadhorn arks such as Lincoln navigated downriver were picturesque, they disappeared within a few brief years, given the competition of steamboats that could carry 10 times the load in a fifth of the time.[19]

But for every 1,000 men displaced by technical advance does more and longer unemployment result today than in the 19th century? We have very little basis for knowing. However, factors that come to mind suggest

---

national Labour Office, "Social Aspects of European Economic Cooperation, Report by a Group of Experts" (1956), p. 99, ch. VI, on "International Movements of Labor and Capital" (and indeed the entire report) is a brilliantly lucid review of problem of factor mobility as it appears in Europe, but in terms that cast a revealing light on American problems as well.

[16] Cf. footnote 8.

[17] Leo Rogin, "The Introduction of Farm Machinery" (1931), pp. 133, 135.

[18] U.S. Department of Agriculture, Agricultural Research Service, "Labor Used for Field Crops," Statistical Bulletin No. 144 (June 1954).

[19] James Hall, "Sketches of the History, Life, and Manners in the West" (Philadelphia, 1935), 11 : 72.

the resultant unemployment may, in proportion, have been shorter in the 19th century. For one thing, a continent is settled only once. The proportion of job opportunities to disemployment then must have been quite high as millions of migrants were drawn successively further and further west. For another, the proportion of the labor force at risk of technological displacement was so much smaller. In 1800 about 10 percent of the labor force were employees; in 1860, about 40 percent were; while today about 90 percent work for others.[20] Moreover, the proportion employed in agriculture fell from 90 percent in Jefferson's day to say 10 percent in our own.[21] Since technological displacement affects employees more promptly than the self-employed, and those in nonfarm pursuits more substantially than those farming, such changing proportions would imply an increase in the amount of unemployment produced by technical advance. Thirdly, and most speculatively, the proportion of skilled workers with links to particular plants and industries may be greater today than then. A 19th century canal lubber, cotton mill hand, or farm laborer who lost his job could find work requiring roughly equal ability without great difficulty — in years of normal production. But when the window glass union dissolved in 1927, when carpetweavers, machinists, and semi-skilled workers lost their jobs during the 1930's, they may well have found it more difficult to find work of equal pay and status than the average displaced worker in the past century.[22] On these points, however, your hearings with industry and labor representatives will undoubtedly produce useful and authoritative information.

I turn now to the third major factor in bringing unemployment — cyclical swings. These are, of course, no novelty. As President John Adams wrote many years ago, "I am old enough to remember the war of 1745 and its end, the war of 1755 and its close, the war of 1775 and its termination, the War of 1812 and its pacification. Every one of those wars has been followed by a general distress, embarrassments of commerce, destruction of manufactures, fall of the price of produce and lands."[23] Let us pick three typical depressions of the last century.

A. The first peacetime economic crisis of this nation is that of 1819. A fraternal order of the time described it in passionate terms: "A deep shadow has passed over our land: a commercial and individual gloom has created a universal stillness. In our remotest villages the hammer is

---

[20] See note 8.

[21] Idem.

[22] "The Passing of the National Window Glass Workers," Monthly Labor Review (October 1929). Gladys L. Palmer, "Union Tactics and Economic Change" (1932), is one of the classic studies in the field.

[23] John Adams, "Works," X, p. 384, quoted V. S. Clark, "History of American Manufactures," vol. 1.

not heard."[24] Can we convert such comments into prosaic statistics? Not at this distance. But detailed contemporary figures for what were then our major manufacturing centers — Philadelphia, Pittsburgh, the state of Rhode Island — may help us make a usable guess.[25] For the number one industry, cotton textiles, they lead to an estimate of a 75-percent employment decline. (To put this alongside a standard of our own time we may note that auto manufacturing employment fell about 25 percent, from 1929 to 1930 and about 37 percent from 1937 to 1938.)[26] What of other contemporary industries? Bricklaying employment in Philadelphia, then our biggest city, fell by 50 percent. Brewery employment in Pittsburgh (and presumably elsewhere) fell by only a third. Taking into account these and other figures, I estimate that manufacturing employment for the nation as a whole might have fallen by nearly two-thirds. The 20th Century cannot match this record, fortunately. But we also cannot match the fact that manufacturing then accounted for less than 5 percent of the labor force.[27] And by reckoning in declines for other industries, based on contemporary reports, we come up with an estimate for this crisis year of not more than 4-percent unemployment of the free labor force.

The crisis of 1857 was one of the worst in the nineteenth century. For the 1857–61 period, according to a speech to the Congress made in 1869 by Representative William Kelley, "not one out of five skilled workmen of the country was steadily employed."[28] Furthermore, he added as symptomatic, that when a Philadelphia contractor advertised for 250 hands at 60 cents a day "more than 5,000 offered, a majority of whom were skilled artisans."[29] (A 60-cent rate was about half that paid in Pennsylvania just before the crisis.) Some figures we have for employment trends in the important manufacturing state of Rhode Island in 1857 indicate cotton textile employment falling by 68 percent in a year, jewelry by 78 percent, iron works employment by 43 percent.[30] All in all a decline of two-thirds in jobs in this key State seems a possible estimate. However, the relief figures for Massachusetts, the leading manufacturing state, rose only a third, and pig iron output, the key product of our third major factory

---

[24] "Address of the Society of Tammany or Columbian Order to Its Absent Members" (New York: George L. Buch & Co., 1819), p. 1.

[25] See note 8.

[26] Office of Business Economics, "National Income," 1954 ed., table 26.

[27] See note 8.

[28] William D. Kelley, "Speeches, Addresses, and Letters on Industrial and Financial Questions" (1872), p. 257.

[29] Idem.

[30] "Transactions of the Rhode Island Society for the Encouragement of Domestic Industries in the Year 1857" (1958). p. 77, quoting the Providence Daily Journal. I am indebted to Prof. Clarence Danhof of Tulane for this reference.

state in that period, fell by only a tenth.[31] In 1857 only about 10 percent of our labor force was in factory work — while farming, ocean shipping, and construction were responding to different demands.[32] Hence an unemployment rate greater than say 5 percent would have been most unlikely.

And finally the major extended depression of the last century, that of the 1880's. For 1886 we have a contemporary estimate by the Commissioner of Labor, of 7½ percent of gainful workers unemployed.[33]

Other crises appear in other years. Lingering depression in the 1840's; 1861 a grim precursor of the priorities unemployment of 1941; a long labored period of depression through the middle 1870's, and shorter runs following 1893, etc. To give an indication of these ups and downs, table I shows year to year percent changes in relief loads, in manufacturing production, and in key price series.[34]

What of our 20th century record? Table II shows the trend, and is based on some laborious but still rough estimates that I have prepared for the years prior to the initiation of the outstandingly reliable and meaningful census series on which we have all relied since 1940.[35] What the

---

[31] Data from Benjamin F. French, "History of the Rise and Progress of the Iron Trade of the United States" (1858). Data summarized in K. D. Lumpkin and D. W. Douglas, "Child Workers in America" (1937), app. II.

[32] The total for free, gainfully occupied, aged 16 and over, in 1860 appears in the 1860 census, "Population," p. 680. From this total the number of students (p. 677) were deducted. The number of gainfully occupied slaves was added, estimated for each state as the same proportion of males plus females, aged 10 and over, as were shown in the separate state data for 1850, for white males 15 and over. Analysis of the 1840 census data indicates that virtually all slaves, aged 10 and over, worked and this procedure was not unreasonable. Minor adjustments were made for certain states. For white and free colored children 10 to 15 it was assumed that the labor force participation rates from the 1900 census for native whites would apply, with adjustment for the 10-15, 10-14 age differences. The total for factory employment is that reported in the Manufacturers Census of that year, reprinted in the 1870 census, "Industry and Wealth," p. 393.

[33] First Annual Report of the Commissioner of Labor, "Industrial Depressions" (March 1886), p. 65. The report estimates, on the basis of many field visits and other checks, that of the establishments in the country "such as factories, mines, etc. * * * about 5 percent were absolutely idle during the year ending July 1, 1885, and that perhaps 5 percent were idle a part of the time; or for a just estimate 7½ percent." The estimate is assumed to apply to all gainfully occupied in agriculture, trade, transportation, mining, mechanical trades, and manufactures.

[34] Relief data per 1,000 population: for New York in the earlier years, shown in parentheses, and for Massachusetts, from K. Lumpkin and D. Douglas, op. cit. Production data from Edwin Frickey, "Production in the United States," 1860-1914 (1947), p. 60, using his series adjusted for secular trend. For earlier years the tonnage imports of pig iron, that master material of modern industry, are used as an indication of production sensitivity. Data from French, op. cit., Joseph Swank, "The American Iron Trade in 1876," Annual Report of the American Iron & Steel Association, p. 182.

[35] Unemployment data from the writer's "Annual Estimates of Unemployment in

table reports is what was pretty well set out years ago in Paul Douglas'
landmark study on Real Wages in the United States, 1890 to 1926.

Can we summarize this mass of lives into conclusions relevant to the
committee's concern? I believe so, and would suggest three.

1. No decade has passed without severe unemployment (over 7 percent of the labor force) occurring at least once. And none, except for
that of the 1930's, has passed without seeing at least one year of what we
may call minimum unemployment (3 percent or less.)

2. More than 1 year in every four, a rate of 3 percent (or less) was
achieved, a rate of 5 percent or less was achieved more than half the time.
True, one executive has asserted that "full employment at high wages in
a private enterprise economy is undesirable and self-destroying."[36] But
I think the outstanding American record shows that such full employment
has not been at all self-destroying — except in the irrelevant sense that
all economic and human affairs change.

3. Perhaps the most important inference, however, appears when we
consider both the 19th century indications and the 20th century figures.
For they suggest a paradox: the proportion of the labor force that is exposed to unemployment has risen notably since 1800, but the proportion
actually has shown no trend whatever.

That the proportion exposed to unemployment has gained can be established without much difficulty. For we know that little unemployment appears in farming, among the self-employed, and it is these groups that have
dwindled. Farming occupied 85 percent of our gainful workers in 1800,
today accounts for less than 10 percent.[37] An almost parallel change for
the self-employed took place. (Most farmers are self-employed, of course,
and vice versa.) At the same time the share of factory employment was
rising enormously, from less than 2 percent of our labor force in 1800 to
26 percent today.[38] But factory employment, and its associated construction and transport employment, compose the most unemployment sensitive
portion of the labor force. (If, for example, one charts the changes in
factory employment against those in unemployment for the years since
1900 an extremely close relationship appears.)

---

the United States, 1900-54," in Universities-National Bureau of Economic Research,
"The Measurement and Behavior of Unemployment," Ed. Clarence Long (1957)
production data, 1900-28 from William H. Shaw, "Values of Commodity Output
Since 1869" (1947), p. 23, production data, 1929-54: U.S. Department of Commerce,
"U.S. Output, 1958 National Income Supplement, Deflated GNP." Price data: BLS,
from Census, Historical Statistics of the United States and 1958 Statistical Abstract.

[36] R. I. Nowell, Journal of Farm Economics. February 1947, p. 143.

[37] For 1880, note 8. For 1950 the population census figures were used (1957
Statistical Abstract, p. 213). The BLS data for more recent years are not directly
comparable but suggest much the same percentage.

[38] Cf. note 8.

That the Marxist conclusion did not follow is obvious — perhaps even to those across the air space. Unemployment over the 19th century ran from a minimum of say 1 percent to such peaks as the 4 percent we have surmised for 1819 and 1957, the 7½ percent estimated by the Commissioner of Labor for 1886. We may infer a close similarity between the average prevailing in the 19th century and that prevailing in the 20th century — excepting the years of the great depression. By close similarity I mean that the average differed by less than did the rates for 1923 and 1924, or 1926 and 1927, or 1953 and 1954. Our conclusion is supported for the years since 1869 by the findings in the massive study by William Shaw on production trends.[39]

What produced this happy result? No higher law of economic stability, we may be sure. The major factors are embedded in the causes of our own economic growth — the settling of the continent, the waves of migration, the steady rise in factor productivity and the competitive influences that poured so much of the gains from productivity back into the nation's stream of investment and expenditure. (And as an aside, quite irrelevant unless we wish to project the trend of that growth, it is interesting how much study is being given today to economic development in every country in the world but the one with perhaps the most spectacular combination of real increase and free labor markets — namely, our own.)

But beyond the basic forces of growth we may note two that worked only in the labor markets, helping to counteract any rise in unemployment over the decades. One is the increasing role of women in the labor force. In 1830, 1 in every 12 white women was gainfully occupied, the proportion rising to 2 in 12 by 1890.[40] And for the period from 1900 to today we find that the proportion of our labor force that consists of women rose from 18 to 33 percent.[41] But a characteristic aspect of female employment in today's market is that it generally tends to supplement family income, rather than provide the very means of existence. Women's lower seniority, often lower skills, makes them disproportionately present among those

---

[39] William Howard Shaw, Value of Commodity Output Since 1869 (1947), p. 23. Excluding the 1929-32 contraction no trend appears in the output of finished commodities. Particular value attaches to Shaw's finding of no increase in the severity of contractions, 1929-32 aside, as his is one of the four of five most comprehensive and reliable statistical historical studies ever made of our productive growth.

[40] Cf. the writer's "Population and Labor Force Relationships," p. 15, a paper prepared for the conference on the interrelations of demographic and economic change (1958) for derivation of these estimates. Data for nonwhites involve definition of the labor force under slavery and are irrelevant here.

[41] Cf. David Kaplan and Claire Casey, "Occupational Trends in the United States, 1900 to 1950," table 1, Bureau of the Census Working Paper, No. 5. Figures for a slightly different age interval, plus an extended valuable discussion of long-term trends appear in a major study by Gertrude Bancroft, "The American Labor Force (1958), p. 24 ff. (1957 Current Population Survey data lead to a similar figure).

disemployed. But instead of entering the ranks of the unemployed, they tend to move directly out of the labor force, hardly affecting the unemployment totals. From December 1948 to 1949, for example, millions of men and women were disemployed. While half the men became unemployed, only 18 percent of the women did.[42] This distinction is a major element in explaining our experience after World War II, when for the first time in our history a massive decline in employment occurred without an almost equally massive rise in unemployment.[43]

A second force has been the increasing role of Government in insuring stability of production and thereby of employment. While George Washington's unprecedented policies on tariffs and land bounties were steps in that direction, certainly something new, and potent, was added in the 1930's as in the Employment Act of 1946.

Where do we go from here? The long term trend has shown major forces that tend to reduce labor mobility. But, of course, we have no need for mobility as such: we desire it to reach one or more of our conflicting goals for technological advance, price stability, neighborhood property values and so on. The economist can say little on the values, but the time is overdue for research on the amount of mobility that may be expected under differing policies that are recommended to the citizen and Government policymaker for their adoption.

What about unemployment? Despite the appalling roughness of the data the record to date suggests no tendency to an increase in the unemployment data. And despite the unwisdom of forecasts it hardly looks as though we need anticipate anything like the worst years of the 1930's. Even a thoroughgoing pessimist must admit the enormity of the advance, within the lifetime of a man, from almost total Government inaction to the immediate concern and swift action in the 1948-49 and 1953-54 recessions. The nation has switched to what one may call the visible hand policy.

But in a dynamic economy the best is not good enough for long. We will continue to spill men out of jobs in consequence. And, in Schumpeter's

---

[42] U.S. Bureau of the Census, Annual Report on the Labor Force, 1949, series P–50, No. 19, table 20. These data relate to gross changes, and while being subject to distinct limitations for other uses the steadiness of the contrast between male and female rates justifies their use here. Unfortunately, we lack gross change data for 1953, and because of the sample revision even the absolute figures on unemployment are in question. However, if one looks to the October-December changes in unemployment by sex (U.S. Bureau of the Census, Annual Report on the Labor Force, 1954, series P–50, No. 59, tables C–1 and D–1) a similar pattern is suggested.

[43] Present definitions of unemployment do not class the receipt of unemployment insurance as evidence of unemployment. Although the writer has opposed this position — Review of Economics and Statistics, November 1954 — it is clear that in this particular period some women receiving unemployment compensation were not looking for work with the intensity equal say to that characterizing male unemployed in most years.

TABLE 1. — Business declines, 1837-1915

[Ranked by relief load rise]

	Percentage changes in —					
	Rate of relief —		Pig iron		Wholesale prices	
	Massachusetts	In New York	Production	Imports	Textiles	Metals
1872-76	+143		—24		—22	—39
1837-38		+102		—14	—6	—10
1860-61	—96		—6		+1	+2
1849-50		+60		—29	+5	—5
1892-94	+52		—22		—16	—21
1913-14	+47		—1		—5	—11
1856-57	+30			—16	+7	—1
1843-44		+15		+188	+10	+4
1903-4	+14		—6		0	—11
1907-8	+13		—2		—14	—22
1896-98	+9		0		+4	—7
1840-41		—6		+122	—4	0

TABLE 2. — Business declines, 1900-54

[Ranked by unemployment rises]

	Percentage change				
	Rise in percent civilian labor force unemployed	Output of —		Wholesale textile prices	Wholesale metal prices
		Finished commodities	Gross national product		
1929-32	20.3		—28	—37	—20
1920-21	9.6	—6		—43	—21
1907-8	7.7	—11		—14	—22
1913-14	5.3	—5		—5	—11
1937-38	4.7		—5	—13	0
1953-54	2.5		—2	—2	+1
1903-4	2.2	—2		0	—11
1948-49	2.1			—6	—4
1945-46	2.0		—10	+16	+10

words, technological unemployment * * * linking up as it does with innovation, is cyclical by nature.[44] How much such unemployment we will

---

[44] Joseph Schumpeter, Business Cycles (1939) II: 515.

put up with turns on many conflicting goals — for unemployment, real wages, price stability, income redistribution, defense expenditure. Resolving these imponderables is one of the jobs ahead for American citizens and their government, and in particular this committee.

LONG SWINGS IN AMERICAN ECONOMIC GROWTH

by Moses Abramovitz *

Summary: 1. The economic growth of the United States has taken place in a series of surges during which growth was especially rapid followed by relapses when growth proceeded much more slowly. In periods of rapid growth, output has increased at rates two, and often three, times as fast as in period of slow growth.

2. These waves of acceleration and retardation stand out clearly in records of output when the influence of the relatively short business cycles has been eliminated as far as possible. Clear evidence of such waves can be found in economic records going back at least as far as the third decade of the 19th century. The duration of the waves has usually been between 10 and 20 years. Since this period is two to five times the duration of ordinary business cycles, we refer to the waves in growth as long swings.

3. The long swings in the growth of output were but one aspect of a more general wave characterizing our economic development. Long swings similar to those in output and occurring at about the same time can be found in the records of population growth, immigration, transport development, geographical settlement, internal migration, the growth of cities, price change, the growth of the money supply, the foundation of new corporations, residential buildings, and in still other branches of economic life and in some aspects of noneconomic activity.

4. The long waves in the rate of growth of output reflect similar waves in the rates of growth of resources, both labor and capital; in the rates of growth of productivity; and in the intensity with which resources were employed. These waves in the factors underlying output occurred in a particular sequence which recurred in approximately the same manner during each successive long swing.

5. In the past, the culminating event of each period of retarded growth has been a business depression of unusual severity and almost always of unusually long duration. These severe and protracted depressions began when the long swings in the volume of investment in durable capital entered the rising phase of a new long swing.

* Moses Abramovitz is Professor of Economics at Stanford University. The material here reprinted are his statements before the Joint Economic Committee, Eighty-sixth Congress, April 10, 1959; the questions and discussions of the Congressmen are included. Hon. Paul A. Douglas presided.

6. Although many features of the long swings in economic development can now be described, the cause of these fluctuations is still to be determined. It is not yet known whether they are the result of some stable mechanism inherent in the structure of the U.S. economy, or whether they are set in motion by the episodic occurrence of wars, financial panics, or other unsystematic disturbances. Their pronounced uniformities, however, make it likely that continued study of long swings will shed light on the process of economic growth and on the origins of serious depressions.

I. GENERAL CHARACTER OF LONG SWINGS IN GROWTH

The most important and the most striking feature of U. S. economic growth is the great upward sweep of total output and of output per capita which started in the first half of the last century, or perhaps earlier still, and which is still visibly going on today. Manifestly, however, this sweep of growth has not been steady. Seasonal influences apart, it has been subject to frequent minor interruptions and sometimes to drastic upward and downward movements of an episodic character, the most important of which were connected with wars. In addition, we have suffered the more or less regular interruptions in growth associated with business cycles, a type of disturbance which in this country has involved waves in output which have generally required 3 to 5 years to run their course.

These fluctuations represent familiar and well-established types of disturbances. They are not, however, the only important sources of unsteadiness in growth. Evidence has accumulated that economic development in this country, and in at least some other industrialized countries, has taken place in a series of great surges, followed by periods of much slower growth. These waves of acceleration and retardation in the rate of growth of output stand out clearly after output indexes have been corrected, so far as possible, to eliminate business-cycle fluctuations. The duration of these larger and longer swings in output growth has generally been between 10 and 20 years, although there have been shorter and longer movements of apparently similar character. Because the fluctuations in output which emerge after correction for business cycles are fluctuations in the rate of growth of output rather than in the level of total production, and because the waves are of relatively long duration, they have sometimes been called secondary secular movements or trend cycles. But I shall refer to them simply as long swings. This somewhat neutral title is intended to avoid any premature commitment to the theory that these fluctuations are self-generating cyclical movements whose internal mechanism produces their own recurrence. There are, nevertheless, certain pieces of evidence which point in that direction, and, in any event, the long swings have been marked by a common set of occurrences which repeat themselves from occasion to occasion and which give them a definite character.

The long swings of acceleration and retardation in economic growth are sharply distinguished from business cycles not only by their longer duration but also by other characteristics which make them dramatic elements in our economic history and in the process of economic growth. In particular, the long swings are marked by very large fluctuations in the rate of resource development. Each of the long swings has included a great wave in the level of immigration and in the total number of people added to the population. Each long swing has also involved a wave in the total number of persons added to the labor force. The long swings also manifest themselves in large fluctuations in the net volume of fixed capital formation, and most particularly in towering waves of residential building and of railroad and public utilities construction. Before World War I, each of the long swings in the rate of growth of output involved a renewed surge in the progress of territorial settlement as evidenced by Federal land sales and by the number of miles of canals and railroads opened for traffic. The upward phases of the long swings are also times when the pace of internal migration of people within the country speeds up and when urban growth, more recently suburban growth, proceeds at an unusually rapid pace, only to slow down again after a time.

One common attribute of all these processes of resource development involving the movement of people from country to country and place to place, the formation of households and the birth of children, the foundations of business, and the investment of capital in highly durable forms is that they involve long-term decisions and commitments. Hence they pick up speed and come to fruition slowly and when they slow down, they are not easily or quickly set in motion again. They give rise, therefore, to long waves of resource development and output growth. These processes involving long-term decisions, on the other hand, respond only sluggishly to the impact of the ordinary short and mild business contractions. By contrast, the most prominent feature of short business cycles is a fluctuation in shorter term investment, particularly inventory investment.

While the long swings of acceleration and retardation in growth differ from business cycles in duration and many other features, they are distinctly not free from fluctuations in the volume of unemployment or, more generally, from fluctuations in the intensity with which resources are used. Indeed, each long swing of which we have a definite record has ended in a depression of unusual severity and, with one possible exception, of unusual duration. In one sense, therefore — unless we are to suppose that severe depressions are merely accidental occurrences — we may regard the long swings as the sequence of events which lead up to these catastrophes. An understanding of the long swings may, therefore, help us not only to understand why our rate of long-term growth is subject to acceleration and retardation, they may also be a path by which we can gain firmer knowledge about the severe depressions which are still, perhaps, the most serious disease with which capitalist economies are threatened.

In successive sections of this statement, I propose to describe some of the more prominent features of the long swings in the U. S. economic growth. Section II tells how we make our measures. Section III deals with acceleration and retardation in the growth of output and of economic activity generally. The succeeding sections take up briefly the various processes which combine to form the long swings in the rate of growth of output. Section IV deals with additions to the population and to the labor force, Section V with additions to the stock of capital equipment, that is, with capital formation, Section VI with the rate of growth of productivity, and Section VII with the intensity with which resources are used. Section VIII presents a general conspectus of the various changes in their relation to the long swings in the rate of growth of output and leads up to some suggestions about possible lines of explanation. Now I propose to go into some of these matters in a little more detail.

II. MEASUREMENT OF LONG SWINGS

Just as one must eliminate seasonal fluctuations from time series in order to reveal business-cycle movements clearly, so one must remove the effects of business cycle as well as one can in order to reveal the long swings. Unfortunately, because business-cycle fluctuations are much less regular than seasonal movements, it is not possible to correct time series for the former as well as one can for the latter. The kinds of adjustments that can be made all involve some sort of smoothing process in which averages are computed from the original data over periods believed to be of the same duration as a business cycle. Moving averages of the original data are a common method of smoothing out business cycles.

Those who believe that the normal duration of business cycles is in the neighborhood of 3 to 5 years are inclined to use 5-year moving averages. This corresponds with, although it is not the same as, the average duration of business cycles as revealed by the widely accepted standard business cycle chronology of the National Bureau of Economic Research. Those who believe that, in addition to the relatively short business cycles identified by the National Bureau, there is also a so-called major business cycle, marked by the occurrence of relatively deep depressions which occur at intervals of 8 to 11 years, have often used 9-year moving averages. Still other methods of smoothing out business cycles by calculating moving averages with other periods and with more complicated weighting schemes have been used.

The method employed in my own work is somewhat different. It is a variant of a method long employed by the National Bureau of Economic Research to make measures of secular movements, defined as changes in economic or other magnitudes which do not reverse themselves in the course of a business cycle. This method starts from the fact that business cycles, though they have been on the average some 4 years long, actually vary a great deal in duration. Indeed, the duration of the individual business cycles identified by the National Bureau of Economic Research has ranged between 2½ and 8¼ years. To smooth out the business cycles of experience, therefore, it seems better to strike averages, not over some uniform period of years, as in the normal moving average, but rather over the actual years included in each successive business cycle.

To carry through this procedure, we make use of the standard and widely accepted chronology of business-cycle peaks and troughs established by Wesley C. Mitchell and Arthur F. Burns (6). To obtain values for a series which are, as nearly as possible, free of the influence of business cycles, we compute the average value of the series for all years between the one business-cycle trough and the next. We compute such averages for all business-cycle periods running from trough-to-trough and then for all business-cycle periods running from peak-to-peak. We then intermix the average standings for trough-to-trough cycles with those for peak-to-peak cycles chronologically to obtain a continuous series of averages for overlapping business-cycle periods. Following the National Bureau's usage we refer to these averages as average reference-cycle standings. They are the successive values of a series after the effects of business cycles have been smoothed away as well as possible.

In many types of economic processes, for example, in railroad construction or in immigration, the average reference-cycle standings themselves fluctuate in long waves, and these waves in the average level of a series, when they appear, are often themselves of great interest. In some kinds of economic processes, however, our interest centers in the long swings which may appear, not in the level of the process but in its rate of growth. In such cases, we compute rates of growth per annum between the average reference-cycle standings. We first compute rates of growth between the reference-cycle standings for trough-to-trough cycles, then between reference-cycle standings for peak-to-peak cycles. Again we intermix the two sets of rates of growth chronologically to obtain a continuous series of rates of growth between overlapping pairs of business-cycle periods.

III.   LONG SWINGS IN THE RATE OF GROWTH OF OUTPUT AND OTHER INDICATORS OF ECONOMIC ACTIVITY

I ask you to look first of all at charts 1-A and 1-B which give us our first view of the long swings in economic growth. Chart 1-A shows the annual figures for GNP as estimated by Simon Kuznets — that is the dotted line on that chart — together with the average reference-cycle standings computed from these figures which represent gross national product after the business cycles have been smoothed away. The graph of average reference-cycle standings supports the observation that when business cycles have been smoothed away, the total physical volume of production in this country has, at least since 1870 when these figures begin, risen without significant interruption, apart from the decline associated with the great depression of the 1930's. In short, there have been no long swings in the volume of output.

At the same time, it is apparent that, business cycles apart, total output has sometimes risen along a steeper trend than it has at other times. It is these alternations between acceleration and retardation which are the long swings in growth of output. They stand out much more clearly if we look, not at the average reference-cycle standings of output, but, as in Chart 7-B, at the rate of change per annum between average reference-cycle standings. Chart 1-B displays the large range over which the rate of growth of total output has swung during the last 80 years. It also suggests that the rate of growth does not fluctuate erratically, but rather rises and falls in wide movements usually lasting for considerable periods.

Such fluctuations in the rate of growth are a characteristic not only of total output but of all the major branches of industry with the sole exception of agriculture. Arthur F. Burns' famous study of "Production Trends" made as long ago as 1934, showed that each long swing in the rate of growth and total output was accompanied by similar long swings occurring at approximately the same time in most individual sectors of nonagricultural production.

In chart 2 I have been able to put together some figures that carry this story somewhat further.

Senator BUSH. Could I ask a question on chart 1-B before you leave it there? Gross national product in 1929 prices. I note that for instance in the period of the twenties there you have the sharpest of drops on that chart. Why is that?

Mr. ABRAMOVITZ. That is because during the great depression we had a protracted period of years when total output was not only growing more slowly, which is the usual reason why this graph falls, but actually declining so that the rate of growth fell to negative figures, sir. I was going ——

Senator BUSH. The line that I refer to begins in about 1923 and ends in 1930, all of which was a period I thought of very substantial growth.

Mr. ABRAMOVITZ. Yes, but the rate of growth from about 1923 began to proceed more slowly. During the latter years of the 1920's year by year our rate of growth was slowing up. That is shown on this chart by a drop in the line. Then after 1929 we began to have an actual decline in output and that, of course, is a negative rate of growth and that is the first time we had that for such a protracted period in this country.

The CHAIRMAN. That is a very interesting point, and your figures seem to indicate that the rate of growth was falling very rapidly in the period when the financial wizards were saying we were in a new economic era and going forward more rapidly than we had ever gone before.

Mr. ABRAMOVITZ. I expect some more of that to come out later. It is characteristic of these long swings that we reach our most rapid rate of growth early in what you might call the expansion phase of the long swing, that the rate of growth thereupon tends to fall, and after some years of growth at a falling rate we suffer or, at least in the past we have suffered, a serious depression when, of course, the rate of growth has fallen to extremely low levels.

The CHAIRMAN. Apparently the rate of growth was negative prior to 1929.

Mr. ABRAMOVITZ. That arises from the fact that this rate of growth is not measured year by year, Mr. Chairman, but measured between average reference-cycles standings and those average standings for business cycles were centered at the middle of business cycle periods. The rate of growth per annum between these average standings was then centered at the midpoint between the business cycle midpoints and that apparently suggests that the rate of growth reached negative figures before 1929. It reached it, so to speak, corrected for business cycles.

It is not true, of course, that literally the rate of growth measured year by year uncorrected for business cycles would have reached negatives figures before 1929.

Senator BUSH. Then what is the value of this information?

Mr. ABRAMOVITZ. Sir, we are trying to take a look at the behavior of economic time series corrected for business cycles in order to center our attention on longer movements. Just as we find that by correcting monthly figures for seasonal movements we have a useful way of looking at data even though it does not tell us literally how output or prices moved from month to month, so I think we are going to find that looking at longer movements in data, corrected for business cycles, is going to be a useful way of arranging and assembling figures for comparative purposes.

Now I refer you to chart 2 in which I would like to try to point out to you how widely diffused these long swings in economic growth are, how many different aspects of economic life they seem to be found in. Chart 2 has 4 pages of graphs. It suggests that the long swings in the rate of growth of GNP and of industrial production since the Civil War were diffused, not only throughout the component sectors of GNP, but that they are matched by similar swings in the rates of growth of a wide range of indicators of economic activity such as wholesale prices, money supply, capital imports, new incorporations, the prices of common stocks, railroad bond yields, and immigration. The list could easily be extended. The main point here is simply to gain an impression of the fact that the behavior of these various elements in economic life is moving along in roughly the same fashion. Indeed the impression of rough similarity I think would have been stronger had there not been some mistakes in the charting. Two of the series in which the original computations were made on a monthly basis were charted on the wrong scale and consequently hardly seem to move at all. In the latter sheets we are seeing some of the series which represent long-term decisions and which represent, I think, the core of the long swing, the kind of process out of which it develops.

Table 1, if you will turn to that, brings out an important feature of the behavior of the series whose rates of growth are shown in chart 2. The table presents, for each series a chronology of the years in which the rates of growth reached their peak and trough levels in successive long swings. Apparently, the long swings in the rates of growth of this wide variety of indicators of economic activity not only conform generally to the swings in GNP and industrial production, but their turning points cluster in narrow bands of years which center upon the turning dates in the rate of growth of total output. There are very few cases, if you glance down the columns, in which a date in one column occurs as early as those in the preceding column or as late as those in the succeeding column.

Chart 2 and table 1 I think carry the strong suggestion that in the absence of actual estimates of aggregate output, we might have detected the existence of long waves in the rate of growth of aggregate output from the behavior of a considerable variety of series taken together and we might use the consensus of their turning points to establish a rough chronology of the peaks and troughs in the rate of growth of aggregate economic activity.

This is the raison d'être of table 2, which we use to indicate the existence of long waves in the rate of growth of economic activity before the Civil War. For this period, there are very few series of production statistics. But one can find series representing the construction of buildings, canals, railroads, and ships, the imports and exports of goods, the import of capital, the transport of goods by canals, wholesale prices, interest rates, stock prices, money supply, and immigration. Not all these activities can be studied in all years, but even in the second decade of the century, there were some important indicators of the growth of activity. Charts of the rate of growth of these series, which I have not reproduced, reveal the existence of long swings similar to those we observed in the post-Civil War period. Again, as table 2 indicates, the turning points cluster in relatively narrow bands of years. This suggests that the waves were general in character and it encourages one to try to fix upon a single set of turning points, which may be said to represent in a crude way the turning points in the rate of growth of aggregate economic activity, by depending upon the consensus of the turning points in the individual series.

This we have done in table 3 which presents an attempt at a rough chronology of the peaks and troughs in the rate of growth of total output since the beginning of the 19th century. Before the Civil War, as stated, it depends on the consensus of the behavior of a wide variety of series. From 1864 to 1881, we depend on Frickey's Index of Industrial and Commercial Production, and from 1886 forward, we use the turning points in the rate of growth of GNP. The chronology permits us to say that in the 124 years between 1814 and 1938, there were nine long swings with an average duration of approximately 14 years. The individual swings varied widely in duration, from about 6 to 21 years, but while that is a wide range it is no wider proportionately than the range of duration over which business cycles vary because they have ranged in duration between 2½ to 8 years. That is a wider range proportionately than the 6 to 21 years within which the durations of the long swings have fallen. The suggestion offered by the table that the average duration of the long swings was shorter after the Civil War than it was before is due almost entirely to the inclusion in our list of two short movements whose admissibility to a chronology of long swings may be thought to be in doubt. One is the short period of retardation which our measures suggest interrupted the spurt of the 1880's. The other is the short retardation association with World War I and its aftermath. Had we considered these movements too small or too short to be admitted to our list, the duration of the long swings would have appeared to be longer on the average and less variable. Closer study may suggest that this is, indeed, the better practice.

For the time being, however, the present method of organizing the investigation seems best. The average duration of the long swings would also appear somewhat longer if we were to take into account the record of recent years. A variety of causes have combined to produce an unbroken period of retardation in growth which has now lasted for some 20 years and whose end cannot yet be determined.

I turn now to some comments about the height and depth of the long swings in the rate of growth of output. Table 4 presents measures of the amplitude of the long wave in the rate of growth of GNP and its major components. Column (1) shows the average difference in percentage points between the rates of growth at the peaks of the long swings, when growth was most rapid, and that at succeeding troughs when growth was slowest. Column (2) records the results of the same calculations made from troughs to peaks, showing the number of percentage points by which growth rose from any given trough to the succeeding peak. Column (3) enables us to compare these differences with the long-term rate of growth achieved over the whole 80-year period. The measures tell us that GNP grew over the entire period at an overall average rate of just under 4 percent per annum. That, of course, is a familiar figure.

During long swings, however, after smoothing out business cycles, the rate of growth rose and fell, on the average, about 4 percentage points. Roughly, therefore, we can think of the long swings in the rate of growth of GNP as being of the same order of magnitude as the long-term rate of growth. They involve a movement of the rate of growth from about 2 percent per annum when it is low to about 6 percent per annum when it is high. I would like to point out that this is indeed a very considerable difference, the difference between 2 percent per annum and 6 percent per annum. It is the difference between the rate of growth during the last few years when I think many people have been concerned and dissatisfied with the rate of growth which the economy has achieved and the rate of growth which we would like to see the economy attain and, if possible, maintain consistently.

The most unsteady elements in the growth of total output are patently in the realm of capital formation. And within this area, the most volatile major division is construction whose rate of growth fluctuates through a range about twice as large as does the output of producer durable equipment and about four times as large as gross national product. On a net basis, of course, the fluctuations of capital formation are still more violent. I would like to point out that this behavior of construction, that is, the volatility of construction during the long swings, contrasts with its behavior in shorter fluctuations in which producer-durable equipment and more particularly, inventory investment are much more volatile than is construction. So we can begin to think, if you like, about these longer swings as being connected with great fluctuations in construction activity as contrasted with the shorter business-cycle movements which are more closely connected with fluctuations in producer-durable equipment and inventory investment.

The broad features of the process out of which these swings in output growth arise can be most conveniently grasped if we consider that changes in output resolve themselves into three elements: Changes in resources —

labor, capital, and land — available for use; changes in the productivity of resources; and changes in the intensity with which resources are utilized. In principle, these various elements of economic change could speed up or slow down independently of one another. One of them might display long swings in growth and the others not.

Actually, it appears that the long swings in output growth arise out of an interlocked sequence of changes in all three elements, resource growth, productivity growth, and changes in the intensity of use of resources. All display long swings, and they do so in a certain order which gives us a first glimpse into the cause of these fluctuations. The succeeding sections present some pieces of evidence about the participation of each constituent element in the long swings of output growth.

IV. LONG SWINGS IN THE GROWTH OF POPULATION AND LABOR FORCE

The long swings in output growth have been accompanied by long swings of similar duration in the growth of the population and of the labor force. Chart 3 brings out some of the essential facts about the fluctuations in population growth. It suggests, not only that population growth was subject to long swings, but also that these swings were somewhat smaller before World War I than they have been since that time. In part, this change arises from the great steadiness in the growth of the native-born population before 1914 and in part from the fact that changes in the growth of the native-born lagged behind those in the growth of the foreign-born and in immigration. So these two sources in change of population growth were to a certain extent counter balancing in the period before World War I but since that time not only have there been much larger fluctuations in the rate of growth of the native-born population but also those fluctuations have occurred more nearly synchronously with changes in the level of immigration, with the result that we have had much total fluctuation in the growth of the population.

The CHAIRMAN. Dr. Abramovitz, to what degree can you make comparisons of the growth of immigration and the period after 1924 as compared to the period before 1924, because we placed very restrictive legislation reducing the total flow of immigration into the country in the acts I believe of 1923 and 1924?

Mr. ABRAMOVITZ. Nevertheless, the changes in the level of immigration have been considerable. Immigration went down very markedly during the Great Depression, it rose again in the period of recovery from the Great Depression and these swings jibed in time with a similar swing in the rate of growth of the native-born population.

Senator BUSH. Is it not true that as the native-born population growth rate slowed down during the war so immigration did also?

Mr. ABRAMOVITZ. Yes; that is right.

Chart 3-A develops these points. It compares changes in the amounts of natural increase and of immigration with changes in the growth of total population. It is clear that before World War I, changes in the level of immigration were a far more important element in accounting for changes in population increase than were changes in natural increase of population. Since World War I, the position is reversed. Table 5 expresses this shift in figures. If you look in the last column of table 5, it tells us that before World War I, changes in the volume of immigration usually accounted for 60 percent or more, sometimes much more, of the changes in the decadal increases of population. Since World War I, however, changes in natural increase have been between 60 and 90 percent of the changes in population growth. This reversal has been due not so much to the fact that changes in immigration have become smaller, but that changes in the amounts of natural increase disturbed by two great wars and by a great and protracted depression, have become much larger.

Since long waves in the volume of immigration have been so prominent, it is no surprise that there have also been long waves in the growth of the labor supply, since of course the bulk of the immigrants were of working age. With one exception, each long swing in the rate of growth of gross national product was matched by a similar swing in the number of persons added to the labor force. The one exception occurs during World War I which interrupted the flow of immigrants and so pushed the growth of the labor force down at a time when the pace of output growth speeded up. Chart 4 shows that the swings in labor force additions reflect the large fluctuations in immigration, and before World War I, at least, it was the waves in immigration which dominated the fluctuations of labor force restriction on immigration, it has been a fluctuation in the degree-of participation of the native-born population which has accounted for fluctuations in the growth of the labor force. The reasons for that shift from relatively stable rates of participation of the native population in the labor force to one of fluctuation in the participation of the native-born in the labor force makes an interesting story and perhaps if the committee is interested later on I could say a few more words about it.

The long waves in immigration go back some time before the Civil War. This fact is portrayed in chart 4-A, which finds such swings as far back as 1851 in the form of actual increases and declines in the volume of immigrants and still further back in the form of acceleration and retardation in the growth of immigration.

Table 6 compares the dates when labor force growth and immigration reached their long-swing peaks and troughs with those when the rate of growth of output did. It is apparent that immigration lagged behind output growth and that the lag of labor force growth has been, if anything, still longer. This is a rather important point for an understanding of the forces out of which these long swings grow and what makes them cumulate because we can infer from this lag of labor force growth behind the rate of growth of output that the long swings in output growth cannot be due to changes in labor force growth alone. The rate of growth of output typically begins to speed up while the growth of the labor force is still declining and begins to slow down while the growth of the labor force is still rising. So there must be some other forces at work which account for the early upswings in the rate of growth of output other than an increase in the rate of growth of our labor force.

Now just a few words about immigration. The great importance of the waves in net immigration, that is, in the balance of immigrants over emigrants, in producing waves in labor force growth, especially before 1914, naturally leads one to ask what controlled the volume of immigration. The most likely answer is the state of the job market as judged, for example, by the rate of unemployment. Several reasons may be assigned for this plausible connection. Although the basic decision to immigrate is one that depends on an assessment of long-term opportunities in this country, the time of immigration is likely to be postponed if jobs in this country become scarce for any considerable period. New arrivals traditionally had the most difficulty in finding work. Secondly, when unemployment rose, the number of foreign-born who chose to return home would naturally rise. Recent immigrants were often the first to be laid off. Thirdly, many immigrants who depended on relatives in this country for passage money, would have found such help harder to obtain when unemployment here was high.

Chart 4 shows that there was a considerable similarity between the long swings in unemployment, which I plotted in an inverted direction, so when unemployment goes down this chart of unemployment rates goes up, and those in immigration since 1900, provided we disregard the time during World War I, when the two indexes naturally moved in opposite directions. This connection also helps account for the lag of immigration and of labor force growth behind the curve of output growth. The unemployment rate naturally falls most rapidly when output rises at the fastest pace. But when the growth of output first begins to decline, the rate of growth is still likely to be higher than that of labor force growth. So, for a time at least, unemployment continues to sink and immigration to rise.

V. LONG SWINGS IN CAPITAL FORMATION

Long swings also characterize the growth of the stock of capital. We may judge this from figures, representing the volume of capital formation, portrayed in chart 5. Here we see that the great waves in the level of capital formation are to be found chiefly in the volume of construction, particularly in residential and railroad construction. These volumes of construction have moved within a range which is double or triple at the peak what it is at the trough. The same might be said of capital expenditures of public utilities which are thrown together with those of railroads in a similar graph in chart 6, which you will look at in a moment. In other branches of capital formation the long waves show themselves only in attenuated form. They appear as waves of acceleration and retardation in growth. Total gross capital formation displays swings of intermediate severity. They reflect the towering waves of residential and public utility construction, but their declines are cushioned and shortened by the milder responses of other kinds of investment.

An interesting sidelight of chart 5 is the behavior of the output of producers' durable equipment. The long wave responses in this category have become progressively more severe with the passage of time and, unfortunately, with the increasing importance of this kind of investment. In the 1870's and 1880's when the mechanization of U.S. industry was first beginning, and when purchases of mechanical equipment were still very small, but growing very rapidly, producers' durable equipment showed no long swing declines at all. In the 1890's the decline was very brief and mild. But the declines after 1907, in the early 1920's and the early 1930's, became progressively deeper and longer. It is plausible to suppose that this behavior reflects the increasing maturity of this type of investment expenditure. It was able to resist long swing declines when its primary growth rate was extremely steep, but became less capable of resistance as its long term rate of growth declined.

Chart 6 is designed to cast at least a dim light upon the causes of the great swings in capital formation in residential building and in transport and public utilities development. Both rise and fall in waves which correspond roughly with those in population growth. The rationale of the connection between population growth and these types of construction is, of course, not far to seek. It would, however, be too simple to consider changes in population growth as the sole or even dominant cause of the waves in building. Nevertheless, the connection is sufficiently important to be worth emphasis even in this brief introduction to the long swings process.

In tables 7–A and 7–B we compare the timing of the peaks and troughs of the rate of growth of output with those of the volume of capital formation. In the pre-Civil War period (table 7–A), we must depend on a variety of indicators to gage the turning points in total capital formation. In table 7–B we have the help of estimates of aggregate ance of the evidence suggests that the volume of capital formation reaches the peaks and troughs of its long swings later, often much later, than does the rate of growth of economic activity at large.

It is the same story in both tables for two different periods. If you just look down the columns you will see the dates in the lower portions of the column which represent peaks and troughs of capital formation are almost invariably later in time than the peaks and troughs in the rate of growth of economic activity.

From this we may conclude, as we did in the case of labor supply, that the long swings in the rate of growth of output cannot be due to the swings in the rate of growth of capital stock alone. It is not just that we are getting to have more capital to work with which permits us to raise our rate of growth of output. The latter begins to speed up when the volume of additions to capital stock is still declining and it begins to fall when the volume of additions to capital stock is still rising. The force of this conclusion is further strengthened by the reflection that we measure additions to capital stock by the volume of investment. The actual completion of workable units of capital stock, installing them in the factories, making them ready for use, bringing them in to a shape in which they are ready for use, however, necessarily lags behind the volume of investment by some time, long or short, depending upon the nature of the capital. So I have pointed out that the long swings in the rate of growth of output cannot depend simply on the rate of growth of stock of labor, supply of labor, nor on the long swings of the rate of growth of the stock of capital, and now I have to say something to explain this gap in the argument so far, and in the next section I am going to try to do that.

VI. LONG SWINGS IN PHYSICAL OUTPUT, INPUT AND PRODUCTIVITY

The fact that the long swings in the rate of growth of total output begin to rise while the growth of our stock of resources, both labor and capital, is still falling and begin to fall while the pace of resource growth is still rising can be accounted for by the behavior of the long swings in productivity growth. Chart 7 displays curves representing the rate of growth of GNP, of an index of physical output (that is, of tangible commodities, not services), of an index of the total input of resources, including both labor and capital, and of an index of productivity (that is of output per unit of labor and capital combined).

Perhaps I ought to say a sentence about the meaning of total index resources that combines both labor and capital. I think the best way to grasp the meaning of such index of total input of resources is to think of it as an index which shows how total physical output would have behaved if the productivity of labor and capital had remained fixed and only the amounts of labor and capital utilized had been changed. We are getting a picture of how output would have changed if productivity had been constant. That is the real meaning of an index of total input. Then by dividing this input into output we obtain an indicator of output per unit of input, that is, of productivity.

Senator BUSH. Do you mind my asking you how you define input? I am not quite familiar with that.

Mr. ABRAMOVITZ. Perhaps the simplest way to think of it is as real man-hours of labor utilized. That is the chief component of this index of total input. It is an estimate of number of man-hours of labor actually used.

With this there is combined an index of the amount of capital utilized and these two components of the resources which we use, labor and capital, have been weighted in a way which expresses their importance in the base period.

Senator BUSH. How reliable are these figures on which you base these charts going back so far? I would like you to comment on that.

Mr. ABRAMOVITZ. It is difficult to frame a brief comment, sir.

Senator BUSH. I will withdraw the question because we want to get on with this statement. I will withdraw the question.

Mr. ABRAMOVITZ. Chart 7 enables us to make a number of observations. In the first place, with minor qualifications, the long swings in physical output have been much like those in GNP. In the second place, the long swings in total input resemble those in physical output. Since the most important element in input is the number of man-hours of labor employed, this is, of course, only to be expected. As chart 7 and table 8 make clear, however, the fluctuations of total input, in percentage points, are smaller than those in physical output. Indeed, the showing of table 8 in this respect would have been much more impressive had we measured the changes in the rate of growth of output for periods strictly comparable with the long swings in total input. The relative steadiness of total input implies a long swing in productivity growth. And as chart 7 indicates, the turning points of the long swings in total input and in productivity occur at about the same time as those in physical output. Table 9 confirms this observation and, indeed suggests that input may tend to move in long swings which are not only smaller than those of output but which also lag behind them by a short period. The result is that there is some evidence for the view that productivity growth tends to rise and fall in waves which precede those of output by a short interval. While these are the indications, the differences in time are neither long enough nor consistent enough to insist upon in view of the general crudity of our measures.

The CHAIRMAN. Dr. Abramovitz, may I ask a technical question on chart 7?

In your measurement of output per unit of input you seem to have that upon a negative scale, namely minus 2, and minus 4. Is that a typographical error?

Mr. ABRAMOVITZ. The scale for output per unit of input is on the right side of the chart, but I ought to have the negative figures on the left side removed, quite right.

Senator BUSH. That left-hand column then would apply to what?

Mr. ABRAMOVITZ. Each of these little graphs, Senator Bush, has its own scale on the left side. You will see that for total input there is a scale running from 0 to 4 more or less on the same level with the graph.

The CHAIRMAN. I suggest you put the unit of input on a different chart.

Mr. ABRAMOVITZ. Let me make an attempt to get the chart redesigned. You are quite right. There was some rush in preparing the charts.

We have it then that the tendency for long swings in the rate of growth of total output to precede those in the rate of growth of resources depends upon an equally early swing in the rate of growth of productivity. We must not suppose, however, that these long swings in productivity growth represent only, or even chiefly, an alternation in the rate at which advances in applied technology or in organizational techniques are exploited. The difficulty is that our measures do not isolate the effects of such progress on observed productivity growth from the effects of changes in the intensity of utilization of employed resources. We have already seen that there are long swings in unemployment rates, and we may take this to mean that there are also long waves in the intensity of resource use generally. Our measures of input and productivity do make some allowance for the intensity with which resources are used, for labor input is measured in terms of the number of man-hours actually employed. But they do not allow for changes in the intensity with which employed workers are used. They do not, in short, allow for changes in the flow of work. This is important even in the case of production workers in industry. It is still more important in the case of nonproduction workers in industry, many of whom are kept on the job regardless of the state of demand.

Finally, the measures of input and productivity make no allowance for idle capital. Since, as we shall see below, the acceleration in the rates of growth of output and, therefore, of input, occur in good part in the course of recoveries from deep depressions, I am inclined to assign an important share of the responsibility for the concomitant accelerations in productivity growth to a rapid rise in the intensity of the use of employed resources. Similarly, I believe that one factor, perhaps the chief factor, which causes the rate of growth of productivity to slow down is that the economy approaches full utilization of its employed workers and of the stock of capital already installed. Thereafter, so long as nearly full utilization of employed resources is maintained, productivity can grow only in the degree that the quality of equipment and the organization of industry can be improved. Still later in each long swing, however, the rate of growth of productivity slows up still more. As we shall see, the culminating event of each long swing is the occurrence of a severe depression during which the load factor, so to speak, upon employed resources deteriorates, and this checks still more the observed rate of growth of productivity and sometimes pushes it down to negative figures.

Now I come to the question of the connection between long swings and severe depressions.

VII. LONG SWINGS AND SEVERE DEPRESSIONS

The connection between the long swings in economic growth and the occurrence of severe depressions was noted years ago by Arthur F. Burns (2). We may describe this connection in the following terms. The retardation phase of each long swing in output growth has culminated in a depression of unusual severity or in a succession of depressions of lesser severity interrupted by only short-lived or disappointing recoveries. The evidence supporting this generalization is somewhat more extensive than Burns was able to produce. Whereas Burns' survey was confined to the period beginning in the 1880's, the observations presented in table 10 go back to the second decade of the 19th century.

To select periods of severe depression, I have relied primarily upon Willard Thorp's famous book, "Business Annals." The manner in which Thorp characterized each year from 1812 to 1931 is reproduced in the appendix note to table 10. I used the National Bureau annual chronology of business-cycle peaks and troughs to determine the peak years preceding the beginning of severe depressions and the trough years preceding the beginning of sustained recovery. My selection of periods of severe depressions corresponds with Burns during the period he covered, that is, since 1870. Burns, however, considered that a depression had given way to recovery at the beginning of any business-cycle revival of whatever magnitude. He therefore took the severe slump beginning in 1892 to have ended in 1894 and that beginning in 1907 to have ended in 1908.

Guided by Thorp's "Annals" and, after 1900, also by Lebergott's estimate of unemployment (see chart 4 above), I assume that the revivals of 1894–95 and 1908–10 and 1911–13 were weak, incomplete, or transient and that sustained recoveries did not begin until 1897 and 1915, respectively. Let me add that this selection of severe depression would correspond to a selection which any economic historian would make, almost without reference to such a standard source as Thorp's "Business Annals." They represent the famous great depressions of our history.

The CHAIRMAN. In 1873 to 1879?

Mr. ABRAMOVITZ. Yes.

The CHAIRMAN. The years from 1893?

Mr. ABRAMOVITZ. That is correct. 1907 and on, 1920–21, and 1929–32. And before the Civil War the depression beginning around 1853 and ending around 1858, and before that 1837 down to 1843.

In table 10, I compare the peaks and troughs of the severe contractions with those of the long swings in the volume of capital formation as indicated by the weight of the evidence in tables 7–A and 7–B, and from 1892, by the behavior of total gross and net capital formation. The rationale of this comparison is the hypothesis that so long as the long-term demand for additional capital is strong and rising, business recessions will not cause, or be accompanied by, serious slumps in investment in durable equipment and construction. Business recessions will, therefore, tend to be mild and brief and recoveries will carry the economy back to full employment. Contrariwise, when the long-term demand for additional capital equipment slumps, depressions will be deep; revivals, if they occur, will be weak or transient and sustained recovery delayed.

If we may assume that the long-term demand for additional capital equipment is rising when the volume of long-term capital formation is in the upward phase of a long swing, then we should expect these periods to be free of serious depressions, but when the peaks of the long swings in capital formation have been reached and passed, we may expect a severe depression to occur. The period of depression, in turn, may be expected to last until the long swing in capital formation has turned up again. In short, the peaks and troughs of severe depressions may be expected to occur at about the same time as those of the long swings in long-term investment.

The general showing of table 10 is clearly consistent with these expectations. Of course, even if this hypothesis is valid, we have gone only a short step toward an explanation of the depth and duration of serious depressions. We still have to explain why there are long swings in the volume of long-term investment. The next section refers to some alternative lines of explanation.

VIII. FIVE BASIC CHRONOLOGIES IN THE LONG SWING PROCESS

It is now possible to draw together a good deal of the evidence presented in earlier sections and to attempt a brief description of the sequence in which certain important processes involved in the long swings take place. We do this by providing in table II a combined chronology of the peaks and troughs of the long swings in the various processes already discussed.

What emerges from a study of this chronology is the conclusion that there is a roughly uniform sequence of events during long swings, at least with respect to the processes and occurrences described earlier. By and large events follow one another in a round indicated by the order in which the various processes are arranged in the table. Sustained recovery from depression brings a period of accelerated growth in productivity and output which is succeeded by retardation in growth fairly early in the course of the long swing.

The rates of growth of labor supply and capital stock, more particularly the stock of structures, however, keeps rising for some years after retardation in output and productivity growth begin. When additions to resources, especially the volume of additions to capital stock, begin to fall off, the economy drops into a severe and usually protracted depression. That of course is because additions to capital stock is another name for the level of investment and the level of investment is a large part of total expenditure.

In the course of that depression the secular rate of growth of output and productivity, that is the rate corrected for business cycles, falls still further. Though it reaches bottom fairly soon, the volume of additions to resources continues to fall for some time. And not till the volume of capital formation enters a new long upswing does the economy enjoy sustained recovery from depression, a development which in turn drives the rate of growth of output and productivity to high levels once more.

The recurrent sequence of events just traced is a logical one, in the sense that each occurrence in the sequence helps account for the next. Let me mention a few of the more important connections.

To begin with, sustained recovery from depression leads to acceleration in output growth. This is, in part, a mere reflection of the increase in long-term investment and consumption which are normal parts of recovery. Still more, however, it reflects the need to build up inventories which were liquidated in the previous depression and are now needed to support higher levels of output and sales. The acceleration, finally, is facilitated by the existence of a large body of idle labor and capital.

Next, the rapid growth of output permits employed labor and existing equipment to be used more intensively. There is, therefore, a concomitant rise in the rate of growth of productivity.

The forces that make for acceleration of output and productivity growth, however, are necessarily self-limiting. The rate of growth of output must slow down after a time if only because existing capacity is becoming more fully employed. Bottlenecks appear, first at isolated points in the economy, and then with increasing frequency as full employment of labor and capital is approached. As the rate of growth output tapers off, inventory investment, which is closely tied to output, begins to decline, and this reduces the growth of demand.

Similar causes also act to inhibit the growth of productivity. Just as acceleration of productivity growth was based on more intensive utilization of employed labor and existing capital, the gradual disappearance of idle capacity and the need to hire additional workers forces productivity growth to depend more nearly exclusively on the progress of technology and organization.

The factors which bring acceleration in output growth to an end and lead to retardation, also act to promote a continued rise in the rate of growth of resources. Foremost in importance are the decline in unemployment and the more intensive utilization of capital. The reduction of unemployment spurs the growth of the labor force, partly by encouraging a flow of immigrants and partly because many marginal members of the working force enter the labor market when jobs become easier to find in convenient places and at convenient hours.

Improvement in the job market also spurs population growth. This is in part the consequence of a rise in immigration. In part also, it reflects the response of the marriage rate and the birth rate to the greater security that accompanies a firm labor market.

The rise in population growth stimulates several important elements of long-term capital formation, namely, housing construction, public utility investment, and the building of community facilities. The gradual disappearance of idle capacity stimulates others, namely industrial and commercial construction. We should also note that when new industrial capacity is installed, it will not be distributed geographically in the same way as existing capacity was. The evolution of technology and markets dictates a geographical shift in production. This requires a redistribution of population and increases still more the need for residential, public utility and local government construction.

Indeed there is clear evidence of long swings in internal migration which accompany the long swings in the growth of resources.

So long as long-term investment expenditures continue to grow fast enough, they generate a rising demand for goods which absorbs our growing capacity to produce. The economy then enjoys a period of steady growth at a pace which is constrained by the growth of resources themselves and by the progress of technology and interrupted only by minor recessions. But if the growth of demand for additional durable capital tapers off enough, still more if it declines, the economy falls into a severe depression. There then ensues a progression of responses in the realms of productivity growth, population growth, and capital formation which causes the economy to operate below capacity for a protracted period.

While we can detect the logic in the progression of events during the long swings, and while it is patent that each event helps explain the occurrence of the next, such a recital as I have just made is woefully incomplete as a theory of the long swings as a whole. The most important missing element, among many, is an explanation of the fact that, after a time, the amounts we are adding to resources, particularly the volume of capital formation, cease to grow at an adequate rate, begin to fall, and so set the stage for depression. Why do these processes not settle down to a steady rate of advance which would sustain steady growth in demand and in output at large?

Several lines of explanation suggest themselves, and these must still be investigated. One stems from the observation made earlier that construction activity, especially residential, railroad, and public utility construction, has moved in long waves of about the same duration as that of our long swings in output growth. This leads to the hypothesis that there is something in the nature of the construction industry and of the real estate market which tends to produce a long cycle in building. This long wave in construction may well be enough to account for the recurrence of severe and protracted depressions and for the long swings in productivity, output, and population growth which flow from them. Needless to say any such theory would need to take into account the reciprocal influence of events in the rest of the economy upon the construction industry itself.

Another line of explanation would place heavy emphasis on changes in money supply and other developments in the financial markets. Professor Friedman, who I understand will appear before this committee later in its sessions, has shown that there have been long swings in the rate of growth of the supply of money which have run along with, but lagged behind, those in the rate of growth of output. He has also shown that, whereas in ordinary recessions, there is mere retardation in the growth of the money supply, severe slumps were marked by an actual decline in the money stock. These facts can be fitted into the story already related without difficulty. We can put the case in the following terms. So long as the stock of money, corrected for business cycles, rises at a sufficient rate, prosperity is well maintained, and output rises steadily, subject only to minor recessions. Presumably, such steady growth would be traceable to the stimulus which rising money balances afford to expenditures of all kinds. But if the rate of growth of money balances falls below a certain level, a fortiori, if money stock declines, demand ceases to rise fast enough to absorb our growing capacity to produce, and investment expenditure then falls.

The CHAIRMAN. Mr. Abramovitz, how do you define the term "stock of money rising at a sufficient rate"? Do you mean that prices were steady or rising sufficiently to cause output to rise, or what?

Mr. ABRAMOVITZ. It has to rise at a rate which is sufficient with prices steady or at a rate which is sufficient, taking account of the rise in prices which may occur. In short, the real demand for output has to grow and the real demand for output in Friedman's opinion is connected with the rate of growth of the money supply. That is with the rate of growth of real money balances held by people.

The CHAIRMAN. I do not want to anticipate what you said but the period 1897 to 1914 was one of very rapid increase in the gold supply and the money supply, a period of rising prices, but I will think you will find it was a period of a slowing down of the rate of economic growth, is not that true?

Mr. ABRAMOVITZ. The period from the middle nineties to about 1900 was one of great acceleration but then from about 1900 on we suffered retardation in the rate of growth.

The CHAIRMAN. Yet that was a period in which the gold supply was rising, the money supply was rising, prices were rising?

Mr. ABRAMOVITZ. Quite true.

The CHAIRMAN. And yet economic growth was slowing down?

Mr. ABRAMOVITZ. Slowing down presumably because we had already mobilized our existing resources and so real output could not increase faster after that point than the growth of resources and productivity.

The CHAIRMAN. I am saying Mr. Friedman's explanation that you have to have an adequate increase in the supply of money certainly was not true in this period. You did have more than an adequate increase in the supply of money and yet the rate of growth slowed down.

Mr. ABRAMOVITZ. But it was sufficient in his opinion to keep demand high enough to absorb our growing resources and so to prevent the recurrence of a serious depression.

The CHAIRMAN. You mean if we had not had this development in the supply of gold we would have had a major collapse.

Mr. ABRAMOVITZ. You would have had a major collapse sooner.

The CHAIRMAN. That is hypothetical, I would say.

Mr. ABRAMOVITZ. These various explanations of the rate of growth, I am afraid, are hypothetical.

Representative REUSS. Is it not Mr. Friedman's point that while an adequate rise in the stock of money currency and demand deposits is necessary to sustain growth, the converse is not necessarily true, that is, you can have an adequate supply of money but for other reasons you may not get growth?

Mr. ABRAMOVITZ. For other reasons we might suffer retardation. That would be a fair statement of Friedman's position and up to that point one which I would support.

Representative REUSS. Do I understand that you and Mr. Friedman are in agreement on this point, sir?

Mr. ABRAMOVITZ. That is right.

Representative REUSS. Thank you.

Mr. ABRAMOVITZ. If one asks what controlled the rate of growth of our money supply, Friedman's answer is that it was a set of accidents in gold discoveries and in the progress of technology in gold extraction combined with the vagaries of an often misguided monetary policy. It seems possible, however, that a more systematic explanation of the long swings of our money supply, and of their relation to the volume of expenditure and investment, may yet be devised when we can take into full account the impact of income growth on our trade balances, therefore, on the flows of gold, on the character of the assets necessarily absorbed by banks and other financial institutions, and on the volume of liquid assets demanded by business and households and supplied by finance and government.

Finally, a third line of explanation would attribute the severe depressions in investment and output to a variety of factors in the nature of accidents or episodic disturbances. In this view, our economy has a built-in tendency to grow steadily — minor recessions apart. But it has been upset from time to time by the after effects of great wars, by speculative excesses of obscure origin, and by financial panics whose occurrence cannot be tied in to the other events of long swings in a systematic way.

No one is now in a position to choose confidently among these possibilities. Indeed, it is certain that episodic disturbances have been and will be important even if there is some stable mechanism which causes long swings to recur.

These great gaps in explanation obviously reflect the fact that there are also great gaps in our empirical knowledge of long swings. My statement has stressed the physical side of these fluctuations. But there are numerous other aspects concerned with prices and costs, saving and finance, external trade and capital movements which are undoubtedly important. They need to be carefully measured and their behavior assimilated into a general description of the course of events during the long swings in economic development.

Thank you, Mr. Chairman.

(The tables and charts follow:)

TABLE 1.—*Rate of growth of economic activity—Peaks and troughs of rates of change between average reference cycle standings, selected series, 1860–1948*

	Peaks	Troughs	Peaks	Troughs	Peaks	Troughs	Peaks	Troughs	Peaks	Troughs	Peaks	Troughs	Peaks	Troughs	Peaks
1. Gross national product, 1929 prices	[2]1864.25	[1]1874.25	[1]1874.25	1886.5	1889.75	1892.25	1899	1911	1914.5	1920	1923	1930.25	1938.5		
2. Index of industrial production		[1]1874.25	1881	1884	1888	1892.25	1899	1906.75	1913.25	1920	1923	1930.25	1938.5		
3. Flow of goods to consumers, 1929 prices			[1]1874.25	1888	1891	1892.25	[1]1899	1914.5							
4. Gross capital formation, 1929 prices		[1]1874.25	[1]1874.25	1884	1889.75	1893.75	1899	[2]1907.75	1917.25	1920.25	1921.25	1930.25	1943.25		
5. Gross construction, 1929 prices		[1]1874.25	[1]1874.25	1884	1889.75	1893.75	1899	[2]1907.75	1914.5	1920.25	1923	1930.25	1938.5	1943.25	1948.25
6. Nonfarm residential construction, 1929, prices		[1]1874.25	1884	1886.5	1889.75	1893.75	1900	1914.5		1921.25	1921.25	1930.25	1938.5	1943.25	
7. Capital expenditure in transportation and utilities, 1929 prices		[1]1874.25	1884		(²)	1899	1904	1917.25	1917.25		1921.25	1930.25			1948.25
8. Urban building	1866.5	[1]1874.25	[2]1877.75	1884	1891	1883.75 / 1892.25	[1]1899 / 1903	1914.5 / 1917.25			1921.25 / 1920.25	1932.25	1943.25		
9. Wholesale prices	1862	1869	1884	1884		1894	1899	1911	1917	1920.25	1924	1928			
10. Money supply			1881	1886.5	1889.75		1899	1907.75	1917.25	1921.25	1924	1920.25			
11. Net capital imports, 1929 prices	[1]1866.25	[1]1874.25	1881	1884	1884 / [2]1886.5	[2]1896.5	1907.75	1914.5	1920.25						
12. New incorporations		1868.75	1881	1884		1892.25	[2]1899	1913.5	1918.25	1921.25	1926	1936.75	(²)	1949.5	
13. Common stock prices		1878	[1]1878		1891	1893	[1]1899	1913	1917	1920	1926	1930	1944.75	1949	
14. Railroad bond yields	1869		1881		1891		1899	1906.5	1913	1918	[2]1923	1930	1944		
15. Immigration	1864.25	1871.25	1877.75	1884	1889.75	1893.75	1899	[2]1917.25			1920.25	1932.25			

[1] Tentative.
[2] Extra cyclical movement in this period.
[3] Series has inverted pattern after World War I.

TABLE 2.—*Rate of growth of economic activity—Peaks and troughs of rates of change between average reference cycle standings, selected series, 1800–60* [1]

	Peak	Trough	Peak	Trough	Peak	Trough
1. Urban building	[2]	[2]	[3]1836	[3]1838.25	1845.75	1858
2. Railroad construction	[2]	[2]	1838.25	1842.5	1845.75	1860
3. Canal construction in New York, Pennsylvania, and Ohio	[2]	[2]	1838.25	1842.5	1848	[2]
4. Merchant vessels built	1814.75	1819	1831.25	[4]1839.75	1845.75	1858
5. New incorporations	1812.5	1816.25	1833.75	1839.75	1849.25	1856.25
6. Federal land sales	1812.5	1821.25	1833.75	1838.25	1852.25	[5]
7. Net capital imports [6]	1814.75	1819	1833.75	1838.25	1849.25	[2]
8. Immigration	[2]	[2]	1831.25	1835.75	1845.75	1856.25
9. Tonnage moved on New York canals	[2]	[2]	[2]	[2]	1845.75	1856.25
10. Anthracite coal production	[2]	[2]	[5]	1838.25	1845.75	1858
11. Bituminous coal production	[2]	[2]	1838.25	1845.75	1849.25	1856.25
12. Federal expenditures, civil and miscellaneous	[3]1814.75	1821.25	1835.75	1839.75	1849.25	1858
13. Federal expenditures, total	[5]	1816.25	1835.75	1842.5	1845.75	{ 1849.25 T / 1854 P / 1858 T
14. U.S. postal revenues	[2]	1819	1835.75	1844	1848	1858
15. Value of merchandise imports	1814.75	1819	1833.75	1838.25	1849.25	1860
16. Value of merchandise exports	1814.75	1819	1833.75	1842.75	1852.25	1860
17. Deflated value of merchandise exports [7]	1821.25	1831.25	1839.75	1844	[8]1852.25	[2]
18. Money supply in hands of public	[2]	[2]	[2]	[3]1839.75	1845.75	[3]1858
19. Wholesale prices	[3]1812.5	1819	1835.75	1839.75	1852.25	1858
20. Bank and insurance company stock prices	[2]	1825	1831.25	1838.25	[2]	[2]
21. Commercial paper rates, Boston and New York	[2]	[2]	[2]	[3]1839.75	1845.75	[3]1858
22. Railroad stock prices	[2]	[2]	[2]	[2]	[3]1845.75	1856.25

[1] Dates expressed in whole years refer to years with midpoints at June 30. Dates expressed in whole years plus fractions have midpoints later than June 30 by the specified fraction of a year.
[2] The series did not cover the period in the neighborhood of the turning point.
[3] Tentative.
[4] 1835.75 slightly lower.
[5] The cycle was skipped.
[6] Based on absolute changes per annum.
[7] An inverted series in most of this period in terms of rate of growth.
[8] 1854 identical with 1852.5.

TABLE 3.—*Peaks and troughs of long swings in the rate of growth of output and economic activity; duration of the long swings, 1815–1940*

Peak	Trough	Duration (in years) of long swings in the rate of growth of economic activity			
		Expansion	Contraction	Full cycle	
				Peak to peak	Trough to trough
1814	1819		5		
1834	1840	15	6	20	21
1846	1858	6	12	12	18
1864.25	1874.25	6.25	10	18.25	16.25
1881	1886.5	6.75	5.5	16.75	12.25
1889.75	1892.25	3.25	2.5	8.75	5.75
1899	1911	6.75	12	9.25	18.75
1914.5	1920.25	3.5	5.75	15.5	9.25
1923	1930.25	2.75	7.25	8.5	10.0
1938.5		8.25		15.5	
Average, all cycles		5.21	7.33	13.83	13.91
Average, since 1874		6.5	6.6	12.38	11.2

TABLE 4.—*Amplitude of long swings in rates of growth of gross national product and its major components, 1871–1950*

Series	Average change in rate of growth from—		Long-term rate of growth	Relative amplitude	
	Peak to trough (1)	Trough to peak (2)	(3)	Peak to trough [1] (4)	Trough to peak [2] (5)
	Percentage points	*Percentage points*	*Percent*	*Percent*	*Percent*
Gross national product	4. 25	3. 80	3. 76	113. 03	101. 06
Net national product	4. 64	4. 17	3. 65	127. 12	114. 25
Consumer durables	6. 98	7. 74	4. 22	165. 40	183. 41
Consumer perishable and semidurables	3. 71	3. 27	3. 57	103. 92	91. 60
Consumer services	5. 82	5. 10	3. 98	146. 23	128. 14
Total gross capital formation	9. 83	11. 51	3. 55	276. 90	324. 23
Net capital formation	27. 81	25. 70	2. 34	1,188. 46	1,098. 29
Producer durables	10. 98	11. 67	4. 66	235. 62	250. 43
Total gross construction	15. 32	15. 46	3. 15	486. 35	490. 79

[1] Col. (1)÷col. (3)×100.
[2] Col. (2)÷col. (3)×100.

TABLE 5.—*Share of changes in net immigration and natural increase in changes in total population increase, overlapping decades, 1870–1955*

Period [1]	Changes in—			Proportion of change in total population increase due to—	
	Natural increase	Net immigration	Total population increase	Natural increase	Net immigration
	Millions of persons	*Millions of persons*	*Millions of persons*	*Percent*	*Percent*
1875–85	0. 17	1. 27	1. 44	11. 81	88. 19
1880–90	. 82	. 93	1. 75	46. 86	53. 14
1885–95	. 68	−1. 22	−. 54	−125. 93	225. 93
1890–1900	. 27	−. 72	−. 45	−60. 00	160. 00
1895–1905	0	. 88	. 88	0	100. 00
1900–10	. 97	2. 02	2. 99	32. 44	67. 56
1905–15	1. 18	. 14	1. 32	89. 39	10. 61
1910–20	−. 54	−2. 46	−3. 00	18. 00	82. 00
1915–25	1. 40	−1. 07	. 33	424. 24	−324. 24
1920–30	1. 35	. 54	1. 89	71. 43	28. 57
1925–35	−3. 02	−2. 04	−5. 06	59. 68	40. 32
1930–40	−1. 90	−. 95	−2. 85	66. 67	33. 33
1935–45	2. 40	. 23	2. 63	91. 25	8. 75
1940–50	5. 44	. 58	6. 02	90. 37	9. 63
1945–55	4. 96	. 82	5. 78	85. 81	14. 19

[1] Figures refer to the change in each category compared with a decade beginning 5 years earlier.

TABLE 6.—*Relative timing of peaks and troughs of long swings in rate of growth of economic activity or output additions to total labor force and immigration, 1846–1940*

	Turning points			Lead (−) or lag (+) (in years) relative to rate of growth in activity	
	Rate of growth of output	Additions to labor force	Immigration	Labor force additions	Immigration
Peak	1846	(¹)	1851.5	(¹)	+6.5
Trough	1858	(¹)	1859.5	(¹)	+1.5
Peak	1864.25	(¹)	1871	(¹)	+6.75
Trough	1874.25	(¹)	1874.25	(¹)	0
Peak	1881	1884.5	1881	+3.5	0
Trough	1886.5	1886.5	1886.5	0	0
Peak	1889.75	1893.5	1891	+4.25	+1.25
Trough	1892.25	1896.5	1895	+4.25	+2.75
Peak	1899	1906.5	1905	+7.5	+6.0
Trough	1911	1919.5	1919	(²)	(²)
Peak	1914.5	(³)	(³)	(³)	(³)
Trough	1920.25	(³)	(³)	(³)	(³)
Peak	1923	1924.5	1924.5	+1.5	+1.5
Trough	1930.25	1935.5	1935	+5.25	+4.75
Peak	1938.5	-------------	⁴1945	(²)	⁴+6.5

¹ Not available.
² Both labor force growth and immigration continued to decline after the upturn of output growth due to causes connected with World War I.
³ Turning point skipped.
⁴ Last observation.

TABLE 7-A.—*Peaks and troughs in the rate of growth economic activity and in the volume of additions to capital stock, pre-Civil War period* ¹

	Peak	Trough	Peak	Trough	Peak	Trough
1. Economic activity (rate of growth)	1814.0	1819.0	1834.0	1840.0	1846.5	1858.0
2. Urban building	(²)	(²)	³1836.0	1842.0	1854.5	1864.0
3. Railroad mileage added	(²)	(²)	1840.5	1844.5	1856.5	1862.0
4. Canal construction New York, Pennsylvania, and Ohio	(²)	(²)	1840.5	1846.0	1856.5	(²)
5. Merchant vessels built	1816.5	1821.5	1834.0	1842.0	1854.5	1859.5
6. Net capital imports	1816.5	1824.5	1836.0	1847.0	1854.5	(⁴)
7. New incorporations	1814.5	1821.5	1837.5	1842.0	1854.5	1859.5
8. Federal land sales	1818.0	1824.5	⁵1836.0	1850.0	1854.5	(⁴)

¹ Dates expressed in whole numbers refer to years with midpoints at June 30. Dates expressed in mixed numbers have midpoints later than June 30 by the specified fraction of a year.
² Series did not cover the period in question.
³ Initial or terminal observation.
⁴ Cycle was skipped.
⁵ Extra cyclical movement in the period.

TABLE 7–B.—Peaks and troughs in the rate of growth of economic activity and in the volume of additions to capital stock, post-Civil War period [1]

	Peak	Trough	Peak	Trough	Peak	Trough	Peak	Trough	Peak	Trough	Peak	Trough	Peak
1. Economic activity (rate of growth)	1864.25	1874.25	1881.0	1886.5	1889.75	1892.25	1899.0	1911.0	1914.5	1920.25	1923.0	1930.25	1938.5
2. Net capital formation, 1929 prices	[2]	[2]	[2]	[2]	1891.0	1895.0	1906.0	[3]1912.5	1919.0	1921.5	1925.5	1935.0	1940.5
3. Gross capital formation, 1929 prices	[2]	[2]	[2]	[2]	1892.5	1895.0	[2]	[2]	1919.0	1921.5	1927.5	1933.0	[4]1951.5
4. Producer durable equipment, 1929 prices	1871.0	1877.5	[2]	[2]	1891.0	1901.0	1906.0	1908.5	1919.0	1919.0	1927.5	1933.0	1946.0
5. Residential construction, 1929 prices	[2]	1877.5	[2]	[2]	1892.5	1901.0	1906.0	[2]	[2]	1919.0	1925.5	1933.0	1946.0
6. Urban building permits	1871.0	[2]	1881.5	[2]	1888.5	1901.0	1909.5	[2]	[2]	1919.0	1927.5	1935.0	[4]1955.0
7. Capital expenditures on transport and public utilities, 1929 prices	1871.0	1877.5	1881.5	1884.5	1892.5	1895.0	1911.5	[6]	[6]	1919.0	[6]	[6]	[6]
8. Net capital imports	1871.0	1881.5	[2]	[2]	1888.5	1901.0	1909.5	[6]	[6]	[6]	1935.0	[6]	[6]

[1] Dates expressed in whole numbers refer to years with midpoints at June 30. Dates expressed in mixed numbers have midpoints later than June 30 by the specified fraction of a year.

[2] Cycle was skipped.

[3] 1909.5 was slightly lower.

[4] Initial or terminal observation.

[5] Series did not cover the period in question.

[6] Omitted because of irregularity of behavior after World War I.

TABLE 8.—*Amplitude of long swings in rates of growth of physical output, total input and productivity, 1892–1953*

Series	Average change in rate of growth between—		Long-term rate of growth	Relative amplitude	
	Peak and trough	Trough and peak		Peak to trough col. (1) ÷ (3)	Trough to peak col. (2) ÷ (3)
	(1)	(2)	(3)	(4)	(5)
	Percent	*Percent*	*Percent*	*Percent*	*Percent*
Total input	4.44	3.70	1.67	265.87	221.56
Gross physical output	4.76	4.93	3.36	141.67	146.73
Output per weighted unit of labor and capital combined	1.73	1.91	1.67	103.59	114.37

TABLE 9.—*Peaks and troughs of long swings in the rates of growth of output, input and productivity, 1892–1953* [1]

	Turning points of long swings in rates of growth of—			Lead (−) or lag (+), in years, relative to turning points in physical output	
	Physical output	Total input	Productivity	Input	Productivity
Trough	(t)1892.5	1893.75	(t) 1892.5	+1.25	0
Peak	1899	1900	1896.5	+1.00	−2.5
Trough	1906.75	1907.75	1907.75	+1.00	+1.0
Peak	1911	1910	1910	−1.00	−1.0
Trough	1914.5		1913.5		−1.0
Peake	1917.25		1918.25		+1.0
Trough	1920.25	1920.25	1920.25	0	0
Peak	1923	1923	1923	0	0
Trough	1930.25	1930.25	1927.5	0	−2.75
Peak	1936.75	1938.5	1938.5	+1.75	+1.75
Trough	1948.25		1944.75		−3.50
Peak	1949.5		1949.5		0

[1] Dates expressed in whole numbers refer to years with midpoints at June 30. Dates expressed in mixed numbers have midpoints later than June 30 by the specified fraction of a year.

Source: See appendix notes.

TABLE 10.—*Chronology of severe contractions compared with peaks and troughs of long swings in capital formation*

Peaks in capital formation	Peak years preceding severe contractions	Troughs in capital formation	Trough years preceding sustained recovery
(1)	(2)	(3)	(4)
1815–18	1815	1821–24	1821
1936–37	1836	1842–44	1843
1854–55	1853	1862–64	1858
1971	1873	1877–78	1878
	1882	------------	1885
1892–93	1892	1895	1896
1906	1907	1912–13	1914
1919	1920	1921–22	1921
1927–28	1929	1933	1932

Sources: Capital formation, tables 7–A and 7–B; severe contractions, see text and app. note to table 10.

TABLE 11.—*A chronology of the peaks and troughs in 5 basic aspects of the long swings in economic growth*

LONG SWING PEAKS

Rate of growth of productivity	Rate of growth of output	Volume of additions to labor force	Volume of additions to capital stock = capital formation	Years preceding severe contraction
(1)	(2)	(3)	(4)	(5)
(¹)	1814	(¹)	1815–18	1815
(¹)	1834	(¹)	1836–7	1836
(¹)	1846	1851. 5	1854–5	1853
(¹)	1864. 25	1871	1871	1873
(¹)	1881	1884. 5	(²)	1882
(¹)	1889. 75	1893. 5	1893–3	1892
1896. 5	1899	1906. 5	1906	1907
(³)	1914. 5	(²)	1919	1920
1923	1923	1924. 5	1927–8	1929
1938. 5	1938. 5	(²)	(²)	(²)

LONG SWING TROUGHS

Rate of growth of productivity	Rate of growth of output	Volume of additions to labor force	Volume of additions to capital stock = capital formation	Years preceding sustained recovery
(6)	(7)	(8)	(9)	(10)
(¹)	1819	(¹)	1821–4	1821
(¹)	1840	(¹)	1842–4	1843
(¹)	1858	1859. 5	1862–4	1858
(¹)	1874. 25	1874. 25	1877–8	1878
(¹)	1886. 5	1886. 5	(²)	1885
1892. 5	1892. 25	1896. 5	1895	1896
1907. 75	1911	1919. 5	1912–13	1914
1920. 25	1920. 25	(²)	1921–2	1921
1927. 5	1930. 25	1935. 5	1933	1932

Not available.
² Turning point skipped or, at end of table, not yet reached.
³ Extra movement makes comparison with GNP impossible.

Sources: Cols. (1) and (6), table 8; cols. (2) and (7), table 3; cols. (3) and (8), table 6; cols. (4) and (9), table 10; cols. (5) and (10), table 10.

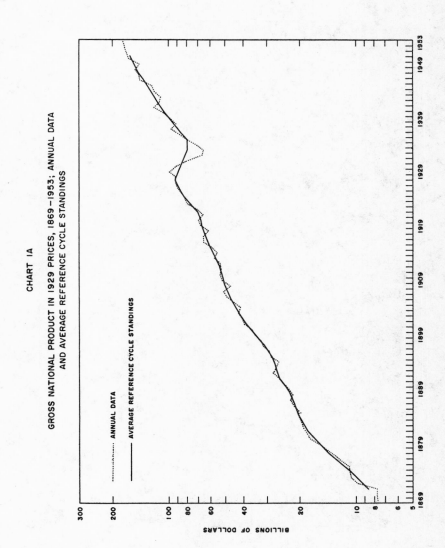

CHART IA

GROSS NATIONAL PRODUCT IN 1929 PRICES, 1869–1953; ANNUAL DATA
AND AVERAGE REFERENCE CYCLE STANDINGS

.... ANNUAL DATA

————— AVERAGE REFERENCE CYCLE STANDINGS

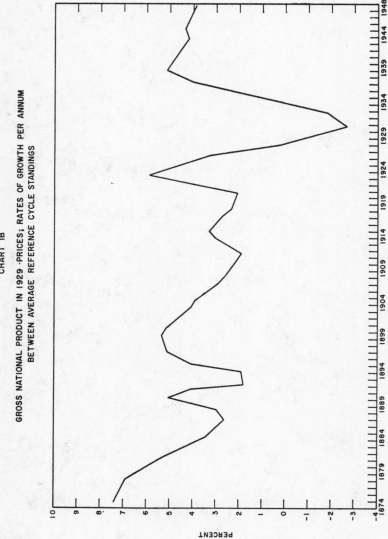

CHART IB

GROSS NATIONAL PRODUCT IN 1929 - PRICES; RATES OF GROWTH PER ANNUM
BETWEEN AVERAGE REFERENCE CYCLE STANDINGS

PERCENT

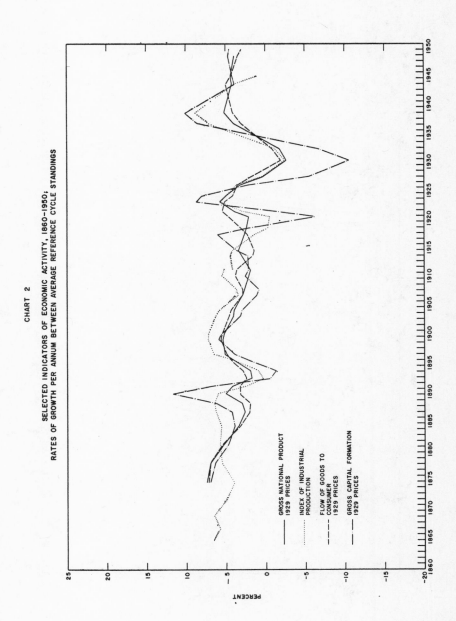

CHART 2

SELECTED INDICATORS OF ECONOMIC ACTIVITY, 1860–1950;
RATES OF GROWTH PER ANNUM BETWEEN AVERAGE REFERENCE CYCLE STANDINGS

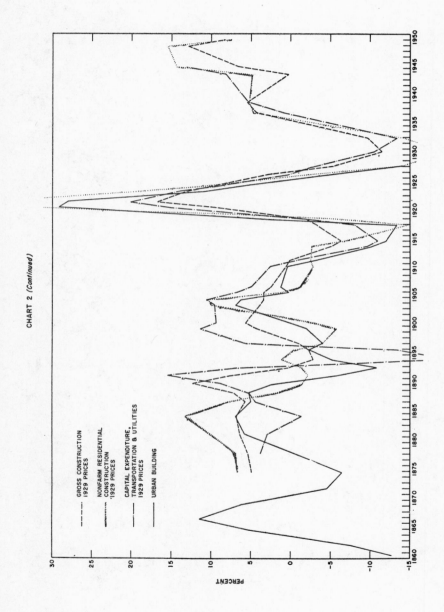

CHART 2 *(Continued)*

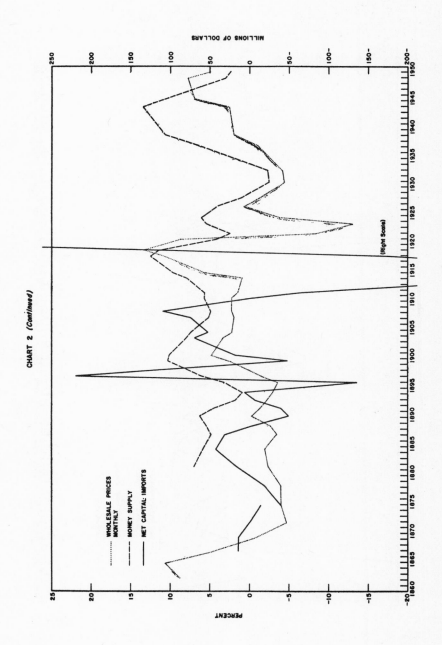

CHART 2 *(Continued)*

WHOLESALE PRICES
MONTHLY
MONEY SUPPLY
NET CAPITAL: IMPORTS

CHART 2 *(Continued)*

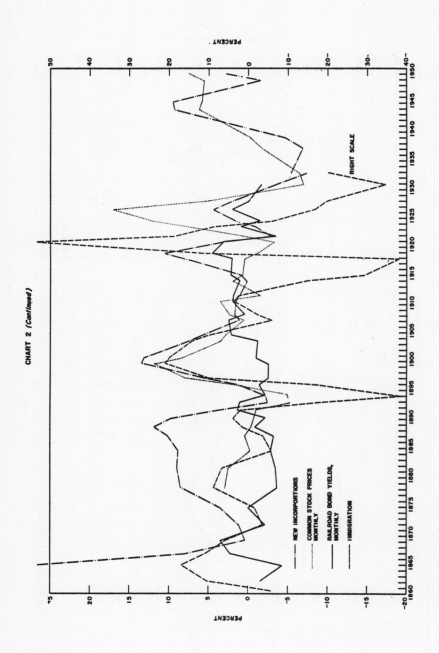

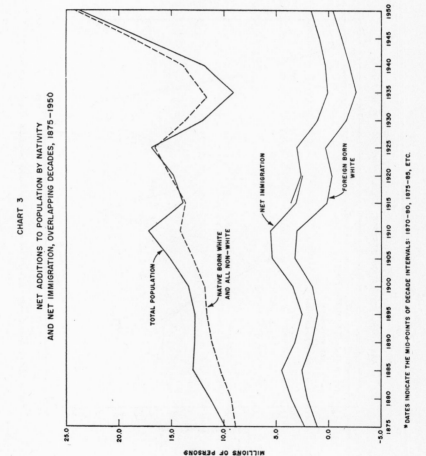

CHART 3

NET ADDITIONS TO POPULATION BY NATIVITY
AND NET IMMIGRATION, OVERLAPPING DECADES, 1875–1950

* DATES INDICATE THE MID-POINTS OF DECADE INTERVALS: 1870–80, 1875–85, ETC.

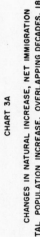

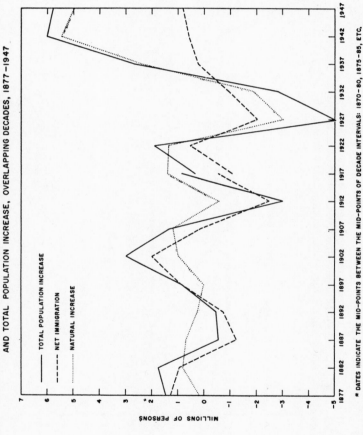

CHART 3A

CHANGES IN NATURAL INCREASE, NET IMMIGRATION

AND TOTAL POPULATION INCREASE, OVERLAPPING DECADES, 1877–1947

TOTAL POPULATION INCREASE

NET IMMIGRATION

NATURAL INCREASE

MILLIONS OF PERSONS

* DATES INDICATE THE MID-POINTS BETWEEN THE MID-POINTS OF DECADE INTERVALS: 1870–80, 1875–85, ETC,

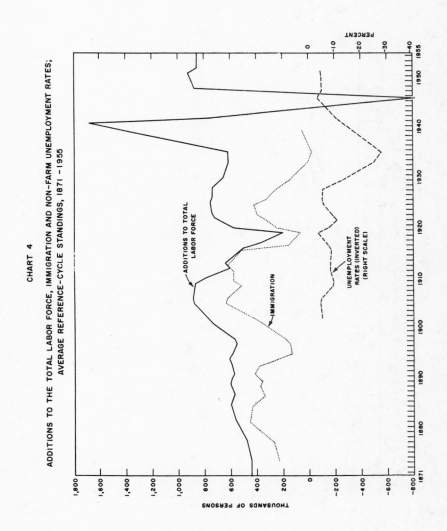

CHART 4

ADDITIONS TO THE TOTAL LABOR FORCE, IMMIGRATION AND NON-FARM UNEMPLOYMENT RATES;
AVERAGE REFERENCE-CYCLE STANDINGS, 1871 – 1955

ADDITIONS TO TOTAL
LABOR FORCE

IMMIGRATION

UNEMPLOYMENT
RATES (INVERTED)
(RIGHT SCALE)

THOUSANDS OF PERSONS

PERCENT

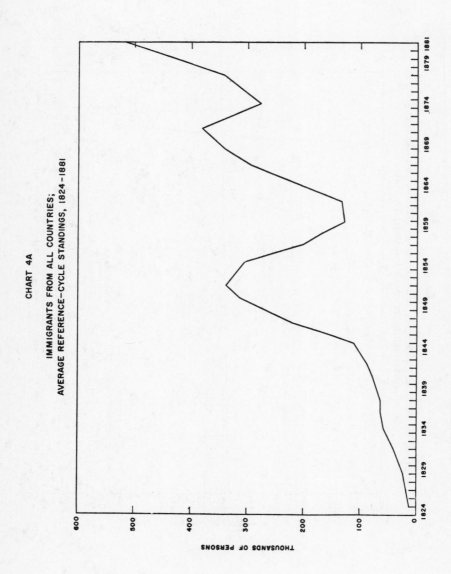

CHART 4A

IMMIGRANTS FROM ALL COUNTRIES;
AVERAGE REFERENCE–CYCLE STANDINGS, 1824–1881

THOUSANDS OF PERSONS

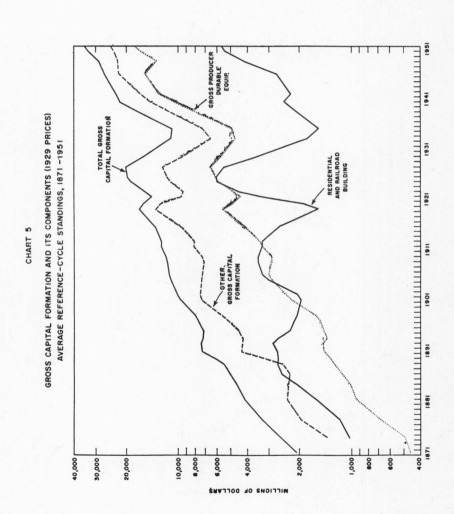

CHART 5

GROSS CAPITAL FORMATION AND ITS COMPONENTS (1929 PRICES)
AVERAGE REFERENCE-CYCLE STANDINGS, 1871-1951

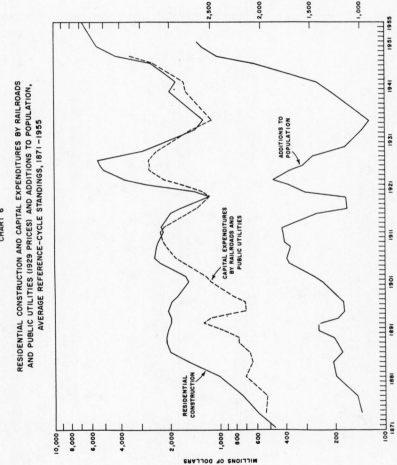

CHART 6

RESIDENTIAL CONSTRUCTION AND CAPITAL EXPENDITURES BY RAILROADS
AND PUBLIC UTILITIES (1929 PRICES) AND ADDITIONS TO POPULATION,
AVERAGE REFERENCE-CYCLE STANDINGS, 1871–1955

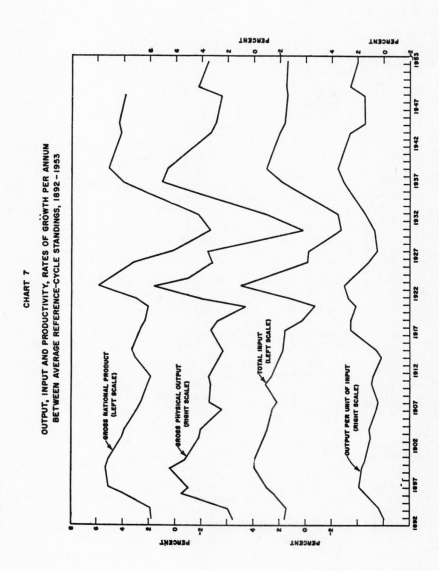

CHART 7

OUTPUT, INPUT AND PRODUCTIVITY, RATES OF GROWTH PER ANNUM
BETWEEN AVERAGE REFERENCE-CYCLE STANDINGS, 1892 – 1953

SOURCE NOTES FOR TABLES AND CHARTS

The following notes identify the sources from which the data underlying the tables and charts were taken.

TABLE 1

1. Gross National Product, 1929 Prices. Simon Kuznets, Technical tables underlying the statistical supplement to Capital in the American Economy: Its Formation and Financing, National Bureau of Economic Research (in press).

2. Index of Industrial Production. Edwin Frickey, Production in the United States, page 127, table 20. Frederick C. Mills, Index of Output of Five Industries, 1899–1951 (unpublished).

3. Flow of Goods to Consumers, 1929 Prices. Simon Kuznets, op. cit.

4. Gross Capital Formation, 1929 Prices. Simon Kuznets, op. cit.

5. Gross Construction, 1929 Prices. Simon Kuznets, op. cit.

6. Nonfarm Residential Construction, 1929 Prices. Simon Kuznets, op. cit.

7. Capital Expenditure in Transportation and Utilities, 1929 Prices. Melville J. Ulmer, Capital in Transportation, Communication, and Public Utilities, Natonal Bureau of Economic Research (in press), appendix B, table B–1, column 4.

8. Urban Building. John R. Riggleman, Variations in Building Activity in U.S. Cities, Doctoral Dissertation, Johns Hopkins University, 1934.

9. Wholesale Prices. Series prepared by the National Bureau of Economic Research on the basis of underlying estimates by G. F. Warren and F. A. Pearson, Wholesale Prices in the United States for 135 Years, for the years 1850 to 1889 and by the Bureau of National Statistics thereafter.

10. Money Supply. Preliminary estimates supplied by Milton Friedman and Anna Schwartz, Money Supply (preliminary manuscript).

11. Net Capital Imports. Mathew Simon, Statistical Estimates of the Balance of International Payments and the International Capital Movements of the United States, 1861–1900, Conference on Research in Income and Wealth, Williamstown, Mass., September 1957, table XXVII, line 32, pages 116–118. Simon Kuznets, op. cit.

12. New Incorporations. George H. Evans, Jr., Business Incorporations in the United States, 1800–1943, table 13, page 34.

13. Common Stock Prices. 1871–1917 from Cowles and Associates, Common Stock Indexes; 1918–1956 from Standard & Poor's Corp., Trade and Securities Statistics, Security Price Index Record.

14. R. R. Bond Yields. Fred R. Macaulay, Some Theoretical Problems Suggested by the Movements of Interest Rates, Bond Yields, and Stock Prices in the United States since 1856.

15. Immigration. 1860–70 from Treasury Department, Bureau of Statistics, Monthly Summary of Commerce and Finance of the United States, No. 12, Series 1902–3, pages 4345–4357; 1870–1945 from Simon Kuznets and Edward P. Rubin, "Immigration and the Foreign Born," National Bureau of Economic Research, Occasional Paper No. 46, pages 95–96.

TABLE 2

1. Urban Building. See table 1, series 8.

2. Railroad Construction. Poor's Railroad Manual, 1912.

3. Canal Construction in New York, Pennsylvania, and Ohio. Harvey H. Segel, Canal Cycles, 1834–61, chapter V, table 1, pages 283–284.

4. Merchant Vessels Built. Merchant Marine Statistics, 1936, pages 42–45.

5. New Incorporations. Index prepared by Moses Abramovitz by combining G. H. Evans' estimates on new incorporations in four sectors. For source of Evans' figures, see table 1, series 12.

6. Federal Land Sales. Walter B. Smith and Arthur H. Cole, Fluctuations in American Business, 1790–1860, appendix D., page 185, table 71.

7. Net Capital Imports. Douglas C. North. The United States Balance of Payments, 1790–1860, Conference on Research in Income and Wealth, Williamstown, Mass., September 1957 (mimeo.).

8. Immigration. Treasury Department, Bureau of Statistics, Monthly Summary of Commerce and Finance of the United States, No. 12, series 1902–3, pages 4345–4357.

9. Tonnage Moved on New York Canals. New York Department of Public Works, Annual Report, 1954, page 198.

10. Anthracite Coal Production. Bureau of Mines of the U.S. Department of the Interior, Mineral Resources of the United States, 1923, part II, table 22, page 549.

11. Bituminous Coal Production. See preceding reference.

12. Federal Expenditures, Civil and Miscellaneous. Annual Report of the Secretary of the Treasury, 1940, table 6, pages 545–549.

13. Federal Expenditures, Total. Annual Report of the Secretary of the Treasury, 1946, table 2, pages 366–371.

14. U.S. Postal Revenue. Annual Report of the Secretary of the Treasury, 1946, table 13, pages 419–421.

15. Value of Merchandise Imports. Foreign Commerce and Navigation of the United States, 1912, pages 43–44.

16. Value of Merchandise Exports. See preceding reference.

17. Deflated Value of Merchandise Exports. Douglas C. North, op. cit.

18. Money Supply in the Hands of the Public. Reports of the Comptroller of the Currency and estimates for 1852–53 by National Bureau of Economic Research.

19. Wholesale Prices. George F. Warren and Frank A. Pearson, Prices, table 1, pages 11–13.

20. Bank and Insurance Co. Stock Prices. Walter B. Smith and Arthur H. Cole, Fluctuations in American Business, 1790–1860, page 174.

21. Commercial Paper Rates, Boston and New York. See preceding reference, pages 192–194.

22. Railroad Stock Prices. See preceding reference, page 182.

TABLE 3

Based on tables 1 and 2. See text.

TABLE 4

The original data from which the calculations in this table were made were taken from Simon Kuznets, op. cit.

TABLE 5

Source: Simon Kuznets, "Long Swings in the Growth of Population and in Related Economic Variables," Proceedings of the American Philosophical Society, volume 102, No. 1, February 1958, table 7.

TABLE 6

Rate of Growth of Output. See table 3.
Additions to Labor Force. See chart 4.
Immigration. See chart 4.

TABLE 7–A

Line 1. See table 3.
Peaks and troughs of the long swings of the series in lines 2 through 8 were identified from charts of average reference cycle standings of these series, the sources of which were cited under table 2 above.

TABLE 7–B

1. Line 1. See table 3.
2. The peaks and troughs of the long swings of the series in lines 2 through 8 were derived from charts of average reference cycle standings. The sources of the data were as follows:

(*a*) Lines 2 to 5. Simon Kuznets, Technical Tables, op. cit., see table 1, series 1.
(*b*) Line 6. See table 1, series 8.
(*c*) Line 7. See table 1, series 7.
(*d*) Line 8. See table 1, series 11.

TABLE 8

From Solomon Fabricant. "Basic Facts on Productivity Change, National Bureau of Economic Research," Occasional Paper No. 63.

TABLE 9

Turning points were selected on the basis of charts drawn from data identified in table 8.

TABLE 10

See text for a general description of the method used to select periods of severe business contraction. The following data indicates the manner in which Thorp's "Business Annals" and the National Bureau's chronology of business-cycle peaks and troughs were used to derive the dates in table 10, columns (2) and (4).

Year	Thorp's characterization	Contraction period selected*	National Bureau's turning points corresponding to beginning and end of selected contraction period	
			Peak	Trough
(1)	(2)	(3)	(4)	(5)
1812	Brief recession; uneven prosperity			
1813	Prosperity			
1814	Prosperity; financial distress			
1815	Prosperity; panic; recession			
1816	Depression	(*)		
1817	Mild depression	(*)		
1818	do	(*)		
1819	Severe depression; financial panic	(*)		
1820	Depression	(*)		
1821	Depression; revival	(*)		
1822	Mild recession			
1823	Revival			
1824	Prosperity			
1825	Prosperity; panic; recession			
1826	Depression; revival			
1827	Moderate prosperity			
1828	Prosperity; recession			
1829	Depression; revival			
1830	Moderate prosperity			
1831	Prosperity			
1832	Moderate prosperity			
1833	Prosperity; panic; recession			
1834	Mild depression			(¹)
1835	Revival; prosperity		(¹)	
1836	Prosperity		1836	
1837	Prosperity; panic; recession; depression			
1838	Depression; slight revival	(*)		
1839	Revival; panic; recession	(*)		
1840	Depression	(*)		
1841	do	(*)		
1842	do	(*)		
1843	Depression; revival	(*)		1843
1844	Revival; prosperity			
1845	Prosperity; brief recession			
1846	Recession; mild depression			
1847	Revival; prosperity; panic; recession			
1848	Mild depression; revival			
1849	Prosperity			
1850	do			
1851	do			
1852	do			
1853	Prosperity; recession		1853	
1854	Recession; depression	(*)		
1855	Depression; revival	(*)		
1856	Prosperity	(*)		
1857	Prosperity; panic; recession; depression	(*)		
1858	Depression	(*)		1858
1859	Revival			
1860	Prosperity; recession			
1861	Mild depression; revival			
1862	War activity			
1863	do			
1864	do			
1865	Boom; recession			
1866	Mild depression			
1867	Depression			
1868	Revival			
1869	Prosperity; monetary difficulties			
1870	Recession; mild depression			

Year (1)	Thorp's characterization (2)	Contraction period selected* (3)	National Bureau's turning points corresponding to beginning and end of selected contraction period	
			Peak (4)	Trough (5)
1871	Revival; prosperity			
1872	Prosperity			
1873	Prosperity; panic recession			
1874	Depression		1873	
1875	...do...	(*)		
1876	Depression	(*)		
1877	...do...	(*)		
1878	Depression; revival	(*)		1878
1879	Revival; prosperity	(*)		
1880	Prosperity			
1881	...do...			
1882	Prosperity; slight recession			
1882	Recession		1882	
1884	Depression	(*)		
1885	Depression; revival	(*)		
1886	Revival			1885
1887	Prosperity			
1888	Brief recession			
1889	Prosperity			
1890	Prosperity; recession			
1891	Depression; revival			
1892	Prosperity		1892	
1893	Recession; panic; depression			
1894	Deep depression			
1895	Depression; revival	(*)		
1896	Recession; depression	(*)		
1897	Depression; revival	(*)		1896
1898	Revival; prosperity			
1899	Prosperity			
1900	Prosperity; brief recession			
1901	Prosperity			
1902	...do...			
1903	Prosperity; recession			
1904	Mild depression; revival			
1905	Prosperity			
1906	...do...			
1907	Prosperity; panic; recession; depression		1907	
1908	Depression			
1909	Revival; mild prosperity	(*)		
1910	Recession	(*)		
1911	Mild depression	(*)		
1912	Revival; prosperity	(*)		
1913	Prosperity; recession	(*)		
1914	Depression	(*)		1914
1915	Revival; prosperity			
1916	Prosperity			
1917	Prosperity; war activity			
1918	War activity; recession			
1919	Revival; prosperity			
1920	Prosperity; recession; depression		1920	
1921	Depression	(*)		1921
1922	Revival; prosperity			
1923	Prosperity; recession			
1924	Mild depression; revival			
1925	Prosperity			
1926	...do...			
1927	Prosperity; recession (III)			
1928	Revival; prosperity (II)			
1929	Prosperity; recession (III)		1929	
1930	Depression			
1931	Depression [End of Thorp's Annals]	(*)		
				1932

[1] Bureau chronology begins.

TABLE 11

Sources identified in footnotes to table 11.

CHART 1A

See table 1, series 1.

CHART 1B

See table 1, series 1.

CHART 2

See notes to table 1.

CHART 3

Source: Simon Kuznets, "Long Swings in the Growth of Population and in Related Economic Variables," "Proceedings of the American Philosophical Society," volume 102, No. 1, February 1958.

1. Total population. Table 2, column 7.
2. Native-born white and all nonwhite. Table 7, columns 1 and 3.
3. Foreign-born white. Table 2, column 5.
4. Net immigration. Table 6, column 5.

CHART 3A

Source: See chart 3.
1. Change in natural increase. Table 7, column 2.
2. Change in net immigration. Table 7, column 3.
3. Change in total population increase. Table 7, column 4.

CHART 4

1. Additions to total labor force. Preliminary estimate supplied by Richard Easterlin, National Bureau of Economic Research.
2. Immigration. Simon Kuznets and Edward P. Rubin, "Immigration and the Foreign Born," National Bureau of Economic Research, Occasional Paper No. 46.
3. Unemployment. Stanley Lebergott, "Annual Estimate of Unemployment in the United States 1900–54," in "The Measurement and Behavior of Unemployment," National Bureau of Economic Research, 1957, pages 215–216.

CHART 4A

Immigration. See table 2, series 8.

CHART 5

1. Gross capital formation, 1929 prices. Simon Kuznets, Technical Tables, op. cit., see table 1, series 1.
2. Gross producers, durable equipment, 1929 prices. Simon Kuznets, op. cit.
3. Other gross capital formation, 1929 prices. Calculated by subtracting the sum of nonfarm residential construction (table 1, series 6) and railroad construction (M. J. Ulmer, op. cit) from total gross capital formation (see series 1 above).
4. Residential and railroad building. See series 3 above.

CHART 6

1. Residential construction. See table 1, series 6.
2. Capital expenditures by railroads and public utilities. See table 1, series 7.
3. Additions to population. Simon Kuznets, op. cit.

CHART 7

1. Gross national product. See table 1, series 1.
2. Gross physical output. Solomon Fabricant, "Basic Facts on Productivity Change," National Bureau of Economic Research, Occasional Paper No. 63.
3. Total input. See reference above.
4. Output per unit of input. See reference above.

The CHAIRMAN. Thank you very much.

Yesterday Dr. George Taylor presented a very interesting index number of wholesale prices and the cost of living for 1800 to the present time and showed the sharp rise in wartime and subsequent fall in peacetime of these price levels, with the exception of recent years—in fact there has been no comparable fall as yet in our price level which accompanied the Second World War.

Have you made any study as to the effect changes in the general price level have upon the rate of economic growth?

Mr. ABRAMOVITZ. I can say this much, and I wish my charts had been better drawn. I hope to have them better drawn before they are reproduced for the committee. There has been a long swing in the rate of change of prices which accompanies the long swing in the rate of growth of output but has lagged behind them somewhat.

This does not appear in my charts, as I say, because the price curves were badly drawn. This need not mean more, however, than that upon recovery from a serious depression we also have a recovery in the level of prices and that the rate——

The CHAIRMAN. I am not speaking of the cyclical fluctuation of prices. I am speaking of secular changes in the price level.

Mr. ABRAMOVITZ. I see, yes.

The CHAIRMAN. You take the period from 1870 to 1896, this or the particular period from 1873, I would say to 1896, you have on the whole a quarter of a century where prices went down, then you have a period of 18 years in which prices rose in peacetime. What about the rates of growth in the quarter century prior to 1896, let us say, and the period subsequent to that?

Mr. ABRAMOVITZ. I think it is perfectly clear that we enjoyed very rapid economic growth in the last quarter century of the 19th century, a period from 1870 to 1890.

The CHAIRMAN. You mean despite——

Mr. ABRAMOVITZ. Despite the fall in prices and that we enjoyed a rate of growth in the first quarter of the present century which was not clearly greater and may have been somewhat lower, in spite of a tendency for prices to rise during that period.

Now this, of course, says nothing about the connection between price movements and rates of growth in output within the two periods. We have to remember that the period after the Civil War was the period of our early industrialization and might be expected to be a period of extremely rapid growth in output regardless of what was happening to prices.

The CHAIRMAN. So you are not ready to generalize on this point?

Mr. ABRAMOVITZ. I will not say that a long-term decline in prices promotes rapid growth in output.

The CHAIRMAN. Nor are you saying that a longtime increase in prices discourages growth?

Mr. ABRAMOVITZ. That is right. And I am particularly not saying that.

The CHAIRMAN. I rather gather that you think that the greatest negative effect on the rate of growth, is a severe depression from time to time, and that if those could be prevented the total output would appear to be larger?

Mr. ABRAMOVITZ. My feeling is that the rate of growth of output would be obviously steadier in the absence of severe——

The CHAIRMAN. The next question I am going to ask is this: Is the rate of growth speeded up later by the fact that it has been preceded by a depression?

Mr. ABRAMOVITZ. Undoubtedly.

The CHAIRMAN. That is used as an argument for having depressions, wouldn't you say?

Mr. ABRAMOVITZ. I think this obviously is an invalid argument. The rate of growth is speed up later only because——

The CHAIRMAN. That argument comes from very eminent sources at times. I would like to have you point out for the record why it is invalid.

Mr. ABRAMOVITZ. The rate of growth speeds up after a great depression only because there are certain temporary factors created by the depression which permit us for a time, and only for a short time, to enjoy very rapid growth. One is the fact that we have a lot of unemployed resources which we can quickly bring back into production. But they need never have been unemployed. And the second is that we have permitted our stock of commodities to run down and in rebuilding that stock of commodities we also produce a great pressure of demand upon the economy which for a time helps stimulate rapid growth in output. Then when those stocks of commodities have been rebuilt to normal levels that stimulus to demand disappears.

The CHAIRMAN. I think the doctors will tell us when a patient has been very ill that his rate of improvement is greater in the early stages than in the later stages but this is not an argument that he should become ill in order that he may later improve.

Mr. ABRAMOVITZ. No, that is right.

The CHAIRMAN. Senator Bush?

Senator SPARKMAN. It is like the modern seizure. The person gets a bad cold, running into pneumonia. So you are getting well.

Senator BUSH. Professor, I certainly have been interested in your statement this morning and congratulate you. There is a lot of work behind this. I appreciate this, as we all do, I am sure.

We are in a strange situation right now of having been through a sharp recession in business and yet having recovered, according to the index of industrial production. Retail sales and other indexes are to new high ground and still we have an unemployment factor which is serious. Even though that is improving it certainly does not seem to have improved commensurate with the other indexes, production, sales, so forth.

Have you any comment to make on that? Could you enlighten us to why you think that is the case? In other words, it was only 2 short years ago that employment was at a peak, you might say, and we had only very moderate unemployment which you might say was always to be expected at the level that it reached then. Yet we reestablished the same levels of operation in most industrial and commercial fields but we have a few mililon more unemployed than we did at that time. What is the explanation of that as you see it?

Mr. ABRAMOVITZ. The immediate explanation, I think, is simple. The rate of growth of output corrected for business cycles after you get back to the same stage so to speak in a business cycle, has not been great enough to absorb the growth in the labor supply and in the stock of capital. We are now passing through a period of low rate of growth, after allowing for business cycles, and it is in that sort of period that we begin to accumulate idle resources, both of labor and capital and you will appreciate that the accumulation of such idle resources of labor and capital is exactly the sort of development which puts us in danger, certainly used to put us in danger of suffering a serious depression.

Senator Bush. Why has there been this lag in development of capital? Why does that exist?

Mr. Abramovitz. Because I believe that there has been a serious change in the conditions controlling the demand for additional long-term investment. You know that we experienced after the end of the Second War, the end of the World War, a great boom in the demand for all kinds of capital equipment. That boom reflected a big gap in our stock of capital which had developed first in the course of the preceding great depression and secondly because of the restrictions during the war on capital investment. It also reflected an amazing upsurge in population growth. For almost a decade, therefore capital investment proceeded at a high level and at an increasing level which year by year increased the total demand for all kinds of goods through the income which was distributed in the course of building the capital.

Now, however, I think we have reached a stage in which the steam behind this great boom has begun to peter out. We have caught up in good part with the backlog of demand for capital equipment, which grew up during the depression and during the war, and, secondly, the rate of population growth has tapered off although it is much higher than we might expect it to be. It is no longer growing year by year as it was doing for 12 to 14 years.

And the combination of these two facts means that the demand for additional capital is no longer growing at the rate at which it was during the first years after the war. When the demand for additional investment tapers off we no longer have that big increase in the total demand for goods which the economy requires if it is to grow enough each year to absorb the growth in the labor supply.

Senator Bush. You said in your statement, the variety of causes have combined to produce an unbroken period of retardation in growth which has now lasted for some 20 years and whose end cannot yet be determined. And then you promised me that a later statement would explain that. Well, I followed you very closely.

Mr. Abramovitz. I meant I hoped to have an opportunity at this point to explain to you.

Senator Bush. Now I would like to give you that opportunity because I was very much interested in that question.

Mr. Abramovitz. Senator, you may have noticed that in the course of my explanation that I said that upon recovery from a deep depression we usually enjoy a period of very rapid and accelerated growth for a time. We did enjoy that period of rapid and accelerated growth during the period of recovery from the great depression of the 1930's. From a period beginning roughly 1933–34, output shot up very steeply and reached high rates of growth. Toward the end of the 1930's, however, and in the early 1940's, partly under the stimulus of defense preparations, we succeeded in eliminating virtually all our idle capacity. We reemployed the unemployed men and we put all or almost all of our stock of capital equipment back to work. From that point on, output growth could go forward only as fast as our stock of resources grew and only so fast as technological developments were exploited and put to work in improving the quality of capital equipment and the efficiency of industry. Since that process of technological improvement goes on in good times and bad, when we reach a period in which output growth no longer can take advantage of idle resources but has to depend solely upon technology and upon growth in the stock of resources, the rate of output growth is going to begin to fall.

Although we maintain a satisfactory and steady rate of growth, the rate of output growth is not as high as it was during the period of recovery from the depression. That is what the chairman was referring to a moment ago.

Output also grew, continued to grow, at a satisfactory though falling rate for two other reasons. One is that after World War II the rate of growth of the labor supply began to fall. A large number of people flowed into the labor force during recovery from the depression and during the war years. But after the end of the war the rate of growth of the labor supply fell off and the labor supply, of course, is the most important element in our total stock of resources.

Secondly, there was a shift ·from war to peace which involved a shift from war industries to the production of peacetime goods. And that shift in the composition of output has a somewhat spurious effect upon our measures of total output because we have been assigning a higher value, so to speak, per unit of output to the output of war industries than we have been assigning to output of civilian goods. To that extent the retardation is spurious.

Senator BUSH. That answers it. Thank you very much, Professor.

Senator SPARKMAN (presiding). Mr. Bolling.

Representative BOLLING. These charts and figures end about 1953. Do you feel that the indications are that we are in a long-term swing that might indicate the threat of potential serious depression?

Mr. ABRAMOVITZ. My feeling is that if our economy were organized, if our economy were now organized, in the way in which it was organized before 1930 we would face the threat of a serious depression.

Representative BOLLING. Now, to follow that up——

Senator BUSH. I do not quite get that.

Representative BOLLING. I am going to follow it up to see if I can clarify the differences he believes exist between the economic organization of the thirties and the economic organization today and then your conclusion on the basis of those differences. If this is not asking too much——

Mr. ABRAMOVITZ. No; I would be glad to say a few words about that.

Representative BOLLING. Fine. I wish you would.

Mr. ABRAMOVITZ. One big difference is that government expenditures now account for a much larger part of total output, absorb a much larger part of total output than they did before 1930, and government expenditures even if they are not made to fluctuate countercyclically are at least insensitive to a reduction in income. So here we have a very large part of our total output which will not fall merely because, say, investment expenditures fall. The Government is at least going to maintain its level of demand for goods.

Secondly, personal income and, therefore, personal consumption is much less sensitive to a change in the level of unemployment than it used to be. Partly this is true because our tax structure is more progressive than it used to be. When income falls, therefore, the effect of this on what people have to spend is less severe because a portion of it so to speak is cushioned by the fact that their taxes are reduced. And, secondly, personal income is protected from drops in output by unemployment insurance and by the fact that many people enjoy old-age pensions. These are people whose incomes might have declined severely in the absence of pensions when their relatives supporting them suffered a decline in their income. We have seen during the course of the last few recessions how well personal income and consumption have held up despite the fact the total output has been going down.

Thirdly, of course, we now enjoy, I think, a more sensitive monetary and fiscal policy on the part of the Government to the threat of recession. The Government acts more promptly now to make money easier than it used to do and acts more promptly than it used to do to readjust its own budget to the threat of recession and so to protect total output and people's incomes from the threat of unemployment.

Fourth, and I think this is extremely important, we have had a major reform in our banking system. I think here particularly of the Federal Deposit Insurance Corporation, which protects the deposits of people from the threat of bank failure which used to be a serious disturbance which accompanied virtually every serious depression in the past.

Fifthly, I think there has been a great growth in confidence of industry generally in the ability of government to take such action as would avoid serious depression. This encourages businessmen to keep up their capital expenditures, not to permit their capital expenditures to fall by as much as they otherwise would, when the business picture changes because they now feel that they are not threatened with catastrophe or the possibility of catastrophe as they used to be when the employment picture and the demand picture became less favorable. The result is that they are willing to maintain at least to some extent their program of capital investment in a way in which they were not willing to do in olden days. Though I think therefore, that many of the conditions which now exist would threaten us with serious depression, I think we are unlikely to experience, happily unlikely to experience, that depression. But this does not mean that we may not have a number of years in which unemployment rates are not higher than we would like to see them because our rate of growth is not as rapid as it needs to be in order to absorb the growth in the labor supply.

Representative BOLLING. Now, finally, the points that you make are that there are certain so-called built-in stabilizers, and this includes everything from social security to a more progressive tax rate. As a result of these built-in stabilizers there is a more optimistic psychology in the elements of the community that must have that relative optimism to maintain certain activities. This, in effect, means that we work within a narrower range in making economic decisions at both private and the governmental level, that while it is unlikely that we will have a catastrophic great depression, that even that in one range of mismanagement would be a possibility and that at the other range or in the middle range there is a possibility of doing a better job of cleaning out the trough, but in effect the range of decision making, in error or correctness is narrower.

Mr. ABRAMOVITZ. I think that is right.

Representative BOLLING. Does that make sense?

Mr. ABRAMOVITZ. Yes, it does.

Representative BOLLING. Thank you very much.

Senator SPARKMAN. Mr. Reuss.

Representative REUSS. I would like to ask Dr. Abramovitz about the material in his prepared statement. You referred to Dr. Friedman's analysis of the growth of money supply.

Is it your point that whatever else may be necessary to assure continued growth, it is a good thing, if not a prerequisite, to have a roughly parallel growth in the money supply?

Mr. ABRAMOVITZ. I think it eases the process, the very complicated process of adjustment through which the economy has to go in order to provide for a growing demand, real demand.

Representative REUSS. To some extent this is a chicken and egg proposition, is it not? If we get growth, the monetary supply expands, but it is also true that the monetary supply is affected by factors other than the rate of growth.

Mr. ABRAMOVITZ. In the economy in which we now live the money supply is essentially under the control of our own Government, the Federal Reserve Board, and of the Treasury.

Representative REUSS. You list other possible causes changing the supply of money on pages 26 and 27. You refer to technology in gold extraction and the accident of gold discoveries. Isn't it true that as a practical matter, in the last 20 years at least, there have been no Klondikes and there have been no radical technological innovations in extraction processes?

Mr. ABRAMOVITZ. Nor would it be important if there were nowadays because we no longer have a free gold standard.

Representative REUSS. So therefore we are talking about the history.

Mr. ABRAMOVITZ. This is historical matter.

Representative REUSS. At the top of page 27, you make a number of statements which I should like to have you explain further. You say:

When we take into full account the impact of income growth on our trade balances.

Then you also say:

on the character of the assets necessarily absorbed by the banks, and thirdly, on the volume of liquid assets demanded by business and households and supplied by finance and Government.

Could you spell those out a little more? I am not sure what you mean.

Mr. ABRAMOVITZ. Yes. In order to enjoy growth in output we have to have growth in demand. One big source in growth demand is growth of investment expenditures. Those investment expenditures are made, of course, by business firms and by households, the latter in particular insofar as they are purchasing homes. Residential construction is, of course, a great source of investment expenditure. Those investment expenditures by both business and households have to be financed. In the course of arranging for the finance of those investment expenditures, businesses and households, so to speak, generate securities. They offer for financing a variety of kinds of financial assets, notes, bonds, stocks, mortgages, and so on.

Growth therefore requires that those financial assets should be absorbed by our financial institutions and ultimately by the general public, if not directly then in some form which reflects the transformation of those assets by the intermediate financial institutions. For example, as a pension fund may absorb the bonds issued by corporations and offer to its own clients an annuity. The process of investment therefore, if it is to proceed smoothly, requires that there should be attractive costs of finance offered to the potential investors. The assets which they issue, therefore, must be absorbed by the intermediate financial institutions at attractive terms and the general public in turn must be prepared to accept the kinds of assets which the intermediate financial institutions are offering to them in return for the funds which they use to finance business or households.

Now, in the course of one of these long swings that I have been describing, the character of the financial assets offered by business and by households changes because in the early stages of one of these long swings a large portion of total investment takes the form of inventory investment. The kinds of financing which must be done in short-term financing and the kinds of assets which are produced by business and offered to the banks are short-term notes of various kinds. Later on, in a long swing, investment comes to depend more and more heavily on long-term investment and upon residential construction and the kinds of assets which then must be absorbed by the market are stocks, bonds, and mortgages.

The willingness of our intermediate financial institutions to absorb those particular kinds of assets, as contrasted with short-term notes, helps to determine the cost of finance to business and to households and therefore the volume of real investment which is made. And the efficiency therefore of our financial organizations can, so to speak, be judged by its capacity to absorb this changing flow of assets, changing in volume and changing in composition and continuing to offer financing at what seems to the investing public to be reasonable rates.

Representative REUSS. This is obviously an important factor of growth. If you have inefficient fianical institutions that do not offer the kind of credit needed, you do not get adequate growth. But I am not quite clear what this has to do with the money supply. It seems to me a different factor.

Mr. ABRAMOVITZ. When a bank accepts the note or other kind of asset issued by a business firm, it is at the same time creating money because it places at the disposal of the investing firm a sum of money equal to the value of the asset which it has accepted and this is in addition to the stock of money balances. These money balances are then expended, distributed to the public, and flow in to the balances of private individuals.

At the same time, when the Government borrows money from the public it is offering to them a form of financial asset which many members of the public regard as equivalent or nearly the equivalent of cash and which therefore stands in their minds as a substitute for a money balance itself and permits them to act, because of the liquidity of theses securities, as if they had cash in the bank.

The willingness, therefore, of our financial institutions to transform the uniliquid types of assets offered by business into the liquid types of assets demanded by the public and the financial operations of the Government help to determine the total amount of liquid assets to the public. They are liquid either because they are actually in the form of cash or liquid because they substitute for cash.

Representative REUSS. Thank you very much.

Senator SPARKMAN. Doctor, we certainly appreciate your appearance before us and giving us this very thorough, enlightening study you have given us.

I think it is something that really requires a study.

There are a good many questions that I should like to ask you but I was not here to hear all of your statement. I should like to read it more fully and more carefully. Therefore, I will waive any questions at this time.

Thank you very much.

And the committee will stand in recess until——

Mr. ABRAMOVITZ. Thank you. I was very glad to be here.

Senator SPARKMAN. The committee will stand adjourned subject to call.

(Whereupon, at 12:10 p.m., Friday, April 10, 1959, the committee adjourned subject to call.)

×